The Jumbled Jigsaw

Also by Donna Williams

Nobody Nowhere
The Remarkable Autobiography of an Autistic Girl
ISBN 1 85302 718 9

Somebody Somewhere
Breaking Free from the World of Autism
ISBN 1 85302 719 7

Like Colour to the Blind
Soul Searching and Soul Finding
ISBN 1 85302 720 0

Everyday Heaven
Journeys Beyond the Stereotypes of Autism
ISBN 1 84310 211 0

Not Just Anything
A Collection of Thoughts on Paper
ISBN 1 84310 228 5

Autism: An Inside-Out Approach
An Innovative Look at the Mechanics of 'Autism' and its
Developmental 'Cousins'
ISBN 1 85302 387 6

Autism and Sensing
The Unlost Instinct
ISBN 1 85302 612 3

Exposure Anxiety – The Invisible Cage
An Exploration of Self-Protection Responses in the
Autism Spectrum and Beyond
ISBN 1 84310 051 7

The Jumbled Jigsaw

An Insider's Approach to the Treatment of Autistic Spectrum 'Fruit Salads'

Donna Williams

Jessica Kingsley Publishers
London and Philadelphia

Definition of Autism (p.13) © National Autistic Society, from *What is Autism?* leaflet. Reproduced with permission. Definition of dyspraxia (p.107) and Tourette's syndrome (p.143) from *Merriam-Webster's Medical Dictionary* © 2005 by Merriam-Webster Incorporated (www.Merriam-Webster.com). Reproduced with permission. Definition of obsessive-compulsive disorder (p.146) from *Merriam-Webster's Medical Desk Dictionary* © 2002 by Merriam-Webster Incorporated (www.Merriam-Webster.com). Reproduced with permission. Definition of trauma (p.270) neglect (p.273) and grief (p.280) from *Merriam-Webster's Online Dictionary* © 2005 by Merriam-Webster, Incorporated. (www.merriam-webster.com.) Reproduced with permission.

First published in 2006
by Jessica Kingsley Publishers
116 Pentonville Road
London N1 9JB, UK
and
400 Market Street, Suite 400
Philadelphia, PA 19106, USA

www.jkp.com

Copyright © Donna Williams 2006

Library of Congress Cataloging in Publication Data
Williams, Donna, 1963-
    The jumbled jigsaw : an insider's approach to the treatment of Autistic spectrum 'fruit salads' / Donna Williams.
        p. cm.
    Includes bibliographical references and index.
    ISBN-13: 978-1-84310-281-6 (pbk. : alk. paper)
    ISBN-10: 1-84310-281-1 (pbk. : alk. paper) 1. Autism. 2. Autism--Alternative treatment. I. Title.
    RC553.A88W546 2005
    616.85'882--dc22
                                2005010899

British Library Cataloguing in Publication Data
A CIP catalogue record for this book is available from the British Library

ISBN 13: 978 184310 281 6
ISBN 10: 184310 281 1

Printed and Bound in Great Britain by
Athenaeum Press, Gateshead, Tyne and Wear

Contents

I'd like to dedicate this book to the following pioneers in this strange field:

The public speakers everywhere who dared to tell their stories and show the world the diversity within the word 'Autism', regardless of fear or social judgement.

The voiceless who spoke via typing in spite of overwhelming exclusion and mockery, and to those who believed in them.

The conventional professionals who dared open-mindedness in consulting outside of their own area where they themselves were limited.

The unconventional practitioners who broke new ground in spite of often having no studies in 'peer reviewed journals' as their safety net, and the publishers who similarly often went out on a limb to give voices to some of the most unheard and marginalised people in our society.

The carers who never allowed a lack of education to get in their way and dared to educate themselves in whatever ways they could.

Those brave enough to own up when the job really was more than their own resources could deal with and let it be someone else's job for the good of all involved.

The compulsive rescuers and perfectionists who dared learn to chill out and give space in spite of it turning their world upside down and redefining the word 'love'.

Those left behind for whom in even minor ways it may never be 'too late' to make life easier or more comfortable.

Malai, for being an amazing inspiration in my work as a consultant.

And Kerry, for sparking interest and research in one of the greatest sources of motivations at the centre of sense of self – personality; and for showing me the circumstances under which personality traits become their extremes.

PART I

Getting Oriented

Introduction

OK, so you landed in the world of those who are developmentally challenged and you're looking for an instruction manual. Most likely you'll get, instead, a label: 'Autism' or 'Asperger's syndrome' or 'PDDNOS' (pervasive developmental disorder not otherwise specified) or some other umbrella term, as though you had one fruit and this type of 'fruit' will always taste the same if it's got the same label.

And maybe you think you all got some kind of apple, like one of you got the Autism apple we might think of as a Golden Delicious. And another one of you got the Asperger's apple we might think of as maybe a Granny Smith. And one of you got one of those 'PDDNOS' type apples we might think of as a Pink Lady.

But what if these weren't single definable variations on one fruit? In fact, what if each were a strange fruit indeed? And the more you get used to it, the more you might find it may have many different flavours and sometimes it is not one fruit at all but a well-disguised blend of fruit salad, and you confused it for a mere apple! What's more, what if the combined ingredients in each of these fruit salads and the amounts of each in each concoction differed slightly in each case? One piece of fruit may be that of information-processing issues, another of sensory-perceptual issues, another of communication issues, another of anxiety disorders, another of mood disorders, another of compulsive disorders and another of sense of self, environmental dynamics, identity and personality issues – and that's just the fruit on top.

Some of you may find that where you thought you had only an 'apple', you will find when you look closer that you also have 'grapes'. Others will not, but might have 'plums' instead. Some will have two types of 'berries' in there and some will have more than one type of 'banana'.

And if you don't like fruit salad, then think in terms of pizza. A pizza is not merely the base. It has lots of toppings involved in what becomes the final pizza experience. So whether you think fruit salad, pizza, stew or trifle, this book is about ingredients – identifying them, giving you the tour and pointing out what this might mean for working most constructively with people challenged by developmental conditions. In the end we may even find that Autism, Asperger's, PDD (pervasive developmental disorder), ADHD (attention deficit hyperactivity disorder), or any other current label for an Autism spectrum condition, is actually a construction, a myth. Oh yes, a condition does exist, but it may not be one condition at all, but a cluster of them – a cluster condition.

This book is all about naming what's in that cluster, that recipe that comes to be labelled a 'developmental disability'. It's kind of like buying a product in the supermarket labelled 'Fruit Salad', but having the contents listed on the side so you know that 'Fruit Salad' might appear to be one thing but it's made up of lots of different things put together. Then, because we know what makes up the fruit salad, what the contents are, then if those contents are causing us advantages or disadvantages, we have a better idea which piece is an issue rather than blaming the entire fruit salad. We might even find that particular fruit salads suit particular tastes and occasions or are best experienced in par-ticular atmospheres where the best qualities of the ingredients come to the fore, a bit like how people think white wine tastes best when it's served with fish, and red wine with meats, and olives with cheese.

When we know what something's actually made up of, then it's like being given an instruction manual, we know how best to work with each of the different parts. But before we look at what's *inside*, let's look briefly at what people see from the outside.

Looking at developmental challenges from the outside

The most important issues are:

- interaction (how people relate)
- self-help (looking after yourself and getting what you need)
- communication ('blah blah' – how chat seems to an Autistic person – and sharing who you are through words)
- learning (taking on new experiences and other people's ideas of important information)
- behaviour (all the stuff that hangs out in what you do)

- imagination (the storylines, movies and mental juggling that go on in your head, or don't)
- emotion (intangible, physical feelings that affect the body)
- sensory perception (how we make sense of what we see, hear, smell, taste, touch; movement through space, muscle feedback, etc.).

Interaction means how we relate to each other. For most developmentally typical people the desire for good interaction is as simple as having their child open to their attempts to join in, to do as they are told, to accept or seek comforting or to respond when they draw attention to something. Instead, the reality is that it can be about living with a child who is full-on, demanding, constantly seeking comfort and demanding their attention; or the opposite – a child who is passive, aloof, independent, unable to conform or to cope with involvement that's started by others.

Self-help skills are about the ability to learn to do things for oneself. This can be as simple as getting a glass of water, taking off a jumper, being toilet trained or asking for help. Because children are often expected to let others care for them, problems with self-help usually don't become too apparent until around the age of two or three. Then a parent may despair in having a puppet-like child who progressively appears unable to dress, feed or toilet him or herself, in some cases even unmotivated to crawl or walk. For others, they may have a child who insists on dressing in the same thing every day, will not change clothes, wears them inside-out or back to front, eats only certain (often problem) foods, excessively overeats, eats non-food objects, drinks excessively or not at all, insists on bizarre toileting routines with tantrums at the slightest redirection of this fierce 'independence' and rejects all external attempts to care, comfort or direct.

Communication means sharing ideas and experiences. For some families, the communication issue comes down to despair over never having heard a child's voice. For others it's about the child never shutting up. For some it's about distant, formal language. For others it's about stuffy, pedantic, seemingly self-interested or obsessive language. It might also be about involuntary sounds, words or phrases said over and over till it drives everyone mad, or communication which doesn't make meaningful sense to most people, or something as simple as having no social judgement in choosing what to say or no apparent ability to keep track of the effect of what is said on other people.

Learning difficulties can mean having a child who doesn't initiate or seems unmotivated most of the time. For others, it's about a highly distracted, impulsive, compulsive, unpredictable or easily distressed child whose challenges interfere with learning. For yet others, it's about a child who either simply doesn't get what meaning is all about or tires of it easily; or the opposite – a child who understands interpretive meaning but appears unable to relate to emotional content or the general theme or feel of what's being learned.

Behaviour challenges can take many forms. Some carers struggle with extreme passivity, rigidity, phobia, or sensitivity as the greatest behavioural challenge presented by their child. Other carers have wild, seemingly untameable, fearless, compulsive, impulsive, sometimes even explosive wild-children with all that that can entail in terms of energy and the judgements of others. Some carers have unpredictable children who swing between both of these extremes.

Imagination is one of the things once said to be lacking in those with 'developmental disabilities', though people in this group continue to demonstrate that their form of imagination may not so much be missing as somewhat different.

Emotion is one of the ways we share experiences. The perception or processed experience of emotion can be seemingly absent, incomprehensible, out of control or wildly hypersensitive. Those who live with this on a chronic level are going to be at risk of developing a disturbed relationship to the whole sphere of the emotional self, the sharing of it with others or even in seeking to understand or develop it oneself. In other words, just as chronic pain may lead people to detach from their sense of the physical or struggle to relate to those who don't have these issues, I believe that chronic severe challenges in the emotions department can lead to a similar disturbance in relation to one's emotional self, the emotional selfhood of others or the sharing of those two worlds.

Sensory perception is about the way we get information from our senses; sight, hearing, smell, taste, touch as well as our sense of body in space. When these are not integrated or are wildly fluctuating, this makes for a rather different experienced reality to the majority of people.

What is an Autism spectrum condition?

The conventional definition

Before dissecting the label of Autism spectrum disorder in a way it may never be seen in its usual conventional terms again, let's take a little wander into the conventional world of Autism professionals and how they have broadly defined Autism.

Most professionals define Autism by external criteria such as the 'triad of impairments' (in social interaction, social communication and social imagination), as set out by the National Autistic Society in their leaflet *What is Autism?*:

> People with Autism generally experience three main areas of difficulty; these are known as the triad of impairments.

- Social interaction (difficulty with social relationships, for example appearing aloof and indifferent to other people).

- Social communication (difficulty with verbal and non-verbal communication, for example not fully understanding the meaning of common gestures, facial expression or tone of voice).

- Imagination (difficulty in the development of interpersonal play and imagination, for example having a limited range of imaginative activities, possibly copied and pursued rigidly and repetitively).

In addition to this triad, repetitive behaviour patients and resistance to change in routine are often characteristic.

The problem with Autism stereotypes

The following characteristic behaviours were mentioned on the Leicestershire County Council Specialist Teaching service website (2003) as being associated with Autism:

- A tendency not to seek out the company of others.

- A tendency to stick to well-tried routines and avoid change.

- A tendency to have a narrow range of interests, often becoming obsessed with a particular activity or subject.

- A tendency to develop irrational fears and anxieties.

- A tendency not to develop a sense of danger.

- A tendency to demonstrate bizarre behaviours and mannerisms.

- A tendency to copy speech parrot fashion.
- Isolated areas of ability.

The problem with such a list is that the features of each of these areas can be caused by very different underlying factors, so in fact there is no one thing called Autism.

The stereotypes associated with Autism are today significantly broader than they were when I was born in 1963. The concept of Autism is being refined all the time to embrace a much broader range of personalities and social backgrounds than in earlier times. With this broadening of the concept of Autism, the 'Autie' population multiplied dramatically.

One previous stereotype was that children with Autism occurred primarily in the families of educated middle-class professionals. Today we are learning that many families previously considered to have maladjusted children, or the products of dysfunctional, uneducated or impoverished backgrounds, are equally likely to have their share of Auties, though they may be less likely to be brought to the attention of professionals and less likely to receive a diagnosis quickly. Once thought to affect more boys that girls, people are now questioning whether Autism spectrum conditions just 'appear' differently in girls so they are not so easily picked up.

Auties always existed, in the cities and in the countryside, in educated and uneducated families, among the rich and the poor and across all races. Some of the so-called 'demented', 'retarded', 'psychotic', 'insane' and 'disturbed' children of the 1960s and before, as far back as institutions recorded having them, were likely somewhere on the Autism spectrum.

I was given the records of a great-aunt of mine institutionalised in 1904 in a mental hospital at the age of 40 with a diagnosis of 'hopeless imbecile'. She was described as having had her condition since birth, that she was oblivious to her surroundings and what was said to her, but chattered to herself in incomprehensible language and had bizarre 'habits'. Where was this woman before she was locked up at 40? How did she finally come to the attention of the authorities? Did she get angry at a neighbour or wander into a house which wasn't hers? Did she become a danger to traffic and walk in front of the horse and carts in her day? Did her parents die and leave her? Where were these people before we had lunatic asylums? She may have been 'a hopeless imbecile' but was she capable of grabbing foodstuffs and eating them, of grabbing something to keep warm and finding places to shelter? How different would she have been from others had she existed in a prehistoric society?

It may well be that Auties became more socially obvious as populations moved toward inner-city living and society developed a demand for more complex life skills and intensive communication than may have been needed in more isolated, rural, pre-industrial times. There may be a few new groups of Auties where the underlying causes are largely environmental, but there are certainly lots of genetic links being found too. And what are we looking at when we say 'genetic'? Are we talking about health issues affecting information processing? Are we talking about mood, anxiety or compulsive disorders compounding to present as 'Autism'? Are we talking about inherited personality traits that are progressively more incompatible with a society which celebrates confident, conforming, competitive, social people as the only desired 'norm'?

Autism in the family: The aerial shot

For some families, living with someone with Autism is an invitation to the endless repetitive routine of the film 'Groundhog Day'. For others it's like never getting off the rollercoaster. For others it is simply 'everyday life'.

Developmental challenges invite the family on an adventure. Often there is mourning as the developmentally typical members of the family realise they have a different child to the one they expected to have. A parent who is also on the Autistic spectrum may not realise what the fuss is about. A parent with Asperger's syndrome might have a child with Autism and, because the two conditions can appear so different, find the child not familiar at all. Sometimes a parent ends up getting a diagnosis once their child is diagnosed.

Many adult Auties and Aspies find the 'mourning' response hard to understand because their 'normality' is 'normal' to them. They often can't appreciate why any family would particularly want one more child like 'the majority' or what the big deal is in having to be developmentally typical. Being an Autie or Aspie in a family that wishes you were something else can be a big emotional burden. Many families release the child from this emotional burden, put their previous expectations aside and create a new, positive and non-judgemental starting point, one that begins with appreciating the child that they did have.

There are good reasons for helping Auties cope better in a world dominated by developmentally typical people, but the pure goal of wanting an Autie to perform a developmentally typical person's version of 'normal' shouldn't be one of them. These are good goals to have for any child if you want them to be more comfortable, stable and able to function with as wide a range as possible of social opportunities in life. Acceptance can still mean helping to reduce the degree of impairment someone has by addressing the underlying causes of developmental challenges. Just because something's 'genetic' doesn't mean some genetic patterns won't play out more healthily in some circumstances than in others, and we still don't usually know just what that word 'genetic' affects. It may be that some genetically inherited challenges or traits are far less likely to impair functioning when the environment adapts to them in one way and far more likely to impair functioning when the environment adapts to them in another way.

Equally, it can be a problem to see the Autism so strongly that you fail to see the person. When a child is severely affected by Autism, it can actually be very hard for families to form a relationship with that child in the usual developmentally typical person's way, especially if a child has involuntary or self-injurious behaviours, emotional fits or epileptic fits much of the day. Under these really difficult circumstances, it might become harder to see the child rather than the condition. Without meaning to, some families end up forming a relationship with the condition rather than the child. Imagine how you'd feel if people behaved as if your personhood, your individuality, your personality, was invisible to them. Imagine who you'd become if you progressively saw this as all you are or could be.

Some Auties see themselves as 'people with Autism' and feel that they are more than just a bag of Autism. Others see themselves as 'Autistic people' and feel their Autism is essential to who they are. Many aspects of Autism are valuable assets which are too often overlooked. Both groups are expressing their own valid experiences and realities. Whilst respecting both views, we can't ignore that there are many Auties who *are* severely disabled and distressed and who will have very limited life opportunities because of some aspects of their Autism.

The 'fruit salad' of Autism

Autism, as one word, is misleadingly used for what is actually a cluster of conditions, a 'fruit salad'. I see Autism as single word for the impact of a collection of different conditions starting in early childhood. This collection is like a cluster of different fruits tightly packed in a fruit bowl. Preserve and tumble that about a lot for three years or more and give each orange time to be affected by the weight of the apple and banana, give the grapes time to be affected by being entangled with the raspberries, give the mango time to be impacted upon by the presence of a few heavy lemons and grapefruit and what you end up with is fruit salad, and identifying the original fruit might be pretty difficult without a guide.

If we take five people with an Autism spectrum condition and focus on a particular area of difficulty among the following:

- communication
- interaction
- self-help
- imagination
- learning
- behaviour
- emotion
- sensory perception,

that area of difficulty could have a completely different underlying cause or combination of causes for each of those individuals.

Take the following examples of conditions which can co-occur in those with Autism spectrum conditions:

- information-processing differences
- social-emotional anxiety states
- impulse-control and mood issues
- personality and identity issues
- environmental and boundaries issues.

Any one or co-occurring combination of these things can cause problems with communication, interaction, self-help, imagination, learning or behaviour. By correctly identifying which underlying conditions affect early childhood development in an 'Autistic' way, we should be able to get a plan of action about which types of help are going to work best for which people. One day we may even have a team of professionals across a wide range of skills who can *holistically* treat individual cases of Autism according to the specific contents of that person's 'fruit salad'.

A new social attitude

A cartoon is one-dimensional, it has only one, surface, level. A film is less flat than a cartoon. It is two-dimensional, but it has another level to it which cartoons don't have. Real life (provided you don't have visual perceptual problems) is usually three-dimensional. It has another level of realness and depth to it which you can't experience in watching a film or cartoon.

Autism has been seen in a one-dimensional way for a long time. I think it's time for Autism to be understood in a three-dimensional way – when we look at the label, how it looks to an outsider and then how it looks from the insider's experience; but then I think we can go further. I think we can view Autism in a *multi-dimensional* way – a condition with a whole variety of different interconnected dimensions or levels.

Treating Autism as something that has many different dimensions or levels involves professionals and organisations getting humble enough to acknowledge:

- that Autism is a word we use to describe a particular kind of 'developmental disability/disorder/difference'

- that a developmental disability labelled 'Autism' may be underpinned by one, two or more of a number of sometimes interconnected conditions/issues

- that each of those underlying conditions/issues on their own may not cause Autism but in combination could compound to amount to a burden great enough to significantly cause a developmental breakdown and delay if not alter future development

- that 'shadow syndromes' of a variety of other conditions may exist, which together can significantly add stress upon development in a variety of ways

- that such 'shadow syndromes' (or even co-occurring conditions in their full-blown form) may have gone undiagnosed because of misassumptions that such conditions don't occur in infants or the misassumption that the overriding label of Autism is some kind of separate, unrelated condition which cancels out the presence of underlying conditions

- that these kinds of misassumption would make the concept of Autism as an incurable, untreatable mystery a self-fulfilling prophecy in the search instead for a single 'magic bullet'

- that 'treatment' may mean a co-ordinated treatment plan involving a team of different professionals from different fields with specific expertise in tackling each of these underlying conditions individually

- that each of the specialists involved should be respectful and supportive in their communications with all involved in the treatment of other conditions existing in this 'cluster'

- that this means changing our conventional, narrow and conservative social view that the teacher, the GP, the paediatrician, the psychologist, the neurologist, the gastroenterologist, the speech therapist and the parent are the only important professionals in working with a child with Autism

- that working with someone in a holistic way may mean thinking 'outside of the box', to include, among others, the naturopath, the opthalmologist, the specialised social worker, the occupational therapist, or chiropractor or the hypnotherapist for that matter

- that with all the best intentions, patterns can happen in even very 'caring' families which can compound the person's developmental problems or mean that the person with Autism is limited in picking up or identifying with alternative ways of coping with his or her disability

- that all this may mean caring for the family, not just the person with Autism; and that this may mean the provision of informed and adequate respite care and also non-judgemental, supportive and empowering help for the carers themselves in developing the social-emotional dynamics, knowledge and skills to best address and cope with their child's particular cluster of conditions in the most empowering way not just for the child but for the holistic health of the family.

Let's now adventure into the exploration of some of the conditions which can underpin the label of an Autism spectrum condition.

PART 2

Into the Depths

CHAPTER 1

Fuel System and Electrical Problems

Health and Autism

You're trying to keep up with the traffic on the motorway but your fuel pump has blown a gasket and the fuel that's meant to run the engine is leaking out. Someone has put sugar in your petrol tank so the fuel running your car is all gunked up with garbage that shouldn't be there. Your carburettor, which is meant to regulate the mixture of things in your car's fuel system, has slipped out of adjustment. Your radiator has developed rust, which has clogged up the works. Your engine is out of oil because of a leaky head gasket and one of the pistons in the engine has seized up and the engine's thrown a few rods, so the whole thing's clunking and smoke is billowing everywhere and the spark plugs are gunked up so the electrics are full of gremlins. At the same time your electrics should be conveying things to you about what's going on but the messages aren't firing and lights are coming on in places you don't need them and failing or flashing in those you do. But you're on the motorway with everyone else and the cars around you are tailgating you, there are horns blasting and someone is shouting that people like you shouldn't even be on the road. Welcome to the world of fuel system and electrical problems.

Most people with Asperger's or at the high-functioning end of the Autistic spectrum may say, 'What health issues? I'm fine.' But among those more towards the Autistic and so-called 'lower-functioning' end of the spectrum, health issues are often obvious and sometimes very serious.

It is nearly impossible to convey to someone who doesn't have these just how much more extremely they can alter information processing, sensory perception, mood, anxiety and compulsive states or exaggerate the tempo of your own personality dynamics so you are way out on a limb in one way or another.

If you think of the brain as a car engine, you will realise that the car engine needs to work efficiently in order to keep the car running. If the car isn't running too well it won't respond well to hazards, to handling corners, to stopping suddenly, to changing lanes... Now a car's engine requires two things to run well: fuel and electrics. It requires not just good fuel but a clean non-leaking fuel tank, good fuel pump, good hoses, good gaskets, a good carburettor, good lubrication, adequate water and clean air. On the electrics side it needs good healthy wiring, no crossed wires, no breakdown of the connections or insulation on the wiring, no blown fuses, healthy spark plugs and electrical points, a good starter motor and ignition switch, as well as a key. If there is a problem with the car's fuel system or electrics, the engine won't run properly and the car won't work like it should. The car also needs rest or it will overheat, break down and blow up.

The fuel system

Auties, most particularly those with significant cognitive and neurological challenges, often have significant fuel system and electrical problems too. The requirements of this fuel system are basically a good clean diet, including food, water and oxygen. The fuel system also needs a digestive system with a healthy non-inflamed gut which breaks down our food into small nutrient particles ready to feed the blood and, ultimately, the brain. The fuel system also needs a healthy pancreas and liver, which produce the enzymes needed to digest food properly and maintain blood sugar levels to feed the brain and, together with the kidneys, to keep the level of toxins low in the body so the brain doesn't get 'hungover'.

Nutrients are food for the brain: brain goodies. The fuel system of the body at every level is the transport system, different delivery trucks for these nutrients, these brain goodies. These delivery trucks include the blood cells that have to be healthy to be able to transport the goodies and not get hijacked on the way by baddies like fungal, viral or bacterial infections or beaten up mistakenly by the body's own immune system.

The immune system is the body's army of soldiers, and a healthy and balanced immune system should help the transport system to deliver its goodies to the brain without being hijacked or attacked on the way. Sometimes the immune system hasn't got enough soldiers to fight the bad bugs. This is called immune deficiency. Sometimes the immune system has another problem, where it is sort of 'confused' and it attacks parts of the self; it attacks healthy parts of the body, it can attack its own gut lining, it can attack its own blood cells, it can attack its own organs, it can even attack its own brain tissue and it can attack good healthy foods, which is what we know as 'allergies' and some food intolerances (though other food intolerances can be caused by faulty detox mechanisms). This 'allergic' part of the immune system is known as the 'auto-immune' system.

The 'essential truck stops' for the transport of goodies to the brain include the heart and lungs responsible for fuelling up the blood cells with oxygen and removing carbon dioxide as the blood makes its journey back and forth between brain and body. Oxygen is an essential and major part of supplying nutrition to the brain, so is adequate blood sugar levels (which we get from digesting all kinds of foods) and enough water to keep blood flowing well, and good exercise to keep circulation going is essential to deliver the goodies and remove the baddies from the body. Low levels of blood oxygen and blood sugar, or not enough fluids (dehydration) mean reduced conscious awareness or fluctuations in conscious awareness. What's more, just because you eat and drink and breathe doesn't mean the fuel system is working properly to deliver these goodies. Also, people often forget that sleep is an essential nutrient, particularly deep sleep, REM sleep. We need REM sleep to download and work through all the emotional and mental events of the day, to detox the brain and repair the body.

Reduced delivery of nutrients to the brain through the blood can mean limited ability to process incoming information and retrieve the information we need to make and control responses: physical, emotional and verbal. It can mean delayed processing of information so that by the time the 'penny drops' the event has already passed. It can mean a backlog of unprocessed information and lead up to information overload and shutdowns, which may be more or less dramatic to outsiders (some people implode silently). It can mean partial processing so one is limited to processing on only one track at a time and may lose a simultaneous sense of self and other or struggle to think and communicate at the same time or to monitor feelings and connect with one's body to express them.

Now even if the gut gets everything it needs to digest food: adequate stomach acid, enzymes, a good acid–alkaline balance, good secretory IgA (gut immunity), good helpful gut bacteria; and even if the important digestion and detox organs of the liver and kidneys and pancreas do their jobs to help digest foods and clean the blood; and even if the immune system is working well and the blood is well hydrated and the lungs and heart are working well, there are still a few naughty things that can happen on the way to muck up the whole delivery.

Now when we think about Autism we think about information processing and that means we think about the brain and how it talks to the body, how it deals with incoming information, how it accesses stored information, how it controls impulses and keeps track of self-expression and all of that important stuff…so with all this going on, what could go wrong?

Well, the brain itself is an organ, an organic, biological piece of machinery if you like. Like the rest of the body it contains veins and arteries – the roads that the delivery trucks need to drive down to get goodies to the brain. Well, even though it usually only happens to old people and alcoholics and smokers, a seemingly healthy young person can inherit 'vascular' problems where these run in a family, or can catch viruses that cause damage 'upstairs'.

Inherited vascular problems can include a tendency to accumulate plaque in the veins and arteries in the brain, a kind of gunk, building up in these pipe-works; this is called cerebrovascular disease. Other problems can include body chemistry issues, called metabolic disorders, that mean certain substances build up too high in the brain or the brain is unable to metabolise (manufacture) enough of certain important ones. Other metabolic problems can mean the walls of the pipe-works in the brain, the veins and arteries, aren't as strong as they are in most people; they can become damaged and lead to fluid accumulation, and occasionally blockages, small leakages that damage parts of the brain or, very occasionally, burst. Viral infections, allergies, the fungal infection of candida, and vascular problems may also cause swelling in the brain, where fluid accumulates causing damaging pressure on parts of the brain. This is called edema. Edema can come and go, which is called transient edema, it can lead to epileptic seizures, which come in many different forms and which can in very rare cases be a serious risk to health and survival. Edema and vascular problems in the brain will cause headaches and a tight pressure in the head called intracranial pressure. Where a person with Autism has seizures and clear neurological issues, and hits himself or herself in the head, it would be worth ruling out issues like edema.

Now the brain has a great rubbish removal, or detox system, and a major motorway for the supply of goodies to the brain. This is called cerebral spinal fluid, or CSF. This fluid runs along the spine to the brain and from the brain. It is the major messenger between the body and the brain. A good flow of CSF to the brain is essential to keep everything working and in balance. Now this CSF enters the brain through an area at the base of the skull. Sometimes this area is too small or tight and just like a squeezed pipe, the flow can be reduced or damaged and that means information processing won't be what it should. Sometimes vascular problems in the brain can mean the CSF doesn't get to flow and do its job within the brain as effectively as it should. If this happens before the age of three, then general cognitive development, how we process information, and the organisation of the brain may be affected. Cranio-sacral therapists are specialists who have trained in an area of medicine called osteopathy. Cranio-sacral therapy is non-invasive, often fairly relaxing. These people assess and work with problems associated with the flow of CSF to the brain. A neurologist is another specialist in the health and functions of the brain and the person who would explore these things. A neurologist may take scans (pictures of the brain) or EEGs, which show brain waves.

The electrics

Now let's turn from fuel system to 'electrics'. A house has plumbing and a house has wiring. Your car has a fuel system and an electrical system. Your car can't run properly when there's a problem in either of those things. The brain is similar.

The brain's electrical system is all about nerves and the messaging system, like a postal service, that conveys messages around the body.

Part of the electrical and fuel systems is a healthy straight spine to pass messages back and forth between the brain and the body. This is why some people with Autism are helped by seeing a chiropractor (a specialist in spinal alignment) who can align the spine to allow messages to be clearly conveyed between the brain and the body.

The electrical system includes something called myelin. Myelin provides the insulation of nerve fibres to protect messages as they pass to and from the brain without getting jumbled, weakened or lost. It also helps maintain healthy connections between different parts of the brain, which is vital for cohesively processing information in a multi-faceted way. Some people don't have enough myelin, and some people have auto-immune problems where the immune system attacks its own good myelin, causing a progressive problem.

Sensory flooding (inability to tune out irrelevant information), being only able to process one track or person at a time, having information-processing delays, having garbled processing or simply backlogging to the point processing is shut down on a particular sensory channel can be normal for people with a myelin deficiency. It could also occur in other people for very different

reasons: gut problems, vascular problems, allergies, and so on. Sensory perceptual problems would be usual. Gait, motor planning, speech and retrieval
problems, short-term memory problems (though serial memory may be a
compensation), attention problems are all common in people with myelin
problems. Problems regulating one's own body functions, including the
immune system, can be normal for those with myelin problems but will occur
in others who have no problems with myelin.

Thin myelin may be inherited, but the actual breakdown of existing
myelin may be caused by environmental triggers like viral infections, or even
casein and gluten in the diet. One of the most well-known auto-immune
disorders causing breakdown of myelin is multiple sclerosis (MS), which is
believed to be fairly rare in areas where casein and gluten are not in the diet.
Some people in this group exclude casein and gluten products from their diet,
even though they have no coeliac disease, simply because this limits the disruptive effect of these particular protein molecules in triggering auto-immune
responses that may worsen MS symptoms.

Identifying the problem and finding the right cause

Fuel system and electrics problems don't always have extreme or dramatic
causes. Lack of deep sleep will mess with health, detoxification and development. Bad diet, excess toxic garbage in the diet, lack of exercise, anxiety
disorders, mood disorders, compulsive disorders and personality or environmental issues and clashes big enough to cause severe chronic stress will com-
promise gut and immune function and that ultimately means an unhealthy
fuel system. So, it's always useful to start with what's simple – sleep, exercise,
water, clean food, low-stress environment.

Here are four essential questions to ask about health:

1. Do I/does my child have health-related problems? (And perhaps,
    What are the simple indications that you/your child likely does
    not have these and does this mean 'the end of the road'?)

2. How would I know? (And perhaps, How might I recognise signs
    of this without spending megabucks in possibly biased tests run by
    the companies who themselves make profit from the treatment?)

3. How can I find out *which* type of health issues I/my child has?
    (And, sometimes, How might I work this out with the least travel
    and expense?)

4. How can I get treatment or management for these? (And, are there home treatments, simple environmental changes and affordable 'food pharmacy' ideas I can bring in without spending a fortune?)

The tool box

Our usual Autism 'tool kit' may have nothing in it for dealing with autism-related health issues. If we do find we have a drawer within our Autism tool box called 'Fuel System and Electrical Problems', we may feel we are ready to tackle these problems. But first we need to know which tools fit which components, and that means knowing which components are in there.

There are certainly many (usually US) companies who are now selling one-size-fits-all fix kits for 'fuel system problems'. But again, the types of fuel system problems are dramatically different for different people, and the tools required to tackle one type of issue will often not be effective in tackling another. And what if we were spending a fortune holding together the health of a child sleeping in a high electromagnetic field which is progressively seriously undermining that child's sleep patterns and health? Wouldn't we first think about moving the bed before spending a fortune? Have airborne allergens been considered? Is the home dusty, damp, sprayed through with fragrances, on a major road with a high level of pollutants or inhabited inside by pets?

I may go and visit a child being treated for immune deficiency, enzyme deficiencies or assumed toxicity issues who in fact has no marked gut/immune dysfunction or toxicity issues at all.

I may visit one who is on a dairy/gluten-free diet with no effect who will respond brilliantly instead to a low-salicylate diet and omega 3s.

I may see a child who is on a quick-fix treatment for candida and five years later is still on the same treatment because the environmental cause of a sleep disorder was not addressed, or a stress-provoking impulse control or mood disorder has been left untreated, or the treatment for an underlying immune deficiency was never put in place so the candida couldn't go away.

I have known of children undergoing extensive, sometimes invasive, testing for bowel 'disorders' when the underlying issue has turned out to be an immune deficiency, metabolic disorder or an inflammatory state triggered by sleep deprivation or too many combined environmental triggers, so it won't be found via a bowel examination. The list goes on and on.

I'm not the ultimate physician to give an exhaustive list, and even if I were it would take another book to cover those areas and do them justice. So just to give you the starting point to ask the questions, here's a brief and limited view of some of the more common health issues that can affect information processing, sensory-perceptual issues, anxiety/mood/compulsive disorders, motor-planning issues and speech issues, and where the subsequent level of burden and stress may also up the tempo of natural personality traits to the degree they become 'dysfunctional'. If you take any of the words below and do an internet search adding the words 'Autism' and 'behaviour', 'learning', 'cognitive' etc., you should be able to access a wealth of information specific to your interests.

ENVIRONMENT-RELATED ISSUES

- 'Sick environments' (high levels of positively charged air particles keeping pollutants airborne and detrimental to health – generally worsened by a combination of poor natural air ventilation and natural light, high use of synthetic fibres building static, and high density of electrical charges from household electrical appliances and their outlets).

- High electromagnetic fields (EMF) affecting the sleep environment (e.g. sleeping with one's head within 1–2 feet of clock radios, stereos, a wall backed onto a fridge, TV, swimming pool motor, meter box or other strong electrical current).

- Sleep deprivation.

- Dehydration.

- Lack of fibre.

- Toxic overload.

- High acidity (impacting on blood health/immune system/oxygenation issues).

BREAKDOWN STATES

- Cranio-sacral problems (impaired flow of cerebral spinal fluid to the brain).

- Candida and 'leaky gut'.

- Auto-immune disease (inflammatory immune state).

- Immune deficiency (various kinds).

- Functional B12 deficiency (shown in a methylmalonic acid test).

- Secretory/salivary IgA deficiency.
- Chronic fatigue/ME/fibromyalgia.
- Heavy metal toxicity.
- Stored viral/bacterial/fungal/parasitic infections resulting in inflammatory states.
- Mycoplasma blood infection/nutrient transportation problems.
- Low blood oxygen.
- Impaired detoxification capacity (i.e. disorders of sulphate metabolism or liver dysfunction).
- Neurotransmitter imbalances.
- Presence of the neurotoxin quinolinic acid.
- Insufficient stomach acid.
- Insufficient enzyme production.
- Pancreas/liver inflammation/toxicity/dysfunction.
- Hypoglycemia.
- Myelin depletion (the protective sheath around nerve fibres).
- Calcium/magnesium deficiency.
- Zinc deficiency.
- B6 deficiency.
- Omega 3 deficiency.
- Selenium deficiency.
- Vitamin A deficiency/excess (including impaired ability to breakdown beta carotene).
- Salicylate intolerance.
- Dairy/gluten intolerance.
- Dairy/wheat/specific food or chemical allergy.
- Coeliac/Crohn's/irritable bowel.
- Spinal alignment problems.
- Left–right hemisphere integration issues.

- Cerebral vascular diseases.
- Viral infection-related edema.

These health issues don't affect all Auties, but any Autie who had these issues would likely be more severely affected if they went untreated. If you suspect someone *is* affected by health issues, the first step is to affordably clean up environment and diet:

- The electromagnetic field affecting the sleep area should read no more than 2.5 milligauss on a triaxial EMF meter. If in doubt, move the bed 60–90cms from the source of any major electrical appliances, electrical motors, meter boxes, transformers, battery chargers, clock radios or stereos, including those directly on the other side of the bedroom wall to the bed.

- The home should have a reasonably low level of airborne allergens such as dust, mould, pet hair, fragrances, traffic pollution and pollens.

- The diet should be relatively non-toxic, easily digestible, have a reasonable level of nutrition and fibre or be supplemented and involve a reasonable rotation of foods to keep allergy levels low.

- Foods should be balanced in terms of alkaline and acid content to avoid imbalanced pH which can lead to health problems.

- A reasonable amount of water should be drunk each day for digestion, blood health and detoxification.

- There should be a reasonable amount of physical exercise and fresh air each day without hours on end of physical stagnation in order to build motor-planning skills, assist neurological organisation, help circulation and digestion, improve detoxification and develop self-help and learning skills.

- There should be exposure to around 10 minutes of direct sunlight at least three times a week to avoid vitamin D deficiency. This is essential for a healthy immune system.

- Sleep, where possible, should not occur regularly in a room with bright or flickering light and night lights should be minimal.

- Address the expectations, feelings, wishes and social-emotional approach of the environment and how these might be contributing to the stress of the person with health issues.

Once you have taken those simple steps, you can sensibly say you might be ready to see what professionals can do to help. Sitting down with a qualified, sensitive, open-minded and holistic practitioner with an extensive background in both natural and conventional medicine, if not also neurology and immunology (tall order, I must be dreaming of an ideal world), and exploring all the signs and symptoms could be a start in wheedling out which health issues might be more likely at work.

Some people may be able to be cured of some of their health issues and others will merely be supported or may require ongoing maintenance. It's just how it is, so be ready and open to accept who is who and what is what. We don't all get the long straw. Some of us get the short straw. I spent my first two decades with health issues associated with primary immune deficiency and auto-immune disease and there have been times that have honestly been like living in hell. Nevertheless, for me, every curse is also conversely a blessing, and I have loved and craved life so much more for it being that bit harder to reach or hold.

Be aware there are many practitioners out there who may recommend an expensive ongoing one-size-fits-all approach, and there may even be those to whom you are a new customer in their money machine. Be discerning. Ask questions. If you are not seeing results after three to six months of sticking to the programme, then don't feel guilty in walking away. No professional is right at all times with all people. Nor do you leave without hope in moving on from what isn't working, you have simply left what is *not* working, no more, no less.

Equally, there will be those who pooh-pooh any suggestion that information-processing, sensory-perceptual, anxiety, mood or compulsive issues, or motor-planning problems could have relatively comprehensible, manageable, underlying physical causes.

My feeling is carers will know if their child:

- is allergic, or regularly has dark circles/puffiness under eyes
- is off their head or confused, disorientated and spaced out
- acts as if on drugs
- seems in pain
- is blocked up or has bowel problems
- is constantly sickly
- is in a dream state

- is often fatigued
- frequently has allergy rashes, eczema or asthma
- frequently gets cold sores or recurrent ear, nose, throat, chest or bladder infections
- has poor muscle tone
- has a strange pallor or flushed cheeks
- is unable to put on weight or get weight off
- craves certain foods or gags at the smell or sight of others
- has little appetite, eats non-food objects or binge eats
- has obvious bowel/gut or immunity problems
- seems to be unable to get the sensory messages efficiently.

Among others, these are some signs which *might* indicate health problems affecting the brain, which might play a part in someone's degree of Autism.

Helping those with information-processing problems
Shopping in the field of nutritional and environmental medicine

The important things to remember in shopping in the field of nutritional or environmental medicine are that it doesn't fit everyone, some people don't need it and the changes should only be justified by the real benefits any particular person will get from those changes. Some people may be much better off first seeing the cranio-sacral therapist to check out the flow of cerebral spinal fluid to the brain, a chiropractor to check spinal alignment necessary for efficient relay of messages to the brain, a neurologist, a pathologist (for tests), an immunologist or a specialist in infectious diseases (someone who tests for and treats viruses and diseases), before seeing the nutritional medicine person to help pick up the pieces. I say, find who you can.

Keep in mind that your GP or paediatrician may pooh-pooh any idea that nutritional medicine, let alone allergy testing, may be of any benefit; and many are still in total denial that gut or immune 'disorders' can exacerbate some autism-related issues. Keep in mind that, according to Dr William Crook in his book *The Yeast Connection* (1986), your medically qualified gurus may actually have about two weeks of training in the field of nutritional medicine in their six years or so of studying drugs and medicine. In other words, given that a naturopath studies nutritional medicine for about three to six years, medical practitioners are really not very qualified to talk about natural medicine; and given conventional medicine places itself higher up the hierarchy ladder, you may not be getting an unbiased opinion.

As far as your GP may be concerned, if findings about nutritional medicine were valid or useful, studies on it would have been written about in 'peer-reviewed journals' – in other words, written about by doctors. Yet, most doctors have never studied nutritional medicine, and the majority of medical studies are funded by drug companies who have no vested interest in nutritional medicine, which they can often neither patent nor make any commercial profit in prescribing.

If you want to ask an expert on hats you go to the hat shop, not the shoe shop and if you want to ask an expert in nutritional or environmental medicine, you ask a naturopath. Saying this, there are some people in the natural medicine fields who do not offer a good or reliable service, have not undertaken extensive and credible studies in the field and may be selling you fairy dust. So don't be afraid to ask for people's qualifications, and don't be afraid to research those qualifications. Ask how long they studied in their field. Ask how their testing works. If someone claims to know psychically, then do be sceptical. Whether you believe in psychic phenomena or not, there are some people who will have some ego confusion or mania in there. And your child's health is a real issue, not just a money-making opportunity, however well intentioned your 'psychic' may be. Similarly, if someone claims to know how to treat your child by virtue of someone's label or by proxy via a third person, you might be better spending your money on a more reliable and individualised service or relying on your own recorded observations in trialling some interventions.

Also, beware of the unwritten loyalty/guilt clauses. A service is like getting something from a shop. It's your purchase and you have a right to shop around and to stop buying and to return at your leisure. You are not obligated to buy, nor are you obligated to remain a regular customer. My own theory is that most change, if it's going to happen, starts to be seen for better or worse within six weeks of making a change. So don't enter into a loyalty programme which expects your ongoing belief if you see no changes after six weeks of treatment. This may not mean the treatment is useless, however. It may be useless or it may be part of the answer. The cost should justify the results.

Sometimes you need to start a number of changes together before a change is seen. Sometimes you will see someone get slightly worse, particularly as coming off allergenic foods or those you are intolerant to can cause withdrawal similar to what drug addicts go through starting around day three off these things. My experience is these usually level out after a week.

Anti-candida treatments, involving the killing off and starvation of fungal infections in the gut, can cause 'die off' symptoms which can last up to two weeks and are reduced with plenty of water and non-acidic vitamin C. Killing off candida and getting off a diet filled with toxic gunk helps lots of people function the best they can, but keep in mind that for some people candida and leaky gut may be part of deeper problems such as primary immune deficiencies, auto-immune disease and myelin issues or the effect of long-term disturbed sleep patterns.

Some people will be cured of their health issues, others merely maintained. This doesn't mean that improving health as much as possible won't help, but it may only help maintain what good functioning the person already has. In a world where people want miracle cures, people don't really think about the importance of simply maintaining what people already have, but it's an investment in that person's future.

It is also important to keep in mind that gut/immune/nutrient/toxicity issues may not be the only causes of information-processing problems. Myelin issues aside, gut/immune/nutrient/toxicity issues may themselves sometimes be a long-term by-product of severe chronic stress when anxiety, mood or impulse-control disorders go untreated.

Imbalances in brain messengers, called *neurotransmitters*, might also produce information-processing issues, so might very altered brain organisation; and there are also cases where some Auties have chromosomal conditions affecting brain development, and other cases where the brain is structurally different to the usual.

The jury is still out on the issue of what came first, chicken or egg, and it might be that in some cases it's the chicken and others it's the egg. Again, the best strategy may be to remain open to a holistic approach that considers a variety of these things at work instead of jumping on any bandwagon that suggests there is only one physiological issue causing one thing called autism.

Addressing underlying health issuess
Health issues could underpin specific issues relating to:

- communication
- interaction
- being in one's own world

- eye contact
- learning and cognitive challenges
- toileting
- sleep problems
- stimming
- meltdowns
- self-protection responses
- challenging behaviours
- food behaviour problems.

Many areas of behaviour (e.g. communication, eye contact, toileting) can be affected by poor information-processing ability, and it is this that can be improvable in some, sometimes many, cases by addressing health issues, if only you can find which one's most likely affect a particular person. Improving health issues can mean:

- improved feedback between the body and brain; in other words, the links start happening or slow links start speeding up

- better relay of messages between the senses and the brain without causing misfirings, flooding of irrelevant information and experiences, by reducing severe information-processing delay or simply allowing relaying of messages; in other words, the world may make sense more fully, more quickly and responses may become more 'on target' and require less immense effort

- an improved ability to make meaningful sense out of what is seen and heard, essential to navigating the world fluently when relying on the recognition of faces, places, things and the language of those around you, which is necessary to all aspects of learning and self-management

- an improved ability simultaneously to express oneself and monitor or keep up with one's own communication for meaning/ pronunciation, keeping track of one's own actions or considering personal or social consequences; this is necessary to learning, reasoning and changing one's own behaviour

- for processing information more quickly or fully, improvements in being able sensorily and emotionally to tolerate things like the sound of one's own voice, acoustics/sounds in different environments, to be less overwhelmed by lights, lighting, clutter and patterns, textures, tastes, smells or physical sensations. This is necessary for relaxing with communication, involvement, learning, having a body, having feelings or being more flexible about one's environment and change

- becoming more relaxed. This is essential to process incoming information, access and express oneself, and have a stable and positive enough mood state to be open to communicate and respond comprehensibly and to find natural motivation to seek out company, dare communication, explore new learning and experiences or challenge old behaviour patterns. Being overwhelmed, confused, fragmented, frustrated and distressed is not helpful to the functioning of any person.

When existing health issues are messing with information processing and these burdens are then managed or removed, all levels of functioning often show some improvement, even though new issues may come up as the person then moves into a new area of development on the progressive, often gradual, road to reaching a higher level of their potential.

CHAPTER 2

Different Ways
of Navigating the World

The System of Sensing versus Interpretation

Two people walk down opposite sides of the street. One side has a bookshop full of text books and technical books and books full of categories of things and their connections. Next door is an electrical store full of gadgets and computers. The other side of the street has a haberdashery, full of buttons and ribbons, fabric and zippers. Next door is a sweetshop full of colourful candies in cellophane and foil wrappers, and a pasta shop full of pastas of all shapes, and a shoe shop with patent leather shoes catching the lights, a glass shop full of ornaments, and a nursery full of plants and flowers of varying smells and textures.

The person on each side of the street is in his/her element. The intellectual mind, fixed, intense, intrigued and interested. The 'sensate' mind, caught up rapturously in the sensory experience of the shops. They cross the road.

The intellectual mind enters the haberdashery and finds the dress patterns, the measuring tapes and the cards showing price per metre. At the sweet store the intellectual mind watches the weighing out of the sweets, their different names and their ingredients. At the pasta shop the intellectual mind wonders about the machines which make all the different shaped pastas, looks at the price lists and reads the labels on the packets. At the shoe shop the intellectual mind explores the foot size and wonders which shoes would be the most comfortable. At the nursery the intellectual mind wonders at the plant families and which are related, when to replant and reads the labels re watering.

The sensate mind, on the other side of the road, now feels the covers of the books and smells their pages, flicking the pages for the different 'voices' of each book. At the electrical store, the sensate presses the keyboard buttons and licks the glass of the monitors, taps the sides of the cases and gets thrown out.

One brain or two?

A sphere is a ball-like shape. 'Hemisphere' is the word we use to describe half of a ball-like shape. Our brains aren't really shaped much like a round ball, but they are divided into two connected sides, called hemispheres; the right hemisphere and the left hemisphere. You could think of them as two separate balls of wool with a few ends connected up to each other in the middle, or mid-brain area.

Although they are connected, it takes a while for all the many different departments in each of these hemispheres to get used to working with each other. This is what happens in child development; these two sides learn to work together, to become what we call integrated. This is like taking those two balls of wool and making lots more connections between one and the other till they end up working more like one larger ball of wool than like two smaller, independent balls of wool.

As we develop through infancy and early childhood, we generally come to use these two sides of the brain together, to integrate them, and we can usually see this connectedness, this integration, in the way we move. Someone who hasn't developed this integration may struggle to learn to walk, may be very clumsy and uncoordinated or use one side of their body relatively independently of the other. It may be like there's an on–off switch stopping them from easily using both sides together consistently. They may find it hard to crawl or march, preferring to pull themselves along on their bottom or walk or run with their arms rigid, pulled up out of the way or flopping about at their sides. Left–right integration comes back to the communication between the different sides of the brain, and that can be altered by so many different things.

It may be worth asking how brain specialisation might illuminate the functioning of some people who struggle to use left–right brain processing in an integrated way. For example, if left-brain processing is about recognising strings of letters and words, about conscious awareness and ability to process language for meaning, and about logic, intellect and reasoning but also about focusing on details rather than the 'aerial shot', the overview then starts to sound pretty strikingly Aspergerian. If, on the other hand, right-brain processing is about 'artism', creativity, intuition and about the non-verbal skills of spatial awareness, pattern, form, theme and the 'feel of something', yet without the ability to sequence, and a tendency to get the global sense of something but lose the details, wouldn't this equate more closely with what often presents us as both the abilities and disabilities of 'Autism'?

Recognising someone with brain-integration problems

A left–right hemisphere integration problem may be evident in how a person uses their eyes, their arms in relation to their legs, how they combine hands in an action, what happens to the hand when it is not being used, how people run and the direction they take when doing an activity, even cases of asymmetry in facial expression where there is no underlying structural condition, and the presence of reflexes which should have become inhibited (lost) in infancy and replaced with new movement patterns. There are specialists who are able to recognise these things and give some ideas what can be done about them.

When I visit a home as an Autism consultant, I am always interested to view the person's childhood photos. Using the hand to divide the face into two, some photos show a consistent asymmetry in the expression on the face, particularly in the eyes. Sometimes there is a different emotion expressed on each side of the face, as though only one half of the brain was processing the emotion or expression at the time of the photo. Often only one of the eyes appears to be reacting emotionally to the photographer or what is being seen, the other eye appearing to be 'staring through' the camera or into space. Sometimes there is one arm contracted back into the body with the hand hanging limp almost in mid-air. At other times, the person appears to be 'in' one arm but the other arm appears to be strangely 'limp' and 'dangling'. Sometimes one half of the body appears to have the person 'in it', but the other part looks almost like the person meant to occupy it has left for a moment.

When I see such a person eat or handle objects, it can be as though the left hand really doesn't know what the right hand has already done or is doing. When such a person runs, sometimes one or both arms are dangling as though the person can't be in them at the same time as being in their legs. Sometimes the arms are contracted in, but the hands hang limp giving a kind of 'begging puppy' posture to the arms and this may be one or both arms. Sometimes such a person will turn their head to look at something on one side as though the eye on that side isn't registering what is seen.

Someone with these problems might only go in one direction or they might only be able to use the left hand over on the left side and the right hand over on the right side, becoming distressed and confused if made to cross over the body's 'midline' to do an action, as though they can't process the feedback when they do.

Personally, I have often 'lost' one of my arms which I've discovered left hanging, sometimes in mid-air, where I last used it before swapping to use the other arm. I have eaten with a fork with my right hand and found the left hand jumping in to eat with my fingers as though it has no idea the right is already doing the job. I have been unable to 'remember' how to skate in one direction yet been amazing in the other, with similar issues in reversing the car as if unable to process properly unless I pull out in a given direction. I have played a board game but been utterly unable to know how to play it when sitting on the opposite side or with the board on an angle to me. When I run, my arms have had little idea what my legs are doing or where I'm going. In washing, I have become confused about how to wash the other side of my body as though awareness of crossing the soap to the other hand just didn't happen 'naturally'. I found it extremely difficult to crawl in a 'cross pattern' but could use each side independently, front and back separately, or both sides together but haphazardly and somewhat random. I learned to do 'cross patterning' when I was 30 years old. I practised it daily for two years, and even at that late age a number of developmental changes did follow.

Causes of right- or left-brain dominance

There are many different causes of these things. One side of the brain may be affected by various conditions more than the other. The flow of cerebral spinal fluid, which nourishes the brain, can be impaired on one side of the brain more than the other. Myelin issues can be greater in certain areas of the brain and develop later in other areas, and brain impairment or damage may affect one side more strongly than the other. Epilepsy can affect one half of the brain more than the other. Some people will naturally have a more dominant side of the brain, and some types of personalities are more naturally oriented toward intellectual tasks and others toward artistic experiences. In other words, personality might be one part of what decides someone is going to be stronger in their ability to be 'interpretive' or 'sensing'.

One of the ways small children with limited information-processing capacity might compensate is to use whatever functions they can or to use those functions which are less taxing in terms of information processing. Left-brain processing involves consciously processing information for meaning: interpreting it. This can be very draining for some people and means they shut down quite quickly. On the other hand right-brain processing is more pre-conscious (a kind of dreamy state), so doesn't involve so much awareness, and it is about gathering and mapping out pattern, theme and feel.

Using the right side of the brain to make sense of the world may allow massive sponge-like absorption of incoming information or experiences (he/she takes all the information in like a sponge). But ultimately the problems may really start when downloading or when beginning to sort and interpret that flood of information. In other words, just because someone takes in a huge load of sensory information and patterns doesn't mean they have understood it.

This could have advantages and disadvantages, with the advantages being that those with such issues might be able to flood their senses with masses of unfiltered information which may later lead to awareness of all kinds of bits and pieces the person may be unable to account for. On the down side, even if they eventually work through this flood of information they may be unable to directly and consciously access or express anything about this because they weren't consciously aware at the time, so they may be more likely to appear learning disabled.

Epilepsy can be another disruptor of cohesive information processing and takes many different forms, from grand mal episodes where the person often drops to the floor and has convulsions, to the far more subtle absence seizures, which can look like someone simply staring oblivious into space. Some forms of epilepsy involve a brief and oblivious repeated action with the hands, a fluttering or blinking of the eyes, and in other types of epilepsy there can be sudden unexplained, seemingly oblivious violence, self-injury or sudden running, even at the wall. Epilepsy is extremely common in those with Autism spectrum conditions, believed to affect around 30 per cent of people in this group, and some specialists feel this is closer to around 50 per cent. Epilepsy may be so interrelated with myelin problems that it may be hard telling where the consequences of one end and the other begin.

This may cause people suffering epilepsy to avoid information processing tasks. Put simply, if someone kept breaking up the movie you were watching with a bunch of static, you'd progressively lose interest in trying to watch a whole movie. If every time you were keeping up with meaning, the slate got wiped and nothing made sense again for the next 15 minutes, it would progressively affect your interest in anything that involved having to keep up with consistent meaning. Most typically developing people know what it is to try and read a book or work something out and be constantly interrupted until they feel 'What's the point?' and progressively don't bother picking up that book because they can't get to enjoy it, to really get into it.

The causes of epilepsy are many and the first test for it is an EEG which is a test that measures brain waves. Some forms of epilepsy are more treatable than others. People may have problems with the flow of cerebral spinal fluid to the brain, spinal alignment issues, nutrient deficiencies, blood sugar problems, toxicity issues, gut dysfunction or immune-system issues underpinning epilepsy. Even extreme over-stimulation or acute anxiety or an untreated mood disorder could be implicated in triggering seizures in those vulnerable to them. Because the underlying causes of epilepsy can be so multilayered and diverse and the triggers themselves can sometimes be reduced, medication is sometimes not the only or best treatment. In this context it may be that treatment for epilepsy may be found from professionals beyond the narrow scope of the GP, pediatrician, dietician, or neurologist, alone. For example, if spinal alignment or issues relating to the flow of cerebral-spinal fluid to the brain were contributing to toxicity issues in the brain then it would be a chiropractor or cranio-sacral therapist who might have something to add. If lack of sleep were contributing to low levels of melatonin and hence a build of toxic irritants in the brain, then a sleep specialist might help explore reducing these problems. The GP, dietician or pediatrician is not an immunologist or gastroenterologist who might best address gut or immune disorders underpinning toxicity issues contributing to both stress and brain irritation. A psychiatrist might be able to treat co-occurring anxiety or mood disorders contributing to over stimulation and chronic stress and hence, reduce some of the triggers in some people. A hypnotherapist or play therapist could work with social stories geared to reducing sources of chronic stress or anxiety contributing to an over stimulated state. A kinesiologist or specialist in sensory integration or environmental adaptations for sensory overload might help improve information processing to a degree so that over-stimulation, as a trigger of seizures, is also reduced. A dietician is not an allergy specialist so an allergy specialist might be able to de-sensitize someone to allergens that contribute to seizures. So it's about thinking more holistically.

In some people there may be a problem with the development of the part of the brain that works like a phone exchange sending the messages back and forth between the two sides. In some people severe chronic stress, biochemistry, immune-system problems, nutrition or toxicity issues are all known to affect the development of organisation of the brain, which would include the development of the communication system between the left and right sides of the brain. When this doesn't develop in the usual way, the ability to keep up with incoming information can be slow, inefficient or simply very different to how the majority of people would process information. In other words people with left–right hemisphere integration issues usually perceive things differently. They are emotionally and sensorily affected differently and, therefore, generally would naturally think and behave differently. You can try to train them to act like they are not different, but, essentially, when left to their own devices, they won't rely strictly on the stored learning of your so-called 'normal' patterns of how they are meant to feel, think and behave, they will eventually revert back to their own natural system.

That doesn't have to be bad news. It may simply mean the developmentally typical persons may have to be open-minded in learning that their own reality is not the only information-processing reality. If they can understand how those with different brain organisation perceive, sense, feel and think in their own natural way, then they can help provide opportunities for these people to do the best they can with their own equipment.

Different jobs

The left side of the brain and the right side of the brain do two different sorts of jobs. As we enter childhood, we usually develop a 'dominant' side, which is what makes us left- or right-handed. Some of us are a mixture, with our right eye being dominant, but left-handed and using our right leg to kick a ball.

The left side of the body is generally governed by the right side of the brain and vice versa, although our society is so used to considering right-handedness as 'normal' that some people who would usually have become left-handed instead use the right, so handedness is generally not considered a highly reliable indicator of the dominant side of the brain.

The right side of the brain is generally the part that absorbs lots of information about things like pattern, theme and feel. It is about experiencing the world, not about thinking about it.

The right brain is more associated with sensing and intuition, feeling one's way and the abstract. Meaning is generally less relevant to the right side of the brain and most activities associated with the right side of the brain are unconscious. Those with a lack of left–right integration but who use their right brain as their dominant processing style might, theoretically, stay enjoyably involved in a pattern others may find seemingly mundane.

The right side of the brain is said to be an abstract world of metaphor and dreams. If X has the feel to it of being like Y then the person may assume without question that X actually 'is' Y. This can be illustrated with examples from my own experience.

As a child I had a green fluorescent plastic ball which had a certain sound when tapped, a certain texture when scratched, and a certain way of catching the light when held before light. After that, anything with the same surface, with the same sound, with the same colour – a fluorescent green ruler, a plastic bottle, a vinyl armrest cover, whatever its nature in the interpretive world of meaning – was somehow '*of*' this original ball and I would be very pleased. By contrast, a child who is almost dominated by a focus on interpretive meaning could be given a thousand objects of a related sensory nature and if they were not actually balls, would feel that they had no similarity at all.

In secondary school I continually lost conscious awareness of the meaning and significance of where I was and often wandered out the gate following one experience or another, only to be found eventually on the other side of town somewhere. Once, I wandered into another school and sat down quite at home in a school uniform quickly recognised as not being 'theirs'; my teachers were then called up. By contrast the more left-brain child with extremely good consistent conscious awareness of location and why he or she was in a certain place may have a similar problem when the activity itself involves everyone just 'going for a wander'. He or she may be utterly lost without exact conscious instruction on exactly how and where to wander.

So when we talk about being '*lost in the pattern, lost in the flow, lost in the rhythm*', we are talking about someone able to do things according to pattern but not able simultaneously to be aware or conscious of the meaning or significance of what they are doing at the time they are doing it. And what's so wrong with that? Many developmentally typical people have these 'moments', this waking dream state.

Right-brain people in a left-brain world

One of the hardest things for those for whom right-brain processing is their primary or dominant state may be that the world of developmentally typical people has no idea how to make use of this form of processing, not as disability, but as *ability*.

Developmentally typical people can be so scared of people functioning, doing, without conscious awareness or proven ability to take account of the meaning or significance of what they are doing, that they often hold these people back tremendously, rather than channelling them into indulging themselves in patterns that happen to relate to self-help, and happen to relate to going out, and happen to relate to being socially involved, and happen to relate to working.

The world of developmentally typical people can be so highly focused on instilling awareness that people who might otherwise bumble along casually from one patterned activity into the routine of the next one, may be overly jolted into self-doubt and fear. Instead of becoming klutzy but independent, they may instead be more likely to become self-doubting, clingy and highly dependent.

It's OK to admit one needs help, or that conscious awareness of meaning and significance are important in some activities, but this is not the same as giving someone the general sense that if they can't hold onto this at all times in all things they should distrust all their other capabilities. Unfortunately, because most developmentally typicals only know how to teach by their own natural style, this is what they may unintentionally instil. Teachers working with developmentally different people may need a good sense of being able to work from within the reality of the Autie to maximise the potential that person has using systems which make sense and are reliable for that person, however foreign these may be to those with different brain function or personality dynamics.

Left-brain people and the methodical scientist

The left side of the brain, by contrast, is generally considered to be the conscious and aware part of the brain, responsible for interpreting or attributing meaning to what is otherwise less processed information about pattern, theme and feel. The left side is generally more associated with intellect and the use of words to convey meaning and concrete thinking and with realisation. There is a left-brain version of creativity but it is generally based on a concrete reality not an abstract one.

Theoretically, those for whom left-hemisphere processing is their primary way of making sense of the world, might even be too constantly aware, too conscious, unable to switch off thought. They may be equally unable to acquire and feel at ease with intuitive reliance on pattern, theme and feel that we pick up with our bodies, unconsciously, without awareness, as part of more right-brain processing.

Those comfortable with, and reliant on, conscious awareness and interpretive meaning might struggle to stay on task with what appears intellectually unstimulating and mundane and may prefer to 'work things out'. These people might theoretically be extremely good at learning what is meant to be right and meant to be wrong and how one is meant to behave and good at working things out involving knowledge. Yet when it comes to bumbling along, trusting to that state of mind involving no conscious awareness, they might also just freeze in such a vast unknown. They may need to know 'the point'. They may be unable to 'just go there'.

Of course many people with left–right hemisphere integration problems occasionally do have lights on in both parts of the brain, but maybe not at the same time.

Left and right without integration

Someone who has very limited integration between the left and right hemispheres can be both very talented or very disabled or both. They may learn to read words or echo speech but be unable to read or hear with meaning, for example. They many be highly sensing, also highly sensual but unable to express themselves verbally or relate in a way most consider learned 'social skills'. They may be very verbal with a good idea of the meaning of words, but with little intuitive idea how to use them interpersonally. They may be able to express themselves, but be unable to make much conscious sense of the feedback. They may be exceptionally artistic, poetic or expressive, but unable to organise themselves to produce anything without facilitation. They may be brilliantly logical and concrete, but seemingly unable to take account of the emotional impact of their behaviour or communications on other people.

As we develop, we may need some degree of left–right hemisphere integration to:

- get better feedback about what our body is doing
- use our eyes properly for depth perception, making out background from foreground information
- keep track of where the edges of things are in order to recognise objects easily and navigate space confidently
- link information in order to learn easily and apply learning from one context to another
- keep track of a simultaneous sense of self and other
- combine sensuality and reasoning, feeling and thought in order to reflect, combine pattern/theme/feel with meaning, and compare and resolve our mental and emotional dilemmas easily (without the use of external representations to help with the process).

As most people develop good integration between the two sides of the brain, then regardless of which side of the brain is the dominant side, the person usually doesn't stand out as 'unusual'. Most people will have a reasonably integrated balance of sensing and interpretation.

There are some people who develop high abilities associated with both left and right hemispheres but have very poor integration between the two. This may leave them highly sensing, intuitive, abstract and generally in a bit of a dream state, but poor at staying aware and conscious of meaning and significance. At other times, they may be very good at consciously learning concrete things involving meaning but really bad at sensing and all the things we do without conscious awareness. It may be that problems in the brain mean that the messages between the body and senses and the brain are so delayed, garbled or flooded with irrelevant information that left–right integration processes are delayed for people with these issues.

A difference between Autism and Asperger's?

Many people see Asperger's syndrome as the 'high-functioning' version of Autism. I think there are two types of diagnosis happening out there. There is one group which diagnoses all those with poor language as being in the Autistic group and those with good language as being in the Asperger's group. Yet among those with poor language, those with good left-brain processing will go on to keep up much better with language and eventually be quicker to use it with meaning than those whose primary system is right-brain processing, the place of feel and experience in which conscious awareness and concrete interpretive meanings are elusive.

It has been my experience that there are some children with Asperger's who appear more Autistic before the age of five but after the age of five or so emerge as children who are very interested in interpretive meaning and catch on quickly. Most Aspies, however, start out in the Aspie rather than Autie range.

The teaching style and education programmes commonly used today are those which rely on children having good conscious processing of information for interpretive meaning; in other words, those with very good left-brain processing. Many Aspies will actually do pretty well academically in this kind of system. It's socially where they are usually most challenged.

Developmentally different people, by contrast, may struggle extremely with academia, either because of severe receptive information-processing challenges or severe communication challenges or both. But there is another reason these people may be more set up to fail in today's mainstream education programmes. This is because today's mainstream education programmes may not be systems which are compatible with a developmentally different way of processing information, of pre-consciously absorbing but perhaps not interpreting, pattern, theme and feel. The consequence may be that these are the children who are set up to most likely fail in a system which doesn't fit them. So it's as if the dice are loaded in a way that will make it harder for them to progress because their own natural skills may not be recognised, not be valued and not be co-opted in developing a more user-friendly learning experience.

Assuming we can take the left-brain/right-brain framework as a basis for differentiating between Auties and Aspies, the 'high-functioning' Autie in a mainstream learning situation may be different again and can be extremely different to the Aspie. Similarly, the 'low-functioning' Aspie may be extremely different to their 'low-functioning' Autie counterpart. Each may have very different developmental needs.

The Aspie may be able to do the shopping according to the long list of learned rules. The Autie, by contrast, may get all the rules and recite them by heart but, in the context in which they are needed, be unable to keep hold of their meaning or application and instead learn best directly through pattern.

One of the catches in learning this way is that, in general, life patterns can have a habit of requiring change. If this is the case, no amount of explanation may filter through because each time the explanation is told it may be utterly embedded only in the moment it was told. Instead of being able to learn from explanation, the person may have to learn *utterly* from the consequences of his or her actions, over and over again until it becomes a physical pattern of experiences which he or she then alters to avoid the consequences. You may say it to the mind all you like, but getting it to filter through to being an experienced new physical pattern of responses is where the problem may be. If you've ever changed a room in your house so something which was always there is now somewhere else you may have found that for some time you keep going to the old place for something even though you *know* the room has been changed. Now multiply that by a lifetime and you might begin to imagine what this is like.

The only less painful effective shortcut to making choices in my experience was to play out the patterns through role-playing actions through the use of representational objects. (It helps to use characterisation to bring these to life so they are not simply 'explained' relationships, but 'demonstrated' ones.)

So for example, if I had to decide which of two people to go with I might use matchsticks to represent them (you might draw faces and hair on them to make it clear they represent people). I would then use stones of two different kinds to represent the advantages and disadvantages associated with choosing to go with one or the other (and you might draw or write on the stones to show the nature of the good or bad things they represent, or just name these and assess them as good or bad, then put them in the appropriate tally pile). Then at the end I would weigh up which side seemed the better deal.

If I had to represent contrasts in different places I might use different coloured pieces of paper to represent the different 'areas' and if there were people I'd meet in those places I'd maybe represent them with the matchsticks, then use the stones to represent good and bad happenings in those places associated with the different people there. So it is like watching a video and I end up unconsciously taking on the patterns I've been exposed to.

So, you want to hear how to get your point across in your own way? Well, does the cat speak dog? Does the plumber repair your electrics? Do you cook with garden utensils? No. You use the tools that best suit even if they are not the ones you know how to use, and even if they don't come with an instruction manual. You use them because they fit, and if they fit then they work.

Many people who are severely affected by Autism may be extremely good at sensing and can be highly sensual. There are certain chemical states which will increase this state, such as high levels of dopamine, which is associated with a heightened sense of pattern. There are certain personality traits which may increase the likelihood of someone being good at pattern, theme and feel, such as an artistic personality which predisposes people to be naturally motivated towards experiencing the world in an 'artistic' way. There may be those who for various health or brain reasons fail to be able to process information much beyond the accumulation and categorisation of sensory experiences in terms of pattern, theme and feel. There may be those who for some reason right-brain processing is switched on and left-brain processing is either more energy consuming or more problematic, or access to it is limited. In any case, I spent my first nine years in the system of sensing and the greatest tragedy was not where I was stuck, but the inability of the world to find alternative ways of relating, sharing and communicating which were compatible, non-invasive and not alienating. Often it can be an adventure or a tragedy, and opportunities can be designed to maximise such a person's strengths instead of mourning perpetually over their weaknesses. I say, be a worrier enough to understand the issues, be a wallower enough to get over self-pity, then be a warrior who knows when to battle, when to adventure and when to accept.

Among those non-verbal people who have managed to communicate via assisted, or facilitated, communication, some of whom have progressed to independent communication via voice communicators, are some wonderfully artistic poets and writers. Some of the most severely affected Auties are as out-standing in the sensing world as many Aspies are in the interpretive world.

Some of the most severely affected Auties map the most subtle shifts in pattern, theme and feel out of new places, people or things, like a snake feels heat. They may be unable consciously and intellectually to interpret facial expression or body language. They may even be generally 'meaning-deaf' and 'meaning-blind'. But, more importantly, they may be excellent at physi-cally picking up shifts in far more subtle behaviours, such as the change in footfall as you cross a floor, the change in how you grasp a cup, the slight increase in your expectation or agitation, the slight shifts in your pace or flow of speech. To write off any group of people as simply globally 'low-function-ing' may say more about the ignorance and arrogance of those making these assumptions, but to do so may also be to be closed-minded regarding what they *are* so good at.

Aspies can be exceptionally 'clever' in the intellectual sense, sometimes highly articulate, extremely logical, concrete and clinical and, in the absence of a good connection to sensuality, they may rely on stored learning for emotional expression. Just as many Auties may have trapped intellect, and struggle to *integrate* what their bodies feel with ideas, consciousness, intellect and mind, some Aspies may have an opposite problem. Many Aspies are extremely emotional people but may have trouble integrating what their bodies feel with thought, behaviour and communication. They may rely instead on mind-emotions. In a similar way some Auties may rely on commu-nicating directly through the less conscious, emotional, often 'functionally non-verbal' world of movements, sounds, sensing and experiencing. Though many developmentally typical people find Aspie social communication a bit Spock-like, many find the less verbal, more sensory social-communication styles of Auties far more foreign or socially 'inappropriate'. If Auties were living in gorilla communities, I think the gorillas might find them a lot more comprehensible.

Most Aspies have started out as children with Asperger's syndrome. Some do not but are misdiagnosed as Autistic by virtue of appearing 'low-functioning' in infancy but growing out of this in childhood. It is also possible that there are some predominantly right-brain people with Autism who develop left-brain skills only in mid- to late childhood and hence, move into being more comparable to those with Asperger's sundrome. Temple Grandin was born in the 1950s, the child of highly educated, professional parents. She was diagnosed as Autistic in infancy but was later re-diagnosed as having Asperger's syndrome. Her behaviour at the age of three would not have had her placed as 'high-functioning', but we cannot say how much of that was the result of personality traits affecting social-emotional and communication development, mood, or information- processing issues. Temple was a healthy child and did not suffer from severe gut or immune disorders, nor did she have epilepsy or tic disorders indicative of brain irritation associated with metabolic or toxicity issues. It's reasonable to assume that cognitively she had most of the equipment in place to reasonably keep up with incoming information to the degree that she did not experience severe receptive-processing problems described as 'meaning-deafness' or 'meaning-blindness'.

A percentage of people once in the 'low-functioning' end of Asperger's syndrome have progressed to the 'high-functioning' end, but their basic underlying system generally remains the same. Their primary way of processing information may always have been very left-brain dominant, very much about concrete thinking, processing information for meaning and reliant on conscious awareness.

Like Temple or like Donna?

Many years ago, in dialogue with Temple Grandin, I encountered her belief at the time that people with Autism required higher levels of excitement and stimulation and that this is what had helped her. Temple has a very high IQ, which might shed some light on why she thrived on such high levels of intellectual stimulation. Certainly there are some people with an enormous capacity for receptive processing who would be understimulated by everyday life and who have the type of personality that craves high levels of stimulation. Temple was absolutely right, about those like herself. But many Auties would work differently too.

I could spend eight hours lost in a pattern, not deep in thought, but in the absence of it as I merged with the pattern. I had the kind of personality which went into social claustrophobia with high levels of interaction. I had the kind of brain that overloaded after hearing five minutes of speech; or I could cross a room, and the processing of my movement would be so delayed I'd have no idea how I got there. When I met Temple, I explained to her that what worked for her would have made me far more low-functioning. I worked best left largely to my own space with limited input and sensory materials or physical/sensory experiences that required no complex explanations and could be explored in a trial-and-error manner with little reliance on interpretive processing. I functioned worst when given multi-faceted intellectual tasks in socially interactive contexts. At 26 and after achieving a higher education my IQ score was just under 70, essentially what was once called 'mildly mentally retarded' and today 'intellectually disabled'. It wasn't that I was more stupid than Temple but that my intelligence isn't of the kind reflected well in conventional IQ tests. The implications this has for excitement and stimulation are huge. If that excitement and stimulation required interpretive information processing I'd have been as quickly distressed as Temple was engaged.

I had a different history to Temple. I was born in the 1960s and from a very different social background, my father with virtually no formal education and nobody in my family having ever completed secondary school. I was diagnosed with Autism in adulthood after a childhood in which I was thought to be deaf, was called psychotic, labelled disturbed and riddled with chronic health issues. I had severe receptive language processing problems into late childhood, but from around the age of nine I began to grasp that people were speaking with meaning. The interpretive world progressively opened up for me, but it was sluggish and slow and shut down quickly, as if that part of my brain had batteries which quickly went flat.

Although I progressively did develop the ability to keep up with the literal meaning of about 50 per cent of what was spoken to me, by the time I hit my teens, my expression remained significantly better than my comprehension. I still struggle to keep up with meaning when reading and don't cope with long lengths of conversation, because the meaning seems to fall away from language. I type and my typed language is complex and quite beyond the level of my general daily speech (at lectures on the topic I'm accustomed to typing about, however, I speak like all my typing). Socially, I struggle to enjoy intellectual stimulation through language, and I often still feel rather isolated because of that; but if someone uses gestural signing I can keep up with language amazingly, as I get to 'hear' it with the 'experiences' intact in the signing so the meaning doesn't fall away. Most people, however, don't use fluent gestural signing, and I feel I am always like a newly arrived migrant. I am highly sensing but I feel this as another language I experience through my body, not just through words to my ears. I experience the system of sensing as my '*original mind*' and experience intellect like my second language, my second mind. At best, in receptive verbal language, I am completely literal. However, for 30 per cent or more of the time I am not literal at all, and words, although heard, are not processed and mean nothing. Non-verbally, however, I perceive pattern at an amazing level. Receptively, my primary system remains that of sensing rather than interpretation.

Today Temple is known for her excellence in engineering. She is quoted as saying that spoken and written words quickly translate for her into pictures in her mind. This affects the way Temple accesses information and how she best learns. I'm sure this is so for most Aspies and many Auties too. But it is not so for all, and I feel those people need to be represented too, especially as it is the receptive issues for these people that makes them the least likely to be able to communicate their reality easily.

Quite differently to Temple, outside of being known as an author and public speaker, I am known for my music and art. I have written and spoken extensively on 'meaning-deafness' and 'meaning-blindness'. Without the use of gestural signing, my brain seems to struggle to keep up with putting any concepts to words and I seem unable to hold them consciously. Even when I do understand them, after three seconds the meaning of what I've heard is mostly jumbled and large chunks of it seem to have fallen away. I also often don't recognise objects when they are not in their expected place, and I can take up to two seconds to recognise the nature of an object. Unless it moves, unless I can experience it, it often doesn't mean anything at first, sometimes it doesn't mean anything for quite some time. It's pattern, theme and feel, without interpretive meaning. My mind switches off, my body switches on. I feel everything and know very little. I don't mind, I'm used to navigating my world this way. But it's far from having words trigger movies in my head.

Taking Temple and me as stereotypes, our dominant systems come through in our greatest strengths and weaknesses and they come through differently. Some people rely largely on sensing, mapping pattern, theme and feel, with meaning either elusive or relatively irrelevant. Others rely largely on interpretation, with meaning as their primary starting point, even to the point where they can't move it out of the way in order to access the pure pattern, theme and feel of what is sensed. More helpful than the visual versus auditory processors division (and neither of these are my forte) I think we could take these two stereotypes as 'interpretives' versus 'sensates'; one relying more on mind and thought (whether visual or auditory is the primary system, the emphasis is on 'meaning'), the other relying more on sensing and experiencing the world directly through body, which I call 'body mapping' (where the emphasis is on 'experience', and meaning may be secondary or irrelevant).

Both groups will have particular issues affecting the development of language, social communication and so-called 'appropriate' behaviour. Understanding these different groups may be essential to recognising the very different cognitive and learning styles, communication paths and social-emotional interaction styles most natural to each.

Sensing and interpretation
Sensing without interpretation

I think that sensing without interpretation is closer to the difference between primal man and modern man. But first let's look at all the things that sensing is not.

Sensing needs to be distinguished from the avoidance, diversion and retaliation responses that can occur in two anxiety-related conditions called exposure anxiety and avoidant personality.

A person who has one of these anxiety conditions can appear 'deaf' yet be known to hear. They may self-protectively be so emotionally unable to dare demonstrate that they have understood that they may be frozen out of expressing this awareness physically or even registering it consciously on a psychological level. In other words, the ability to process information is there but the ability to demonstrate any awareness of that processing may be severely impaired due to an acute chronic anxiety state.

An extreme self-protective anxiety state and a severe problem interpreting incoming information can coexist in the one person too and helping someone like this would involve addressing both issues.

Extreme states of depression can result in thoughts so fixated on sources of worry, fear and negativity that there may be little ability to process much else, and extremely poor self-motivation to do so. Extreme states of mania, by contrast, can result in racing, even distracted and fragmented thought, such that being able to keep up with or control a stream of thought may be impossible. Such a person can be not only very quick to self-protect, very fixated on potential 'threat' and 'invasion' but also so overstimulated, so overloaded that there may be little potential to process incoming information.

Extreme compulsive states such as those seen in severe cases of chronic vocal and movement tics such as Tourette's or severe obsessive-compulsive states can leave a person so compelled and distracted there may be little ability to focus on the processing of incoming information and extremely reduced ability to respond coherently to it. The compulsive state itself may be so chemically driven by unchecked high dopamine levels to be oversensitive to pattern, theme and feel rather than interpretive meaning that actually keeping up with the meaning of what someone is saying or showing you can be extremely challenging.

Where a person simply has an information-processing problem that stops them being able to get meaning from what they see and hear, this could also be due to a sensory-integration problem or dyspraxia. So the person may be able to understand what they see, but not at the same time as interpreting what they hear, for example. They may be able to express themselves, but not be able simultaneously to process incoming information. Or such a person may be able to cross the room or do something physical, but unable simultaneously to process what is seen or heard. These are integration issues, which have a number of quite different underlying, sometimes treatable, causes in different people. But this is not the same as someone being in a state where they process everything for pattern, theme and feel but are unable to process information for interpretive meaning. Again, someone can have both conditions and both need to be addressed independently.

Sensing without interpretation can affect all areas of functioning or only single areas. Sometimes it affects only hearing. So someone who can hear perfectly well but be unable to keep up with the meaning of what's being said is effectively meaning-deaf. If this is the case, then a central auditory processing disorder might be the real problem, and there are many underlying causes of this.

Interpretation without sensing

Interpretation without sensing has fascinated me because in my case it is the interpretive mind that always shuts down. As an intuitive artist, sculptor and composer as well as a writer of not only poetry but also wordy intellectual text books, I know what it is to be in both of these states to the exclusion of the other – sensuality and sensing without mind but also mind without sensuality. Theoretically, one may still be sensing by being right-brain dominant in a split-brain state. It's also possible those with personality traits such as the artistic personality may also feel 'right' spending far more time indulging in right-brain perception and processing states. Yet, theoretically, the same person might also develop (perhaps later) interpretive ability and leanings by virtue of other fairly mind-related personality traits such as conscientious or vigilant personality. If this happened in someone still unable for some reason to achieve a level of left–right hemisphere integration, this person could still experience information-processing problems because processing is more efficient where there is reasonable left–right hemisphere integration. But the type of information-processing problem would be different in each of these different functions. Just because someone has the capacity to process information for interpretive meaning and function with 'mind' doesn't mean there isn't a significant information-processing problem. To be so caught up in detail you can't achieve an overview is still as much of an issue as it might be in reverse. In an overloaded state many very intellectual people with Asperger's who keep up fluently with interpretive meaning still struggle to move from purely literal interpretation to the wider 'significance'. They get the 'what' but lose the 'why'. Mapping combinations of left-brain dominant and right-brain dominant processing in relatively split-brain individuals may hold exciting promise for future individualized programmes, helping people more easily reach their fullest potential according to their own natural realities.

I was intrigued to meet people diagnosed with Asperger's syndrome who were sometimes remarkably interpretive to the point I couldn't stand all the words. They could go on listening to each other as if their brains were eager and hungry for the input, but I felt like my brain was about to explode. Yet they were eager to have me converse with them and to do so face-to-face and verbally, perhaps because some had the visual thinking that allowed them to keep putting concepts to words.

I'm a wonderful video recorder able to store huge strings of actions and words. At the same time I have sat as a passenger in the car and watched my hands on the dashboard swing between being recognised as hands to being mere fleshy pink forms with external space forming a pattern around them. I grew up largely knowing almost only sensing for my first nine years. I learned the interpretive state like a second language. Today I am at home in my first 'language' (a dreamlike, drifting, abstract world of sensing based on body mapping and absorbing pure pattern, theme and feel), but highly proficient (albeit with batteries that go flat quickly) in my second 'language' (a concrete, literal, detached, conscious world of awareness, mind and interpretation).

Someone who has interpretation without sensing may be like Spock: dry, purely intellectual, absolutely logical, yet neither decidedly callous nor empathic, almost functioning as a 'thinking machine'. Though I experience myself as being something like this when I write text books, I am not aware of thought or consciousness when writing, as though the process is automatic and could almost work without 'me'. Unlike most Aspies, I have no idea what it must be like for those who live with conscious thought their entire day, week, month, lives. This is a space I can step into for short bursts, and in between the meaning drops away and I'm back in 'my world', a world of pattern, theme and feel; a world of sensing.

Yet there is a difference between sensing as 'body mapping' and sensing as 'sensuality'. 'Body mapping' is like being a computer which can store and categorise huge strings of pattern, theme and feel, but which is relatively 'mindless' and unable to interpret them at the moment they come in. Watching someone who is 'mapping', most people would likely have no idea what the person thinks or feels, because at the time of mapping the person is not quite 'there'. They are just being, but it is a kind of beingness in which the flood-gates are open and the information taken in is being dealt with in a detached, objective, machine-like way. They may be on 'autopilot' at the time or simply appear to be staring through things or 'in their own world'. Mapping has nothing to do with 'sussing out' a situation. To suss, one has one's thinking switched on, there is conscious awareness, there is judgement happening, con-clusions being drawn, relative significance being assigned, and there is sub-jectivity and a sense of self in relation to other. With 'mapping', processing for relative significance is absent, it is merely about category, there is neither a sense of self, nor a sense of other being experienced, it is more like being a machine and purely open to absorbing information. It is as objective a state as a human being could ever have. In this sense, 'sussing' is to do with 'mind' and 'mapping' is basically 'sensing' pattern, theme and feel in its pure form.

Sensuality, on the other hand, is about the body and how one uses one's senses. Where mapping is a detached cognitive state involving an utter lack of self-consciousness or interpretation, sensuality can also be a detached (though for most it is not detached but personal) yet equally indulged emotional state involving a similar utter lack of self-consciousness or interpretation.

When someone looks at art, they appreciate it from a distance. When someone senses art, they merge with the object as though self and other have no boundaries. The person stuck in an interpretive state without the ability to use sensing will have little idea of the absolute mindlessness and abandon-ment of this kind of sensuality. In a sense, one can't get off the surface and the other can't get out of the deep.

Certainly an overdevelopment of interpretive, intellectual ability can be associated with intelligence, but so can extreme sensuality. These are merely different types of extreme intelligence. Some of this will be affected by personality too. A solitary personality may be far less likely to indulge sensuality and a sensitive/avoidant personality may struggle with it socially, but an artistic personality may be extremely sensory if not sensual, an idiosyncratic personality very much in their own world and sensual.

Psychopaths and sociopaths

The stereotypical 'psychopath' has sometimes been described as a person unable to feel a broad range of emotion, though able to learn intellectually both how to recognise it and how to perform it. Not well connected to their own felt emotions, they may be confused that others have felt rather than performed emotions, and so they may also be more likely to have a morbid fascination with the emotional responses of others and more likely to confuse an adrenaline rush with the only emotional experience they know.

This doesn't mean that all people with problems processing emotion are psychopaths or that all psychopaths are dangerous. Some people in the field of psychopathy would argue there are many harmless, even helpful and certainly often highly intelligent, psychopaths living among us in society and that they are over-represented in intellectual and scientific fields such as information technology! Some of these people are highly motivated to fit in, be liked, and do 'the right thing' according to society's rules.

True psychopaths, unlike Aspies, have often been found to be missing areas in the brain necessary to the processing of emotion, and this distinguishes them from those with Asperger's syndrome alone. Aspies generally have a usual range of emotion but simply struggle to identify it or easily know how to use or resolve it. If we are to embrace the productive contribution that 'everyday psychopaths' may have to society, we need to distinguish psychopathy from Asperger's syndrome, whilst recognising that some people may have both conditions. To fail to distinguish one from the other or recognise where someone has a combination of both states, is to fail to provide services most appropriate to those people. Failing to distinguish one group from the other runs the risk of Aspies being seen socially in terms of the rare but always memorable headlines that can result from the occasional psychopath gone 'wrong'.

For Aspies, interpretive processing may simply be their dominant state and some are capable of not just intellectually learning, but coming to experience and indulge in a degree of emotional closeness, sensual abandon, sensuality and sexuality.

The stereotypical sociopath is sometimes described as a person who doesn't reason, who acts without thought for the consequences. But a narrower definition of sociopath might be someone who acts with intent for self-gain with no respect for the consequences for others. So whilst on the surface some rather feral sensates might fit a broad stereotype of sociopath, on a more refined level most would not.

Central auditory processing disorder: implications for sensing and interpretation?

Some of the features of central auditory processing disorder (CAPD) begin to look very like the sensory and receptive processing problems of those with Autism spectrum conditions. Speech sounds can be distorted in both CAPD and Autism. For both groups background noise can interfere with the ability to keep up with language or understand a lesson. In CAPD it may be common for words to be heard as arbitrary sounds which the person struggles to connect to meaning; this is essentially 'meaning-deafness'. This, too, is what we often see in people with Autism. Could it be that these things are simply CAPD occurring in someone with certain personality traits and when the two come together we are more likely to call it Autism? Could it be that when someone with the sensitive-avoidant or solitary-schizoid type of personality traits also has or develops CAPD, then the burden on personality is so increased by the anxiety and frustration of this type of communication disorder that the person is so much more extremely avoidant or schizoid to the degree that we see them as Autistic? And if you were not merely 'meaning-deaf' but also had 'receptive processing disorder' (yes, there is such a condition), amounting to a combination of meaning-deafness and meaning-blindness, how would you calm yourself, entertain yourself or give the environment the clear message you were overwhelmed? Would you 'stim'? If you happened to have the anxiety, mood and compulsive disorders associated with a high degree of chronic stress, would you look even more 'Autistic'?

It's easy to question in this context whether Autism as a singular condition rather than a process actually exists. If CAPD or receptive processing disorder is the real challenge, perhaps we are better off addressing those conditions directly, rather than addressing a label like Autism. If the CAPD and receptive processing disorder are reduced, it may be that much of the 'Autism' seems to go with it.

The development of the part of the brain used to associate sound with meaning can be deprived of building these associations in the same way that someone who doesn't exercise might end up with weak muscles and unable to play sports well. Some of the things which can deprive the brain of the experiences needed to link sound to meaning could include:

- chronic ear infections due to underlying food allergy or immune deficiency issues
- problems with the flow of cerebral spinal fluid to the brain or spinal alignment
- myelin problems affecting the insulation of nerve pathways in the brain
- specific problems in the area of the brain involved in processing speech and telling apart different sounds
- competition with the hearing disorder of tinnitus
- a pattern of uneven hearing which distorts incoming sound
- jumbling effects, where the processing of earlier information has been delayed but is then processed a few words or sentences further on so these concepts are then perceived to occur tumbled into later sentences they don't actually belong in
- a failure of the links between the part of the brain which produces mental images or pictures with the part of the brain which produces spoken or written words
- secondary effects of scotopic sensitivity syndrome.

A problem getting meaning from what one hears can also be a brain problem such as receptive aphasia, in which the part of the brain specifically involved in processing sound for meaning isn't working properly.

Scotoptic sensitivity syndrome: Implications for sensing and interpretation?
Where a person with sufficient eyesight appears meaning-blind but has a good ability to interpret what they hear, there can be a range of dynamics at work. Scotopic sensitivity syndrome (SSS) is a visual perceptual problem often addressed through special tinted lenses. SSS is often underpinned by food intolerances, food allergies, nutrient deficiencies and toxicity problems, and can result in visual perception being affected. What this can mean in some cases is that what is seen is effectively 'in bits'. Someone may look at a face or

body but have to scan it piece by piece and have little perception of it as one whole integrated cohesive thing. Meaning-blindness can also have an underlying brain cause such as agnosia, in which the part of the brain used to put interpretive meaning to what is seen is not working properly.

Other causes of left–right integration issues

Where someone with adequate hearing and sight is both meaning-deaf and meaning-blind, it could well be that there is a different condition underlying the meaning-deafness to that underlying the meaning-blindness, but one condition which may link the two may be salicylate intolerance.

There is also a range of shared causes which can underlie the simultaneous presence of these two issues. These include brain problems affecting both the area of the brain involved in interpreting what the eyes see as well as that affecting the processing of what is heard. Most atypically developing people, however, are not actually 'brain damaged' and most are generally not found to have actual receptive aphasia combined with actual agnosia.

Other shared underlying causes could include relatively treatable toxicity, and nutrient or immune issues affecting the brain's general ability to process incoming information. This basically means the brain may be not so much damaged as significantly affected by what can amount to 'poisoning' (toxicity), 'starvation' (functional nutrient deficiencies impacting on the supply of nutrients to the brain; e.g. gut problems) or 'inflammation' (immune function problems resulting in inflammatory states in the body including the 'blood brain barrier' which can result in undigested proteins, toxins and blood infections directly affecting the brain).

But toxicity issues are not the only reason why one style of processing may be so dominant to, or unintegrated with, the other. The flow of cerebral spinal fluid to the brain, that messenger which sends messages back and forth, detoxes the brain and supplies nutrition to it, can be more restricted, its flow more impaired, to one side of the brain than the other. A cranio-sacral therapist works with this. Even certain types of personalities may be more naturally predisposed to developing skills more associated with right-brain or left-brain learning; and if these traits are extreme, there's no reason not to imagine a situation where someone would stick fairly insistently to what comes most naturally to them and what they excel in, especially if that person is burdened with a whole range of other issues. Whether they are the artistic personality excelling at passionately mapping the form of rocks, the sound of gravel or the patterns in ice, or they are the more solitary or conscientious personality who excels at verbal logic and detachment, may depend on the individual, but it may make quite some difference to the diagnosis.

There is a difference between being 'brain damaged' and being 'brain affected'. There can be developmental issues affecting brain organisation. If something like an untreated anxiety condition, severe mood disorder, severe compulsive state, an untreated gut/immune dysfunction, toxicity issue or even severe abuse/trauma or deprivation, dramatically interferes with the brain's ability to organise information, then the development of left–right hemisphere integration, as well as other brain links, might be affected.

Helping those with left–right hemisphere integration issues
If 'interpretives' are more left-brain dominant and 'sensates' more right-brain dominant, how might we set about helping people to have an integrated level of both?

Babies start out without much left–right integration. What's important is that, with the brain getting the right feedback, most people start to develop this in infancy and are fairly on track by early childhood and usually quite well integrated by late childhood.

It's possible that many of those who have not managed a reasonable degree of left–right integration may eventually be noticed because of learning difficulties, attention problems, sensory perceptual problems, co-ordination and motor-planning problems and, more controversially, even mood and 'personality disorder'.

A left–right hemisphere integration problem is not the only brain issue that can underpin someone being 'interpretive' without 'sensing' or 'sensing' without the capacity to 'interpret', but it might be one of the most common. Others like gut and immune system dysfunction can also be a major cause of information-processing differences. Whilst it's common for people to swing between states of sensing and interpretation depending on the activity, they can, if needed, draw on both systems when full processing of the experience requires it. However, there are those on the Autistic spectrum (who may be the least likely to be diagnosed) who swing between being all sensing and no interpretation and then all interpretation and no sensing. Unlike their non-Autistic counterparts, these people may (sometimes after the first five to 30 minutes) only be able to process information fluently in one hemisphere at a time, so they get stuck in one mode or the other with each being intermitently not just offline but inaccessible.

In order for the brain to get good feedback about sensory, emotional, cognitive and physical experiences, it needs fuel. This means the supply of nutrients reaching the brain has to be fairly consistent and sufficient. If the brain is starved of those nutrients because of a gut or immune-system problem or if the messengers in the brain, the neurotransmitters, are imbalanced because of nutrient or toxicity problems, the brain doesn't get feedback the way it should. So if this was a shop assistant, then he or she would struggle to keep up with the work tasks. In a department store full of challenged shop assistants the general pattern of organisation in the whole store might take longer to organise or get into a great working routine. And the brain can have similar issues. Not only can brain health affect the day-to-day running of things but if the messages aren't flowing like they should, the brain can't get itself organised and into a pattern.

This might also have an impact on the body's ability to heal itself where there are gut and immune-system problems, so it can be a cyclical problem, one of those chicken and egg things. Sometimes it's the chicken, sometimes it's the egg that comes first.

Sensory impairment, as found in deaf-blind children, could mean a decreased level of feedback needed to stimulate left–right integration in the brain, and certainly Auties can also commonly be found in this population.

Occasionally, children with no clear sensory impairments have been seriously abused, deprived and neglected by families with unrecognised emotional or mental health issues, drug or alcohol dependency or social work issues. Children with developmental conditions are not immune to being born into such families any more than any other child. These challenged families need help as much as, if not more than, well-adjusted families with children with developmental conditions. They should not be further marginalised, shamed and rejected by the wider special needs community or the professionals who serve it.

I have met many who prefer to think of Autism as being some kind of pure category somehow exclusive to children with families who have no obvious mental health, substance abuse or social work issues. A child with a small dose of autism-related issues born into a family where he or she is seriously abused, or seriously physically or sensorily deprived over a period of time, will potentially have a greater developmental delay than they otherwise might have had. Where severe ongoing abuse or trauma is present before the age of two, such repeated shocks to the system are now thought to alter brain development leading to developmental difficulties in these particular children.

The Autism world is so traumatised by the old 'refrigerator mother' accusation that it has sometimes gone to another extreme, portraying its own group as incapable of harbouring occasional seriously troubled and damaged families in which some children with Autism have added developmental burdens. We need to get honest and open and realise that abusive, dangerous and extremely troubled families occur right across society in all educational and economic social groups, and some of these families will have children on the Autistic spectrum. Sometimes the child's Autism will put such a strain on the family as to cause it to break down. There will be other cases where a child with Autism will be born into a family which already had little ability to cope healthily.

There is still a common assumption that if a child's Autism has been made more severe by virtue of something like neglect or trauma, the child is not a 'pure' case of Autism. Furthermore, there have been some extreme cases of forced compliance used in a fixated and militant way on particularly emotionally hypersensitive children to the point where their families reported that their child developed a post-traumatic stress disorder response to learning. So just because a child experiences something as 'abusive' doesn't necessarily mean it was intended that way. Previously, such 'regressions' were blamed on the severity of the child's Autism rather than on the incompatibility of the programme being used or the inappropriate nature of its delivery. Whatever the source, post-traumatic stress disorder will far from decrease a child's developmental and information-processing issues.

Extreme sensory fluctuations, such as those in ultra-rapid cycling bipolar in infancy, could conceivably flood the body with adrenaline, among other things, interrupting and confusing the feedback that would otherwise lead to left–right integration in the brain.

It is possible for a so-called 'good' family to develop such fear of blame, and such social praise for their 'self-sacrifice' in fixating on their child's needs, that their child is in danger of developing pathological responses to such extreme co-dependency. If a child then develops progressively greater self-protective instincts in defending against what he or she perceives as persistently 'invasive' external control, this will not help the child's developmental problems. If the child develops extreme self-doubt and learned dependency in the face of the parents' apparent dependability and quickness to take over, this will not help the child's struggle to, in spite of their difficulties, progressively overcome some of the challenges.

Some children are so overprotected from germs and being outdoors or playing in the street that they have little physical activity compared with children before the era of TV and computers. The use of the body in playing, climbing, crawling, rolling, running and catching are essential parts of building left–right integration in the brain. Some children, however, can be missing the part of the brain essential in building left–right integration, and have connections which are too densely packed to efficiently pass messages between the different sides of the brain, or have too few connections. Spinal misalignment has also been cited as one of the issues that can affect proper feedback to the brain necessary to developing left–right integration. This can be addressed by a chiropractic examination. The flow of cerebral spinal fluid to the brain has been associated with problems where pressure at the base of the skull restricts this important flow of messages to and from the brain. A cranio-sacral therapist would examine for this.

The truth is that some children with left–right integration problems will be more easily helped than others.

- There may be some with *motor-planning problems* who may improve with cranio-sacral therapy, chiropractic or 'Brain Gym' (a form of physiotherapy involving patterning exercises for the body which may help train hemisphere integration in the brain, which may thereby improve associated information-processing and learning difficulties). As socially non-invasively as possible, these people may need to be put through the motions of physical activities until these become natural to them. Because integrating information into actions may be a big problem for them, telling them what to do and waiting for them to make the connections to do these things may not be enough to help their brain put the connections together into action.

- There may be those with such *anxiety, defensive and personality states* sabotaging their development that they may need to be assumed capable and left helpless to the point where they struggle for themselves. These people may be so caught in defending themselves against 'invasion' that they cut off from identifying with or learning from whatever they are forced through under a compliance model. They may fail independently to dare the use of that which they've appeared able to do through forced compliance. These people may need to chase experiences from their own motivation. That can often only be achieved through an indirectly confrontational approach outlined in a later section.

- There may be those with signs of primarily *health issues* who will likely benefit from environmental changes and an individualised treatment programme from a specialist in gut/immune 'disorders' and a background in both natural medicine and medical expertise. Some of these people may have gluten/dairy issues, some may have salicylate intolerance, some may have specific food allergies, some may have blood sugar problems, toxicity issues, nutrient deficiencies, candida or immune deficiencies of various kinds. Each child may need a different treatment. Some may need a complex, long-term treatment plan, others need only a short-term intervention to get them developmentally on track.

- There may be those with signs of *imbalanced neurochemistry* that in some cases medication may address. This may come under headings of obsessive-compulsive and tic disorders, mood disorders and anxiety disorders. The psychosis seen in schizophrenia may or may not be common among those with Autism. Often it is wrongly assumed to be present where information-processing issues or mood, anxiety, tic or personality disorders have not been understood. But having Autism doesn't make you immune to having a psychosis, and manic psychosis can commonly affect people with bipolar disorders, which may be common in those with Autism. Certainly, if you did have a psychosis, the presentation of your Autism may well be worse. So keeping an open mind about the co-occurrence of any psychiatric conditions may help some people be less affected by the overall picture of what gets put down to 'their Autism'.

This list of left–right integration problems is not exhaustive, and there will be many things I haven't mentioned. It is, nevertheless, a starting point. Without identifying that brain organisation issues may be at work, however, you can't even begin to weed through the underlying causes of these issues themselves.

Left–right integration and health

The body has a remarkable ability to heal itself provided:

- it gets adequate deep sleep and regular healthy sleep patterns
- it is not structurally missing some of the parts required to do so

- it is not chemically missing some of the requirements to do so
- it is not nutritionally missing the resources to do so
- it is not overly taxed in its use of resources through the burdens of allergy, anxiety, stress, emotional/psychological trauma, toxicity or overindulgence in physical or mental activity, emotional burden or particular extreme mood states to the point of exhausting its resources
- nothing is standing in the way of it getting feedback.

The body needs to get clear cohesive messages about what is physically, mentally and emotionally going on, and to be able to process those messages cohesively and effectively so that the body can adapt and eventually heal itself.

There is another potential complication of a lack of left–right integration on Autism spectrum conditions. If left-brain processing is associated with concrete thinking and conscious awareness, what would happen to us emotionally if this were never balanced by the chill-out factor of the dreamy right-brain world of abstraction, metaphor, sensing, sensuality pattern in which conscious awareness barely figures? Would we have some people who feel they can't quiet their mind, feel too consciously aware of everything they say and do to the point they can't bear attention, and fear making the slightest error? After all, in such a state, would errors not provide the fuel for fierce compulsive thought, full of potential for self-conscious embarrassment and awareness of limitation and mental self-criticism? Perhaps this is a foundation for understanding some of what appears as the dynamics of 'avoidant personality disorder'. Perhaps we could even go further and say that thinking too much predisposes some people to depression; and if one also has a tendency towards obsessive-compulsive disorder, this is very fertile ground for it to take root.

And conversely, if one is largely in a dream state, happy to bumble along obliviously caught up in pattern and familiar with a world devoid of conscious awareness and interpretive meaning, would one not run the risk of being the sleepwalker jolted overwhelmingly harshly into conscious awareness with every external piece of praise and attention, and external attempts to draw attention to your 'achievements'? Would this not be akin to being woken with ice water? And what of the freezing effect of making the right brain consciously aware of a generally unconscious action? If it had little ability to shift to that realm of conscious awareness that is left-brain process-ing, would the function simply not 'abort'?

Imbalances in the brain chemical serotonin are associated with poor impulse control, and high level of the brain chemical dopamine is associated not only with acute awareness of pattern but also aggression. Theoretically, could this be part of the makeup of some acutely 'right-brain' people who not only are frozen out of the ability to continue an action when jolted into conscious awareness of it, but who can respond in a highly self-protective fight-flight way to such 'invasions'? Perhaps this is one basis for understand-ing an interrelationship between left–right integration issues and the anxiety disorder I call exposure anxiety.

Raised levels of dopamine are associated with a euphoric state and high levels are associated with aggression. Could this mean chronic exposure to high adrenaline levels, such that adrenaline addiction may become more possible? If this were so, the person with this may continue to manifest threat or 'invasion' where others would usually find no problem. High levels of adrenaline in cocaine addicts inevitably lead to crashing lows before the next high. Could the presence of a large number of 'Autistic' children being recog-nised with the mood swings of rapid cycling childhood bipolar (manic depression) be explained this way? Serotonin and dopamine imbalances have been commonly found in Tourette's. Could some of the vocal/motor tics associated with Tourette's be what are commonly seen as 'bizarre behaviours' in those with Autism? We don't know but I think these are good questions.

In both avoidant personality disorder and exposure anxiety (if not also in conditions with the solitary nature of schizoid or schizotypal personality), if an indirectly confrontational approach is not used with these people, they can experience acute chronic stress, which will not help their gut/immune function at all. Once gut and immune function is suppressed, the fuel supply which runs information processing in the brain is going to be affected, and information processing is going to pay the price. It could be that anxiety-related health problems would then be more common in those with certain personalities and anxiety disorders than others.

A disorganised brain may be less likely to have the healthy immune system to heal itself, less likely for someone to use thinking and action to resolve the stress of extreme mood states, less likely to have a stable consistent experience of thought or volition, less likely to be able to co-ordinate a range of functions in performing complex actions.

All difference and 'mutations' can lead equally to abilities as to disabilities. If we all had a reasonable state of brain organisation, we might have a bland society but probably also one with a relatively consistent level of multi-track functioning. I do want to see people reach their greatest potential, but I'm not sure I want such a bland world, and we would likely lose much that makes life interesting in wishing too blindly for it.

Sensing versus interpretation and IQ tests

Interpretive processing may be more associated with conscious awareness, language and processing language for interpretive meaning. 'Interpretives' might do better on language-based tasks involving the need to access responses consciously.

Most IQ tests do not test for things like intuition or the type of empathy that comes from the ability to resonate with and feel the other person's emotional reality (although not interpreting that consciously). So interpretives would be fairly likely to do better on today's IQ tests than sensates.

It may be that sensates function at their best when the tasks do not involve conscious awareness, are not primarily language-based, rely on triggering responses rather than expectations of good conscious accessing skills, and involve intuitive 'understanding' essentially based on pattern, theme and feel. I have not yet come across an IQ test which tests for these kinds of abilities, nor have I come across many educational programmes which use these strengths instead of holding people back on the basis of their being weak at 'interpretive' processing.

There are some aspects of Montessori teaching which have credited the ability to learn through body rather than directly through mind. The first phases of Steiner education also acknowledge the sensual phase of childhood development in which intellect (interpretive ability) is not the primary strength. Some community schools have developed discovery learning pro- grammes which could be further developed to tap into this style of learning. There is so much yet to be developed for 'sensates' within current educational programmes and practices. This may be partly because the designers, the head teachers and the class teachers themselves may be far more proficient in inter- pretive processing and fixated on its inflated (and perhaps culturally biased) importance in the social hierarchy, and perhaps poorly aware of their own sensing capacities and how these might progressively also be channelled into life skills, particularly in the absence of a connection with reliable, fluent, interpretive processing skills.

Sensing versus interpretation and specific behavioural issues

Now let's look specifically at how sensing versus interpreting as a dominant system could underpin specific behaviours such as:

- communication
- being in one's own world
- eye contact
- sensory responses
- learning and cognitive challenges
- toileting
- sleep problems
- self-stimulating behaviour (stimming)
- meltdowns
- self-protection responses
- challenging behaviours
- food behaviour problems.

Communication will be affected by someone having all-sensing and little-interpretation or vice versa in several ways. The ability to comprehend language with meaning relies on not just absorbing the pattern, theme, feel of communication but also linking these with mental concepts and social uses.

Those living by the system of sensing may accumulate strings of television advertisements, jingles, songs and simple phrases they may emotionally associate with a variety of moods, physical and social situations, emotional experiences and, sometimes, vague topics. So a children's song about pirates may actually stand for 'we're all feeling quite adventurous aren't we!', an advertisement recommending a particular product may stand for 'so you think this will be good for me?', a phrase associated with a food product may mean 'so, I've done a good job haven't I', the almost inaudible 'foosh' sound produced when patting a cat may actually mean 'nice cat' or 'want to pat'.

It is sometimes possible to keep a diary of the mood or situations in which expressions occur so you can build up a set of interpretations for sensing-based emotional expressions or verbal expressions. Over time you may even be able to use some of these to bridge the divide between sensing-based language and interpretive language such as 'yes, Palmolive, the vitamins are good for you', 'hmm, foosh, very nice cat-ness'.

The ability to comprehend literal language in the absence of sensing may mean that the general pattern, theme or feel may need to be shown visually with the rest of the information then slotted in. This may mean drawings, diagrams, or a combination of gesture, signing and using representational objects.

There are great strengths and intelligence in those in both of these groups. However, both of these groups may struggle significantly with information overload because we generally process information most quickly and cohesively when we have a combination of sensing and interpretation.

People who are all-sensing, little-interpretation or vice versa will be '*in their own world*' in different ways. We usually define 'being in one's own world' partly meaning 'not in the same world as the rest of us'. People who rely on pattern, theme and feel, and struggle to keep up with meaning, may be quickly confused, frustrated, bored and overloaded when constantly presented with tasks that require interpretation and understanding rather than doing and experiencing. More and more, society depends on overt expression of intellect and certain personalities who rely on sensing can more easily give up on that world than others. If non-Autistic people understand and appreciate the equality of the system of sensing they can learn this 'language', meet these people on their own terms and progressively build bridges.

Interpretive people who lack sensing can be so 'Spock', so 'intellectual', so 'mind' and so 'literal' that they can also find themselves unable to relate to others or feel others can truly accept, appreciate and relate to them. Non-Autistic people who continually lament or stress that someone extremely 'interpretive' can't sense may compel these people to spend far more time 'in their own world' where acceptance and belonging is less of a sore point. There is much society can do to understand this processing style, appreciate its strengths, support people facing its weaknesses and avoid teaching some of these wonderful 'apples' to judge themselves as 'failed oranges'.

Eye contact can be an issue relating to those who sense without interpreting and those who interpret without sensing. Without understanding the significance of what you pick up indiscriminately as pattern, theme, feel, it is impossible to know why eye contact is such a big social issue for non-Autistic people. If you use smell, tactile sense, acoustics or movement as your primary way of testing familiarity, recognising or establishing closeness, eye contact may be a foreign system. Being made to look at people's faces when presented with a new experience may seem utterly distracting and pointless to the 'experience' and the 'doing'. Actually 'seeing' the other person's eyes, without processing this for meaning, may be no more than that, just eyes. For those who additionally have fragmented vision problems, eye contact can be an annoying, pointless distraction from the real attempt to get a cohesive experience. We can actually all interact and survive quite well with or without eye contact. Whilst learning it may be a useful social skill and please others, it may be important not to overdo the emphasis or forced compliance in the eye contact department if that puts people off more than it connects them.

Interpretive people who lack sensing may give you eye contact but experience this on a very literal level. They may do this because it makes you feel better or because they may have learned that this is the social sign that they are being listened to. But expect fireworks to go off or great deep emotional connections to happen, and you may as well be waiting to find a pair of shoes to buy in a hat shop: wrong place. Interpretive people may connect deeply with you if you explain (perhaps with visuals) your feelings and give them a list from which to choose and identify their own. Remember, this may be Spock. They may be deeply moved by you, but it may be because you know every type of tropical fish, because you introduced them to train magazines or explained the solar system. It may be because you are so 'useful' and 'helpful' and 'kind' and 'tolerant', not because of what they sense.

Sensory responses can be dramatically different for people who work by sensing rather than by interpretation, even though the senses themselves may not be affected. This is because it is our mind or our emotions which tell us what we see, hear, feel. If we experience things without forming concepts, or we form very broad concepts, this will greatly affect how we make sense of what we experience. Someone who senses without much interpretation may struggle to distinguish the use of things if they share a number of similar features. So drinking out of the toilet, the bath or the sink, for example, or lying on the floor, on a table, along a shelf or on a bed may be relatively interchangeable; a concave shaped object of any nature may become a bowl; a toilet brush may just as easily become a hairbrush; a plate may become a spinning thing; a series of wires may become something to flick; colours on a white background may seem to be floating in space rather than known to be part of a painting; a shopping mall may be called a circus; a tiled elevator may appear to be a mobile toiletless toilet cubicle. Someone with poor or little interpretive thinking may have very different sensory responses to the world around them from those of someone who interprets fluently but struggles to sense.

Someone who interprets without much sensing may have a very good sense of what is being experienced but may be very specific and struggle to generalise. They may not realise connections till these are pointed out, and may not notice similarities. But at least similar won't be assumed to be 'same'.

Learning and cognitive challenges have very different faces when it comes to sensates versus interpretives. Sensates may learn best through pattern, theme and feel in activities which are:

- not dependent on interpretive language
- dependent on doing rather than understanding
- learnt through patterning in a hands-on experience
- learnt through trial and error rather than by verbal instruction
- in an environment without multiple sensory distractions, particularly where the 'misuse' of these could be dangerous
- where triggering techniques (actions, statements, omissions, modelling) are used to motivate action, rather than accessing techniques (questions, instructions, teaching)
- where movement through an action follows a pathway (a line, a square or a circle), so body mapping can become a helpful part of the activity
- where relationships do not depend on sharing minds through verbal language (though some of these people, for some reason, may use typed language interpretively whilst all other functions work on the sensing level)
- where extra processing time is allowed to compensate for the inability for interpretive thinking to help assist information processing.

Interpretives may learn best when:

- instructions are overt, and clearly and preferably visually set out
- literal language and explanations are used
- the activity involves thinking without an expectation to intuit
- social dialogue is upfront, to the point, has a practical purpose
- social time is structured and intuition or picking up subtle cues is not expected or needed

- there is no overt abusive behaviour and social 'manners' are overlooked, and there is an agreed acceptance not to take any personal offence or insult at these natural omissions

- relationship expectations and the desire of others to have emotional responses or understand the person's feelings are made upfront and overt without personal judgement or offence if the responses are honest but non-abusive

- extra processing time is allowed to compensate for the inability for sensing to help assist information processing.

Toileting can be affected by whether someone senses or interprets. Someone who senses without much interpretation is a hedonist (all about what's enjoyable in the now). In the moment, when taking action, they may be unable to grasp or retain the significance of why it is better to use a toilet than go in one's pants, particularly if they enjoy the sensation or smell or feel or entertainment at the social impact of their own excretions. They may use unusual places to do their toileting which makes certain types of 'sense' to them at that time. They may be unlikely to care whether they are squishing excrement or clay, but the clay may smell less pungent and be, therefore, less enjoyable or familiar; or unlikely to care whether they paint the wall with the brown pigment that's immediately available rather than the acrylic paints you offer them instead. They may not be self-conscious of where they take their clothes off on the way to the toilet or at what point they get around to pulling their pants back up. The idea of a toileting routine involving pants down, sit, go, wipe, pants up, flush, wash, dry, leave may be too complex, too challenging and, without each step involving some sensory enjoyment, unlikely to be thought about. Those parts which are found enjoyable may be done to the exclusion of the others without being part of a toileting routine at all. Even teaching these people a song may help them link actions to patterns but not necessarily actions to understanding or meaning.

Interpretive people are more likely to get to grips with the mental concept of a toileting routine, what it is, how to do it. Their downfall may be in intuiting which sensations are signalling the need for the toilet and then mentally organising (for the natural instinctual actions may not happen) how to act upon this before an accident happens. As these people live in their minds, they may equally struggle with how to put one thought out of their mind in order to focus on the task of recognising their sensation, determining which one it is (or telling the physical from the emotional), working out how to respond to it and taking the action to let go of the current task in order to attend to it. As getting to the toilet involves more instinct than thought, these people might struggle most with getting there. Once they are there their mind will usually help them through the actual toileting routine itself, and even those with sequencing problems can usually learn well through charts and lists up on the wall or back of the door.

Sleep problems may have specific relationships to sensing and interpreting. Some sensates may be unable to control their hedonistic, in the moment, enjoyment to get to grips with what time of day it is, while others may sense 'body time' extremely well. They may learn by pattern about a sleep routine but the concept of the purpose being to sleep may be secondary to the feeling that they are caught up in a, hopefully entertaining, enjoyable ritual. Once in bed, however, they may not link tiredness with a need to sleep and, perhaps, seek instead to wake themselves up with a high level of arousal and excitement (just like someone else might have a coffee). They might be likely to experience stillness as a lack of activity requiring action or entertainment to fill it. Just as an interpretive may stay awake downloading thought or with the racing thoughts and provoked feelings that that may involve, the sensate may download the enormous mass of sensory flooding they've accumulated throughout the day, even resulting in an extreme mood state in the process. The sensate may take self-calming action in such a state through jumping, pacing, rocking, flicking, sounds or tunes. Music and rhythm may help them download and stabilise. Some may need mood levellers to help. Those who are relaxed may lie exploring sensory experiences in the same way an interpretive may lie thinking. The sensate may deeply experience the darkness or the floaters on their own eyes, the patterns in the room and how these move as they move.

The interpretive may be better at registering what time or day or even minute it is. He or she may be preoccupied with the enjoyment of mental stimulation to the degree that the physical sensations of tiredness are left uninterpreted and almost part of a 'distant world'. Recognising bed-time may be more likely to trigger a sleep routine than realising he or she is tired. The idea that a person goes to sleep because they are tired may be stored learning rather than real observation. To the interpretive its far more likely they'd know a person goes to sleep because it is 10pm (or whatever time). Once in bed, the intuitive experience of sleeping when one is tired may be replaced with a niggling, annoying feeling, as thought becomes harder to keep a grip on. The interpretive may be kept awake by thoughts they are unable to download fully or easily because the capacity to sense or intuit is missing and, hence, half the tools for resolving unresolvable thoughts may not be there.

Stimming may relate to sensing versus interpreting in the a number of ways. Some stimming is the result of poor information processing, so a person may have to do an action over and over again to achieve a heightened sensory or emotional effect. This may be the case where someone can get the 'doing' but can't process the concept intellectually. By improving the messages to the brain, some cases of stimming may sometimes decrease or even stop.

Some stimming is the result of a need for self-calming or 'downloading' and is the result of information overload or problems with regulating mood or anxiety states. When good feedback between the body and brain is restored as best as possible, the person should be better able to keep up with information more interpretively and resolve and regulate things like mood and anxiety issues so the self-calming and download functions of stimming should be less required than before.

Some stimming is the result of feeling alienated from the environment. Alienation is what we feel when we feel we are alone and have no belonging with those so different from ourselves. We can feel alienated for all kinds of reasons, but inability to keep up with interpretive processing is one of those, just as many interpretive people feel alienated from their highly sensing but non-interpretive child. For sensing people who feel alienated from the interpretive people in their world, offering more than just intellectual tasks and interpretive verbal language may lead to less need for self-stimulation.

People who sense without interpreting may become so acutely tuned to the patterns around them that they pick up the distress or stress or invasiveness of others very easily. Stimming can be one way that highly sensing people shut themselves off, by reinforcing a sense of their own world again. When the environment addresses its own distresses and stresses, this may decrease the need for a sensing person to have to use stimming so much to create those boundaries.

Interpretive people may become bored with activities reliant on intuition or sensing, so they fill in their time with self-calming strategies or self-entertainment called 'stimming'. Many interpretive people on the Autistic spectrum refer to activities like reading as a 'stim' which basically means they have found ways of entertaining themselves, perhaps whilst others are more interested in social interactions which are far more reliant on a combination of interpreting and sensing. In other words, they instinctively choose what they excel in.

Meltdown is the word given to a temporary 'breakdown state', maybe seen as a tantrum or shutdown caused by overload. Meltdowns may relate to sensing versus interpreting in the following ways.

Meltdowns can happen when information processing backlogs to a point where there is a dramatic instability. This can happen where someone is all-sensing and little-interpretation or all-interpretation and little-sensing as we actually best process and organise information and resolve thoughts and feelings based on that information when we are able to use a combination of sensing and interpreting as our resources. Left–right patterning exercises can help some people with downloading and many will naturally do things like head weaving (moving in circles from left to right), body weaving or hand weaving, which are believed to help with left–right integration, but there are many left–right cross-patterning exercises which do similar. Most people simply need time out to download and tackle the instability and chaos in a safe space with no more incoming information before getting back into things.

Meltdowns can be the result of social-emotional distress where others have not understood or appreciated that those who rely on sensing may be unable to cope with a lot of interpretive input, or that those who rely on interpreting may be unable to work on an intuitive level.

Equally, meltdowns can happen when others wrongly assume that just because a sensing person cannot interpretively keep up in the moment, they therefore don't use interpretive thought at all. Many will have interpretive thought, but this may not be easily consciously accessible. However, given a trigger and access to a communication device other than verbal language (which requires more conscious processing and body connectedness), many do have plenty to communicate. Meltdowns can happen when others think these people don't think at all or have anything to communicate.

Similarly, many primarily interpretive people may have as much emotion, even sensing, as anyone else, but it is often dominated or blocked by the extreme emphasis and reliance on interpretive processing. When these people are treated as though they have no feelings and can sense nothing, they may not instantly pick up that they have been treated this way but progressively they may become distressed by this without realising what they are experiencing. This can also result in meltdowns.

Self-protection responses might also have a relationship to sensing versus interpreting. People who are highly sensing may pick up the patterns of others at an extremely sensitive level. We often hear of someone being 'open to influence' or 'closed-minded'. In fact, sensing is all about being very open, almost too open. Because it is about feeling the impact of the world through one's body rather than mind, it means that boundaries between self and other may become blurred. People with these kinds of blurred boundaries may easily merge into sensory experiences with objects, places, space, or even other people, but equally, they may learn to overly self-protect in order to achieve or maintain any separate sense of self at all. In an almost hypersensitive manner they may remain in a high self-protection state because the fact they are so sensing makes the threat of social 'invasiveness' such a heightened issue. If sensing people were offered more than just intellectual tasks and interpretive verbal language, they would be so much less alienated from the 'interpretive world' that they may need less of the self-entertainment others call 'stimming'. It's like the cat sensing the pouncing and invasiveness of an eager dog. If the dog becomes more 'cat', the cat can relax because invasion is no longer an issue. People can learn to 'simply be' in parallel dialogues, in parallel self-expression, without it all having to be directly confrontational. Much more can often be achieved with highly sensing people when others change their interaction style to stop triggering chronic self-protection states.

People who are mostly interpretive may become highly self-protective for very different reasons to those who are highly sensing. Moving in a world that they know uses intuition and sensing, interpretive people may feel they are 'different' and have learned through bullying and the experimentation of others that they are vulnerable specifically because they are missing an intact ability to sense and intuit.

Challenging and self-injurious behaviours may relate to sensing and interpreting in many very different ways. Information overload, alienation and frustrations in communication and social interactions can all lead to challenging or even self-injurious behaviours in any despairing person. People who are all-sensing and little-interpretation or vice versa may be more prone to these problems and frustrations than others who have integrated interpreting and sensing. Addressing the causes and planning solutions to overload, alienation and frustrations in communication and social interaction should reduce a lot of challenging and self-injurious behaviours.

Sensing without interpreting can lead to many sensory-based and body explorations which can be labelled challenging or self-injurious behaviours. Helping people to explore their senses and body safely is preferable, where possible, to trying simply to stop all natural exploration and self-entertainment, which only causes any of us to fixate on countering these external attempts to control or suppress our own natural drives. Programmes can be created to sensitise or desensitise people to certain experiences so they can be less damaging in getting their sensory experiences and more easily get over fixations on them.

Being interpretive without being sensing may mean that people won't pick up facial expressions, body language or subtle hints about when a behaviour is challenging the rights and needs of others. Many interpretive people will care about this, and won't mind a clear, practical, open and non-judgemental explanation and redirection, often preferably using visuals rather than relying simply on telling them. Some personalities will naturally struggle with this more than others.

Food behaviour problems can arise where there is an imbalance of sensing and interpreting. If we have sensing without much interpreting in the moment we experience things then we are going to be far more involved with food on a sensory level than thinking about what it is or why we need to eat it. This means we are more likely to eat what we crave or are even addicted to (and many allergic people will crave what causes their food allergies etc.). People who rely on sensing may intuitively associate foods with mood states and crave the foods that keep them in particular mood states, not necessarily to the benefit of their own behaviour management or development. People who rely on sensing may be far more likely to eat non-food objects, simply because they have good colours, shapes, smells or textures, or because they associate enjoying a sensory object with devouring it (which on an intuitive level is what we do when we enjoy an experience, though most people's interpretive thinking stops them from being too primal about this and seeking to mouth or orally devour a nice polished table top).

People who rely on sensing may be acutely aware of change and seek replacements of what they've been attached to with something the same, so changing things may be a bit of a struggle. Others won't mind as long as the key 'attachment feature', such as smell, texture or colour, is maintained, but not necessarily the whole lot. Linking new foods with already enjoyable experiences may help some sensing people accept new foods. So if they like rabbits and rabbits eat lettuce, for example, they may come to associate the lettuce with the enjoyment of patting rabbits. If they like water, they may like coloured waters and then accept jelly. If they like pebbles or beads, they may accept mixtures of beans. If they like sand, they may go for eating linseed. While Social Stories™ work for interpretive people (Gray and White 2002), play therapy and videos linking sensory experiences with food substances may help those who struggle with receptive verbal language.

Those reliant on interpreting with little sensing or intuition at the time they experience things may fixate on the concepts that things stand for. So packaging may matter a lot because it has been ascribed a particular meaning, and changing food products may often mean first weaning people off the packaging! Interpretive people may develop fads they associate with logical but maybe narrow ideas. So they may have heard carrots are good for eyesight so want to eat a bag full of carrots a day regardless of the fact this may cause them liver stress from excess beta carotene. They may have heard sugar gives them energy or that people who eat a certain chocolate bar are more popular, and so insist on these food habits to the exclusion of healthy ones to their own detriment. Interpretive people who struggle with sensing may be less likely to recognise the connections between the foods they eat and their own mood or physical sensations, and so may be more likely to continue to eat foods that affect them badly, especially if some concept or idea about that food overrides any focus on how it actually makes them feel. Social stories may help overcome some of these issues as might lists and visual healthy eating programmes.

CHAPTER 3

Issues of Overload

Being Mono and Delayed Information Processing

A child sits in front of the TV pressing the remote control buttons at random. The TV channels flick quickly from one to another every second or so till the division between topics is lost and everything seems in a jumble. The child hits the volume button, then the contrast, the brightness and finally lands on a channel with nothing but static. This is what it is like to be mono-tracked.

A mono-tracking pupil and a multi-tracking pupil watch the teacher giving the lesson. Both are eager to fit in, as enthusiastic as each other about the topic, both like the teacher and respect those around them. Both children start to hear and see the same thing. After the first few sentences, one child begins to get restless. The teacher's voice seems to be getting faster and a few of the words don't mean anything. The teacher has something in his hand but the child can't work out what it is now. The teacher appears to be moving very suddenly and more quickly, almost becoming cartoon-like in his movements. The child giggles a little but is also getting anxious. The child's heart starts to race a bit and suddenly the lights seem much brighter and the room looks kind of 'bitty' and the teacher's voice is now not only faster but louder and the words sound jumbled and make no sense, like the meaning has fallen away. Even all the other children in the room just look like 'things' now. It's like who, and even what, they were has fallen away. The child has started rocking and making patterns which feel much calmer in all the chaos. This is an example of what delayed information processing can feel like.

Assume you are told over the phone you are to build a house. You might assume you simply pack up your usual tool box and you are equipped to do the job. But what if the details of the job included that it was a miniature house for a model railway? Or a straw bale house? Or you were building it from mud bricks? Or it would be simply a cave built into the ground? The details of the job will change how useful your standard 'one-size-fits-all' tool box will be in building such a house.

The same is true of working with Autism. You may have a standard tool box you think 'works' in helping those with Autism, but then you may find out you are working on several specific conditions which require different specialised tools for each job and that collectively these conditions come together to give a way of functioning we call Autism. OK, so imagine that your Autism tool box has several different drawers within it. One of those drawers has an 'improvement kit' for 'information-processing problems'. But then you are told which specific information-processing problems are happening. And now your tools look a little bit crude for the job, a bit like expecting all spanners to fit all types of bolts. They don't. So now you need more specific tools.

Similarly, the best approaches for each type of information-processing issue will be different so working out which issue might be most likely at work in a particular case is important. So let's start with an overview of the general experiences which can occur in having information-processing problems.

Being mono-tracked

Most developmentally typical people are fairly multi-track. In other words, they can keep up with what's going on on several channels at once:

- When they are speaking, they can usually simultaneously keep up with the meaning of what they are saying.

- They can usually keep track of where their body is in space and what it's doing, even the facial expression, body language and intonation of the other person, at the same time as they are speaking or thinking.

- They are usually able to express themselves and keep track of what they are saying at the same time without things wandering off everywhere and without losing the ability to understand their own speech.

- They are usually able to read out loud and also understand the meaning of what they are reading.

- They can usually listen to someone and not only map the meaning of what the other person is saying but simultaneously keep track of their own thoughts and feelings about what is being said or that they are tired, hungry, cold, need the toilet or are in social or physical danger.

- They can usually be told something and not only think about what that means for the here and now but even think quickly beyond that to how this information might be useful or affect other situations in other places and at other times.

- They may be so good at multi-tracking that as they are busy speaking, moving or doing something they can not only simultaneously take account of the responses of others around them but easily modify their own track or behaviour accordingly.

Most Auties or Aspies, however, work in a more or less 'mono-track' way:

- Sometimes they struggle to look and listen at the same time.

- The visual distraction of someone moving about or an animated facial expression can compete with the ability to keep up with the meaning of what's being said.

- When focusing on what's being said, it can become very hard to simultaneously make any use of the facial expression or body language coming from the person at the same time.

- Someone who is mono-tracked might be so busy keeping up with what they are saying or what's being said that they may not have noticed what their body is doing at the time.

- They might be kept so busy with processing other information they may not realise they need the toilet, haven't had a drink all day, are shivering from the cold, sweating from the heat, desperately tired or really want to leave the situation.

- They might be unable to simultaneously keep up with a sense of self and a sense of other. Effectively, they may be in a kind of all-self/no-other or all-other/no-self state. When they tune into being on the self track, the simultaneous feedback of the other person may go unprocessed, as though it's just a bunch of noise and movements that don't have any real significance. Sometimes even the meaning of what they are seeing is lost, so the other person just seems to be 'something'. In this state of all-self/

no-other the person ends up going on and on simply on their own track. The opposite state is one in which the person is so focused on listening or watching or climbing into the feel or patterns of the other person, they may have no simultaneous idea of what they, themselves, think, feel or want at the time – all-other/no-self.

A lack of a simultaneous sense of self and other may be what some non-Autistic psychologists have mistaken for 'mind-blindness'. This 'mind-blindness' was the basis for the 'theory of mind' which was used to explain what is perceived (generally from a non-Autistic perspective) to be lack of empathy. In fact, many empathic people on the Autistic spectrum take offence to this theory. I've met a handful of Auties who do seem to lack any empathy at all, but I generally see that as a function of something else which happens to be in their particular 'cluster' getting called Autism, such as depression or certain personality traits, rather than their information-processing nature. I've met many wonderful, beautiful, and extremely empathic, if not highly sensing, Auties, verbal and non-verbal, with all manner of other challenges.

Back to our present topic, the underlying causes of being mono are many but essentially it comes down to how we spread our resources. Some people with dementia, Alzheimer's, chronic fatigue syndrome, multiple sclerosis, myalgic encephalitis, multiple food or chemical allergies or intolerances, those with functional malnutrition and gut disorders and those in a state of low blood sugar, even those with impaired immune systems or impaired flow of cerebral spinal fluid to the brain or spinal misalignment, for example, may also have experienced a shutdown in their ability to multi-track, finding themselves progressively mono-tracked in their information processing. So we can be pretty sure that 'fuel system' problems and 'electrics' problems are two of the issues that affect information processing. But being mono-tracked isn't just about what happens under these circumstances, it's an adaptation, a way we compensate. So in this chapter we will look at 'being mono' in its own right.

Imagine someone starts a new department store but it only operates one or two departments at a time, with the lights being out in the other departments. Over time, the manager of the department store may be very proud of this functioning department store. It may not be like other stores but to him it's running 'normally' and as well as possible given the natural organisation structure that developed as it became established. Now imagine some other manager comes in and says, 'Nah, this is all wrong, this isn't efficient' and sets about making the department store run in a multi-track way. Well the staff aren't designed to work that way, the store isn't stocked to suit that format, the very structures underpinning the building can't support those changes and, whether this multi-track system is more efficient for others or not, when applied in the wrong place it causes nothing but far greater disorganisation, chaos and distress among the staff. When someone develops in a mono-tracked way since infancy, this style feels 'natural' and progressively becomes part of how their brain organisation develops. It is the least chaotic way such a brain can most cohesively process information and whether it is 'normal' or not to the majority of people doesn't change that.

Where other burdens come in

When we can't keep up with the rate of what's coming in, we process it one track at a time – we become mono. Sometimes this is because of 'fuel system' or 'electrics' issues, sometimes this is because the environment produces a degree of information overload, sensory overload or social-emotional invasiveness that creates such a degree of burden the result is being mono. Sometimes it's a matter of how many other straws are on the camel's back; in other words, what's taxing the person's resources.

Becoming mono has happened to some people in breakdown states, and some people with depression experience the same, so it's always worth exploring whether an Autie is, for some reason, in a breakdown state or suffering from depression. I would add to that the burdens of chronic severe stress, extreme impulsivity and constant compulsive distraction at work in conditions like severe Tourette's syndrome (a condition causing involuntary movements and vocalisations), obsessive-compulsive disorder (OCD), bipolar disorder (manic depression) or the acute or chronic fight-flight states of exposure anxiety as being capable of such an energy and focus drain that in extreme cases there may be little processing space left to function as anything other than mono-tracked. Could some of these mechanisms be at work in underlying the severity of someone's Autism? Conditions such as gut and immune disorders, blood sugar problems, Tourette's, OCD, depression, bipolar and anxiety disorders can exist from infancy onwards and are found in a considerable percentage of those diagnosed with Autism.

If we lack the ability to keep up with processing what we see and hear at the same time, then the ability to pick up and use language will likely happen late and in some cases not at all. Some people are so overwhelmed by visual clutter and patterned walls or floors, or the effects of overhead lighting that it becomes difficult, maybe impossible to think easily or respond verbally.

If, because we are mono, we lose our connection to our body as soon as we are processing something else, we may have all kinds of automatic movements or noises going on which can distract and put the listener off. Some mono people may also be so busy keeping track of their body and its movements, in crossing the room or doing an action, that they simply cannot speak, cannot keep track of what they are saying, or cannot understand what is being said to them whilst they are moving. It is also easy to see why some severely mono people may feel they keep up better when they limit the world's opportunities to sabotage their information processing through the added 'burden' of language.

If we stick with a state of all-other/no-self we may have no idea what we think or feel and be limited to copying expected or prompted responses. If we stick with a state of all-self/no-other, we may have big gaps in what language skills we do develop. Our language may be so individual to us, so idiosyncratic that other people don't understand it. It may be so addressed as if for our own benefit that nobody else can make it out. It may even be relatively functional but relentless, obsessive and annoying to others who are looking to 'converse' (converse meaning to chat back and forth with someone as though that person has a simultaneous multi-track sense of self and other).

Furthermore, without a simultaneous sense of self and other, the concept of 'with' may be absent because language is experienced as 'at' or 'in front of', not 'with'. It is this experience of 'with' that underpins one's concept of what 'sharing' and 'being social' is all about. When I was 30 years old, after a lifetime of all-self/no-other and all-other/no-self, I finally held a simultaneous sense of self and other (thanks to 30 days on glutamine in my case – again not for everyone). I described it as to have touched the heaven of shared 'social', to know what it is to be 'with'. Without this experience, you can learn to 'do' developmentally typical social communication, but it is near impossible to grasp perceptually and emotionally the usual social communication values of developmentally typical people and why these matter so much to them.

Similarly, if someone can either express themselves, or keep track of what they are hearing, but not do both at the same time, they may have great difficulty even understanding their own speech and where it's going. Some may happily trundle along into lengthy litanies, a boggling verbal jumble they presume is still intelligible, perhaps unaware that they have increased their speed or volume to an intolerable or incomprehensible level. Others, and perhaps particularly those with the 'sensitive' personality type, might be more frightened than most to trust what they cannot keep track of and so limit their communication to one-word sentences they are able to keep up with. Other personality types such as the 'solitary' and 'vigilant' with these information-processing challenges may be far less socially motivated to develop interpersonal communication than others, and those with the 'idiosyncratic' personality type may be less motivated to accept or take on corrections to whatever idiosyncratic, perhaps self-directed language they do develop.

Ask yourself how you would be if you were challenged with these issues, but do so in the context of your own personality traits. If you are a try-anything, confident or adventurous type of personality, or one to whom social relationships are natural and not daunting, then you'd maybe fare better than those who didn't have these traits. But just imagine if you didn't have these resources. How motivated would you be to encourage others to speak with you when you knew you would either struggle with keeping up with what they've said or that when you replied you couldn't understand yourself and had little or no idea if you were actually making any sense? Now imagine if the *same* person also had a very poor simultaneous sense of self and other as well. Listening to someone else speak could easily shut you off from any experience of yourself as a person, and in any case you may be unable to respond in any way you, yourself, could keep up with. Now imagine that as your stress level went up, your adrenaline went with it, and everyone sounded louder, faster and seemed more invasive, the lights seemed too bright, the patterns around you seemed to be dragging your attention and almost swallowing up your sense of where you were in space. All round, it may simply look like the verbal language that is so desired by carers and professionals is an invitation to confusion, loss of control and overload.

Typed communication is much easier for some people because, unlike spoken words, they can hold onto the visual word longer. They may be able to see the words being out there in the world and better able to trust whether or not they are making sense. Some people can type-speak and at various times meaning may shut down for them too. This is not the same as saying they can't intelligibly type-speak in short bursts under favourable circumstances.

Recognising someone who is mono-tracked

The mono person takes many forms. It may be the person who:

- appears to get only 'bits' of what's going on

- appears to take in everything except 'the point'

- can only manage consciously to do or keep up with one thing at a time

- seems at times to be 'meaning-deaf' or 'meaning-blind', or experience an intermittent 'body connectedness' (where this is a constant state, consider dyspraxia)

- always appears to be 'at' or 'to' or 'in front of' but somehow lacks that feeling of being actually 'with'

- focuses on the part and loses the whole or who grasps the whole but has no idea of the significance

- is constantly surprised by the reactions and responses of others

- is so busy keeping up just in the moment that there is little or no wider awareness of consequences, implications or alternative ideas beyond the one track he or she is on

- behaves as though everything is constantly changing and is very entertained and at ease with feeling finally able to predict that storybook story played over and over and over again

- tells you the same thing a hundred times, each time feeling it's the first

- is suffering from overload and shutdowns, who is off in a dream, under the table or completely off on another track or making up his or her own track

- does not recognise you when you've changed clothes, worn glasses, been seen in an unexpected place

- does not recognise a familiar place or object when they've come at it from a different direction, time or day.

Recognising someone who is multi-tracked

Everybody is a bit mono sometimes; when they are in grief, extremely rushed, getting over the flu, had too much to drink the night before, have low blood sugar levels, because of allergies, because of chronic fatigue, when living in a state of chronic threat, when too much has happened in one day... So being mono *is* something that multi-track people do know about. What they don't know about is what it's like to have been born in that state, or for that state to have been the only reality they've ever known. In other words, being mono is not just about information processing, it's about how living constantly in that state affects social development, identity, and sometimes even personality.

Those who are multi-track are equally affected by this being their constant state. If you grow up multi-track you have more chance of:

- enjoying playing group sports
- being out as part of a group bigger than two or three people
- being able consciously to manipulate people in a diverse range of ways (which requires a simultaneous sense of self and other)
- being consciously aware of fashions and trends and how these reflect on you
- grasping the developmentally typical version of 'manners'
- being able to organise your household, negotiate in your relationships and resolve conflicts
- recognising a person when they've changed clothes, worn glasses, been seen in an unexpected place.
- recognising a familiar place or object when you've come at it from a different direction, time or day.

You might also be more likely to take for granted how easy certain things are for you. You might be more likely to make comparison-based judgements of others as 'stupid' or 'weird' if they aren't like your majority. You might be more likely to take for granted as 'normal' that much in this world is really designed for the majority – multi-track people – or even that that's how it *should* be.

When multi-track people stand in a queue with mono-track people, they may struggle to understand why that person can't get their money out ready for the purchase or why that person takes so long when they do get served. When multi-track people get served by someone mono-tracked at a counter, they might feel the person is not as competent as themselves, because every-thing is done in a much more 'one thing at a time' style and, when it's not, some part of the service gets in the wrong order, something meant to be there is missing or on the floor and the expected words may or may not be said.

It is natural for multi-track people to judge a mono-tracked person by their multi-track standards (Auties also often judge developmentally typical people by Autie standards!). In other words, to judge the apple as though it is a bad orange rather than recognising that it's doing really great as an apple coping in an orange type of job. This is one of the biggest obstacles to employment for people on the Autistic spectrum; not their own capabilities, but the unfair measurements of multi-track people who naturally assume everyone is 'like them' because that's what 'normal' is, and that if you can't function as 'one of them' you shouldn't be given places within their structures. Competence is important but there are different styles of competence and the great strengths of having an Autism spectrum condition are often forgotten when people fixate only on how well someone can mimic non-Autistic styles.

When multi-track people do actions, they often think ahead, often without the need for a list to plan out every step. They just hold and juggle it all in their heads. They might provide a whole lot of verbal context with no clear 'point', then give you the information yet not remind you of the subject itself. This is because they hold the subject in their head whilst they 'waffle' with all the rest of their information, assuming you'll hold the subject too until they've finished with the 'frills'! They consider reminders of the actual subject to be redundant. When multi-track people converse they have a better chance of keeping track of turn-taking, and they can usually listen and think their own thoughts at the same time, and they hold over what the subject is without having to make that overt. They are more full-on than a three-ring circus!

These struggles are all aside from the added issue of processing delay.

Recognising someone with a lack of simultaneous self/other

Everybody gets a bit self-absorbed and on their own track some time. Stand-up comedians almost totally run their own show. Manic and obsessive people can be unable to contain themselves. People with control dramas can wind you into controlling dialogues in which they may ask the same thing over and over again to distract you from moving them elsewhere. But none of these really capture the person who jabbers away at you, perhaps even plays both their own role and yours and may even invite your response, but then appears to do nothing at all with it. Or consider the emotionally balanced person who appears utterly oblivious of their impact on others, because when they are on their own track, the processing of why you are there, who you are, perhaps even what you are, may fly out the window for a while.

Then there's the opposite, those people who sit or wander about as if objective, or a mile away, who perhaps stare through you but have that Mona Lisa smile that gives away that they are registering what's around them, but why aren't they responding to it? In the absence of a social anxiety condition, something which would cause a self-protection or fight-flight state, they might be depressed and withdrawn, or obsessive and having made a rule not to respond. But they might be none of these things, merely someone mono-tracked who has moved into a state of all-other/no-self, in which one may struggle to connect with one's own body in responding, or, more deeply, struggle to think or feel anything, but merely be mapping everything, as a computer might.

Cognitive and behavioural implications

People with a lack of simultaneous self and other can be worlds unto themselves. Life may be one big movie or one big stage. Those who have this intermittently may feel suddenly estranged, distant, disconnected, anxious or simply lost without being able to grasp why. Some may seek proof they continue to exist, compelled to create a dramatic or shock response, others may become distressed and suddenly cling inconsolably as the social world effectively 'throws them out'.

Much of the problem of this aspect of mono is the responses of others. When someone they have closeness with suddenly seems a world away, staring through them or oblivious to their expression as they continue endlessly on their own track, many developmentally typical people take this as rude, or inconsiderate, or feel they had bad judgement in choosing someone who wasn't as considerate, polite or interested as they thought. In other words, they can take offence at the person's disability, take it personally and make judgements based on projecting their own processing reality onto the person with an Autism spectrum condition. It is always best if you know you have this mono issue to be upfront on meeting new people and tell them that you slip out of gear at times and lose pieces of information, and that they shouldn't take these things personally when they happen or assume they are intentional or simply bad manners or lack of caring. It's like explaining upfront that you have some different customs and they become apparent sometimes and there is no need for anyone to take offence.

Information-processing delay

Not only can someone be utterly mono in a whole variety of ways, but the information which does come in may be delayed in the ability to make sense of it. For an Autie, this might mean they don't instantly understand what the object given to them is, or even what the literal meaning of a spoken word is, unless, perhaps, accompanied by actions. My processing delay on what I was seeing depended on whether it was being used when I saw it (in action), whether it was positioned in a place that linked its meaning for me and whether I got to tap it (the acoustics gave me its 'nature' from which I could get its meaning) or move it (lots of objects roll or rock a certain way). Without these it used to take me anywhere from 30 seconds to recognise an unfamiliar object if at all. These days this processing delay is reduced to sometimes taking me around two or three seconds before I know what I'm seeing. As a result there are times I feel like an animal more than a person; when I can still respond to the pattern, just not the meaning.

My ability to process 'blah blah' up until late childhood was delayed by anywhere up to five seconds, if processed at all. This meant most of the words remained meaningless at the moment when I heard them. These days some words are processed at around the time I hear them, others are delayed by two or three seconds before they mean anything, and some are simply not processed at all. The impact is that in terms of sound, the sentences I hear sound fine; but in terms of meaning, they are often jumbled with the quickly processed words getting through first and the later ones hanging about so they end up in a different, often meaningless, order. If you ask me to repeat back to you not the string you said to me but the meaning of what you said, you'd often get a very sketchy or fairly altered version of what you thought someone would have understood.

When there is jumbled meaning the emphasis can change completely. Even the meaningful bits of earlier sentences can be jumbled in with the most recent ones. I have a great sense of surrealism, humour and natural creativity. Most of the time I don't bother to struggle a second or third time to under-stand or get clarification of the meaning of what was said (and to ask such a question would be an organisational challenge anyway and involve having to stop receptive processing in order to move to expressive mode). I'm OK with a very sketchy 'rough idea' or general 'feel' or 'theme' of things. But what if I was a serious or highly self-conscious and fearful personality, someone who relied on interpreting rather than sensing? How much more distressed at myself, my life, or others might I be in this situation?

Until my 30s the progressive backlog of unprocessed and jumbled 'blah blah' would overstimulate my system and my adrenaline would peak. Not only would I hear meaningless 'blah blah' which robbed me of connection with my own thoughts or feelings and the security that gives any of us, but also this adrenaline peak caused the pitch and volume to appear much sharper, the pace much faster. So the harder I listened, the more often people appeared to be speeding up in a screeching voice and shouting at me. Not really the invitation to communicate you might imagine you are calmly offering.

Those who failed simultaneously to use any gestural signing to augment the meaning of their words left me feeling 'meaning-deaf'. To achieve good consistent ability to keep up with what people were saying and have space to think and feel and shift enough to reply, I needed the other person to slow down and simplify language, leaving two- to three-second breaks between ideas, and preferably augment their language with gestural signing or the use of objects or diagrams.

Whilst it is true for some, the idea put forward by Temple Grandin that (all) 'Autistics think in pictures' may mislead people into imagining that those with severe receptive auditory and visual processing issues all think in pictures too yet many may need gestural signing or communication via representational objects for the concepts to gel. My experience is that some people with Autism have extreme difficulty in automatically making mental pictures, let alone linking experiences or concepts of any kind to static pictures or incoming words. These people may need to see the experience of the cup being used, not just a flat symbol, picture or even photo of a cup. In other words they rely on the experience, not the mental concept. Perhaps those who can easily put words to pictures are more likely to develop comprehensible speech, so we are yet to hear more from those who live in a world where meaning is far more elusive.

The literal and the significant

A similar processing delay may be at work for many Aspies though for many it may not be the literal meaning that is lost, but the *significance* of what they see and hear. Perhaps this is a requirement to be able to 'think in pictures'. As someone still struggling to hold consistent literal meaning, the struggle to realise the significance of what I see and hear in my everyday life seems rather invisible. Whilst Aspies may feel a great loss in not keeping up with the significance beyond the literal, I don't have a great grip on what all the fuss or loss is about because literal meaning is struggle enough. But I feel I have an advantage that many Aspies don't have. I am extremely highly sensing and navigate pattern, theme and feel brilliantly. I don't feel I need much of a mind because I feel I'm very good at being an animal. For me, this compensates for an inability to be more than literal in my everyday life.

The Aspie may love books and conversation, keeping up brilliantly with the literal meaning of what they see and hear, but 'the point' involved may be consistently lost. They may know all the facts, but the motives, the implications, and the reason may be invisible. They may get a gift and wonder what they are meant to do with it. Some Auties, on the other hand, may even struggle to know what it is.

The Aspie may open the gift, recognise what it is, but not know what they are meant to do about that. He or she may like or hate the present, without realising the implication that they maybe shouldn't say that it's horrible in front of the person who gave it, or that the giver might appreciate hearing a thankyou. This is perhaps especially so for the Aspie with a solitary, rather self-owning personality type to which such social-emotional needs don't seem natural.

Of course, there are many people on the Autism spectrum who fluctuate somewhere between the Autie and Aspie types of challenges. Nobody is a 'pure case' unless we tune out seeing what doesn't fit our assumptions. Many people are at all kinds of places on the continuum, and those different combinations will have an impact on the type of language and communication issues at work as well as indicating potential ways to work with solving some of these.

Meaning-deafness as part of being mono

Meaning-deafness can be confused with a self-protection state such as exposure anxiety or avoidant personality in which it can be difficult to dare social acknowledgement of others when they initiate. Meaning-deafness can also be confused with mood disorders such as the oblivion in a manic state in bipolar or the withdrawal state of depression. Meaning-deafness can be confused with chronic compulsive disorders in which the person is kept so busy with tics or caught up in obsessive thoughts or compulsions that it can be nearly impossible to pull away to attend to what has been said. Obviously, meaning-deafness is most easily recognised where it occurs independently of these things. The problem is that many people with Autism spectrum conditions have meaning-deafness and combinations of these other things. So the best way to help some people with their challenges is to address each of those things, including the meaning-deafness if this exists too.

People with meaning-deafness can have this for a whole range of reasons. If the meaning-deaf person is sensitive to overhead lights or direct sunlight, appears to see the part and lose the sense of the whole, appears to have vision which flits from one thing to the next as though there is no real line of tracking as one looks around the room, then the visual perceptual issue of scotopic sensitivity syndrome (SSS) has a reasonable chance of overloading the ability to keep up with what one is hearing. Treating the SSS can dramatically decrease how mono some people are and help them keep up with what they hear.

If someone is meaning-deaf in some places, but not others, observe what is common to those places, perhaps a patterned carpet or wallpaper (this floods my senses and shuts down a lot of my ability to understand what I hear). Are the overhead lights flickering or buzzing? Is there a fan or fridge motor whirring away in the background? Is there lots of movement or is the person expected to move and listen at the same time? Do people in one environment speak more slowly, make things more visual and concrete than in other places? Are people less directly interpersonal in the environments where he or she appears to have less difficulty? Is the person simply less anxious in the places he or she appears to be less meaning-deaf?

Meaning-deafness can affect the person who appears to guess what you have said from a handful of key words but misses the specifics. It can be someone who gets all the words but is utterly literal and has lost all deeper processing of what has been said for its significance. It can be someone who has not yet discovered that words are used not simply 'in association' with the sensory experiences they relate to but are used meaningfully to 'represent' those experiences.

Cognitive and behavioural implications of meaning-deafness

If someone is consistently meaning-deaf, it means they hear sound but it is all just patterns, 'blah blah'. This has big implications for information overload, because without being able to discriminate between what is meaningful to you and what is not, your senses are simply flooded indiscriminately with the lot. Imagine being on a train and taking in every bit of 'blah blah' from all the people on the train, together with the sounds of the train itself, the hum of any fluorescent lights, the sounds of people scuffling about...all of it is treated as 'equal'. Now imagine that on top of that you are expected to act like language is something user-friendly you would love to promote and want to hear more of, something you are expected to initiate to stimulate others to give you even more of this cacophony. And imagine on top of that that as you become over-loaded and distressed, as would be understandable and normal in your reality, you are then chastised for not controlling yourself and acting 'normal' according to someone else's information-processing reality. Enough to drive you mad? Add to this the fact that your possibly unaffected intelligence is then judged on the basis that you can't understand what people say, follow an instruction, etc. On the basis of your assumed lack of intellect and control-lability, imagine you are then excluded from a large number of opportunities and environments, so you are perhaps overly controlled, taught to be more dependent than you'd perhaps have otherwise been and, after all, it's because there's something 'wrong' with you. And people may wave their arms about, show you the occasional picture, but they won't fluently sign for you. Why should they? You're not deaf.

Seems a little stupid? But those who have never known consistent meaning-deafness have little idea that without hearing with meaning, you can't learn the relationship between seeing and hearing unless it's overtly linked at the moment when each word is actually heard. Yet the only signing delivered currently in the Autism field is that of Makaton, a piecemeal signing system requiring *interpretation*, as opposed to gestural signing (more akin to that in deaf signing), much more of which requires no interpretation for those with interpreting problems!

The other alternative offered currently is PECS, a picture exchange system. This is limited to which pictures you can find and show at a given moment and for some people who might be capable of comprehending fluently when gestural signing accompanies slow speech, this is akin to speaking to older children and adults as though they are receptively three years old. You can't have complex discussions through PECS, you can through gestural signing. But because thinking in gesture, movement, and so on isn't natural to those who've never known consistent meaning-deafness, they seem to find it too hard to learn this 'second language'.

A similar thing exists expressively in that those who grew up consistently meaning-deaf have generally demonstrated no ability to use fluent functional language. But the brain can process words outside of the moment they were received, beyond conscious awareness in a similar way to how we pick up sub-liminal advertising. Given a keyboard and a non-invasive push start (and physical support where necessary for those with motor-planning disorders) some meaning-deaf people have, controversially, sometimes dramatically, surprised people as much as they've surprised themselves when typed dialogue emerges in someone with no 'in the moment' receptive awareness of interpretive language. Obviously, this doesn't fit developmentally typical processing reality, so even seeing is not believing for many and the field of facilitated communication (assisted typed communication) is certainly the hotbed of this debate, with those with Autism often paying the price and having their only link to the world of meaning removed.

Intermittent meaning-deafness is even more confusing. Surely someone who could follow an instruction an hour ago, couldn't just lose that facility in the next hour, only for it to be back on by the end of the day? Surely this must be an attitude problem, bad behaviour, laziness? These are often the assumptions. The person with intermittent meaning-deafness may revert to the only bottom line they *can* guarantee: that language will not consistently make sense and, therefore, why should they socially encourage others to expect otherwise? The natural consequence is to discourage others from using language with you and often either to speak all the time so your processing problem is hidden or not speak at all because you can't guarantee you'll be 'online' to answer. Again, it would be so easy to train people to ask/sign 'Are you overloaded? Have your language batteries shut down?', and then revert to visual language to get the meaning back; but no, it doesn't work that way.

Often I find when those with only intermittent meaning-deafness stop speaking, their carers, teachers, etc. reduce language at *all* times to something like PECS. Naturally, the isolated, alienated, bored and frustrated child has behavioural problems, or more to the point, from the child's perspective it may well be that the environment has behavioural problems. In terms of learning, unimaginative teachers who have themselves often never struggled with meaning-deafness, create lessons utterly dependent for delivery and message on verbal language. Yet there are ways of feeling, smelling, even hearing the patterns of maths, sensory explorations in science, nature studies, music, art, cookery which require little or no language, and typed communication that can be done with very minimal spoken language, not to mention classes in which modelling gestural signing as natural and incidental can also be done non-verbally and in a self-owning, socially non-invasive way.

Meaning-blindness as part of being mono

People who are meaning-blind use objects in an unusual way. But then so might those who are 'stimming', so might those with obsessive-compulsive disorder, so might those with Tourette's; and even those with exposure anxiety may be compelled to use objects in ways the environment 'doesn't

want' – but struggle to dare show they can use them in the way the environment 'does want'. So recognising when the unusual use of objects is an issue of
meaning-blindness is a bit of an art, and to get it as right as possible you have
to recognise what all those other conditions might look like when interacting
with objects. And remember, one person may have a cluster of such conditions, only one of which is actual meaning-blindness but several of which
may involve an unusual use of objects. So, in referring to those with
meaning-blindness, what exactly do I mean by 'use objects in an unusual
way'?

There are two issues that I know of which underpin meaning-blindness.
The first is that of limited left-hemisphere processing, which theoretically
might account for someone who is stuck in the world of pattern, theme and
feel in which 'interpretive meaning' may be 'invisible'. So if you look at a
young baby playing with a spoon, for example, most babies will watch how it
moves in their hands, feel the metal in their mouths or the handle for that
matter; some might notice how the metal catches the light; and if the baby
happens to knock the spoon against something, it will hear the noise the
spoon makes and may notice the spoon has traces of smell from where it has
been.

This isn't too different to the meaning-blind adult who is given an object
and checks out its nature in terms of surface texture, acoustics when tapped,
how it bounces back when pushed or shaken, how it catches light when
turned, the experience of its form when felt within the mouth, the tongue
sensation in relation to the substance it is made from, its smell, its visual form.
These are valid ways of making sense of a visual object in any person who has
limited sight or visual processing. As a person who spent much of my first nine
years in this state, and one for whom severe shutdowns in the ability to use
interpretation meant these were the only avenues left in establishing 'familiarity' and use in those states, I think we do 'Autistic' adults an injustice to equate
this type of recognition and familiarity behaviour with mental retardation
simply on the basis that it can look so much like a baby's exploration. A blind
person would take such an assumption as an oversight if not an insult, so why
should the same not be true of the sometimes very truly but differently intelligent Auties who use the same behaviours because of meaning-blindness?

Then there is a second issue underpinning meaning-blindness: that of the
fragmenting effects and loss of visual context inherent in some severe cases of
scotopic sensitivity syndrome. Scotopic sensitivity syndrome (SSS) is often
related to diet, and some people have found that (hopefully safely) raising

levels of omega 3s has reduced levels of visual perceptual problems. Salicylate intolerance can result in a decrease in omega 3 levels in the body, and I've found that many children with signs of scotopic sensitivity syndrome have lost much of this when they start a regime of glutamine, omega 3s and a low-salicylate diet.

Tinted lenses are available for those who can be tested, give feedback (even observable body responses in some cases) and cope with wearing glasses. The Irlen Institute has centres around the world and tests people for scotopic sensitivity syndrome, but Brain Power International (BPI) is an alternative company run by opthalmologists which has a smaller but, in my view, equally effective range of tinted lenses, and the entire test range can be purchased for around the same cost as one pair of selected Irlen lenses (which may well need updating later). I personally would like to see schools purchase sets of the BPI range so children could self-test in their own time and space in a familiar environment at no cost and simply send glasses off for tinting once a tint is selected from BPI's smaller range.

Scotopic sensitivity syndrome presents as someone who often struggles under fluorescent lighting, is often hypersensitive to direct sunlight and who, when looking around a room, appears to stare straight through things, often using peripheral vision (but this also occurs in those with exposure anxiety, and Tourette's can also cause a tic involving sideways looking). Their eyes often flit haphazardly from one thing to the next with little 'linear tracking' (they generally don't look around in a smooth visual line).

People with scotopic sensitivity commonly focus on the part to the exclusion of the whole and appear to notice tiny detail. The same people will sometimes place objects away from them, observe them and then come back, alter the pattern, stand away again to view it as a whole, come back, etc. Auties who have scotopic sensitivity syndrome may be curious about dropping objects through space and can appear to walk blindly up or down stairs as though their vision is irrelevant, or appear a bit strange when doing so (some will hunch a bit, hold on tightly as they use stairs, scrunch up their face or appear deeply concentrating), as though they aren't sure about depth and space. They may be fixated on the edges of things, following lines (these two can also happen in obsessive-compulsive disorder), or use echo-acoustics (using sound to bounce off the surface of objects in testing the nature, shape or depth of objects).

Scotopic sensitivity means seeing everything bit by bit by bit so areas full of movement, or movement through crowds, can be overwhelming (but this can be an issue with exposure anxiety too). This can cause shutdowns in other areas of information processing, so the same person can become progressively more meaning-deaf or lose all sense of where his or her body is in space or lose whatever sense of simultaneous self and other he or she has. So, suddenly, such a person may appear to have 'disconnected', shut down, and that can mean panic for some, oblivious 'mania' for others, attack for others.

There are certainly lesser effects of scotopic sensitivity. Some people may have partial shutdowns in the ability to process information. This means that the sensory flooding caused by scotopic sensitivity (for one scene can be instead thousands of seemingly unrelated 'bits') can make information processing pay the price. So someone who at one time understood the relevance or significance of what they were looking at or hearing may now only get the literal meaning. So they may still know what they are seeing or hearing but have little idea now why it's important or what they are expected to do about it (this may also occur in other information-processing issues, depressive mood disorders and personality disorder and be unrelated to SSS). Similarly, the person may feel progressively detached from the activity and drift out of any simultaneous sense of self and other back into that of all-self/no-other or all-other/no-self. Other information-processing issues can also cause this, including nutrient issues like irregular blood sugar levels, vitamin or mineral deficiencies, food allergies, food intolerance, issues involved in immune disorders, etc.

Cognitive and behavioural implications of meaning-blindness

Meaning-deafness and meaning-blindness have big implications for language, interaction, behaviour and learning on different levels. If someone has gut or immune problems affecting their ability to process information, then the best way to get these out of the way is to treat the underlying health issues as best as possible.

If someone is meaning-blind, they may be unable to recognise 'what' an object is unless it is in current use or unless they were actively at that moment seeking something to fulfil a use and therefore had a ready-made concept to slot the sensory experience into. For someone with meaning-blindness, recognising the 'what' of what's around them may otherwise not 'just' happen as it all becomes simply 'stuff'. So making things visible may not be enough. Some people have to actually see the thing in use before they can attribute meaning to it. Something similar can happen when language development has been greatly affected by such a thing. Imagine a teacher sending the children off to their table to use scissors in making their pictures. Without saying 'use your scissors to cut things out and make pictures' the relationship between scissors and cutting may not occur for some people. When you show the scissors and show the cutting and the use of these cut-outs to make a picture, the words may only then have meaning. This is usually purely an information-processing issue.

Other people have a lesser loss of visual or auditory processing. They may get the 'what' but have no idea of the 'why'. They may know they are meant to use the scissors to cut things out and make a picture but have no idea at all why anyone would want to do this and what they are meant to think or feel about it. This could be a cognitive information-processing issue, but it's just as possible that it can be about levels of arousal, about social-emotional reality or about personality disorder affecting a person's social-emotional repertoire. If it were an information-processing issue then pointing out the wider significance of what someone might think or feel about what they've made or what its later use might be might set things straight. For someone for whom it's more of a social-emotional reality issue, you might be better off finding out what, if anything, *does* have significance and purpose for that person.

Information-processing issues will not only have an impact on behaviour in terms of struggling to keep up or deeply grasp the wider connections or significance of what's going on, but the stress of feeling so out of control, so overloaded, confused, is enough to make most of us divert away from 'work' into 'play', enough to make most of us bring in self-calming and download strategies (and sometimes doing something very repetitive can be a download strategy), enough to make most of us want to scream or withdraw. Saying that, there are personalities in there too, and it's important to keep a clear balance between being sensitive to someone's overload and reinforcing that the slightest distress will let them off the hook at all times. A change is as good as a holiday and sometimes changing the activity in a way that is less overloading, more playful and more about pattern, theme and feel than about meaning, helps someone to stay involved and keep up at the same time until the person is again able to cope with the activity in its usual form.

Recognising someone with delayed information processing
Delayed processing can look like nobody's at home. It can look like someone struggling to repeat your words as though trying to imagine what they'd mean had they said them themselves. It can be someone who suddenly blurts out or demonstrates awareness of information that even they had no idea they

had till it was out. Asked to repeat it, they may be unable to. When we process information consciously, we are relatively in control of it. Delayed processing happens beyond conscious awareness; and when and if the evidence of it pops out, it can surprise the person themselves too, who may have no idea where that information came from.

Cognitive and behavioural implications of delayed information processing

When you have wandered through a supermarket and a song is playing, you may not notice at all because you were too busy on another track. The next day you may find yourself singing this song in your head or out loud and have no idea where this has come from. You had taken the song in pre-consciously, and something had triggered it out into conscious awareness.

One of the effects of delayed information processing on language is that someone may accumulate lots of language awareness, but it may not be consciously accessible immediately. Because many people with this kind of state in which information processing has shut down might look so 'out of it', 'unaware', 'nobody home', it's too easy to assume the person is mentally retarded. Many Auties who went on to communicate through assisted typing, some of whom became independent communicators, often expressed that they had peripherally picked up how to read although they overtly showed no sign that they could do so. There are many topics which I have no conscious awareness of knowing about and if you ask me directly I can't access any information on them. But if I talk to myself or address someone else about them they seem to spring up and sometimes blurt out of me before I've even realised I've said anything. I call this process 'unknown knowing'. Similarly, those who cannot begin to answer open-ended questions can often still respond to multiple-choice questions. Those who appear unable to spell will sometimes re-order letters left behind on a letter board when placed in the wrong order. Yet in a directly confrontational world in which the majority have conscious access and awareness of what they know, most educational or social situations will assume we are all the same.

Can someone fluctuate in their ability to process information?

Most Auties are not 'offline' all the time. It's more like their 'batteries go flat'. Some people with conditions like low blood oxygen, or other physical conditions which rob the brain of nutrition on a fairly constant basis, may be fairly offline most of the time, but there are many physical and health issues which can fluctuate really sharply, including the interaction of certain foods, stored viruses, allergies, food intolerances, blood sugar and immune disorders, to name but a few – but this does not mean nobody's home.

There are people in comas who have been able later to recall things said to them whilst in the coma. There are those who may simply be robbed of the motor planning to communicate what they are experiencing and who may need an alternative assisted non-verbal communication technique to do so. But most Auties simply slip in and out of gear in terms of information processing.

The optimist sees the cup half full. The pessimist, the worrier, the phobic, the person who needs to be needed, sees the cup half empty. If an Autie is having regular 'flat batteries', the pessimist may well see this as the person's usual state and the person with Autism who resonates with this will be left to identify with their condition. If the same person is viewed by the optimist, they may see this purely as a 'download' state before the person bounces back again into being able to process information for a while.

The person with Autism can identify with the pessimist or the optimist. If the person with Autism identifies with the optimist, he or she may not identify with the Autism as 'self'. If the person with Autism tends to be more of a pessimist, he or she would identify selfhood with Autism and could pull against this sense of himself or herself, playing on his or her inabilities and pressuring those trying to help into being co-dependent or 'rescuers'. So, to a degree, identification and the 'music of beingness' one resonates with or pulls against in the immediate environment play together in determining the pattern of how someone will behaviourally and emotionally respond to their own overload and shutdowns.

Information-processing 'batteries' go flat on different levels. For many Auties, flat batteries means the meaning has fallen away, it is still being accu-mulated, but it has stopped being conscious. So it's like the 'what' may have disappeared. Even literal meaning may have slipped out of gear. Some of the signs may be that the person appears not to 'realise' he or she is being spoken to (anxiety disorders aside) or may repeat your words as if trying to work out the meaning of what was said. Losing attention, fidgeting, self-entertainment, self-calming, even distressed self-injury are all common indications someone has shut down on this literal level. It's like watching the world fall away, being closed out, plunged into chaos, and often when receptive processing falls away, expressive ability disappears with it. Pauses in speech, slowing down pace, making things visual, reducing all unnecessary input, providing a rhythm, sensorily familiar objects or simply giving download time are all useful tools. What's usually not so useful is complex questioning, discussion or interference which can all add to the chaos at the worst possible time.

On an Aspie level it is mostly the 'why' that falls away so the person may still get a reasonable level of the 'what', still be reasonably literal, but the significance, the wider connections of what has been seen, heard, done, falls away. And the categories of Autism and Asperger's syndrome are not pure. There are those on a sliding scale from one end to the other.

Information-processing problems and IQ tests

The ability to participate in an IQ test is often dependent on the ability to:

- combine your senses in completing a task
- hold a simultaneous sense of self and other:
  - in interacting with the tester
  - in being able to understand and think/feel at the same time or communicate and monitor communication at the same time
  - in being able to think/feel and communicate at the same time
- move and think at the same time (necessary to writing, etc.)
- stay on task and keep up with the interaction of multiple concepts involved in comparing, contrasting, shifts in time or situational context and relationships between characters or events in a story or dialogue
- keep up with processing information for interpretive meaning in a fluent and ongoing, if not interactive, way.

In any of these areas, some people with severe information-processing problems could do badly in IQ testing without this having anything to do with their actual intelligence. An IQ test which was not culturally biased against those with these challenges would have to be designed in a way that could not wrongly assume any of these information-processing challenges to be reflections of intelligence. To date, I do not know of such a test.

Information-processing problems and health

At first glance, most people wouldn't imagine that having information-processing problems would have an impact on health. Health issues like gut/

immune breakdowns might cause some information-processing problems, but having cognitive problems surely couldn't affect the health of the body?

We know that those with information-processing problems usually suffer from chronic stress, and we know that chronic stress eventually breaks down the health of the body. Things like 'oxidative stress' are made worse by high anxiety and can lead to impaired blood flow and limit the capacity of red blood cells to transport nutrients around the body, and that includes supplying nutrients to the brain. High chronic stress will eventually reduce people's immunity, so those with pre-existing health problems will run the risk of these health problems coming to the surface. Reduced immunity can lead to inflammation in the body, a kind of inflamed rawness, and this can affect the lining of the gut so a child might develop bowel issues. Chronic stress will exacerbate conditions such as mood disorders, obsessive-compulsive or tic states. Chronic stress will bring out the worst in most people who also have personality disorders. Chronic stress will exacerbate social anxiety states and will usually adversely affect communication problems. So the chronic stress caused by constant experiences of uncontrollable overload and shutdowns has the potential to create a vicious cycle.

What about dyspraxia?

Where gut/immune issues are ruled out as the underlying cause of information-processing issues, dyspraxia may be worth considering. But it is important to recognise that there are conditions such as exposure anxiety, avoidant personality or dependent personality where someone may be unable to dare acknowledge or show the skills they have, and that this could be confused with dyspraxia when the dyspraxia element of the Autism alone is not enough to account for the degree of 'disability'. Nevertheless, here's the definition of dyspraxia given by *Merriam-Webster's Medical Dictionary* (Merriam-Webster, Incorporated 2005a): 'impairment of the ability to perform coordinated movement'. There are also associated problems of perception, language and thought. For example, people with dyspraxia may have difficulty understanding the messages that their senses convey and difficulty translating those messages into actions. They may find organisation hard and may have trouble learning and retaining physical movements. The progress at which they acquire language may be delayed, and language and speech may be impaired (see Dyspraxia Foundation n.d.).

Available therapies for information-processing issues

Most of the current big one-size-fits-all approaches are aimed at behaviour management or interaction skills, rather than at reducing information-processing issues or speeding up information processing.

Some of the programmes aimed at improving information processing include Brain Gym, which addresses brain organisation and brain patterning. Up-to-date international lists of Brain Gym specialists or therapists are available on the internet.

Biofeedback is also being used where children and adults can use computer games specifically designed to reward re-patterning of brain waves associated with impaired information processing. Such programmes are rare and experimental. They are generally run by a special type of psychologist called a neuropsychologist. An internet search on biofeedback used in addressing behaviour and learning might bring up any up-to-date listing of therapists in your own country or state using this technique.

There are also natural medicine programmes which address gut/immune function to tackle information-processing problems. These can be provided by naturopaths, doctors who are also trained as naturopaths, specialists in gut disorders, immune function, inflammatory states, allergies and food intolerances, etc., as well as by chiropractors (chiropractic relates to spinal alignment affecting feedback to the brain), cranio-sacral therapists (cranio-sacral therapy relates to working with the flow of cerebral spinal fluid which relays messages to and from the brain) and osteopaths (osteopathy relates to working with deep tissue manipulation and is used to treat toxicity and immune system issues).

There is treatment by opthalmologists (who specialise in what the brain does with what the eyes see) for scotopic sensitivity in reducing sensory flooding caused by overload when the brain is unable to see things as a whole. There are self-calming programmes, sensory rooms, hypnotherapists, play therapists, art therapists, music therapists and dance/movement therapists, who all work in different ways to treat chronic stress associated with information-processing problems among other things.

There are alternative communication techniques such as facilitated communication, and home techniques including communication via objects and gestural signing which can help some very overloaded people communicate where they otherwise would be unable to. There is a wide range of suggestions to make the environment less overloading which are detailed in my book *Autism: An Inside-Out Approach* (Williams 1996).

In a nutshell, information-processing problems might mean any of the following:

- Sleep deprivation associated with light, noise or high electromagnetic fields affecting the sleep environment.
- Brain organisation differences, including dyspraxia and left–right integration issues.
- The compensation of being mono, processing delay, overload and shutdowns.
- Gut/immune/nutrient/toxicity issues.
- Neurotransmitter imbalances, such as may occur in mood, anxiety and impulse-control disorders (and may sometimes be underpinned by gut/immune issues affecting the brain's chemistry).
- Central auditory processing disorder.
- 'Psuedo' processing issues, such as environmental patterns, identity issues or personality disorders.

The most appropriate treatment in reducing information-processing problems which cause someone to be mono-tracked or have delayed information processing will depend on which underlying issues are at work.

Being mono-tracked and specific behavioural issues
Being 'mono-tracked' could underpin specific issues relating to:

- communication
- toileting
- sleep problems
- stimming
- meltdowns
- self-protection responses
- challenging behaviours
- food behaviour problems.

When one is mono-tracked, verbal *communication* may be put on hold whenever the person is on a different sensory track. So if they are moving or looking at something else or busy thinking/feeling they may be simultaneously unable to process what they are hearing (but others who rely on sensing may absolutely need to be doing something else whilst listening, because if they tune in too directly they shut down). It is essential to tell the difference between whether distraction helps or hinders a particular person. It would be harmful to assume that self-distraction isn't essential for some people in order to stay 'tuned in', even though they may appear not to be. For others it would be essential to remove the 'distractions'. One person's food is another's poison, and both may have the label 'Autistic'. There is a difference between sensing people and shut down people who are experiencing boredom or alienation because of being mono- tracked in a multi-track world and who distract themselves to compensate emotionally.

The ability to comprehend with meaning relies on being able to keep up with processing that 'blah blah' for meaning and simultaneously process the meaning of what one is seeing, including its wider context. It means maintaining a sense of self and other, a connection to and feedback from one's own body and emotions and holding thoughts consciously in one's mind whilst continuing to breathe, walk, talk or do…a tall order for some people who are severely mono-tracked.

When information processing is slow, the meaning can seem to 'drop out' leaving the person simply with the pattern, theme, feel of what is being said. So information-processing delay can be one cause of intermittent or constant meaning-deafness, meaning-blindness, poor body-connectedness, a lack or loss of simultaneous sense of self and other, a struggle to express oneself and simultaneously hold thought or to hold emotion and access verbal language at the same time without one or the other going 'offline'. It's easy to see how distress, confusion and fragmentation would arise and how behaviours related to making functioning simpler, self-managing stress or simply reacting extremely to the environment might all be improved by reducing the levels of overload and facilitating information-processing time for people who are severely mono-tracked.

In Aspies this dropout of information-processing ability can mean they lose the significance of what's being said or handled, or of what is happening (lose the 'why' but still get the 'what'). Auties may lose the 'what' of literal meaning but still be able to sense in terms of pattern, theme and feel.

The mainstream version of social 'normality' requires a simultaneous sense of self and other. If you swing between all-self/no-other and all-other/no-self, this may happen because of personality issues but can also happen if you are generally mono-tracked in your information processing. Being mono-tracked will lead to different social communication, learning, self-management and behavioural styles to those of mainstream people, and these styles may appear to be quite lacking in social skills. The mono-tracked person may in fact have both a lack of social skills as well as a mono-tracked processing style. In this case, teaching social skills will not stop them being mono-tracked and they will continue to demonstrate social communication styles that will not be multi-track and may well still be seen to be lacking in the application of what has been taught to them. An information-processing problem can be compensated for, but learning to act like a multi-track person will not fix the processing issue. It *is* acceptable to be mono-tracked if that is what you are, even though developmentally typical people may pressure you to learn at least to *act* as if you have a simultaneous sense of self and other. It is *not* acceptable for others to make character judgements about any Autie on the basis of them being mono-tracked in their processing and struggling to hold any simultaneous sense of self and other. This is as unacceptable as discriminating against employing wheelchair users because they don't walk, sight-impaired people who don't make suitable eye contact or hearing-impaired people who don't respond 'properly' when you speak to them. Unfortunately, society has a long way to go in getting to grips with this and continues to see what are often mono-tracked styles as 'lacking social skills', 'behavioural disturbance' or 'character faults'.

Part of being mono-tracked may mean you can only think and feel when not simultaneously speaking, so that when you speak the thoughts or feelings behind the communication are easily lost track of. The use of representational objects and gestural signing may help with this. However, there is still huge social ignorance about this issue and people's intelligence and character is still judged on how well they can communicate.

Most multi-track people can think and feel about what they are hearing at the moment they hear it, whereas many mono-tracked Auties may only be able to switch to what they think or feel once the other person has stopped talking. Then multi-track people generally expect a response, and if they see the mono-tracked person appearing to think or feel nothing instantly in response to their communication, they often assume this to be a reflection on that person's capacity for empathy or thought when, in fact, in their own time and space, these functions may be quite intact.

Part of having delayed information processing may be that you may struggle to understand the meaning of your own language or behaviour, so that after you start speaking or acting you don't know what you are saying or doing. This can be especially so when having to juggle thoughts, feelings, vocalisation, word retrieval and the use of one's body all at once. Many people with these issues will use typing to communicate instead, which requires different pathways and far less diverse manipulation of the body in co-ordination with everything else. Unfortunately, largely multi-track society still cannot get to grips with this experience or the need for some people to use this form of communication.

Part of having delayed information processing can be that incoming words or even your own words can sound jumbled or fragmented (as the spaces between words may be processed as though they occurred in the middle of words, even if they actually didn't).

The natural adrenaline impact of progressive backlog due to delayed information processing may dramatically alter the perception of the speed, pitch or volume of other speakers' voices or one's own voice, affecting motivation and openness to communication.

The impact of visual chaos on someone who is mono-tracked may be so extreme that it can shut down the capacity to understand or use verbal communication, explore new activities or environments or have mental space or relaxation to consider changing existing behaviours.

Mono-tracked people may cope best when:

- they are given one task at a time
- they are given the components of a task in one continuous line of movement
- they are in an environment with minimal visual distractions (e.g. no fluorescent lights, no fans or other noisy motors or electrical appliances)
- they can stick to what they've got to know
- they use the same workspace each day
- they have a clear timetable if there are multiple tasks involved
- they are given visual instructions/charts to follow and are not expected to rely on holding things mentally

- being part of the social atmosphere is not an essential part of learning or working

- eye contact and physical contact is a choice not an expectation

- people speak slowly with pace breaks between presenting changes of topic or new tracks

- visuals are used to help keep track with spoken language

- alternative communication techniques are accepted and provided

- at least a handful of peers with the same processing reality are present within the school or workplace

- being mono-tracked or having delayed information processing is not taken as a reflection on one's potential, intelligence, worth or equality.

Toileting is a very multi-track task, and delayed processing can certainly play havoc with it even after toileting is 'learned'. This is because information-processing is different to having a learning problem. One may be good at learning but terrible at information processing in the moment when expected to respond or organise oneself, and the result will be the same as with someone who is learning disabled. Unfortunately, because this is not under-stood, those without learning disabilities who have marked information-processing challenges are more likely to be blamed for not acting upon what they appear to have learned.

Toileting in modern western cultures is one of the most multi-track life skills. It requires:

- being aware of both one's present activity and bodily sensations

- being able to tell one bodily sensation from another

- being able to tell a bodily sensation from an emotional one

- being able to connect a bodily sensation to a thought related to action

- being able to relate those two to actually moving the body in the direction of a toilet

- co-ordinating the pulling down of clothes in sync with which side of the bathroom door you are on (it is far more instinctual and natural to begin undressing at the point of the thought)

- opening a door and making one's way to the toilet whilst staying on track of the original intention

- putting on a light on the way (often simultaneously putting on a fan built into the light, which then fills one's head with noise so it's not possible to think)

- associating the need to let go with the restriction of having to sit somewhere over a hole before letting go and keeping clothes out of the way at the same time

- pulling clothes back up but then stopping from acting on the natural impulse to 'get on with it' and instead retrieve and (often without any visual chart to follow) follow a regime of flushing (more noise to compete with thought), running water (and telling left from right tap, if not regulating temperature), putting hands under the water, returning to soap, rubbing hands, putting hands back under water, turning off tap, drying hands, turning off light, opening door.

Being mono-tracked means struggling to switch from current activity, thought or disconnection from body to everything required to respond to the need for the toilet. With delayed information processing this feeling can hover about for quite some time until it simply takes care of itself, or is so urgent there is then a panic in organising how to get to the toilet and get the task done. Those with certain personality traits will be differently affected by this experience, and those with anxiety disorders may be more burdened still.

Sleep problems have a particular relationship to being mono-tracked and having delayed information processing. A multi-track person takes in a huge amount of information but processes it as one chunk. A mono-track person may process the same information one piece at a time. In other words, they experience far more stress in their capacity to process information than the multi-track person does. But there's also a secondary effect. When people are multi-track they develop a progressive sense of what is *significant* information and what is not. They automatically filter out what's irrelevant to the task or topic. I believe we need to hold many concepts all in the context of each other on a constant basis to be able to build up this filter. When people have been mono-tracked all their lives they may never have developed this filtering capacity. So not only do they process each piece of an experience one track at a time, hence taking longer to process the thoughts, feelings and experiences about this than others, but they may also fail to filter out a lot of the information that the developmentally typical person will. The result may be a double dose of information overload.

Now different personalities will react differently to being overloaded and not fully grasping their experiences. Some will fall apart, others will carry on regardless and there are all the shades in between, but it is sleep where we work through all our unresolved stuff, all the peripheral information we didn't fully work through when awake and all the links this may have for our past or future. So imagine for a minute the very different impact that disturbed sleep patterns would have on each of these groups. Imagine then also how much precious dream space would be taken up with mundane processing or mostly irrelevant stimuli if you were someone who was mono-tracked and had spent your day backlogged in a state of delayed processing. You would barely have kept up with the day before by the time you woke up. The developmentally typical person would not only have worked through the day before but have begun delving into connections with past and future which will have an impact on how the two then go on to respond to new information today.

Add to this that stress and unresolved conflicts are one of the things that keep us awake and cause us a restless or disturbed sleep and you have an idea of the links between sleep and these aspects of information-processing challenges.

Self-stimulatory behaviours (stimming, or stims) can have all kinds of different underlying causes, but here are the aspects where they directly relate to being mono-tracked and delayed information processing. The repetitive actions of stimming can be:

- used as a self-calming tool when overloaded
- a way of finding the wholeness of a mono experience, through replacing complexity with repetition
- a way of countering alienation in a multi-track world
- used by some people as a tool for getting through backlogged information processing.

From the psychologist's view, stimming is seen as something going on within the individual and is generally attributed to their own dysfunctions. From the sociologist's view, however, stimming can be viewed in a wider social, cultural and environmental context. There is truth in both perspectives. Stimming may be as much about what is happening in the individual as it is about the clashes between the social, emotional, sensory and communication differences between Autistic and non-Autistic versions of 'normality', self-management and coping.

Meltdowns can have many different causes, not only those associated with information processing. People can have them because of sensory-perceptual problems, mood disorders, anxiety disorders, frustration and distress related to compulsive disorders, from the pressure and confusion of mental disorders as well as because of overload associated with being mono-tracked in a multi-track world and progressive backlog that happens with information-processing delay. It's important not to assume that these meltdowns have the same cause at all times and in all people regardless of whether they have an Autism spectrum condition.

Self-protection responses are normal in any extremely stressed person who feels confused, overwhelmed, overloaded, frustrated, alienated and stuck in a world which often doesn't understand or know how to help in an Autie-friendly way. But this alone is not the only cause of self-protection responses in Auties and in many cases self-protection responses are driven by mood disorders, anxiety disorders and even personality disorders such as avoidant or schizoid personality. When someone with any of these issues also has extreme struggles because of information-processing problems, the impact on self-protection responses is multiplied and is bound to be much more extreme than it would be in a person who had only one of these issues.

Challenging and self-injurious behaviours can flow quite naturally from being mono-tracked or from delayed information processing. We need to feel like we are keeping up in order to feel included, equal, in control, relaxed. We need to have cohesive experiences and hold them mentally in the context of previous and possible future experiences in order to learn easily from past experiences and make decisions to take action to handle things differently. Without this, we can feel helpless and caught up in a simplistic cycle of experience and reaction without working out other solutions or taking action to avoid or resolve our situation. These are some of the ingredients of self-injurious and challenging behaviours.

When these occur in someone who has little fluent relationship between selfhood and body, selfhood and mind, selfhood and emotion or any ongoing sense of simultaneous self and other, there is less of a concept of 'harm'. For example, the question 'who are you hurting?' and why it should matter can be a big part of stopping self-injurious behaviours. If in a moment of distress you experience only feeling without thought, or experience thoughts and feelings but are cut off from any felt experience that your body is you, and have little of the self-consciousness that would come of a simultaneous sense of self and other, then you'd be more likely to self-injure than others, and it would be much harder to make all the connections necessary to stop naturally. You may be unable to reason intellectually with some people with Autism about their self-injurious behaviours, but there are still social stories, hypnotherapy stories, diversions, alternative models for stress management, alternative communication devices for those with severe communication challenges, ways of altering the environment so such episodes are less frequent or severe. There is also still the possibility of reducing any co-occurring mood, anxiety, compulsive, personality, environmental or mental health issues which increase the impact of information-processing challenges on self-injurious and challenging behaviours.

Food and eating when you are mono-tracked or have delayed information processing can be a bit different. Being mono-tracked can mean a struggle to:

- recognise hunger when on a different track
- easily tell hunger and thirst from other physical or emotional sensations
- eat and hold utensils at the same time
- eat and keep track of what the food is at the same time
- tell food from non-food
- tell the food on a plate from what it is in the packaging
- tell when you are still hungry or when you are full
- co-ordinate the need for food and drink with the seemingly unrelated track of asking, saying 'please' or thanking people for it (for in nature it is natural simply to find food and drink and take it)
- have any ongoing feeling of why what you do as self in your eating behaviours should have any direct relevance for anyone else (other) such as is required by 'manners'.

When you've worked something out, you stick to it because it's quicker and more reliably recognised that way. So, when you eat in a certain place at a certain time, it is easier to retrieve and process information about eating in that place/time. The problem is that this is mapping rather than learning and so the components required for the same tasks may not connect in other places and at other times. Mapping may have its limitations but so does learning. If

mapping is recognised as a tool used by those who struggle to learn intellectually, then teachers could facilitate students in a broader range of mapping
skills instead of focusing on the intellectual learning of skills that the same
person may be unable to retain, hold in sequence or retrieve with any consistency. I have become brilliant at mapping but I'm still very impaired at
learning.

CHAPTER 4

Experiencing the World Rather Differently

Sensory-Perceptual Issues

Three people visit the local supermarket. One goes in and does the shopping without noticing the overhead fluorescent lights, the hum of the air-conditioning, the hum of the fridges, the smell of people's perspiration, the sound of people chattering. The second one becomes progressively overwhelmed to the point that shopping becomes near impossible without extreme stress, even dissociation if not a panic attack, and needing to exit the store. Progressively, even the thought of going to such places may cause such dread that more and more things are avoided. The third one ends up forgetting why he is there, is busy buzzing obliviously from one wild sensory experience to the next before experiencing sudden terror over something seemingly utterly mundane.

This is a glimpse into different sensory-perceptual realities. But to understand sensory-perceptual realities, you need to understand their interrelationships not only to information processing, but also to mood, anxiety, personality and environment.

Sensory heightening

Before I was 25 I knew I was experiencing some kind of drug-like effect but had no idea where this was coming from. The same behaviour that had had me labelled 'disturbed' and 'mad' in childhood, had a different social reaction when I was a teenager and young adult. Generally, I was now seen as being 'on drugs or something'. I appeared 'off my head' without having taken anything to be in this state. People would laughingly say things like 'I'll have what she's on' and ask what I'd taken. Some of the behaviours they were commenting on were caused by mania and part of an untreated bipolar disorder I'd had all my life, some of it was part of my personality in which idiosyncrasy, surrealism and seeing the world around me as 'art' came totally naturally, but these natural traits were being pushed over the edge by immune-system chaos.

Someone oblivious to the reactions of those around them, walking over furniture in public places, singing obliviously, orchestrating moving traffic, playing wildly with buttons in elevators, revolving doors or getting to great heights with the euphoric urge to jump and 'fly' can look very much like someone on drugs, especially in their teens and early twenties, growing up in a social environment where drugs were rife.

At other times I was mesmerised by lines, patterns, organisation, symmetry, coloured lights, spinning objects, structures, textures of surfaces, smells and noises. They could mesmerise me, send me into inexplicable hysterics, manic bliss or an acute and phobic sense of invasion. I called this 'sensory heightening'. This type of sensory heightening is common in those with acute anxiety states, and essentially raised adrenaline heightens our senses. In those with mania, sensory heightening may cause overstimulation and fascination with particular objects, though later may lead to a phobia of the same things.

In those with depression, by contrast, the stimulating nature of sensory heightening may be met with feelings of intolerance. Whether a sensory experience is met with intolerance may depend not only on whether adrenaline levels make the perception so sharp and refined as to make the sensory experience extremely uncomfortable, but also on the person's social-emotional makeup.

If the sensory experience, say noise, was initiated by outsiders and one had exposure anxiety or avoidant personality, the noise might 'feel' intolerable, but this may well be more on a social-emotional (or, if you like, a phobic/self-protective) level, rather than truly sensorily extreme. When we believe something is uninvited and invasive, we can believe it to be far more sensorily extreme than it actually is. It's effectively a perceptual illusion, but it's very real to the person experiencing it. Treating a social-emotional problem caused by an underlying anxiety disorder as a sensory problem can waste people's hope, time and money on techniques that don't address the real problem. Saying that, there are certainly others who have true sensory issues, such as sensory crossovers, jumbling of sensory information, sensory flooding, scotopic sensitivity, tinnitus, or extremely uneven hearing. Some of these things will be linked to health issues which may be more or less treatable for some people.

High levels of dopamine are believed to make people particularly drawn to and sensitive to pattern. Dopamine is believed to be implicated in conditions such as Tourette's and to have some relationship also to obsessive-compulsive disorder. Those with these conditions are generally particularly sensitive to perceiving pattern.

Health issues can impact on information processing, but they also affect the balance of brain messengers (neurotransmitters) which control emotional responses and impulse control in reaction to sensory information. If these are unbearable or dramatically reducing functioning they may still, nevertheless, be manageable if not relatively treatable in some cases once you know which issues are at work, but to change this in someone who has never known any different may mean to alter their Autism, which some would argue is an attack on Autistic *culture* or done out of fear of eccentricity. My view is that if a person is affected so extremely by a treatable neurotransmitter imbalance that they have few self-help skills, and cannot be self-supporting or independent, then they have a right to get their best shot at changing that. If, at the end of the day, one chooses to lick surfaces, stare hypnotically at coloured lights or collect textured objects, that's a life choice and one can choose that regardless of a label, but having a label is no reason to deny anyone the opportunity to reach a state in which one can truly choose.

Perceptually, other things were happening for me. The world was visually somehow 'in bits': a fragmented reality in which it was hard to perceive the wholeness of anything and even harder to make any sense of something or someone in the context of its wider surroundings. There were losses of depth perception with the compulsive fascination and fear of watching things drop through space or fear of being expected to move through what appeared to be a 2D world as though it were 3D.

Today, these things are known as part of scotopic sensitivity syndrome or Irlen syndrome, a generally treatable visual-perceptual problem, with sometimes treatable underlying metabolic issues at work. It can often be addressed with the right tinted lenses to reduce enough of the particularly problematic wave lengths of light coming in through the eyes to leave time for the brain to process what's left cohesively. Unaddressed, this condition can mean anything from clumsiness to lack of fear (you can't fear what you don't perceive), from reading disabilities to scan reading and hyperlexia, from an inability to read facial expression or body language to a general functional agnosia – essentially meaning-blindness in which one cannot visually work out the meaning of what one is seeing, especially when it is still or in an unusual place or one is unable to tap or smell the object. Again, there is the question as to whether correcting such perceptual differences is interfering in Autistic culture. My answer is that such people can as adults make an informed decision to choose to take their tinted specs back off, they can choose to eat more of the foods that increase this perceptual problem or not.

Other perceptual problems were happening to me that were more akin to the effects of LSD. Background would appear to shift place with foreground, so what was far away could appear suddenly close and vice versa. The ground appeared to bend and bow. The sense of movement and speed felt exaggerated and highly fluctuating. Halos appeared around things and colours and pattern felt somehow overwhelmingly beautiful, sometimes overstimulating to the point of that stimulation becoming painful. Fascination and phobia were able to shift without boundaries. It was a place of the greatest beauty and terror, an amusement park I hadn't asked to be in and couldn't get out of till it was over. This turned out to be caused by acute allergic reactions to particular foods and was treatable and preventable.

In spite of living with this and the other sensory-perceptual extremes, confusions, adventures and instabilities, I was utterly left alone with it and expected to function, sink or swim, whether I could or not. Some drunks and drug addicts can continue to function, dressing, cooking, taking their children to school, wiping their own bottoms and sometimes even washing their clothes and bodies and feeding themselves; some even hold jobs short term, even have the occasional friendship and catch public transport. We can't pretend we don't notice their flaws and wish someone more 'together' in their place, but some function so well we hardly know of their problems unless we live with them. Others have no such self-expectations, have never learned them and are utterly dysfunctional, becoming ever more incapable. The treatment plan for these people should be a multidimensional one that addresses the problem in a holistic way. The same is true for those whose sensory-perceptual problems are put down to Autism.

Having severe sensory-perceptual problems through no fault of your own can be like this too. For some, this may mean a low salicylate, dairy-free, gluten-free or sugar-free diet. For others, it may mean avoiding foods and substances causing specific allergic reactions. For some, it means treatment for underlying gut or immune disorders, toxicity problems or nutrient deficiencies. For some, it means any of this and small amounts of medication. It may mean addressing visual-perceptual problems. It may mean altering the nature of the wider social environment or one's own mindset and what reinforces it, in order to alter stress, anxiety, overstimulation or depression as compounding factors in making these things worse. It may mean working to restore the flow of cerebral spinal fluid to the brain, addressing spinal alignment problems or moving where one sleeps so that sleep patterns that have been affected by high electromagnetic fields are progressively able to normalise. Ultimately, treating sensory-perceptual problems means finding which treatments best address which problems to empower individual children to become empowered adults. It does not mean hating Autism. It does mean respecting that *balance* rather than 'normality' is a humanitarian and respectful goal and believing that we all have a right to reach our greatest potential.

Sensory-perceptual issues and the environment

Before discussing the relationship between sensory-perceptual issues and specific physical and psychological disorders and conditions, I believe there are a handful of things in the physical and social environment which might have an impact on sensory-perceptual issues.

- Fluorescent lights can increase visual fragmentation issues in scotopic sensitivity syndrome as part of Autism.

- Fluorescent lights, computer screens and flashing lights may set off epilepsy-related sensory-perceptual experiences.

- Fluorescent lights, refrigerators, fans, dryers, washing machines, vacuum cleaners, air-conditioners, overhead projectors, computer fans, etc. create humming noises at particular vibrational frequencies which some people are overly sensitive to. They also interfere with processing receptive language in some people with central auditory processing disorder as part of their Autism.

- Overuse of pattern in carpets, wallpaper and home furnishings can overload visual processing for some people to the degree that this may cause compensatory shutdowns in other functions, such as general visual processing, simultaneous sense of self and other, body-connectedness or auditory processing.

- Some environments regularly provide exposure to food and chemical substances toxic to the gut/immune systems of particular people; others fail to provide enough exercise, exposure to sunlight or access to good nutrition and water to a degree that these limitations affect brain development, information processing and sensory-perceptual issues.

- Chronically socially invasive interaction styles may exacerbate anxiety states in someone who is challenged by sensory-perceptual issues.

- Socially damaging environments may be unable to provide a reasonable degree of safety, stability and positive experiences from the perspective of the person with Autism.

- Environmental expectation that a child will not cope may be to such a degree that the child cannot feel or envision any other feeling about his or her chances than that he or she will not cope.

- Environmental over-protectiveness and co-dependency may be to such a degree that a child might be denied the self-discovery necessary for becoming responsible for the management of his or her own sensory-perceptual challenges.

- Environments that deny children equal access to life experiences from which to learn directly may affect children's sensory-perceptual development.

Sensory-perceptual issues and specific disorders and conditions

Exposure anxiety

In states of acute exposure anxiety, I reacted to a feeling of social claustrophobia as though everything were a threat of 'invasion' and my adrenaline levels were physically overwhelming. Blood rushed in my ears making the muscles of my inner ears go into contractions and a 'voom' type of sound like ocean waves was rushing inside of my ears. Lights would appear to be overwhelmingly bright. Touch could provoke me to attack instantaneously or shut me down. Any of these can be called sensory heightening. But the treatment in this case is not to overly worry about the symptoms but to treat the cause; to address the exposure anxiety.

In states of information overload, my adrenaline levels would also peak, and this had the effect that voices sounded suddenly louder than usual, lights seemed suddenly too bright and the visual chaos was suddenly suffocating. Standing on a patterned carpet would suddenly make me feel dizzy, and I felt like my connection to my body was being wiped out by the overload of the patterned carpet flooding my senses. To treat this type of hypersensitivity you would seek to reduce where possible both the environmental sources of information overload and the physical underlying causes. The combination of exposure anxiety and information overload, of course, doubled the impact of the problem. When also affected by mood extremes this effect was multiplied even further.

Gut/immune disorders

Food allergies, particularly a dairy allergy, affected my sense of colour and pattern, and these were heightened to a hallucinogenic level. Travelling in the car, dips and rises could feel like the big dipper. Travelling at 30 mph felt like I was going at 150. Background and foreground would shift places randomly. Colours would split so that an orange colour would pulsate between yellow and red instead of being one colour. Whites would fragment into pastel rainbows and lights had halos (before I was nine all objects and people also had halos). On top of this gluten made me more obsessive and irritable and salicylates made me physically restless, racy, reactive and manic. Obviously identifying health issues underpinning gut and immune conditions is so important: what is the environment like? is it non-toxic? is the sleep environment healthy? is the atmosphere socially invasive? is it alienating? is it stable? are there clear personal boundaries? After this, treating gut/immune conditions is clearly essential for some people as part of addressing sensory perceptual issues.

Epilepsy

Many people with epilepsy are entirely unconscious of their attacks. Those with temporal or frontal lobe epilepsy, however, may have sensory experiences before or during an episode.

I had an EEG in my twenties which showed what was described as 'a highly marked central abnormality' and was diagnosed as 'atypical epilepsy' (after dietary interventions my EEG tested as normal). Mostly I had brief blackouts and shutdowns, and there were times I had repetitive behaviours I was unaware of until I was coming out of them. But a few times these neuro-logical challenges had an amazing sensory effect. One moment I was fine, the next moment I felt a bit strange and then I experienced the entire room quaking as if I were caught up in an earthquake. It lasted only a few seconds but was obviously pretty shocking and whilst it was as though the entire room was shaking, nothing actually shifted in the room. I also have times when I have flashes of fluorescent colours, almost like 'blanket lightening', occurring inside my head which is hard to describe as these are not seen by one's eyes at all; they usually occur when I'm tired or occasionally in response to being touched. Dietary changes, treatment for gut/immune issues, and finally medi-cation for mood/impulse control problems really cut down on these types of experience. Many people are not this lucky, but there are certain things which may be sensible in maximising the brain health of any person with epilepsy such as the following:

- Check the environmental health of their sleeping area to ensure they are not sleeping in high electromagnetic fields.

- Have a cranio-sacral therapist ensure the proper flow of cerebral spinal fluid to the brain.

- Have a chiropractor check that spinal alignment is what it should be.

- Reduce airborne allergens, dietary and environmental toxins and sources of emotional stress.

- Ensure there is adequate exposure to 10 minutes of direct sunlight a few times a week, which is essential to healthy immunity.

- Check blood sugar levels are regular and improve diet and supplements to keep them that way.

- Ensure regular exercise and calmtime, good water intake (around six to eight glasses a day), and regular meals and consider dietary interventions if allergies or food intolerances are messing with blood oxygen levels, particularly in the interaction with stored viruses.

Scotopic sensitivity syndrome

Scotopic sensitivity affects people differently. In some people it merely affects reading as the page may pulsate through the print, or colours may appear on the white page, or print may swirl. In my case it affected not only reading but also the environment. I couldn't see a face or body as a whole, often failed to recognise objects I hadn't already got to know, found visual chaos overwhelming in its impact on sensory flooding and spent much of my first seven years hypnotised by dancing air particles I could see because of extremely hypersensitive vision. Movement through space, the supermarket and crowds, were like being in a bag of icing sprinkles. I was so overstimulated. Dietary interventions have helped some people with this, including omega 3 fish oils, but also a low salicylate diet has helped some people reduce visual fragmentation, and affordable tinted lenses have helped many people with this issue. These cut out certain light frequencies, allowing the brain more time to process what is left so the effect is greater cohesion and less sensory flooding.

Brain organisation

Poor brain organisation can result in sensory hypersensitivities, and literature on the motor-planning problem of dyspraxia is full of information about this. I have had left–right integration problems all my life and was assessed by the Brain Injury Rehabilitation and Development Centre in Chester in the UK. They assessed me as having infantile reflexes which were meant to have been inhibited soon after birth. These infantile reflexes were still present as an adult, indicating that my brain wasn't getting the feedback it was meant to in order to inhibit these earlier reflexes to make way for those meant to replace them.

Assessments aside, in real life all that I knew was that I was either all mind and struggling to combine this with anything personal or emotional, or I was the opposite, utterly emotional and unable to experience or kick start thought, let alone express or unravel this stuff in verbal language.

The result was not only overload relating to the loss of meaning shutting down, but also its opposite, where I would experience a great sudden flooding of confused conflicting emotion which had been on hold whilst I worked through meaning. The impact on sensory heightening was terrible. When this used to happen in infancy and early childhood, I would be so overwhelmed there were times I had no idea what or whose my own body was and tried to pull my own skin off and run away from my body. When I screamed I had no idea it came from me. When I struck the thing stuck on me (my body) I had no idea this was 'me'. These episodes happened several times a day in the early days, but by adulthood were much rarer and by my thirties they were very subtle if not gone. I did two years of patterning exercises at the age of 30 (many people feel Brain Gym and patterning exercises are of limited use after age 10) and two years of cranio-sacral therapy and a year of McTimoney chiropractic. At the same time I went on the 'smart drug', amino acid glutamine. When I started I was constantly losing one half of my body and had difficulty doing things in certain directions and couldn't use cross-pattern movements unless directly following someone else. After these particular interventions all these issues were greatly improved. I still end up with two competing hands trying to feed me, each not aware the other is working. I still indicate with my wipers and try to wipe the windscreen with my indicators. I still get some confusion because of these issues, but it is much, much less.

Impulse-control issues

Obsessive-compulsive disorder can involve being extremely sensitive to pattern. Some of the most common compulsions other than cleaning and checking are to do with order, evenness, perfection, symmetry and numbers. Whilst these are not sensory hypersensitivities they can look like it. The need to tap things in odd or even rhythm patterns, to circle objects certain amounts of time, to have to complete activities in certain 'circuits', the need to pick all the fluff off something, these may be mistaken for sensory-perceptual issues.

Clothes can impact on these compulsions, as can one's placement in a room, the nature of the table surface one is sitting at…the list goes on. Obsessive-compulsive disorder is caused by neurotransmitter imbalances and is at least partially treatable in some cases through medication, but there are other techniques including biofeedback and cognitive behavioural therapy. Some people report 1000mg taurine as helpful with obsessive-compulsive disorder. Treating gut/immune disorders might reduce the degree of OCD for some people. Certainly reviewing the health of the sleep environment, as part of addressing stress levels, would also do no harm.

Bipolar disorder

Mania as part of bipolar can cause extreme sensory heightening. In a state of euphoria, sensory experiences can be almost 'orgasmic' in their extremity. But I found that extreme euphoria always gave way to extreme sensory discomfort and distress, and what was in one moment deeply moving in the next was too moving, too impacting. My body would sometimes go into tremor from the overstimulation, the blood would rush in my inner ears, sound was overwhelming, light was too bright, and touch was so hypersensitive it was like being stuck with pins.

By contrast, in a depressive state I was so geared for feeling that everything was an entrapment impinging on 'my world' that I was equally intolerant because the stillness and withdrawal were at times almost hypnotic.

Treating sensory hypersensitivities in people with mood disorders involves treating the mood disorders.

Omega 3s have been used in mood disorders as a natural mood leveller or natural lithium. A low salicylate diet has levelled things out for some people. For others, going dairy-free, gluten-free or treating the gut/immune problem of candida has helped them stabilise, as has addressing nutrient deficiencies, balancing blood sugar and addressing gut/immune issues. Some people require sensible doses of appropriate medication, and whilst there are warnings about side effects associated with most medications, severe chronic stress itself has severe long-term side effects on lost development and physical health; and mood disorders can be not only seriously disabling but also life threatening in some cases. Sleep deprivation and disturbed sleep patterns are not good news for hormone regulation underpinning mood balance, so checking that light, noise or high electromagnetic fields in the region of the bed are not disturbing sleep patterns, or the deep sleep necessary to mood health, would also be worth considering.

Depression

Depression is worth considering as an underlying cause of what are sometimes assumed to be merely sensory hypersensitivities.

Depression can underpin phobic states and constant worrying, social withdrawal, lack of confidence, rigidity and reluctance to cope with, let alone adapt to or embrace, change. A depressed person may find many more reasons to feel distressed and uncomfortable than someone who doesn't suffer from depression. People with depression may be more likely to see themselves as passive and helpless and to fixate on small annoying details, to work themselves up and be less likely to optimistically employ self-calming strategies to help themselves constructively rather than tantrum. Whilst some people with Autism have depression as part of a bipolar state, unipolar depression has been a major feature of the Autism of some people, contributing to resistance to change, lack of interest in surroundings, passivity and irritability, introversion and social withdrawal, lack of confidence and lack of self-initiation.

Clinical depression can happen regardless of environment, and it is only recently that a percentage of very young children have been recognised as having inherited unipolar depression. After all, clinical depression is about an imbalance in brain chemistry; and there is no reason why a toddler is exempt from such a physical thing, except that we find it hard to conceive of in those we think should be healthy and balanced by virtue of youth.

Sensory hypersensitivities can be underpinned by emotional imbalances and lowered nutrient levels associated with suppressed gut/immune function, commonly going hand in hand as much with the extreme stress of bipolar as with unipolar depression. Nevertheless, sleep deprivation and disturbed sleep patterns can also set off depression, so checking that light, noise or high electromagnetic fields in the region of the bed are not disturbing the patterns of deep sleep necessary to mood health would be worth considering.

Personality disorder

Personality traits are normal. When people are under all kinds of burdens, those traits can become extreme to the point of being called 'disorders'. Personality disorders can be seriously disabling for those who have them. Yet it is standard policy that they are not diagnosed until adulthood, and these adults have to have come from somewhere. They were once children, and surely some have had the same features affecting their lives all along.

Whilst there are extremely sensible political reasons not to label children as having personality disorders, overlooking their presence is not the answer either. Perhaps there is a middle ground between ignoring and diagnosing which is merely to indicate that a child may presently have the characteristics akin to a certain adult 'personality disorder' in order that environmental strategies can be put in place so the child's particular needs can be most constructively met and their traits constructively channelled, before these patterns have become entrenched and lifelong.

The Autism field is only now beginning to acknowledge co-morbid conditions as affecting the severity of someone's Autism; the issue of personality disorders is still a hot potato that most therapists will not calmly and open-mindedly consider in helping the children in their care. Nevertheless, here I will explore some possible relationships between personality and sensory-perceptual issues, looking at specific personality disorders within the four personality types or 'temperaments' (see www.geocities.com/ptypes/):

- hyperesthetic (desiring superiority, fearing inferiority)
- anesthetic (desiring power, fearing weakness)
- depressive (desiring belonging, fearing rejection)
- hypomanic (desiring pleasure, fearing pain).

HYPERESTHETIC PERSONALITY

Obsessive-compulsive disorder is the exaggerated extension of the *conscientious personality*. Obsessive-compulsive personality is not the same as obsessive-compulsive disorder, though the two are often confused with each other. Those with obsessive-compulsive personality can be perfectionist, rigid, stubborn and fixated on detail. It might be easy to imagine how an Autie who also had these types of personality traits might be assumed to have sensory hypersensitivities, and that someone who had this type of personality and sensory hypersensitivities might be a lot more intolerant about these and more fixated on controlling the sensory environment.

Avoidant personality disorder is the exaggerated extension of the *sensitive personality* type. Avoidant personalities are extremely sensitive to embarrassment, criticism or rejection and because of this may be extremely reluctant to try new activities or enter new social situations they cannot be certain won't lead to a feeling of inadequacy. It can be imagined that an Autie who also had this type of personality might be more likely to avoid new sensory experiences, and this could easily be confused with being sensorily hypersensitive. Someone who was both sensorily hypersensitive and had avoidant personality might be more likely to fear being ridiculed because of their hyper-sensitivities and be more likely than others to develop phobic responses to being in the social situations where this might happen.

Paranoid personality disorder is one which fears submission and desires autonomy and is an exaggerated version of the *vigilant personality*. Paranoid personality could mean that an Autie could, as part of their 'fruit salad', develop paranoid responses to particular sensory experiences leading them to fear or fixate on these things, particularly if they felt their life was controlled by others who would force them to submit to sensory experiences they had not autonomously chosen themselves.

Histrionic personality disorder is the exaggerated extension of the *dramatic personality*. Those with histrionic personality have exaggerated expression of emotion, are highly suggestible and may be uncomfortable in situations where they are not the centre of attention. Given this outline, it is imaginable that an Autie who had this type of personality might have a more extreme emotional reaction to sensory hypersensitivities than most people, and be more likely than others to take the opportunity to draw attention to their distress. If they are also assumed to have sensory hypersensitivities associated with their Autism, their suggestibility may increase the belief that they have these issues whether they in fact do or do not.

ANESTHETIC PERSONALITY

Sadistic personality disorder is the exaggerated extension of the *aggressive personality* for whom retaliation and physical interaction is natural. Sadistic personality is associated with enjoyment in causing discomfort, pain or harm to others. Saying this, there are many Auties who have caused these things to others who are in no way sadistic individuals. This does not mean there will not be an Autie who does also have this type of personality disorder and we need to be open-minded on that. But, given the nature of this type of personality disorder, it is not easy to imagine someone with sensory hypersensitivities who would deliberately cause painful or distressing sensory experiences to others.

Schizotypal personality disorder is the exaggerated extension of the *idiosyncratic personality*. Schizotypal personality involves 'magical thinking'; conceivably, an Autie who had this as part of their 'fruit salad' could develop a belief about particular sensory experiences powerful enough to develop intense fear, fascination or identification with these things.

Compensatory narcissistic personality disorder is the exaggerated extension of the *inventive personality*, which is about competition and one-upmanship. Compensatory narcissistic personalities have a natural tendency to look down on, ridicule or degrade others, a tendency to exaggerate and boast. Because of this, it might be imagined that those with Autism who have this type of personality may be more likely to mock the sensory hypersensitivities of others.

Schizoid personality disorder is the exaggerated extension of the *solitary personality*. Those with schizoid personality are asocial, in that they have little desire or interest in close relationships with others and may have few activities they enjoy. This type of profile in someone with a diagnosis of Autism might be confused with being sensorily *hypo*sensitive, or it might equally be assumed that someone like this might be socially avoidant because of sensory hypersensitivities, whether they do or do not in fact exist for that person. If someone with schizoid personality disorder as part of their 'fruit salad' labelled Autism was also challenged with sensory hypersensitivities, it is conceivable this would only further justify the lack of enjoyment in social activities beyond the person's own direct control.

DEPRESSIVE PERSONALITY

Passive-aggressive personality disorder is an exaggerated extension of the *leisurely personality* and is associated with passively resisting fulfilling everyday social and occupational tasks. Those with this type of personality may continually fall back on complaints of being misunderstood and unappreciated by others. At the same time someone with this type of personality may appear to envy and resent those he or she sees as 'more fortunate' than themselves and may exaggerate their own sense of 'misfortune'.

Given this description, it is imaginable that someone with this type of personality might play on perceived hardship, setting up a kind of 'go on...make me do it' situation, in which they almost force others to push them and then justify their procrastination on the basis of feeling 'pushed around' and 'pressured'. This could be perceived as actual hardship rather than a personality dynamic, and resistance put down to sensory hypersensitivities which may or may not actually exist. At the same time, an Autie who had this type of personality and also had sensory hypersensitivities may find even more fuel to indulge in an attitude of self-pity and resentment of others who 'don't know such hardship'.

Depressive personality disorder is an extension of the *serious personality* type. It is the personality of the pessimist, the critic, the cynic. These people may be predisposed to see themselves as severely limited, focus on their failures, and exaggerate their sense of helplessness in situations they cannot control. They need to think things through before taking any action, avoid taking risks and find impulses and passion unwelcome distractions.

Given this description, it may be easy to imagine that an Autie who had this type of personality would be more likely to demonstrate behaviours that were designed to avoid excitement, interest and arousal. These types of response could be assumed to be about sensory hypersensitivity whether, in fact, they are or not. It is also possible that someone who chronically fixates on discomfort is possibly more likely to experience an exaggerated sense of the invasive nature of such things.

Masochistic personality disorder is an exaggerated extension of the *self-sacrificing personality* type. They are reluctant to admit enjoyment, tend to thwart the attempts of others to help, may respond to positive achievements not with pleasure or pride but with guilt, dread or a behaviour that effectively causes themselves self-punishment. They struggle to achieve things on their own behalf in spite of the ability to help others achieve the same. Given the nature of this personality disorder, an Autie who had this pattern of responses might be very emotionally confusing to others who are trying to help. Someone with these issues who also had sensory hypersensitivities might be less likely than others to address these needs, and might actively resist, perhaps even seek to undo, the attempts of others to help them even at their own expense.

Dependent personality disorder is an exaggerated extension of the *devoted personality*. These people struggle extremely in making even everyday decisions without the opinion or reassurance of someone else, may have great difficulty disagreeing with anyone or initiating any activity on their own, and need others to take responsibility for them. People with this type of personality may have intense fears of being left to take care of themselves and may exaggerate their own incapability in order to avoid imagined abandonment.

Given the nature of this personality disorder, it is imaginable that an Autie who also had this might appear extremely reluctant in trying new sensory experiences and might place others in the position of continually being responsible for them. It's imaginable that others may be confused as to why someone like this can't 'get over it' and each time needs the same level of support in order to take on a challenge which was already assumed to be conquered many times over. It is imaginable that someone with this type of personality might be assumed to have sensory hypersensitivities when in fact these are manifestations of their personality state. It may also be possible that someone with this type of personality has actual sensory hypersensitivities, which would possibly only exacerbate the nature of their personality in assuming incapability in the face of these sensory issues. Removing the sensory hypersensitivities in such a person, however, would not treat the personality issues.

HYPOMANIC PERSONALITY

Narcissistic personality disorder is the exaggerated extension of the *self-confident personality* and is associated with having unreasonable expectations of getting especially favourable treatment and expecting automatic compliance in having expectations met. This personality disorder is also associated with a lack of empathy, and those with this type of personality are cited as unwilling to recognise or identify with the feelings and needs of others. It may, therefore, be reasonable to assume that an Autie who also had this type of personality disorder as part of their 'fruit salad' may be more likely than some to throw a tantrum if he or she experienced sensory hypersentivities and perhaps more likely to experience these than those without such emotionally extreme states. Someone with this type of personality might, theoretically, also be far more intolerant of the needs of others in insisting that disliked or unfamiliar sensory experiences be removed, regardless of the enjoyments or needs of others in these experiences. If someone with this type of personality took the compliance of others to be a reflection on his or her 'specialness', then by contrast, someone seeking to help such a person get used to undesired sensory experiences could be taken to be denying acknowledgement of that 'specialness'. Reintroduction of the same or similar sensory experiences might, theoretically, then meet resistance not simply to the sensory experience itself but to what these dynamics might emotionally stand for in this power dynamic.

Antisocial personality disorder is the exaggerated extension of the *adventurous personality*, though for many people antisocial personality is fairly synonymous with irritability and aggressiveness. This is not to say this is the only source of such feelings, but it may mean that an Autie who had this as part of their 'fruit salad' might be more likely than some other personalities to unempathically express intolerance and aggression in the face of sensory hypersensitivities, rather than try to find ways to stay calm or cope with them. It may also be that such a personality disorder could be more associated with a tendency to high adrenaline states, and it is in these states that people are more likely to find sensory experiences more extreme. The antagonistic nature of antisocial personality may also mean that someone with this may be more likely than others to be intolerant to a sensory world they feel has been imposed upon them, or assumed to be comfortable by others. It may also be that in an irritable and aggressive state an Autie who also had antisocial personality may be more likely to seize on a range of excuses to justify the venting of irritability, and be without the kind of social empathy which would otherwise hold someone back.

Borderline personality disorder is an exaggerated extension of the *mercurial personality* and is associated with emotional instability and extreme mood reactions in which intense regular episodes of distress, irritability, anxiety or anger are more common than in most people. This is not to say this is the only condition which can cause these feelings. It could be imagined that an Autie who also had this type of personality disorder might also have a greater tendency than most people to experience high adrenaline levels which could increase sensory heightening. In such an overstimulated state, someone with this type of personality disorder would be more likely than most to have acute, if not sometimes explosive, emotional responses to these things.

Cyclothymic personality disorder is an exaggerated extension of the *artistic personality*. Bipolar disorder is cited as common in those with this personality type, but one could have this type of personality with or without also having a mood disorder. This type of personality disorder is akin to the dynamics of bipolar though, unlike bipolar, it is a patterned response which is generally not treated by medication and is not associated with the more full-blown irrationality and confusion which bipolar can entail. Cyclothymic personality disorder is associated with an all-or-nothing state of fluctuation between blind optimism and blind pessimism.

An Autie who had this type of personality trait might be quite confusing on a sensory level and it is imaginable that they may fluctuate sharply between enjoying and indulging in a particular sensory-based experience and then suddenly appearing to have developed the opposite response of phobia and dread or vice versa. Again, sensory hyper- or hyposensitivities could potentially be wrongly assumed, but it's also possible that the sensory hypersensitivities of someone with this type of personality may become the target of emotional fixations in both types of mood state.

Effects of sensory-perceptual issues

Sensory-perceptual issues and health

Nothing that causes persistent destabilisation, feelings of entrapment, confusion, discomfort or alienation from the external world or from our own body is ultimately good for our health. Sensory-perceptual issues, stemming from one or more of a variety of underlying causes, are one of the things that can cause any or all of these things. Sooner or later these experiences have the potential to contribute to a chronic state of stress and all that may mean for collapses in psychological, emotional and physical wellbeing with the cyclical impact this may have on information processing.

Sensory-perceptual issues and development

There are those with severe sensory-perceptual issues who learn to manage them and function in spite of them, and there are those who do not. This difference may depend on a range of things such as:

- how many combined challenges that person had to contend with
- the personality and mood states of the person living with these challenges
- environmental modelling of how each person is responsible for issues that affect their own world

- whether a carer is present so that the person is left to save themselves

- whether the person learns that managing their own stuff is a matter of utter survival.

No matter how well an individual learns to compensate for or manage severe sensory-perceptual challenges, these will have an impact on development.

If you can't see things as a whole, and you are provided no other means of linking words to meaning other than visuals, you will struggle to conceptualise words visually.

If you can't hear people fluently with meaning or their words or sentences are jumbled, distorted or meaningless, you may eventually learn to grasp the system of language, even if only through writing, but the everyday world of conversing may always seem like a chore and a struggle.

If you are pained and shut down by common sensory experiences, you may find your links with the external world limited.

If you struggle to think, process receptive information and use your body at the same time, you may suffer harsh social judgements, exclusion and wrong assumptions about your equality, intelligence and capacity to experience.

Nevertheless, if you wish to seize life, regardless of the challenge, in whatever ways are still open to you, then you will, within the confines, motivations and orientations of your own personality traits. You may never run the whole mile, but for many even the few steps become a great achievement, and as a one-size-fits-all society, we have so much further to go in supporting people in a way that respects their diversity and taps in to their potential.

Sensory-perceptual issues and testing

Colleges and universities have recently allowed people with exam nerves and dyslexia to take their exams in a private room with extra time. Those with hearing loss, loss of sight or mobility problems have compensations made to allow them inclusion. Yet the sensory-perceptual needs of those with Autism are only recently being acknowledged, and these are also equal-opportunities issues about real inclusion.

A person who is severely affected by fluorescent lights may be unable to process information, co-operate or control their own behaviour during testing under such conditions. Those who cannot keep up with processing 'blah blah' for receptive meaning may have visual cues but if they also have visual fragmentation issues, this may be of little use to them unless there is gestural signing to show not the picture but the *experience* associated with the static image.

Those who cannot connect with their body whilst thinking or processing a question may not be given the alternative of communicating through a movement as simple as a pointed finger on a letter board.

Those who can only manage to use their senses peripherally may be forced to focus directly and lose the ability to process information as a result.

These are only a handful of the challenges that can face people with sensory-perceptual challenges when faced with IQ testing under conventional circumstances. And a low score on an ability test will often then decide their fate, even though it may be far more reflective of the lack of understanding and accommodation of the tester.

Sensory-perceptual problems and specific behavioural issues

Sensory-perceptual issues could underpin specific behaviours/issues relating to:

- communication
- being in one's own world
- eye contact
- learning and cognitive challenges
- toileting
- sleep problems
- stimming
- meltdowns
- self-protection responses
- challenging behaviours
- food behaviour problems.

Without good visual cohesion, the picture representations of seemingly whole objects will be difficult to recognise and put experiences to. Without this, *communication* can be severely interrupted. Unless communication is linked to other sensory experiences outside of the visual, such as patterns of movement, acoustics, texture, form, smell or taste, the links between words and experienceable concepts may not develop fluently. Severely sight-impaired people can learn language and so can those with visual-perceptual fragmentation or meaning-blindness, provided those teaching them understand and specifically cater for their deficit.

Without clear, undistorted, sensorily tolerable perception of voices, people will struggle both to acquire language and to be motivated to tune in to other people's language or be socially encouraged to speak to them. The same applies to hearing your own voice. If what you hear sounds unclear, distorted, sensorily intolerable or without meaning, it can become very difficult to find active motivation to continue to speak, rather than, perhaps, type or sign.

If you are easily sensorily overwhelmed in certain sensory environments, it can be extremely difficult to attend to the communication of others or keep reasonable track of your own communication in those places. Over time this can diminish confidence and you may find it is simply more consistent and easier not to bother. If communicating brings eye contact or touch which you are unable to cope with, you may progressively become actively avoidant of initiating communication as a means of keeping these other things at bay.

We all *retreat into our own world* when anything strongly sets us apart and make us feel estranged from the assumed 'normality' of the majority around us. That developmentally typical people actively relax with sensory experiences we don't cope with, can be so large a part of feeling alien that it can justify feeling so much better 'in our own world', rather than reaching out within a world which doesn't fit us.

The extreme sensory confusion, unpredictability and overwhelming nature of sensory-perceptual challenges could send any person to seek refuge and sanctuary. This will affect different personalities quite differently. Some will cling, some will indulge these extremes, some will avoid and some will isolate themselves. When extreme challenges happen to someone with solitary personality, for example, they will seek refuge and sanctuary in solitude and isolation from others. The compelling, mysterious, amusing, fascinating, even hypnotic, nature of sensory-perceptual experiences, by contrast, can make the job of being in one's own world so much easier than opening up to the inclusion of others on their terms. The artistic, idiosyncratic and leisurely personalities might be particularly likely to respond this way.

If you don't see a face as a whole, *eye contact* may have little meaning in the context of a face you see only as a series of unrelated moving pieces. Visual fragmentation may be much worse when under fluorescent lighting or when processing lots of other auditory information or distractions, including fans and motors, in the background. Eye contact relies on feeling comfortable with others and being able to perceive the face as a whole.

Learning involves being in an environment that does not dramatically exacerbate sensory-perceptual challenges and can adapt to them. Even mainstream schools, if willing, are capable of doing some of this. The behaviours of people with sensory-perceptual challenges can also commonly lead to some being misjudged as having more learning/cognitive challenges than they actually have. Similarly the personality traits of specific individuals may lead them to appear to cope far beyond their actual capacity to understand and keep up.

The sensory atmosphere of the *toilet* may need to be considered if lighting, acoustics, fan sounds, temperature or other atmospherics are putting the person off using the toilet area. Sometimes fear of someone turning on the lighting or exhaust fan, or the sound of flushing can put someone off.

I remember my nephew confiding in me that he *couldn't sleep* because a voice was whispering to him. I asked what it was saying and he said 'ws-ws-ws-ws-ws'. I noticed a fridge on the other side of his bedroom wall and took him to the fridge and opened the door. 'Is the voice in there?' I asked him. 'Yes,' he replied excitedly. I explained that it was the 'voice' of the fridge and was caused by the ice melting and the 'voice' was actually the sound of water. My nephew only had two words at the age of three but spoke by four. What if he'd been non-verbal? How might he have told anyone he was kept awake by a mysterious whispering voice?

Many Auties have the most acute hearing and may be kept awake or distressed by sounds most people simply reason about and tune out. Many Auties see floaters on the surface of their own eyes, which appear as though they are sparkles floating in the air, often especially at night. It may be OK to distract from some of these things with music or fairy lights, but it is equally important to sleep that there is no other light or sound disrupting the capacity for deep sleep.

Sensory-perceptual challenges are not the only underlying cause of *self-stimulatory behaviours* but are often assumed to be. Tics are often confused for self-stimulatory behaviours. It is especially essential not to confuse tics with self-stimulatory behaviours, as having other people fixate on or seek to overly control someone's tics can make them more entrenched and severe.

When we fear things, we may seek to desensitise ourselves to these experiences. When something has control over our lives, we may seek to master it and take control over these experiences. When something is a mystery we

can't solve, we may be naturally compelled by it. When something is mesmerising or provides comfort or escape from something more difficult, it can be
hard to pull away from it. Self-stimulatory behaviours can start up where
sensory-perceptual experiences cause fear, loss of control, an unsolved
mystery, or are mesmerising. The goal is to respect these feelings, accept
stimming where it does the person no harm and help them compensate for
these feelings in ways which make sense to them so that stimming isn't so
compelling or necessary.

Meltdowns happen when people are severely overwhelmed or distressed or
both. Because of this they can happen for all kinds of reasons, including
sensory-perceptual challenges. One person may have meltdowns for a range
of different reasons at different times or because of the combined effect of a
number of different causes. Different personalities will behave very differently when experiencing meltdowns. Some personalities will openly 'lose it'.
Others may simple 'disappear' and continue on auto-pilot because the terror
of drawing attention to themselves counters any clear external expression of
this experience. Others may become wacky and surreal and 'back in their own
world'.

Sensory-perceptual challenges are only one cause of *self-protection responses*
and it is important not to blame someone's self-protection responses entirely
on sensory-perceptual challenges simply because they have an Autism
spectrum condition. The ability to rely on our senses and perception is
an essential part of trusting our body, trusting ourselves, trusting others
and trusting to life. Extreme sensory confusion, the unpredicitability and
overwhelming nature of sensory perceptual challenges could send any person
to seek refuge and sanctuary. But different personalities find 'sanctuary' quite
differently. A dependent personality may assume their own incapability to
cope and cling to others, and a dramatic personality may play on the drama for
the reward of attention. An adventurous, obsessive-compulsive, artistic or
vigilant personality may indulge these extremes to master control over them,
for the adrenaline of the experience or from pure fascination with the sensory
world. An avoidant or solitary person may seek refuge and sanctuary in
solitude and isolation from others. Sensorily altering the environment is one
answer, but empowering people to use their own coping strategies and compensations is also very important.

Challenging and self-injurious behaviours are common in zoo animals in
captivity under severe stress. There are many things we can feel trapped with –
our body, our emotions, our mind, our senses and perception, our mood state,

our anxiety state, our tics and compulsions, the discomforts of our own personality state. When we feel we are not trapped with the inescapable, we are usually very different. Even when we are trapped with what is inescapable we can still develop a playful, even constructive, relationship with it.

Food and eating behaviours are often put down to sensory-perceptual problems when they can just as easily be related to zinc deficiency, food allergies, food intolerances, mood, anxiety, compulsive and personality issues. We all have our sensory preferences when it comes to food smells, textures, appearances, tastes, combinations. Stressed people are more likely to make an emotional big deal out of these preferences than unstressed people, and different personalities will fuss in different ways. Extreme sensory responses to certain textures, tastes and smells can be psychological and emotional rather than purely sensory. Sensory-perceptual issues are more likely to affect the ability to recognise food when in an unfamiliar presentation or situation or when other distractions detract from the ability to keep track of what is food and what it's for.

CHAPTER 5

Losing Control of One's Body

Impulse-Control Problems

Two dogs are taken for a walk, one with fleas, one without. The one with no fleas greets other dogs, smells telegraph poles, scrounges about, interested in the external world, comes when called. The other dog is distracted and struggles to stay outwardly focused as its fleas compete for attention with the external world. This dog is called. It fails to respond, distracted by its own fleas. It's person says 'stop that' and this compels the dog even more strongly toward its own compulsions and makes the fleas even more distracting, for however annoying the fleas are, the dog's even greater fear is that of feeling it has no control over its fleas. Attending to those fleas may feel like a matter of sheer survival.

Conditions such as Tourette's and obsessive-compulsive disorder affect the ability to control one's impulses. Reward deficiency syndrome and oppositional defiance disorder are also worth looking at as part of the topic of 'impulse-control problems'.

Tics and compulsions

Tourette's disorder

Here is a brief outline of Tourette's taken from *Merriam-Webster's Medical Dictionary* (Merriam-Webster, Incorporated 2005a):

> a familial neuropsychiatric disorder of variable expression that is characterized by multiple recurrent involuntary tics involving body movements (as eye blinks, grimaces, or knee bends) and vocalizations (as grunts, snorts or uncontrolled utterance of inappropriate or offensive

words), that often has one or more associated behavioral or psychiatric problems (as attention deficit disorder or obsessive-compulsive behavior), that affects many more males than females, and that usually has an onset in childhood and often stabilizes or ameliorates in adulthood – abbreviation *TS*; called also *Gilles de la Tourette syndrome, Tourette's disease, Tourette's disorder.*

I've had various tics over the years, including a combination of stomach tensing and compulsive coughing, blinking tics, a wincing tic (involving screwing up the face and shrugging so it looks like I'm in pain), lip pursing, face stretching, grimacing, breath holding, sniffing, nose clearing, throat clearing, spitting, fist clenching, lunging, hand weaving, clapping, hand shaking, head shaking, face slapping, stomach punching, hair pulling, hand and arm biting, sideways looking, throwing of arms into air, squealing, sound tics, word tics, phrase tics, tapping, smacking, pinching, jumping, running at furniture, falling on things and people, whistling, covering my face with an open hand, running thumb and middle finger down the middle of my face to meet in the middle, the 'popping' of inner ear muscles, flicking light switches (which has been listed as a Tourette's tic!).

Some of these tics entertained me but that didn't make them voluntary. One can be entertained by the surprise of one's own farts, but that doesn't make farting a stim. There were certainly times when I had sounds and word phrases as stims, but that didn't exclude the fact that in other cases they were tics and involuntary. I certainly had obsessive-compulsive issues with symmetry and number as well as visual-perceptual problems which affected the flicking of light switches, but this didn't exclude the fact that at other times this was involuntary and merely a tic. I often enjoy whistling. This doesn't mean that at other times it hasn't been a tic. Many of my tics have only lasted a few weeks or months before giving way to a different one. Many have returned for repeat phases over the years. Some of the breathing-related tics have been overwhelming and taken up 50 per cent of my waking day and a few times when I've had viruses these have escalated to around 80 per cent of my waking day to the point that I've wanted only to sleep just to feel free of them. At other times I will only tic perhaps less than 20 times over an entire day, and I'll then have days, weeks or months without tics at all before they suddenly show up again. Others are not so lucky, and I've seen people diagnosed with Autism for whom tics will drive them mad for up to 80 per cent of their waking day. Whilst most cases of Tourette's are not so severe that they require medication, some cases are; and there is no reason why having a diagnosis of Autism should exclude such people from this treatment.

Obsessive-compulsive disorder

Briefly, obsessive-compulsive disorder (OCD) is an impulse-control disorder driven by anxiety, so it's more likely to be found in people who for one reason or another are chronically overwhelmed or more sensitive than most people. When people think of OCD they often think of hand-washing or checking rituals in which something is checked over and over again. But people with obsessive-compulsive disorder can focus on things like perfection, balance, order and symmetry to the point that they might be unable to relax in a usual classroom, enter or exit a room, eat, sleep or breathe as most people would who weren't compelled to notice every imbalance, imperfection or aspect of 'dis-order' or asymmetry. But OCD is not only rituals. More recently it has been understood that OCD can involve persistent and repetitive disturbing mental images or thoughts. Most of us have had a repeating song going around and around inside our head some time. Imagine having the same broken record about the topic of the impending death of your loved ones, about how everyone thinks you are a sexual deviate, about how you are contaminated or have killed or harmed someone without knowing and imagine if these disturbing intrusive broken records go around and around day-in day-out or attacking you in sudden bursts in the middle of your lessons, whilst working, in the middle of a dinner or romance with someone or whenever you encounter strangers in the street. This perhaps gives you some idea of the discomfort and distraction that can be suffered by those with OCD.

THE DIFFERENCE BETWEEN OCD AND OBSESSIVE-COMPULSIVE PERSONALITY

Obsessive-compulsive disorder is an impulse-control disorder underpinned by chemical imbalances in the brain. Obsessive-compulsive personality disorder is an extreme personality trait and can occur as part of a cluster of 'personality disorders' which include avoidant, dependent and obsessive-compulsive personality. Whilst OCD can be an 'associated condition' commonly occurring in certain personalities more than others, interestingly it's associated more with the vigilant-paranoid personality than it is the obsessive-compulsive one.

Whilst OCD is called 'ego-dystonic' – meaning it is experienced as 'invasive' and not part of the self – obsessive-compulsive personality disorder is 'ego-syntonic', meaning the person experiences it as part of their selfhood. This doesn't mean someone with OCD can just let go of their condition, because their condition has hold of them! What's even worse is that even though OCD is experienced as 'invasive' and 'non-self', those who've had

OCD since infancy may have known no other life consciously before OCD so it's easy for them simply to figure, 'so this is life', 'this is what I am' and not seek help for or challenge their OCD in spite of truly suffering developmentally, socially, emotionally, psychologically in being eaten up by it.

Where those with obsessive-compulsive personality disorder are perfectionists, fixated on detail and control, and can be rigid and inflexible, those with OCD can have any range of personality. Someone with OCD may not be a perfectionist at all and still have to check the same thing over and over again, wash their hands 10 times in a minute or trace a pattern over and over again until it 'feels right' or count and count to the point it almost drives them mad, and be unable to stop doing these things no matter how despairing it makes them to be out of control like this.

Where the person with obsessive-compulsive personality may love 'perseverating' on their favorite topic, the person with OCD who experiences persistent invasive thoughts generally feels plagued by them, uncomfortable, wound up, anxious and sometimes frightened and even suicidal at having the same anxiety-provoking thoughts going around and around over and over. What's more, the nature of the thoughts for someone with obsessive-compulsive personality may be very much that these are experienced as 'my thoughts' where the invasive compulsive thoughts of the person with OCD may be experienced as hideous, anxiety provoking, alien and 'not me'. Where those seeing 'Autism' as a 'culture' point to the perseveration and fixations of the obsessive-compulsive personality in many people with Asperger's syndrome and some with Autism, this should never be merrily projected onto non-verbal people with Autism who may instead be genuinely suffering from OCD and be unable to communicate the difference.

Merriam-Webster's Medical Desk Dictionary (2002) definition of OCD is: 'a psychoneurotic disorder in which the patient is beset with obsessions or compulsions or both and suffers extreme anxiety or depression through failure to think the obsessive thoughts or perform the compelling acts.'

Tics and OCD should not be mistaken for 'stims'

Tourette's can occur from the age of two, and a percentage of folks on the Autie spectrum are thought to have Tourette's or obsessive-compulsive disorder. For some, vocal tics are so severe that they take over their communication to the point that it becomes utterly dysfunctional and they may lose faith in pursuing communication at all (there is a prevailing myth that these are always swear words, but only a small percentage of those with Tourette's experience the swearing tics). Further, the Tourette's researcher Dr Angela Gedye (1991) associated Tourette's with 'speech arrest', which can last from moments to minutes, and is associated with seizure. Also, unrelated to speech arrest, the freezing up of speech common in selective mutism (found in otherwise developmentally 'typical'children) is also found in children with learning disabilities, stuttering and compulsive disorders such as OCD (and OCD is common to a very high per cent of people with Tourette's).

Many children with Autism are known to have tics, and because others have 'stims' (self-stimulatory behaviours), actual involuntary tics can often be mistaken for voluntary indulgence in stims, many children with severe and disabling levels of tics and OCD get no medical treatment for these as they are simply assumed to be stims and part of Autism.

OCD often co-occurs with tics. These are more complex and ritualised and are not stims nor should they be confused with obsessional interests. Stims and obsessional interests involve volition. OCD and tics do not (even though one may enjoy or be amused by some of them at times, though mostly they are exhausting, annoying and invasive). They are involuntary and compulsive and, like tics, if suppressed, OCD rituals often become entrenched and more severe.

Bipolar disorder

Bipolar disorder is certainly another condition affecting impulse control, but will be mentioned in Chapter 6 on mood disorder. Personality disorders, which include antisocial, borderline, narcissistic and histrionic personality, can also result in impulse-control problems.

Effects of impulse control disorders

Impulse-control disorders and psychological and social wellbeing

Compulsive states are often annoying, often alienating, usually draw the wrong kind of attention and can severely disrupt one's ability to pay attention, stay on task (let alone stay in a seat) and keep up with information processing when driven mad by these 'fleas'.

Compulsive states can have an effect on inclusion and opportunity as many places feel more 'OK' about someone with an Autism spectrum condition who does not have 'bizarre' behaviours than they do about one who does. Finding the confidence to initiate meeting new people is often harder for these people because they not only have to introduce themselves but also introduce their 'fleas' so that others don't simply recoil once these start to appear. Children who have had an impulse control disorder since infancy don't have the luxury of this clarity. They don't remember a time before these compulsions, so they are less likely to be suppressed and more likely to be seen not so much as invasive but as part of one's 'self'. There is a need here for social stories through which children with compulsive disorders (as opposed to obsessive-compulsive personality) can learn that their compulsive disorder is not the same as their 'self', that 'compulsion' is not the same as 'want', that one can learn to calm and divert and co-opt and disobey one's own tics or compulsions more comfortably.

Other people can simply feel alienated by the compulsions of those with tics or compulsive disorders, embarrassed by them, distracted by them or see them as the person's weakness, especially when sometimes the person with them may be able to suppress them for short bursts in certain situations or when on particular tasks, but they flare up when anxiety, excitement, overstimulation, even slight boredom sets in.

Impulse control disorders can have an effect on identity in several ways. Where tics and compulsions may severely govern someone's external appearances, communication, interactions and inclusion, this can cause a split between the internal self and external self that is more extreme than it might be for those without these challenges. A sense of one's own world as a place of acceptance, sanctuary, even company with one's memories or 'playing out' of an imagined self, can be a great source of guaranteed success that far outshines the jaded allure of taking real risks in the external world.

Compulsive states can also affect identity when one is so governed by compulsive thoughts and actions that there is a poverty of one's volitional self-generated stuff. In other words, some people with these 'fleas' can feel they are simply a big bundle of their 'stuff'. It is even worse when others see them in the same light. It's like the coffin lid gradually closes, and hope for freedom, volition, selfhood, belonging and the feeling of really being known as a person is progressively lost; hope disappears with the last piece of light as the coffin lid closes on this invisible imprisonment. It is a lucky child indeed who has a parent, teacher or friend who can still see them as a person far more than a walking manifestation of a 'condition' even when the condition may govern 50, 60, 70, 80, 90 per cent of their waking day. It is little wonder that conditions like OCD usually go together with depression. But it must be remembered that many children with compulsive and tic disorders have bipolar disorder as well, even though the tics or compulsive disorders may, themselves, provoke depression.

Impulse control disorders can have an effect on alienation from others who can take these things personally. There are people who will take it personally if you are unable to shake their hand or if you wash after contact. There are people who will be greatly offended if you have a spitting tic, or feel threatened if you suddenly lunge. There are people who will be so annoyed by compulsive noises or so offended by a lack of response, that they progressively stop talking around you. There are those who feel you can't possibly be listening or watching peripherally, or feel they have personally disturbed you if your compulsions are driving you to straighten everything they've touched. There are people who will think you have no interest in them if you are compelled to ask the same question over and over again to placate your compulsive thoughts. The forms of alienation go on and on.

Severe compulsive disorders may make you alienated from your body or your voice, which seem to take on a life of their own. If your severe tics or OCD compulsions cause you physical discomfort, you can wish you didn't have a body so you wouldn't be driven mad by it. It can be hard to care sometimes whether you dress the body, feed the body, give it sleep. Involuntary tics and compulsions may so appear to take over your life that when you get the chance, you ignore the body's needs. You may so often associate your voice with involuntary noises that you give up on the idea you have volition over it or that anyone would still have faith or be interested in you should you manage somewhere in all the involuntary stuff to utter the simplest statement of volition. Even if they did notice or assume that, for a change, you had uttered something with volition, would you be able to follow it up, reply to the response or would the arousal simply imprison you for yet another round?

Severe involuntary impulse-control disorders may create fear of being entrapped in the body of someone who looks 'nuts' or suffocated, especially if they involve almost constant breathing-related tics like breath holding, teeth grinding, humming, compulsive throat clearing, compulsive sniffing or compulsive coughing. Because they may have no apparent physical disability, those without communication may gradually realise that their intelligence, sanity or capacity for empathy may be judged by their condition.

Severe involuntary impulse-control disorders may steal the time otherwise spent communicating, interacting, learning, socialising, playing and becoming a more well-rounded self. Those with these may miss out on a degree of the same social, emotional and communication development that other people would usually have, so on top of everything else they may feel socially awkward, socially backward, left behind.

Severe impulse-control disorders may alter family relationships and home stability. Imprisonment with impulse-control problems may make someone reactive and oppositional even where their natural personality would not be. You need to relax and unwind somewhere, and that can mean that all the suppressed compulsions now come flying out where you feel you run the least social risks. Then the very people you most need support from may progressively become those most alienated from you, most externally controlling of you, most apologetic on your behalf, or they may inadvertently pass you an intense emotional burden in simply covertly wishing and praying that you get over your stuff so they can 'get on with life'.

Severe impulse-control disorders may dramatically alter behaviour-management approaches because you are dealing with people who have a higher degree of stress than others, who may feel constantly robbed of control over their own thoughts, bodies and voices. What are very simple demands, simple adjustments to most people may be like the straw that breaks the camel's back to the person already struggling with a severe compulsive disorder which follows them everywhere. They can feel as comfortable as a drug addict seeking to get on with life in the grip of withdrawal clutching at the gut and the mind.

Severe impulse-control disorders and health

Put simply, a dog with fleas will progressively get worn down – emotionally, cognitively, psychologically and physically. Impulse-control disorders can be like invaders in one's own body. When severe enough, these 'fleas' may put someone into a similar struggle with their body as those struggling with involuntary movements of some movement disorders. Imprisonment, disempowerment, distraction and despair do nothing to stabilise any of us and without stabilisation, we may live on a choppy ocean of chronic stress which eventually wears anyone down. If those with impulse-control disorders tend to have a short fuse, ask yourself how well you'd cope living with fleas.

Severe impulse-control disorders may not only have a huge direct impact on chronic stress and depression but also, progressively, on gut/immune function and general health because, quite simply, bodies can only take so much stress. People with chronic stress are more prone to burn-out, to cycles of hyperactivity and fatigue, to poorer digestion and lowered immunity and, progressively, to associated toxicity issues and subsequent neurotransmitter imbalances. In other words, sometimes things can cascade from bad into worse and severe compulsive disorders in early infancy could conceivably become part of the breakdown process, which ultimately may also affect the development of brain organisation and subsequent information processing.

Impulse-control disorders and testing

Whilst most people with impulse-control disorders are not severely affected by them, there are some who are. These may be so severe that staying sitting in a seat or remaining on task can take considerably longer for these people than others and some may take many short bursts of self-control to be able to finish a task in snatched opportunities of successful self-management.

There may still be those less experienced test-administration assistants (and perhaps some people with even less of an excuse for ignorance) who have an unspoken unconscious assumption that, surely, if the person being tested was 'all there' they'd control their problems long enough to do the test.

Because those with severe impulse-control disorders may often look or, in the case of involuntary vocalisations or movements, sound or appear so bizarre to those who don't have them, it may be too easy for testers to make wrong assumptions about the intelligence or psychological/emotional stability of the person with severe impulse-control problems. To make matters worse, impulse-control disorders like oppositional defiant disorder or Tourette's may sometimes compel people actually to do the opposite to their true intention, and without anyone to check that the answer given was in line with the person's intention, it may be very easy for these conditions to affect ability testing. This may be even more likely where the overriding label is Autism and the co-existence of an oppositional state affecting impulse control is not recognised.

Available therapies for impulse-control disorders

Every person diagnosed with Autism adapts differently. The same is true of compulsive disorders. Some people learn to suppress these impulses till they have a time and space to let them fly. Others find that suppression merely heightens them. Some people learn to identify their selfhood as separable from their compulsive disorder, others do not. Some people can take on self-calming strategies, utilise biofeedback programmes, respond to social stories, to appropriate low doses of medication, to cognitive behavioural therapy in dealing with OCD, or to hypnotherapy in addressing compulsive thoughts centring on phobias. Others do not cope, comply or respond. Some people's compulsive disorders may be triggered by information-processing problems such as overload, and when this is addressed the tics and compulsions decrease. For others, compulsive disorders underpin the information-processing issues. Some people will have mood, anxiety or personality disorders underpinning chronic stress or overstimulation and exacerbating tics and compulsions. For others, these issues are secondary or not at work. In some people these impulse-control disorders may be more prominent in some environments or phases of life than others. In other people these issues will be ongoing and relatively unchanged. The range of professionals involved in the treatment of impulse-control disorders is vast but, among others, can include neurologists, neuropsychologists, cognitive behavioural therapists, psychiatrists, hypnotherapists, gut/immune specialists in holistic medicine, stress management counsellors, a peer group, people who model humour and surrealism in the face of chaos, and the wonderful medicine of those accepting people with a respect for equal rights, inclusion, advocacy and an ability always to see the person first before the condition.

Compulsive disorders and specific behavioural issues

Severe impulse-control disorders could underpin specific issues/behaviours relating to:

- communication
- being in one's own world
- eye contact
- learning and cognitive challenges
- toileting
- sleep problems
- stimming
- meltdowns
- self-protection responses
- challenging behaviours
- food behaviour problems.

OCD is different to obsessive-compulsive personality. People with OCD may be incredibly distracted or distressed by their OCD, which may affect their *communication*; but those with obsessive-compulsive personality are more likely to rant on their own interest topics obsessively. Those with OCD may have obsessive thoughts, but these are usually troubling to them and distressing, whereas obsessive thoughts in obsessive-compulsive personality may cover the whole mood range from distress to enthusiasm, dogmatism and excitement, depending on the person's mood at the time. Severe OCD can cause depression which can be so overwhelming it could reduce communication, and those with OCD and anxiety disorders, particularly social phobia or avoidant personality, may be more likely to develop selective mutism.

People with severe Tourette's may struggle to communicate fluently without the interruption of tics, and if this occurs in a person with social phobia and avoidant personality the chances of them progressively developing selective mutism and becoming too inhibited to use speech would perhaps be significantly higher than it might for most people.

A young Autie with Tourette's may learn that the more they join in or use speech the more they become emotionally or sensorily overwhelmed, and that this makes their tics worse. It is not a big step from here to developing communication problems.

An Autie or Aspie with OCD or Tourette's with severe impulse-control problems may be a more overwhelmed, possibly an even more alienated, Autie or Aspie than they might otherwise have been. As OCD and Tourette's can become additional sources of self-consciousness, and become the basis for ever greater attempts by others to try to control you, and increase your likelihood of being set apart or bullied, there are reasons why compulsive disorders may increase an Autie's natural compulsion towards *being in their own world*.

OCD generally shouldn't affect *eye contact*, but if someone had developed an OCD-related phobia about eye contact then it would be affected. OCD is generally full of 'if I do X, then the dreaded consequence of Z will happen, so I'll avoid X so Z won't get me'. So, for example, someone may desperately not want you to leave them because they fear you will die if they aren't with you. They may develop a belief that you won't leave till you get eye contact and, therefore, if they avoid looking at you they will be saving you from certain death. As irrational as this may seem, people with bipolar or schizophrenia may also have strange beliefs affecting eye contact. I have heard from people diagnosed with Autism spectrum conditions who have believed they had special powers and it would harm others if they were to allow them to make eye contact with them.

Eye contact problems in Auties with OCD may also centre around compulsive thoughts, particularly those associated with extreme shame or fear of sexual impropriety or committing violence. Imagine if you feared others could somehow see you were having thoughts which you yourself abhorred, had no interest in and would never act upon, but which you couldn't control. Compulsive and troubling thoughts in OCD are commonly associated with irrational fear of loss, fear of losing control, fear of contamination and fear of rejection.

The visual disarray of an environment might set off OCD compulsions to sort, order, tidy, balance and create symmetry. Touch and tactile experiences with substances can set off OCD compulsions associated with fears of contamination. An Autie who is sensorily overwhelmed may be more likely to move from this feeling of a loss of control into their OCD compulsions. The same may be true of Auties with Tourette's where a sensorily overwhelming atmosphere is capable of then setting off a feeling of being so 'out of control' it sets off the tics.

It may be very uncomfortable for anyone to *learn or pay attention* when they are distracted, and compulsive disorders are all about distraction. If you had to deal with an extreme impending tragedy it would be hard to sit and pay attention to the maths lesson. OCD obsessions and compulsions can trigger a feeling similar to an extreme impending tragedy. Many people with Tourette's can feel the tension prior to a tic or run of tics firing, and this can make it very hard to focus or stay involved in an activity.

There are also the social-emotional effects of compulsive disorders. Most people cope well with learning and paying attention when they feel socially accepted, understood and comfortable in a learning environment. If compulsive disorders have led to you being seen as 'alien' to others or a disturbance to the class, then on top of the compulsive disorders themselves the social-emotional impact of this kind of exclusion will only make learning and motivation harder. Some personalities will be more challenged by this than others, but those with both compulsive disorders and the sensitive-avoidant personality may struggle most to cope with these things socially.

Compulsive disorders can affect any aspect of life, but a fear of germs, contamination by surfaces, or even fear of breathing where there are smells, may all have the potential to affect *toileting*. Whilst hand-washing is the most known OCD compulsion, it is certainly not the only one. Nor does a fear of contamination always result in handwashing. It is just as possible someone may develop a great fear of touching the tap or flush button if they fear others have touched it, and avoid touching the soap if they feel others have already used that bar. There may be particular wiping rituals and an excessive use of toilet paper. Symmetry and order compulsions in the toilet can involve counting or folding numbers of sheets of toilet paper or making sure these feel they have been gathered in even quantities rather than odd quantities. The number of times the toilet has been flushed or the spacing of each flush may continue until there is a feeling of symmetry achieved.

Checking compulsions may involve checking and rechecking whether the toilet has been flushed, the opening and closing of the door and its lock mechanisms, the opening and closing of water taps.

Tourette's tics can occur in any place and at any time but some people can teach themselves to suppress them temporarily for short bursts (though typically the greater the external attempts to suppress them the worse they become). The toilet is one of the most personal spaces of one's life. This means it is a place where lots of tics can come out. It would not be unusual for a student with Tourette's tics to purge their tics whilst in the toilets. The impact on others, however, may be difficult. People with clapping, shouting, whistling or other noisy tics are likely unintentionally to draw attention to themselves even in the toilets. People with facial tics, which can include tongue thrusting, facial stretching and grimacing or twisting, slapping or lunging tics, may appear pretty scary to others who are relatively isolated with them in the school's toilet block. Even though the tics generally make a person no more or less harmful than anyone else, they can look pretty unpredictable and even scary to those who don't understand. Explaining tics to others can be socially very important to avoid both fear and bullying, and this may be especially important if the person with the tics has Autism and is functionally non-verbal so their intelligence and sanity is not judged by their tics.

The checking and symmetry compulsions of OCD can make it difficult to *sleep* or stay asleep. Compulsions to check the room constantly for anyone hidden, to open or close the door, turn the light switches on and off, check handles, open and close drawers are common. The fear of breathing unevenly as one falls asleep or the fear of losing one's perfect place in the centre of the bed due to falling asleep are usually not felt as whims but as necessities to survival. Not obeying compulsive drives may bring on panic attacks, as though one's life or safety actually depended on complying with the compulsions.

Tourette's tics may have been suppressed on and off all day, and sleep time is the one time when a person can be alone in their own space. This means that bed time easily becomes the natural time when a person may purge their tics and it can be normal, even preferable, for someone with Tourette's to get their tics out of their system before sleeping. It is not usually possible to get to sleep or stay asleep with a gut full of adrenaline from suppressing tics. Purging them can be the best way to get the body ready and able to sleep. Most people with Tourette's will not tic in their sleep, but some will have twitches and flexing in their sleep.

Tics are often mistaken for *self-stimulatory behaviours*. You might think of one as a fart and the other as having a scratch. The fart is involuntary though you can suppress it for a while and if you do the pressure builds up. The scratch, on the other hand, is completely voluntary, however compelling the associated itch is. It's important to realise that some tics may be fairly entertaining to the host even though the tics themselves are involuntary. We may laugh at having farted, even try and make it part of a joke. But that doesn't make it voluntary.

Often the person with tics is oblivious to them, or is distracted, annoyed or even distressed by them. Self-stimulatory behaviours, on the other hand, are basically voluntary indulgences which serve some kind of safety, enjoyment, download or social control purpose. Stims can be replaced with experiences that bring greater safety, pleasure, control over others or download capacity when overloaded. Tics can often be distracted from or co-opted and very subtly morphed into something less disruptive. Attempts to suppress someone else's tics directly will often make them more entrenched and more severe.

Any dog with fleas is going to lose their temper or throw a tantrum more easily than one without. Any camel already weighed down with plenty of straw will collapse more easily when the final little straw is placed on its already overburdened back. OCD and Tourette's can create dramatically elevated levels of overload, and so cause *meltdowns*, in those who are already challenged by information-processing issues and other fruits from the 'Autism fruit salad'. Counselling people, creating an accepting and understanding environment, providing non-punitive time-out spaces, modelling self- calming strategies, providing cognitive behavioural therapy, dietary interventions to reduce stress levels, if not small amounts of appropriate medication where necessary, may be essential to helping people with compulsive disorders function as best and completely as they can.

People with OCD or Tourette's suffer from anxiety and stress more than those who don't have these 'fleas'. Adrenaline can be thought of like a type of fuel. Fuel can drive very different vehicles and machines. Adrenaline in people can have different effects in different individuals. In one it will mean hyperactivity and diversion behaviours, in another aggression, in another anxiety and phobias, in another obsessions and compulsions, in another mania. The only thing that can commonly be said about adrenaline is that it doesn't relax you.

Self-protection responses are going to be higher in people with high levels of adrenaline. The more sources of high adrenaline at work, the more self-protective the person will be in a whole range of ways. In terms of self-protectiveness, OCD or Tourette's on their own would only result in obsessive or compulsive states. But when combined with information-processing and sensory-perceptual challenges, anxiety or mood disorders, a dose of identity confusion and social alienation wrapped up in a personality package which runs counter to the environment or approach currently used, you will have a recipe for highly developed self-protection responses. The solution lies in working with each of the components involved to lessen the load.

Highly stressed people are more likely to have *challenging and self-injurious behaviours*. The agitated states of both depression and mania can be associated with this level of stress, and those with OCD and Tourette's often also have mood disorders, with OCD commonly crossing over with depression and Tourette's commonly crossing over with both depression and bipolar.

Symmetry and perfection-related compulsions in OCD can lead to compulsive skin and scab picking and hair pulling known as trichotillomania. Contamination phobias and washing compulsions in some cases of OCD can become so excessive that the hands crack and bleed.

Tourette's tics can include seemingly self-injurious behaviours of face and head slapping and punching, head banging and biting, pinching, but also challenging behaviours such as smearing, exposing oneself, spitting, sniffing, tapping people and objects and licking surfaces.

In terms of despair and distress, people with OCD or Tourette's are more likely to experience extreme social rejection and external control by others. Both of these things could burden these people almost as much as the conditions themselves and lead to challenging and self-injurious behaviours that are then secondary to these conditions.

Symmetry, order and perfection compulsions can have a big effect on *food and eating behaviours*. People with these may become distressed if foods are mixed up together and may insist on eating their meat separately from each vegetable, or may even insist on only eating one food at any one time. People with these compulsions may have particular rituals in eating bread or biscuits such that the object is kept relatively complete all the way to the end, and they may distress if they get a biscuit or chip which is 'broken'. People with ordering compulsions may become very distressed when expected to eat things in a different order to the usual or even at a different time.

Some people with OCD who have contamination phobias may become distressed if given 'messy food' or if expected to touch or handle the food. They may become distressed at using cutlery others have used before. There are those who may develop phobias about food and have to pull it apart or check it in minute detail before feeling comfortable with eating it.

The eating of non-food objects is called pica and is common both in Autism and Tourette's, and is listed as a Tourette's-related compulsion. Tourette's tics often centre on taboos, so if people are expected to eat with their mouths closed, for example, it may be that someone with Tourette's may unconsciously fixate on not opening their mouth when eating to the point it triggers a feeling of suffocation, when they may be compelled to open their mouth, particularly when its full of food, simply to relax the distress. If someone with Tourette's is told to stay seated, this may trigger a feeling of being trapped and lead to a compulsion to leave their seat. If someone is told not to touch their food, they may develop a distress that they are unable to use their hands, and so become compelled to tap the food to dissolve the distress. Smelling compulsions are common in Tourette's, including the smelling of objects, people and one's fingers, but the more you seek to stop someone with Tourette's doing this the more you are likely to simply fuel the compulsion.

CHAPTER 6

Strange Emotional Spaces

Mood-Regulation Problems

Two aliens arrive from different planets to planet Earth. One notices the absurd and intimidatingly outgoing, social, invasive and incomprehensibly flexible nature of the Earthlings. Another fails to notice their more subtle emotional states and assumes they must think and feel very little, is struck by their limited emotional range, their bland equilibrium, their relative absence of extreme individuality and reliance on 'common sense', 'protocol', 'patience' and 'permission'.

Mood disorders: Childhood depression and bipolar disorder

In this next section I will discuss childhood mood disorders as it is still commonly assumed that infants can't develop clinical mood disorders. Nevertheless, it's important to remember that as an infant with an untreated mood disorder grows up they become a child with that mood disorder then an adult with that mood disorder. Hence, whilst I refer here to childhood mood disorders, this term is being applied to those who developed these mood disorders in infancy and early childhood as an exacerbating factor in their autism. Many adults with Autism spectrum conditions also develop later-onset mood disorders of the same kind. In other words, as a medical condition relating to a chemical imbalance in the brain, a mood disorder may have its onset at any age.

Recognising someone with depression

I guess the first thing to clarify is what depression is not. Just as OCD is not obsessive-compulsive personality disorder, depression is not 'depressive personality disorder'. You can have a depressive personality and feel safer when negative, defeatist and looking on the bleak side of things and yet not have depression.

That aside, we need to distinguish between depression with no apparent external cause (called endogenous depression) and when we develop depression because of something which has happened to us (called reactive depression). The two are not easy to tell apart, perhaps especially in Auties and Aspies. The needs of Auties or Aspies may be very different to those of developmentally typical people, so it may appear to outsiders that there is no external problem when in fact the nature of the external problems is simply such that most people would not have found a problem with these.

Similarly, there are Auties who don't understand or relate to Aspie realities, and vice versa. What distresses one may not distress the other. Because two fruit salads with the same label may in fact contain very different combinations of fruit, there are even those with a shared label who may be unable to see the source of each other's justifiable, if not treatable, reactive depression.

So in the context of all that, and as Autism spectrum disorders are often diagnosed in childhood, let's have a little look at what childhood depression is meant to be. The symptoms of depressive disorder in children may seem like those which happen to all of us and they are. The difference is in the frequency, intensity and duration of those experiences. Just as adults with depression may experience fatigue, aches and pains, stomach aches, headaches and problems concentrating that are very physically real, children with depression can experience the same. Just as adults with depression may consider leaving their family, children with depression may consider running away. Just as adults with depression may be chronically bored, irritable, despondent, indifferent and uninterested in company and communication, children with depression can experience the same things so chronically that it is more than just 'part of growing up' – it may be getting in the way of development. Just as adults with depression may isolate themselves, lose interest in previous skills, lash out at those trying to get close to them or be flat or teary, children with depression can have the same problems on a more regular basis than it being 'just kids'.

The relationship between Autism and childhood depression

Childhood depression in itself is not Autism, but certainly having depression would not help a child to find the motivation and initiative to challenge their own limitations. So we could reasonably expect that if two children with Autism had exactly the same fruit in their fruit salad with the exception that one had depression and one did not, the one that did not would be likely to cope better with their other autism-related challenges, explore adaptations, and have a greater potential to build bridges to a higher level of functioning than the one who additionally had the burden of chronic depression.

Any and all of us can experience depression if we are put through experiences of extreme frustration, pain, intimidation, confusion, loss, entanglement, entrapment or alienation to the point where we lose hope, become despondent and enter despair. Here we begin to pull in, to withdraw or to put on a false front and function, perhaps in the absence of an internal, connected, self; buried alive. We have lost our *joie de vivre*, our love of life, our spark of interest, our comfort in belonging. We are experiencing not our life force, but our death force, an attraction to the void which extinguishes our world, petrifies it, produces stagnation and progressively strangulates out of existence the flow of life. We may no longer care about others or our effect on them, about appearances, about ourselves, about our body, about the future. Fortunately, most of us can break free eventually from these things and begin, if not too far gone, to unravel. Many Auties, however, may have no control over their life choices in any way and may experience themselves as extremely powerless. The truth is, for many of them this is an objective reality.

There are also personality types which will predispose people to depression, such as the extreme instability of identity and chronic fear of abandonment associated with borderline personality disorder, the inability ever to feel recognised or celebrated enough which may be a source of chronic dissatisfaction, self-pity and despair in narcissistic personality disorder, the tendency to see the end of the world and blow that emotional experience up to grand proportions as seen in histrionic personality disorder, the self-imprisonment within inability that can be part of dependent personality disorder, the isolating and alienating detachment and aloneness of schizoid personality disorder, the entrapment within one's body of avoidant personality disorder or selective mutism, or the inability to relax and trust inherent in paranoid personality disorder.

There are tic and compulsive disorders, anxiety disorders, learning disabilities and severe physical disabilities which can be so frustrating, aggravat-

ing, annoying, distracting, embarrassing, alienating and imprisoning as to be
a basis for depression if not addressed.

Origins of depression

As already mentioned, there is a difference between depression attributable to
life circumstances (reactive depression) and depression which occurs regardless of life circumstances (endogenous depression). Some people are simply
depressive no matter what lengths the environment goes to to empower or
understand them, and it might be of great benefit to the Autism field not only
to recognise childhood depression but also to differentiate this from those
cases where a child has a depressive personality disorder rather than a clinical
depression. There is no rule which says people with Autism are immune to
either issue: children are subject to genetic inheritance, picking up patterns
from those around them and reacting to life experiences the same as any
human being.

Clinical depression may be a matter of neurotransmitter imbalances set
off by gut/immune dysfunction or abnormalities in the area of the brain associated with depression, the hippocampus, or metabolic abnormalities which
predispose the person to lower than normal levels of the mood regulators
serotonin or dopamine. My own view is that we could say that the basic forms
of depression might be divided into two, often interconnected areas, which
are:

- chemical imbalance
- life experiences and life circumstance issues which give very
  subjective reasons *particular to the individual* which are sufficient to
  lose hope.

From infancy onwards one may have one or the other but there is no reason
why there can't actually be a combination of both. Tackling withdrawal,
introversion, rigidity, resistance to change, passivity, lack of initiation and
sometimes aggression can be personality rather than depression issues, but
there will be other cases where treating depression is the answer and that may
mean locating the type and basis of the depression.

If the basis is largely chemical then the interventions will address neurotransmitter imbalances either directly or indirectly through addressing gut/
immune issues or a combination of both approaches. If the basis is the burden
of a treatable anxiety disorder, a tic or compulsive disorder, or even the mood
instability of something like rapid cycling bipolar, these too can usually be

addressed on a biochemistry level to a large degree and the secondary depression should sort itself out once the burden is removed.

If the basis is a personality disorder, these are certainly harder to treat but not impossible. There are 'mood foods', Bach/Bush Flower Remedies, cognitive behavioural therapy, biofeedback, stress management, assertiveness training, social stories and hypnotherapy which may help some to a degree. But the environment can also decrease alienation, empowering and redirecting the abilities of these children in ways that are more compatible with their personality challenges. For example, if you live with someone solitary or avoidant whose depression is increased when they are constantly expected to share their feelings, confide or enjoy intimacy, then you could ease some of that burden by providing them with ways of expressing themselves and enjoying activity that doesn't involve a lot of direct exposure before other people – like computer games, walking, drawing or typing to themsleves. Conversely if you have someone adventurous or dramatic who loves excitement, daring, or attention, you could stop perceiving them as needing to suppress their naturally 'out of control' nature and look at things like skateboarding or character acting. If you had someone idiosyncratic for whom it is natural not to conform and who freely goes off into their own world, you could learn to value innovation and eccentricity and learn to play in an improvisational and even surreal manner within your own world, allowing them to join and leave as came naturally to them.

If the basis of depression is an inability to communicate, there are a range of new communication techniques which do not rely on verbal ability or even complete control over one's own body movements. There are triggering techniques for those who shut down when expected to access responses. Ultimately, for those most severely impaired there is often still the ability to learn the language of sounds and behaviour as a key to their likes, dislikes, choices. Even if seemingly incapable of speech, many can organise thought. Even if incapable of organising thought, virtually nobody is utterly incapable of some kind of expression of feeling. I can feel someone's mood in their breathing and muscle responses. It's a matter of what we expect as 'communication'. Sometimes we are so fixated on what isn't there we become blinkered to the possibilities of what *is* there.

If the basis of depression is a lack of control over one's life or socially claustrophobic being the constant focus of caretaking and fixation on your incapabilities to the point you are never responsible for anyone else, these things can be changed by the environment. Even those with no apparent proven ability to help themselves can feel important and empowered when given the job of watching out for someone or something else.

Those whose depression is based in extreme guilt, shame or self-hatred at feeling a burden upon those who are waiting, watching, wanting, praying for a miracle may be most magically helped into seizing their own lives when others remove this incidental emotional pressure and burden and clearly just get on with their own lives, discover themselves and develop humour, silliness, surrealism, regardless of the apparent 'tragedy' they had previously, claustrophobically, invasively, co-dependently been fixating upon.

In today's society we put so much faith in conventional medicine we often forget about the real environmental medicine: the effect we have on each other. We talk about the positives of music therapy but forget about the music of our own beingness which is forever being picked up by those in our company. What tune are we playing around the person struggling with their own challenges? Chaotic? Afraid? Fixated? Waiting? Disappointed? Mourning? Trapped? Overwhelmed? Alone? Lost?

Autism, depression and the environment

A few decades ago, children with Autism were believed to have withdrawn into an 'Autistic' state because of such things as grief, neglect or abuse. Carers were often blamed and the children even removed in order to 'recover'. These were dark days for the field of Autism and there has been a knee-jerk reaction in which these things are now utterly disregarded as underpinning the severity of some children's Autism.

But maybe we have thrown the baby out with the bathwater here. Some children with Autism may be more highly sensing, more emotionally hypersensitive, even more prone to particular personality disorders and communication challenges than most people. These might disempower or overwhelm them to the degree that they consciously comprehend less and therefore *cope* less easily on an emotional level with complex physical experiences of feelings like entrapment, guilt, self-hatred, social claustrophobia, aloneness and alienation than other children. In *their* experience, these feelings may well amount to the equivalent of grief, neglect and abuse without those around them ever imagining their often well-intentioned actions could be experienced this way.

This is not to say that most families abandon, neglect or abuse their Autistic children, nor that depression is the whole of any person's Autistic 'fruit salad'. It is just that some Autistic children may not cope well with the emotional impact of some environments and this might sometimes underpin depression and withdrawal.

An Autie may have very different reasons for developing a depressive state because of the 'normal' actions of developmentally typical people including:

- being seen as a 'case' far more than just a person

- being fixated upon as 'having problems' to the point where this is all they see as their identity and perceived social image

- being always the one 'cared for' to the point where they might feel they would rob others of their identity or lose their 'affection' if they improved or developed independence, yet feel intensely trapped with their 'incapacity'

- never being given the empowering responsibility for anyone or anything outside of themselves to the point where they never get to feel like 'the capable one'

- being assumed incapable until proven otherwise by those with power over their life

- being constantly 'helped' and corrected to the point where they can only see themselves as a bundle of incapability and 'incorrectness'

- feeling intense guilt, shame or self-hatred for not feeling grateful to those who 'care' and 'love' them, for all the constant 'help' or for not meeting the expectations/desires/prayers that they would 'recover'

- feeling incapable of being accepted as equal to any developmentally typical child even though they may be full of equal but different potential as themselves

- feeling others cannot understand their ways, and they cannot relate to other's ways, and this is socially all that is on offer.

Because the field is overly focused on the problems of Auties there is often very little counselling given to those who are suffering more than they should be specifically *because* it is they who are seen to have the problems.

What's needed and generally overlooked in the field are techniques like counselling, social stories and play therapy designed for the level and nature of the Autie. These should:

- help the Autie in better understanding, coping and where possible communicating their own needs regarding the social/emotional attitudes and patterns of their carers and friends

- help the Autie and their family better appreciate the Autie's own uniqueness, potential and equality.

There should also be training for carers in helping them not merely to grieve and share that grieving with each other but to constructively move beyond that to facing up to the adventure of what they do have, embracing diversity and learning from the Autie how to build bridges between their different realities.

'One man's food is another man's poison'

It is always tempting for families to believe that there is nothing emotionally damaging about their own well-intentioned efforts, their own 'grieving process', the sympathy of those who support the family or the patronising attitudes or approaches of those involved in education. Yet just because a certain pattern of social-emotional communication doesn't progressively fling you into depression, doesn't mean it won't be so for someone else. In other words, one person's food is another person's poison. Take, for example, a case where a child with personality traits that would naturally make him or her extremely asocial and a loner is brought up in a home where cuddly, sociable, friendly carers provide constant attention and show a progressively desperate need for social-emotional interaction and communication. Or take someone with obsessive-compulsive personality who was brought up with carers insistent on the great values of a flexible day-to-day programme, sense of adventure and enthusiasm for the unfamiliar. Or the idiosyncratic or adventur-ous personality with a phobia of conforming and tendency to boredom being brought up in a highly structured, conservative, conformist atmosphere of forced compliance!

Take, for example, a case where a child who is a hands-on kinesthetic learner in need of a discovery learning programme involving trial-and-error learning is brought up in a conservative home where there is a constant expec-tation 'not to touch', where any new learning experiences are withheld until the explanation is proven to have been understood, and there's an over-eagerness to 'correct' or even take over from the child at the first 'mistake'.

Take, for example, a meaning-deaf child with central auditory processing disorder who is brought up in a highly verbose environment with the TV and radio also constantly running and no provision of visual cues whatsoever to provide any fluent meaning to this cacophony of 'blah blah'. Or the case where someone with severe visual fragmentation and epilepsy grows up in a household and school environment full of fluorescent lighting and an insistence these be left on, where visual learning is provided but useless to them, and the opportunities for kinesthetic learning is not introduced. Or someone unable to close out the sound of fans who lives in a home with a noisy fridge in the kitchen, a noisy heater in the sitting room and an air-conditioner all day at school. Or the extremely mono-tracked person being responded to constantly and only in a fuse-blowing multi-track manner. Or the person working by sensing who is only ever offered a social/emotional/communication reality of those living by interpretive thinking.

Take, for example, the case of someone with anxiety disorders, compulsive disorders, impulse-control problems or motor-planning problems, but otherwise an intelligent and feeling human being who is not provided with, or is denied, the capacity to communicate through typing or electronic media and is effectively 'silenced' by an ignorant or conservative environment which assumes that 'if he or she could communicate he or she would do so verbally like the rest of us'.

Any of these things would not be a problem, except where they come together in the wrong mix. The treatment here is not to treat the child for depression so much as to alter the environment so the child's depression lifts. This might mean working with the expectations or alienation of the environment itself. It might mean building alternative social, emotional and communication avenues for the carers or partners of an Autie to fulfil elsewhere the needs the Autie can't meet for them. It might mean simple environmental adaptations that make life more compatible for everyone. It might mean building social networks so an Autie can have more positive and fitting, less alienating, experiences elsewhere. It might also mean social stories in repairing the damage that had been done beforehand and modelling or training someone in how to assert their needs or explain their own 'reality' where being unable to do so is a major source of depression.

Depression and brain chemistry

Sometimes, however, an Autie might struggle with depression in the absence of any of these environmental issues.

Until recently, depression was considered something that only adults experienced. Today children are known to be capable of inheriting the same gut/immune/metabolic and brain issues underpinning this type of non-environmental depression in adults. Today even some toddlers are being addressed for depressive states underpinning motivational, social, emotional and communication issues as part of their Autism, but there are some who will respond badly to antidepressants, shooting from depression into equally unmanageable and destabilising 'mania'. It is also not clear yet which medications can be considered 'safe'; and whilst many children have been helped through medication for depression, some antidepressants have resulted in quite the opposite, such as suicidal feelings.

The 'quick fix' promises of medication do not mean this should be the first line of intervention, and blaming everything on biochemistry too quickly excuses families and the community from some serious attitude and interaction work. There are also those children with Autism for whom depressive states are not central to their Autism. The fruit in the fruit salads will be different, and what works for one child will not necessarily work for others with the same label. Any family history of substance abuse, suicide and depression, however, may be a reason to explore the possibilities of biochemistry issues underpinning depression, even though in some families this apparent 'depression issue' may be the product of generations avoiding or not knowing how to address anxiety disorders, tic or compulsive disorders, personality disorders or simply passed-on patterning which comes out in challenging environmental 'stuff' being passed down the line...and both issues may coexist. The best medicine in treating issues related to depression may be that of getting our heads out of the sand and facing up to the wide range of possibilities, and recognising that whilst 'depression' may be a single word, it may have many different underlying causes with very different treatments.

Recognising someone with childhood bipolar disorder (manic depression)
Bipolar is not simple 'naughty behaviour'.

It is not the same thing as attention deficit hyperactivity disorder (ADHD) though a percentage of children diagnosed with ADHD may instead or additionally have childhood bipolar.

Childhood bipolar is not to be confused with severe behavioural changes and challenges seen with child abuse, though that is not to say the two can't co-occur in the one child. Of course, children with bipolar are not immune from child abuse and it may be that such abuse might be hidden by blaming behavioural and emotional changes instead on the child's bipolar.

Childhood bipolar is not to be confused with histrionic, narcissistic, borderline, antisocial or schizotypal personality traits in children, but there's also no reason why someone with these personality disorders couldn't also have childhood bipolar, and childhood bipolar is capable of upping the emotional volume on anyone's already erratic, even disoriented experiences and behaviour to a degree it might be confused with some personality disorders.

Childhood bipolar may co-occur with, or be mistaken for, something like the involuntary avoidance, diversion and retaliation responses of exposure anxiety, but in itself is not the same thing as exposure anxiety.

Bipolar is more tightly defined than depression but it is still a condition that can be confused with, can co-occur and interact with, other conditions and that can also occur on its own.

Childhood-onset bipolar, often called rapid cycling childhood bipolar because of its differences from adult-onset bipolar, is a relatively new discovery with the first publications on it beginning to appear in the 1980s and 1990s. However, the DSM criteria for adult bipolar are said to not be suitable for diagnosing it (NeuroPsychiatry Review 2000), and DSM criteria for the childhood form are still being developed. Whilst I generally had at least one or more episodes of full-blown giggling euphoria a week, apparently children with rapid cycling bipolar tend to have episodes of high irritability or rage attacks. Unlike bipolar in adults, rapid cycling bipolar in children is apparently more continuous, with episodes between several a week up to every 45 minutes. So, with children, bipolar may be more likely to be considered 'just how that person is'. In an adult, the sudden shift to a bipolar episode once or twice a year would stand out far more distinctly as being strikingly different to how that person 'usually is'.

The symptoms of childhood bipolar can be extremely similar to those of ADHD, and it is believed that a large percentage of those with ADHD may actually have rapid cycling bipolar or have both conditions. You can just imagine the effect of amphetamines on a child with rapid cycling bipolar who has been misdiagnosed with ADHD because of impulsivity, attention problems and hyperactivity. Imagine the tragedy when a psychiatrist, convinced that this is ADHD because it looks nothing like adult bipolar, then increases the medication! Other symptoms of childhood bipolar include extreme difficulty sleeping at night and trouble getting it together in the morning. Nightmares, phobic states and extreme fight–flight responses are common in children with bipolar, and grandiose behaviours or self-injurious reactions may also be common.

Effects of childhood mood disorders

Can mood disorders mess with inclusion and development?

Bipolar disorder in childhood may be extremely destabilising, and it is easy to imagine that having this in infancy with no ability to ask for, or cope with the interference of, help could instil a fear of unpredictability and change because the child is persistently in a state of unpredictability. Similarly childhood depression might instil such a withdrawal from one's body, inclusion and self-expression that the mind may not be 'driven' to make connections and everything may feel like a strain and imposition, provoking a very natural response of 'rigidity' and resistance.

When emotions suddenly leap to extreme proportions this might conceivably have secondary effects on a child's attitude about meeting new people and going to new places even, perhaps especially, when the child is in a stable moment. The obvious question in the child's mind may be 'What if I lose it and everyone else freaks out?' This would have clear implications for inclusion and learning opportunities. Childhood depression, too, might have effects on meeting new people because in the absence of an internal motivation, social offerings may be bound to look like impositions demanding 'compliance'.

Childhood bipolar means that emotions so easily get wildly out of control that it may be easy to develop a fear of being 'affected' by others. Where bipolar is left untreated, it may be a natural self-regulation method simply to limit the opportunity of the environment to get too close, to be able to 'reach you', to be in a position to cause overstimulation that may lead to mood cycling. Childhood depression, by contrast, may leave you so alienated by the seemingly motivated world which embraces new experiences that you naturally seek to protect yourself from these aliens with so different an emotional reality and who are so much more connected to their bodies than you might be.

Childhood bipolar may mean subtle emotions get lost because the extremes leave such a strong impression. It's like someone who always eats strong-tasting foods. Soon the subtler tastes may be harder to notice. By contrast, someone with childhood depression may see none of the contrasts in a world in which virtually everything may be flat and incapable of touching or moving him or her.

Childhood bipolar may alter the ability of the environment to trust you in society at large. Instead, people may over-control you on the basis that you can't control yourself and over-focus on you to the point of heightening feelings of social claustrophobia and self-consciousness (not the same as self-awareness), and instil the sense that control is what they do for you yet your loss of control is 'your fault' alone. Childhood depression by contrast may create burnt-out, co-dependent 'martyr-like' carers who have sacrificed their own passions, motivations and freedoms, yet (however caring they may be) may feel internally burdened and tired by constantly trying to be the motivator to someone who can't seem to come to the party. The irony is the more co-dependent they become (and as a culture such carers are often hailed as 'saints' for their determination), the more a child with depression may self-protect from or give in to such good intentions. Sometimes, clearly getting on with your own fun is a stronger tool of inspiration than determinedly seeking to give this to someone who didn't ask for it. Being left to chase is the key to finding want, and want is the key to so much.

Childhood bipolar may limit your ability to form friendships when other children find you bizarre, highly unpredictable or frightening in your extremes. At the same time it may attract others towards you with the same types of problems or who are seeking thrills, perhaps at your own expense. The irony is that it may be these people you finally find you have belonging and a peer group with, yet these may be the people least equipped to help you maintain equilibrium and the most likely types of links to be rejected by your family or carers. Children with depression can seem 'spooky', 'distant', 're-jecting', just as kids with bipolar can seem wild and unpredictable. People will take a depressed child's depression personally or read too much into it, in the same way as they will with a child with bipolar. Judgements need to be put aside. Having a card that warmly and kindly reminds people of some of these mistaken assumptions and thanking them for daring understanding and tolerance, may go a long way.

Childhood bipolar may instil despair that nobody will ever give you a position of responsibility for others, and others may be so on guard against your unpredictability they won't relax and just see 'you', even when you are in between cycles. Childhood depression may instil despair that the flatness, the emptiness, the boredom will be taken personally by others but also that life may feel like a prison sentence in such a place yet always threatening to give you something much worse – the alien nature of change.

Childhood bipolar may mean you accidentally destroy things you like and enjoy, sabotage friendships and relationships you value, and leave you questioning your worthiness to exist. Childhood depression may mean you struggle to show a self-initiated interest in anything or anyone, and others may consider you ungrateful of all they have to offer.

Severe childhood bipolar may so severely fragment your ability to stay on track or come off a single track that your sanity, your intelligence, or the integrity of your personality may be unfairly judged by others, and you may be utterly unequipped to prove otherwise until your bipolar is managed. Depression may so distance you from your body and so dull your senses that you don't make the wealth of connections others would, and your intelligence may be measured by the outward expression of your motivation.

The sensory extremes associated with high arousal states in childhood bipolar may be an adventure in the sensory heaven and sensory hell of sensory flooding and instil an alienation from your own body. The sensory flatness of depression may feel like a life sentence, yet the impinging nature of sensory experiences designed to stir or reach you may be invasive, foreign, and an alien stimulation from an external world you are miles away from and cannot emotionally or socially relate to.

Childhood bipolar may exhaust your family and you. It can be such a drain on the immune system and such a source of chronic stress or acute anxiety as to reduce gut/immune function and set in motion a progressive toxicity cycle, further neurotransmitter imbalance, interruption to the development of brain integration (e.g. dyspraxia) and progressive information-processing challenges. Depression can equally suppress your vitality and has long been linked to lowered gut/immune function.

Childhood bipolar may compel a child to do something impulsively which may unintentionally cause harm or endangerment to themselves or others. Mixed states may be extremely dangerous as they may have all the drive and activity of mania combined with the negativity, fear and hopelessness of depression. Whilst the lack of motivation and drive inherent in unipolar depression may stop some people from achieving suicide or life-endangering actions, the imprisonment of depression can be dangerous if a child finds a way to escape the burden of existence.

Childhood bipolar may be a source of extreme creativity, surrealism, inventiveness, ingenuity, individuality, diversity and inspiration, even once it's brought back to a safe and manageable level. Some of the most amazing and inspirational figures in history across all walks of life have been people with degrees of bipolar disorder. The actors Robert Downey Jnr, Ben Stiller and Jean-Claude Van Damme have all been reported to have bipolar, as have the writers Virginia Woolf and Syvia Plath, singer Axl Rose of Guns and Roses and the rapper DMX as well as the astronaut Buzz Aldrin (McWilliams 2005).

Childhood bipolar may have an extreme effect on the ability to tune in and control impulses long enough to learn or express that learning consistently in a cohesive manner. It may have a big impact on the nature of social development and information processing, as it is extremely difficult to process information receptively when you are flying off distracted in several directions at a time. Depression, by contrast, may make it extremely difficult to find motivation and interest which drives expansive thought and the forming of connections between new information. Depression can pull someone away from connection with their voice and expression through their body to the degree that it can have an equally profound effect on information processing, communication, inclusion and learning. The achievements by those with depression may be great but often single-tracked, perhaps less expansive than those in people who have achieved a manageable level within bipolar in which mania is a major feature. Even small steps from those with unipolar depression are great achievements. In either case, there's the saying 'What doesn't kill us, makes us stronger.' It may be for some people that the impact of childhood bipolar on the self may be one of those things, and when a child is released from those challenges, they may be a remarkable child nevertheless. The impoverishment of the depressed child may release a different kind of potential once that obstacle is treated. Both are equally worthy of support and recognition.

Childhood bipolar is not simply mania, nor is it simply depression. Childhood bipolar is usually rapid cycling in nature which means the mood extremes can cycle anywhere from several times a month, to several times a week, even several times a day. This is called rapid cycling childhood bipolar.

Ultra-rapid cycling bipolar can cycle up to every 45 minutes. This cycling is a rollercoaster which can swing from manic states to depressive states and also mixtures of the two, called 'mixed states'.

Depression as part of bipolar is dynamic, acute, sudden and part of a fluctuating condition. Unipolar depression is not like the depression that occurs in rapid cycling bipolar. Until treated, unipolar depression is a much more constant, fixed state.

I have met children with patterns akin to a depressive type of bipolar, those with a manic type of bipolar, those dominated by mixed states and those with unipolar depression. The first three have one thing in common. Their condition is dynamic and fluctuating. Only those with states akin to unipolar depression have a history of far more static, fixed kinds of interactions, communications, responses.

Is it possible that children with unipolar depression, depressive personality disorder or avoidant personality disorder, may be more likely to be recognised as having so-called Kanner's Autism? And if so, what do we do with the old concept of Kanner's Autism being some kind of 'pure Autism'? With around 30 per cent of children with Autism now believed to be affected by a childhood bipolar condition, the idea that those with depressive states as part of Kanner's Autism have some kind of 'pure Autism' seems to make little sense. Those with various bipolar states, however, may be more commonly found as part of a new expansion of the word Autism but also, because of their potentially more fluctuating, even outgoing nature, be found in groups labelled PDD (pervasive developmental disorder), PDDNOS (pervasive developmental disorder – not otherwise specified), and (if they have developed a degree of verbal communication) mislabelled ADHD.

Mixed states can be a combination of euphoria or extroversion, and simultaneous negative and dark moods. A person in a mixed state may be laughing yet extremely distressed. They may appear extroverted yet suicidal. In my own personal experience, in a manic state I was excitable, frenetic, felt God-like, untouchable, with no sense of fear, an absolute blind optimism, flying from one track to another and challenged in stringing the steps of an activity together. In a depressive state (which for me, though acute, were fortunately brief) I could be gripped with doubt, worry and certainty that I was unlikable, deeply struggling to dare, to find intent or take action. In mixed states I felt like I was being split between two emotional extremes and I would become extremely uncertain of what I felt as both extremes would be firing and competing at the same time. I'd still appear outgoing, even bubbly, yet an extreme negativity, self-doubt and fear would be in there too. Manic and depressive states may feel extreme yet so 'one colour' that they might give a feeling of relative stability compared to the experience of mixed states. In the grip of a mixed state, one feels incredibly unstable, fragmented and torn. When in this state I cannot cope at all with anyone around me who is also unstable, nor do I cope with taking on any new experiences. One of our greatest sources of security, I would say our greatest source of security, is in feeling we have some kind of stable emotional reality. When one is splitting into being two opposite extremes simultaneously, it is like shaking the foundations of a house. The house cannot feel supported until the foundations are again relatively settled.

I have been blessed in my chaos and my extremes to know a fluctuating life often of intense passions and only ever to have had one long-term severe experience with a depressive state, which lasted months at a time over a period of about two years. It is from this distant window that I reflect on some of the feelings and experiences of those in a more fixed, stable depressive state, and on the effect on communication, thinking, feeling and connection with one's body. The experience of acute shorter depressive episodes as part of rapid cycling bipolar felt quite different to the much longer depressive state. A deep and stable depression can be compelling enough to find no ripples and nothing that would inspire you to struggle back against it. In acute (perhaps dangerous) depressive episodes one lands with a crash and the feeling of acute instability still seems to hover like an aura. In the end only someone with unipolar depression can really speak on behalf of a reality only they have known, and I'm sure many lost speech and connection to their body as children slipping, unrecognised, into this state with it being labelled part of their Autism.

Mood disorders and health

Any form of severe chronic stress will eventually take its toll on the body. Some people are more vulnerable to physical breakdown. Some people are more vulnerable to mental breakdown. Some people are more vulnerable to emotional breakdown. The fact is that when we are under sustained chronic stress, something starts to give. For some this is sooner, for some this is later. To understand the greatest sources of chronic stress we must understand the greatest sources of security, for it is when that security is extremely undermined that we often experience the chronic stress.

We often falsely assume that the greatest source of security is others. But when we have an extremely unstable experience of reality or self, then external comfort has little place to connect and often can't help us. Sense of self is one of the most major foundations for internal security. Without it we might only be able desperately to cling to others, get 'lost' so we tune out to the problem or find release in rage or self-injury.

One of the most essential bases for a stable sense of self is having a reasonable level of consistent information processing. Another is having a reasonable level of calm in which we do not feel constantly on edge. This might break down in those with extreme anxiety disorders and certain personality disorders as well as some of those experiencing bipolar. Another is having a sense of connection to our body and voice through which we can experience selfhood expressed and connected in a flowing way to the external world. This might be an issue with those trapped because of severe anxiety disorders, particular personality disorders, severe dyspraxia, severe cases of Tourette's or OCD, or those suffering from severe depressive states. Another is having a tolerable level of emotional 'colour' and reasonably predictable levels of emotional fluctuation and flow to the degree that we can feel comfortable with life affecting us and experience some continuity of selfhood. This might break down in those with severe levels of something like rapid cycling childhood bipolar.

Any of these conditions left untreated might potentially progressively impact to some degree on gut/immune function and lead to a cycle of toxicity, inflammation, disturbed brain chemistry and an increase in challenges as the cycle continues.

Can people become addicted to their own chemistry?

There are several conditions of which constant adrenaline rushes are part. It is not enough to say these conditions are merely the result of imbalanced neurotransmitters, or that those imbalances might be aggravated, even in some cases caused, by underlying gut/immune issues. Part of the severity of a condition can also be shaped by how the environment responds to you in those states as you develop, but also how you embrace these conditions. These high-adrenaline states may become an integral part of your identity and sense of self or your view of the world and its relationship to you, and you may feel strange when *not* in the grip of these states.

Thyroid issues aside, some of us inherit a tendency to addictive patterns. This may be especially true of the children of carers with the same qualities and where children have been exposed to addiction before birth, but it is not limited to these people. It is not just environmental substances or foods we can become addicted to. We can also become hooked on our own chemistry extremes. The severity of a condition involving adrenaline addiction might, therefore, also depend on whether the child with that condition has become addicted to their own adrenaline. Behaviours, attitudes and beliefs all involve chemical processes. Some Auties who are addicted to certain chemical highs may in fact be overly predisposed to tune in to, or fixate on, the very experiences and behaviours that cause the types of arousal to produce these chemical highs. This is not to say that addiction to one's own chemical extremes alone could cause childhood bipolar, but it may be that those children with bipolar who are predisposed to addictive behaviours through inheritance, exposure or environmental modelling, where others in the family also struggle with these issues, might struggle more severely in managing their own bipolar patterns.

Perhaps the same is in fact true of unipolar depression. Adult Auties and Aspies I've spoken to have expressed that they were 'addicted' to their own depressive state. This is not to say all people with unipolar depression are like this, just that it can happen.

I remember speaking to someone who had had a mental breakdown who also said she had become drawn into the magical thinking of this state, almost like a drug. Those I've spoken to about these 'addictive' experiences with extreme mental/emotional states have expressed that there was a morbid curiosity with seeing how far or deep these things could go.

I have known this in myself of both manic and depressive states. In the manic state I wanted to get higher and higher regardless of the consequences (which was sensory pain, cognitive shutdown, a loss of control over my nervous system with regard to my body and utter blind panic). I have experienced the addictive call of withdrawal into such depth that I felt miles from my body and voice, and it is only once you become aware that what you gave into is a trap that you are at all able to do anything about it, if in fact you can.

Certainly environmental medicine is essential in the form of the modelling that's around you, but safely and sensibly changing things chemically for people so they are pulled out of such states regardless is sometimes the only solution when their own addiction to such states may run so counter to them helping themselves.

Presently in the Autism field there is a lot of emphasis on merely teaching people to act as if they don't have these issues. This type of compliance-based programme has its place, but using it as the only approach when dabbling with these challenging and serious issues is, in my view, folly. It merely drives the issues underground, where they sooner or later generally break through to the surface.

Reactive depression and the reality of 'damage'

Auties come from all kinds of background. It is a simple social fact that some of those backgrounds might involve carers with substance-abuse issues, carers with mood disorders, carers with personality disorders, families struggling with financial stress, lack of social supports, major childhood or background baggage of their own or be living with abusive partners.

There are some Autie children who have witnessed regular domestic violence or a parent suffering from emotional abuse or have experienced the loss of an essential carer at an important crossroad in development, or who have even been sexually, emotionally, psychologically or physically abused themselves. Autism should never be a label that leads people to believe abuse could never have happened, nor a reason for society to turn a blind eye assuming the Autism would somehow 'protect' the child from such experiences. Even if a child with Autism may not register these things consciously or express them outwards, children with Autism may still *feel* these patterns and be affected by them. Their Autism does not make them immune. We need to acknowledge that abused Auties exist. Depression, chronic anxiety, anxiety-related suppression of gut/immune function, sleep disorders or severe interruption to important neurological and developmental phases may have a range of possible causes and may all potentially contribute to exacerbating the severity of someone's Autism. All these things also have the potential to arise more commonly in children who have been severely abused. If these things occurred in someone already vulnerable to developing Autism, their Autism could, theoretically, be exacerbated or complicated by abuse and improved by addressing those challenges. This wouldn't make them any less 'truly Autistic' than any non-abused child with Autism. It is merely that different circumstances can combine to result in the same type of results and one of those circumstances, for some people, may be abuse.

Can mood disorders come and go?

Children with depressive states as part of childhood bipolar can continue to peak and trough – these episodes for one child may be once a year, for another several times a year, for another once a month or once a week, for another several times a week or several times a day. Some of these children may switch between one of these cycles and another. Some of the things which may trigger and affect cycling may include:

- experiences and levels of stimulation
- information overload
- heightened sense of social invasion
- marked changes in the structure of one's day or environment
- a build-up of unresolved issues
- dietary and hormone patterns
- fluctuations in immune/gut function and stored bugs
- some types of epileptic seizures.

Children can be taught to suppress the expression of a mood disorder to a degree; and, to a degree, some depressed children can be taught to behave socially, to initiate physical contact and to smile; to a degree, some kids with bipolar can be taught to behave like 'normal' children. None of this is to say the child who can supress the full-blown expression of their mood disorder can simply stop having a mood disorder at will or that the child doesn't continue to suffer inside or in the privacy of his or her own space.

Theoretically, children with unipolar depression that is not a reaction to experiences (rather being associated with brain or neurochemical differences) may be less able to learn to disguise, suppress or cover up this emotional state and its social-communication reality. Unlike those with bipolar who may have experienced the spectrum of emotional states or those with a reactive depression who knew a different emotional reality before they sunk into depression, those with a state akin to unipolar depression may have no such 'body memories' to draw on in expressing anything other than the more one-tone reality they have always known.

Treating mood disorders
Where to find help
If someone has developed a reactive depression following loss, abandonment or trauma, techniques like music therapy, art therapy, movement therapy and play therapy may be an important, non-invasive part of getting back in touch with one's body, mind, emotions, communication and the social world.

Some people can dare to type where they cannot dare to speak. Some do this through communication software using pictures that form sentences for them. Others progress to using word grids or letter boards. Some need a facilitator who physically supports them through the process of typing with the goal of progressively fading out that support. Some people with Autism progress through this avenue to relatively independent typing. Others do not. Therapists who advise in this include enlightened speech therapists and those in the field of facilitated communication.

If someone had a depressive or wildly fluctuating mood state as part of a personality disorder, then the environmental approach may need to be altered to better address the mood disorder and a form of counselling employed both for the carers in coping with these changes and for the person (perhaps through specially designed social stories) in presenting choices and consequences, dispelling emotional/social/psychological myths and introducing

new social patterns. Bach Flower Remedies may help address extreme personality states and some naturopaths deal with these (Bush Flower Essences are a
similar Australian product).

Taking the focus off the condition and putting energy into modelling
'doing things', 'being' and being 'silly' for one's own sake, instead of endless
wrangling in an environmental clash, may be even stronger medicine. The
therapists working in these areas can include some clinical psychologists and
cognitive behavioural psychologists. Hypnotherapists have helped some
carers with tackling their own co-dependency issues which might have a
positive flow-on effect on a child with personality issues affecting mood.
There are also hypnotherapists who have specialised in developing 'stories'
for people with personality disorders to help them consider and relate to new
patterns.

If someone has depression because of an impulse-control problem such as
OCD or Tourette's, then it is this that needs addressing through counselling
suitable to the person, management strategies for the condition, advocacy in
the community in raising awareness to make life easier, biofeedback, and
sometimes sensible medication appropriate to the underlying condition.
Some of the therapists working in this area might include neuropsychologists,
neuropsychiatrists and cognitive behavioural psychologists.

If someone's mood disorder is made worse because of information-
processing challenges, sensory issues, anxiety disorders, gut/immune issues
or lack of access to alternative communication devices, then the focus should
be on treating the underlying issues; there is a wealth of books covering
self-help approaches in these areas. There are specialists in gut/immune
disorders affecting those with Autism spectrum conditions, and most practise
'holistic' medicine, which combines natural and conventional approaches.

Sometimes, after the garden has been weeded, one can see what it left.
Some mood disorders can be treated through a combination of dietary interventions, nutritional supplements and sensible doses of medication appropriate to the type and nature of the mood disorder. Only psychiatrists are
qualified to prescribe conventional medication used in the treatment of mood
disorders, but they will usually not advise on dietary interventions or
supplementation, and most presently do not yet respect those who do.
Nobody should assume that medication will work for all people with mood
disorders or that medication alone is the only answer, because the underlying
causes can be many and only some of these respond to medication.

Can the environment be medicine?

The environment can certainly act as medicine to some degree in being part of how someone with a mood disorder will respond or function. Using the environmental approach to the best advantage, however, depends on the individual.

Those cast aside as 'unmanageable', 'disturbed' or 'too much hard work' will see themselves this way, and use this as a justification not to seek to manage their mood disorder or will assume such views are 'valid' and 'right' because those who make these judgements are more 'stable' and 'normal' than they are. They may assume only others can help or that there is no responsibility to help themselves because clearly they are assumed incapable of that job in the eyes of those so obviously more 'capable' than them. Others may use such assumptions as something to swing against and disprove the opinions of others by trying to manage, hide or seek help for their mood disorder and its related behaviours and issues.

Environments which constantly rescue or assume responsibility for an Autie's challenges may do that person no favours. Over-controlling someone who already feels out of control isn't good environmental medicine. If someone is withdrawing from the claws of forced compliance and so-called 'inclusion', what they may need instead are models who are getting on with their own focus, involved in their own lives, responsible for their own stuff in order to know what these emotional social realities even look like. There may be no point leading an Autie to a social-emotional reality you yourself are poorly modelling. So carers getting back into a sense of their own lives, their own interests, their own needs and personality may be very important, regardless of the chaos, because doing so may be part of facilitating the chaos slowly (when the heat is off) and progressively to subside.

Auties with mood disorders may be socially limited because carers become alienated from the community, afraid of looks and judgements, 'advice' or pity, embarrassment, shame and the isolation and guilt that goes with it. Introducing the Autie and their challenges to the community through an 'introduction card' (perhaps giving a website address for further information) may be part of seeing the community as less of a bogey man. This is so important because any child with mood disorders may need more than anything to feel understood for who they are and what their challenges are, and be accepted as an equal member of society in order to feel more than just their 'condition'. One can be 'different' yet feel so accepted for the person inside that they assume their 'differentness' is part of the 'normal' diversity of society in general and *that* is great environmental medicine. Those in the community who don't cope with this diversity can then more easily be explained as being 'attitude disabled'.

None of this means that environmental changes alone can cure a severe mood disorder, only that in some cases environmental issues can be part of a remedy or can stop other emotional, social or identity issues from making things get worse.

Mood disorders and specific behavioural issues

Mood disorders might underpin specific behaviours/issues relating to:

- communication
- being in one's own world
- eye contact
- learning and cognitive challenges
- toileting
- sleep problems
- stimming
- meltdowns
- self-protection responses
- challenging behaviours
- food behaviour problems.

Communication problems are frequent in people suffering from depression or depressive states. They are more likely to speak as little as possible and some will feel 'safer' disconnected from the world, so mutism is commonly associated with severe depressive states. Someone in a depressive phase of a bipolar disorder could also withdraw and be uncommunicative. Those with depressive states might also be likely to be less physically communicative, less animated in their communication on all levels, generally more passive as a communication participant and less independent in initiating. Communication topics in a depressive state may be more likely to fixate on anxieties, fears and worries.

Mania, by contrast, can involve such a racing of ideas, such an expansion of thoughts and feelings that someone may be unable to organise their language properly or keep track of it, may be relatively incoherent because of the speedy change from one topic to the next, speak non-stop with little regard for those on the receiving end, or seem to talk compulsively to themselves. In a manic state, passivity might be far harder, and independent initiations might be overwhelmingly disruptive. Communication topics in a state of mania may be quite different to those the person would have when in a more balanced mood state and may be more likely to fixate on a fierce topic of interest if not excitement. In rapid cycling bipolar it might be common for someone to switch from a manic to a depressive style of communication in a very sharp and sudden shift. Mixed states may also cause a mixture of the features of manic and depressive states in communication.

Extreme mood states, manic or depressive, can both give a feeling of *being in one's own world*. Depression can give a feeling one is inside oneself, cut off from the external world, removed, distant from it. Mania can give a feeling of urgency and a feeling of going very fast. Some people experience euphoria as though the usual, more mundane aspects of life become irrelevant or take on a level of major significance. As much as depression can make someone 'in their own world', so can mania and mixed states.

I was certainly quite a 'mood monster' as a child and my father would say he knew when I was about to go feral because my eyes would start 'flashing' about. The *eye contact* of someone in a manic state might be described as 'glowering' or 'distracted'. By contrast the eye contact of someone in a depressive state may appear 'lost', 'withdrawn' or 'avoidant'.

Depression is known to blunt sensory experiences and may be associated with sensory hyposensitivity. At the same time, those in depressive states may be more likely to feel intolerant of what they experience as intrusions or impositions, which could mean being more intolerant than others to intrusive sensory experiences. This could easily be mistakenly assumed to be the same as sensory hypersensitivity.

Mania, on the other hand, is generally associated with heightened sensory experiences. Those in manic or agitated, highly aroused states are more likely to seem to be hypersensitive to sensory experiences or to fluctuate sharply between hyper- and hyposensitive responses depending on the dominant mood state at a particular time.

Depression is associated with fear, anxiety and obsession, as well as intolerance, blunted affect and low motivation. None of these things are going to improve someone's orientation towards *learning*, or their learning capacity, or have them use their cognitive abilities to their greatest possible potential.

Mania is associated with distraction, agitation, aggression, even elation and fragmented thinking. It is hard to learn when you can't relax, can't sit still, can't pay attention, can't control yourself or are drawn towards far more captivating thoughts, feelings, actions and experiences than those in the learning situation, or are unable to hold information together or retain it. Someone with manic depression would experience a fluctuation between both of these extremes.

Regression is a symptom of sudden or severe depression and losing *toileting* skills may be one way regression can show itself. Depression is also about low levels of motivation and flattened affect, meaning that neither praise nor punishment may have much effect. In this context, depression might make it more difficult for a child to learn or care about attending to toileting needs. In a manic state, being highly distracted, strongly driven toward other more exciting and compelling tasks or simply being unable to organise or sequence the thoughts and actions involved in toileting may be more likely.

In general, depression is associated with low energy levels and *sleeping* during the day. Mania, by contrast, is usually associated with high (adrenaline-driven) energy levels and insomnia. Rapid cycling bipolar may have features of both of these.

People initiate *self-stimulatory behaviours* for all kinds of reasons and in all kinds of moods. One of those reasons may be to distract from or comfort oneself in the presence of feelings of fear or anxiety associated with depression. Another may be to break through a flat affect and hyposensitivity in order to experience something in spite of a depressive state.

Mania is a high-energy state which can be unpredictable, over-arousing, uncomfortable and a place of hypersensitivity and agitation. It is equally possible that some people will involve themselves in more self-stimulatory behaviours to comfort themselves in an approaching state of mania, and others will use these same self-stimulatory behaviours to reach a manic high.

Whilst mood may play a big part in self-stimulatory behaviours, the particular way this manifests itself will be different with each person. On the one hand, the flattened affect associated with depression may mean less appearance of *meltdowns* and a greater tendency to implode rather than show these problems more outwardly. On the other hand, depression is associated with greater rigidity and inflexibility and a lower ability to tolerate intrusions so this could increase meltdowns.

Mania is a more energetic, sometimes aggressive, perhaps more agitated, more fragmented and hypersensitive state, so meltdowns might equally be increased in manic episodes as they might, for different reasons, be increased in depressive ones.

Depression can involve a natural *self-protection response* in withdrawal. Mania, because of its extremity, unpredictability, loss of control and potential to create a feeling of fragmentation, might also cause self-protection responses to trigger in those personalities who fear these things or the social consequences they might bring, such as the over-involvement or external control by others.

Hypo- and hypersensitivity associated with depressive or manic states might increase some *challenging or self-injurious behaviours* where people fail to notice or care about self-injury or self-injure in response to agitation, distress, despair or being emotionally overwhelmed with mood extremes. Extreme reactions to social invasion may be more extreme with people in a depressive or manic state, and fixation on the extreme lows of something bothering you can escalate quickly and dangerously to absolute extremes in a sudden depressive swing within a general bipolar condition. The extreme self-protection of someone in a depressive state and the extreme high energy of someone in an agitated manic state mean that some challenging behaviours may be more extreme in those with untreated mood disorders.

Depression is associated with reduced appetite as well as with comfort eating. Hyposensitivity, low levels of self-care and rigidity and preference for the familiar when in a depressed state may mean that someone's *eating behaviours* when depressed are quite different to how they would be when not depressed. By contrast, those in a manic state may be more energetic in how they pursue and attack food and some will happily devour food in a manic state whilst others will be too distracted or feel little appetite and may sail through the day without noticing they are hungry. Specific eating disorders, including anorexia, binge eating and bulimia, can be associated with mood problems.

CHAPTER 7

Invisible Cages

Anxiety Issues

A traveller came across four beasts during her travels through the city, the forest and the jungle. The first beast was running and running but the traveller could see nothing chasing the beast. The second beast seemed distracted, almost drawing attention to itself before flitting off to another point and doing the same. The third beast suddenly charged at the traveller though she had done nothing to provoke it. The fourth beast simply played dead and it was only until well after the traveller had passed that she realised it had been real.

Anxiety issues occurring in Autism spectrum conditions can be divided into two groups: primary and secondary; but almost all anxiety responses can be broadly categorised into avoidance, diversion, retaliation or freezing.

Some examples of primary anxiety disorders and secondary anxiety states follow.

Primary:

- exposure anxiety
- social phobia/social anxiety disorder
- selective mutism
- avoidant personality
- separation anxiety disorder
- generalised anxiety disorder
- panic disorder

- post-traumatic stress disorder
- phobias.

Secondary:

- anxiety due to overload/sensory issues
- anxiety due to impulse-control issues
- anxiety due to untreated mood disorders
- anxiety to do with environmental issues
- anxiety associated with other personality issues.

Primary anxiety disorders

Exposure anxiety

Exposure anxiety (EA) is my own term for the anxiety disorder I lived with all my life. Since I wrote *Exposure Anxiety: The Invisible Cage* (Williams 2002) many very relieved people have written to me thanking me for finally describing this experience they also shared but were unable to communicate about.

Exposure anxiety is an involuntary self-protection mechanism. Whilst many people with avoidant personality disorder might relate strongly to the experiences of those with exposure anxiety, they have their differences. Similarly, exposure anxiety may share impulse-control problems with pathological demand avoidance syndrome except that those with what I see as severe true EA struggle to follow through with their own simple desires when the only person demanding anything of them is themselves. It is for this reason that I see there is true EA and other EA-like conditions. I see true EA as best described as a kind of emotional equivalent of cerebral palsy, a state where intentions and desires cause involuntary blocking of actions, exacerbated by additional heightened stimulation, such as exposure before others. It is because of this that I see true EA as most likely caused by a potentially treatable underlying imbalance in brain chemistry.

Exposure anxiety can be like taking severe shyness and multiplying it by 50, even though, at first glance, many people with exposure anxiety may appear far from shy because exposure anxiety can equally compel you to divert attention and retaliate without apparent provocation. It can make it difficult to dare 'expressive volume' in a directly confrontational (self in relation to other) world whose culture is geared towards making you notice you have noticed: something they call communicating, sharing and interacting.

Exposure anxiety can be about feeling your own existence too close up, too in your own face, so it can cause you to have an instinctual involuntary aversion to conscious awareness and responsibility for your own expression.

As with conditions like agoraphobia, the more the person themselves leaves their exposure anxiety unchallenged or reactively over-challenged, the more it can become hard to stay motivated to initiate speaking or looking, to express a need or want, to share an interest or even dare to stay aware that you have one.

For some people, exposure anxiety can create such an emotional obstacle to connection to mind or body that they 'can't do for themselves', 'can't do as themselves', or 'can't do by themselves'.

Fighting back against one's own severe chronic fight-flight states isn't easy either. Pushing beyond the limits of what their own self-protection response can withstand as 'threat of exposure' or 'threat of inviting invasion', exposure anxiety can result in, and heighten, islands of involuntary aversion, diversion and retaliation responses. For some people, this is a permanent state across all situations. For others, the exposure anxiety targets specific activities, places, situations, people. So one can have less, even no, exposure anxiety in one situation, for example, but be crippled by it in another.

Exposure anxiety is not something foreign. It affects us all to some degree, and that's the key word, 'degree'. We all have known a height of excruciating self-consciousness that compels us to pull away, divert attention, or retaliate as though we would otherwise suffocate. Everything that occurs in Autism occurs to a degree under certain conditions in those who are not Autistic. The difference is simply degree and frequency.

The degree and frequency of attacks of exposure anxiety affect everything. It affects how we appear, how we experience the world, how we experience ourselves and it affects how our personality, language, behaviour and social-emotional skills develop through adaptations within our prison and between the spaces made by the bars.

Exposure anxiety can be a disabling, acute, chronic and persistent fight-flight state. In exposure anxiety, the focus of this adrenaline-driven state becomes fixated upon self-protection of one's own world. That means there is a fierce, instant, pre-conscious compulsion to protect oneself against loss of control and the initiations of others to 'invade' – which they call communicating and sharing. Exposure anxiety can fixate on one's own initiations where these threaten to invite in the initiation of outsiders to 'invade', such as eye contact, initiating verbal communication or even allowing people to see what one is capable of doing.

Exposure anxiety is much more about anti-motivations than motivations. A person with severe, chronic exposure anxiety can be desperate to communicate, yet the self-protection avoidance, diversion or retaliation responses may be so strong and quick that they beat the person out of the starting gate every time. Essentially, the anti-motivation caused by the self-protection response overrides whatever other motivations the person has to 'join the world'. Those who do manage some degree of functioning or freedom from their exposure anxiety usually do so by engaging one of the rules: 'can't do it as myself', 'can't do it by myself', 'can't do it for myself'. In terms of communication this may mean they may be able to communicate using a put-on voice or that of a TV character, or through singing, or as a copy of you, but not as themselves. It may mean they can communicate as long as they have their special object or special person with them, or as long as you are doing it too; but they won't stand alone in their own expression (unless of course there is no threat of exposure, such as no one watching, waiting, wanting). It can mean the person with exposure anxiety may be able to communicate in some way to the prompt for a compliant response, for to do so is not to do 'for oneself', or in helping someone or something perceived as less capable, but then will return to the exposure anxiety state when expected to initiate communication on their own behalf when in the perceived proximity or company of others.

One of the keys to reducing exposure anxiety as a tool to expanding communication is that of reducing any aggravating sources of stress. This can mean manipulating brain chemistry directly through small doses of a medication appropriate to the problem (and there is much overdosing and use of drugs not appropriate to the condition underlying someone's autism-related issues). It can mean tweaking dietary issues such as food allergies, intolerances, fungal infections, immune deficiencies, nutrient deficiencies and basically taking away the aggravating burdens that can contribute to imbalances in brain chemistry in some people. It can mean environmentally reducing information overload in those people who are also severely mono with delayed information processing so they can begin to lower their general stress levels. Often, reducing exposure anxiety means getting out of these people's faces and finding ways to be more cat-like, aloof, playing hard to get and self-owning in our social communication with someone with exposure anxiety, and less dog-like, watching/waiting/wanting, desperate to 'invade' (i.e. rescue, save, help, prove, join, 'share', 'care', 'love'). Environmentally reducing exposure anxiety means becoming less and self-in-relation-to-other with people in a severe fight-flight state. In other words, learn to speak the language and build bridges instead of exacerbating the person's involuntary war. If you charge at the gates, the prison warder just strengthens the gates and the person being overprotected inside is then even more heavily imprisoned.

One of the problems with current applied behavioural analysis, and unfortunately also in some conventional speech therapy approaches is that when it is used in this very dog-like way with those with severe, chronic exposure anxiety it can drive this deeper, making the condition worse. Instead of being nonchalant, self-owning and 'fly on the wall', they are too often clearly eager, very self-in-relation-to-other in their social-emotional style and rather 'bull at a gate'. Unfortunately, rather than blaming the lack of fit of the approach itself, often the person's Autism is blamed and the person merely labelled 'low-functioning' or said to be regressing.

Social phobia/social anxiety disorder

Social anxiety centres around fear of social embarrassment or humiliation. Like most phobias, realising the fear is exaggerated or irrational doesn't make it disappear. As a result, those with social anxiety disorder avoid the places, situations or encounters with people where these things may happen and, as a result, reduce their inclusion with others. This may reach the point where, without treatment and sticking to countering this condition on a day-to-day basis, it can interfere with development in general, and also jeopardize education, employment and relationships.

Social anxiety disorder can be a crippling condition which can condemn people to loneliness and social isolation. They may be unable to eat in front of others, initiate or join in in a conversation, unable to ask for help, seek service in a shop, cope with social get-togethers or cope with being asked a question or getting attention in class. They may be gripped with nausea and feel physically ill at the threat of such things, experience palpitations and sweat as if facing a life-threatening situation. There is a large crossover with selective mutism and many children with social anxiety disorder may be unable to communicate at all in social situations or even be extremely inhibited in the ability to use gesture to disclose their thoughts and feelings in these situations. Many will have other anxiety disorders along with social anxiety disorder. On my mother's side of the family there have been a number of women with agoraphobia. Whilst alone these things are not Autism, perhaps such an inheritance may be part of a collective package that comes together with other things in some people's autism.

Treatment may involve cognitive behavioural therapy, in which small steps are negotiated in very gradually, reality-testing the basis for the anxiety and helping the person prove to themselves they can calm themselves and overcome the anxiety. This is not always possible, is time-consuming and, unless covered by health insurance, may be expensive if accessible at all. Not all cases will respond to such therapy and many people will turn to small doses of appropriate medication to help someone get a grip on an anxiety disorder. Certainly, it may be self-defeating to treat the someone's anxiety disorder if their carer is continuing to have one themselves, which reinforces the old patterns.

The incidence of social phobia is different in different countries and most of the diagnoses and studies are done on adults. However, it has been found in children and is thought to be noticeable from around 12 months of age. Because diagnosis is usually in adults, the incidence in adults is naturally reported as higher and social anxiety disorder seems to be reported to appear later in some people than in others. Whilst it may be noticeable in some children from 12 months old, there may be others for whom the onset isn't noticeable until they are toddlers, and others who might not develop it until school age. Nevertheless, just acknowledging that this may be part of someone's Autism 'fruit salad' empowers us to bring in the strategies to reduce the burden this might have on social and communication skills, development and inclusion. The underlying causes of social phobia and social anxiety disorder are considered to be a combination of inheritance and environment.

Environmental factors include things which diminish confidence in emotionally hypersensitive children, including speech or language problems, mobility or gait problems or physical disfigurement, and there is a higher incidence of speech and language problems in those with social anxiety disorder than other groups. A dual diagnosis of Asperger's syndrome and social anxiety disorder is not uncommon.

Experiences of acute social embarrassment such as vomiting or wetting oneself in public are also believed to contribute to the onset of social anxiety disorder in some children. Traumatising experiences can certainly cause things like post-traumatic stress disorder so we shouldn't be surprised if a significant percentage of those diagnosed with social anxiety disorder have also suffered abuse (including humiliation) or neglect. It is, however, equally feasible that particularly children with social anxiety disorder may be more likely than others to become targets of abusers and bullies. There will, however, also be many where the anxiety disorder can't be accounted for in this way. In researching my father's side of the family I met with a cousin my father had once described as being 'like me'. I met with her and she certainly had severe challenges as a child, barely able to dare speak or look at other children, but grew up to have a family and go to work (though still felt very socially anxious). She went on to describe her mother as a woman struggling to leave the house, who at times couldn't even dare to walk to the letter box. On my mother's side one of my aunts reported that there were several women on that side who she felt had been 'agoraphobic'. It is easy to imagine how hard it might have been for those in their environments who were more assertive and socially confident. There are abusive people of all kinds and people tend to abuse what they can't relate to, empathise with or understand. Unempathic people occur in families with and without children with anxiety disorders. It wouldn't be surprising to sometimes find both social anxiety/social phobia and abuse occurring in the same families, although one could clearly exist without the other.

Some social environments are considered more likely to contribute to the development of social anxiety disorder in children, such as growing up with very socially anxious, nervous carers, which may be a combination of genetics and social patterning.

By contrast with exposure anxiety, those with social phobia may be outwardly less physically hyperactive, excitable or manic. Whilst both groups may be highly agitated or distressed, those with social phobia may be more likely than those with exposure anxiety to be described as withdrawn, irritable and lonely. Those with social phobia may also differ from those with exposure anxiety in that they may respond better to gentle praise and encouragement whereas for many with the over-stimulation of exposure anxiety, this may be felt as an 'invasion' and may lead to the person doing even less of what the environment desires. Whilst exposure anxiety seems to me more common in those with bipolar states and impulse control disorders such as Tourette's, I feel it also has a personality component to it. Whilst I feel it's more common in those with the solitary and avoidant personality types, people with those types don't always have what I'd recognise as exposure anxiety. As social phobia is more common in those with solitary and avoidant personlity types it would be reasonable then to assume that one person can have both exposure anxiety and social phobia and certainly I would identify with both issues and have seen some clients with one, other or both.

Selective mutism

Back in 1934, before Autism was known about, the term 'elective mutism' was coined by an English doctor by the name of Trammer. It was used to refer to children who had acquired speech but stopped using it around the ages of three to five years old. At the time it was seen as a wilful and oppositional response on the part of the child. Today, the term 'elective mutism' has been generally been replaced by that of 'selective mutism' with the cause attributed to anxiety.

Website information on this condition varies wildly with reports of 'elective mutism' affecting up to one per cent of school-aged children, whilst other websites, referring to 'selective mutism', estimate that this occurs in as few as 1 in every 10,000. Some websites exclude those with Autism as being capable of having selective mutism on the basis that language disorders in Autism are seen as purely information-processing or motor-planning issues, whereas those in selective mutism are seen as a form of anxiety disorder. Other sites appear to contradict this, stating that as many as 69 per cent of people with selective mutism will have a developmental delay, and that whilst half of all children with selective mutism will begin speaking, some with and some without therapy, another half will still be selectively mute by secondary school.

Sites also differ in the degree of selective mutism, with some sites stating that these children almost always retain speech at home though are unable to use speech outside of the home. Other sites mention that a minority of those with selective mutism will progressively expand the numbers of people they are unable to communicate with.

Regarding gesture, again the sites differ. People with selective mutism are described on some sites as being able to use pointing and gesture to indicate needs, but elsewhere cases are described as so severe that they also restrict the child's ability to gesture in social situations or that the only use of gesture will be eye 'pointing' (the use of the eye to indicate a need), a nod or a smile. Difficulty sustaining eye contact is very common in this group.

Anxiety disorders are cited as extremely high in this group with some sites suggesting that up to 70 per cent of this group also qualify for a diagnosis of social phobia, a condition common to those with the solitary and sensitive personality traits. Similarly, a high number of those with selective mutism (reportedly associated with the sensitive/avoidant personality) have been treated with antidepressants and anti-anxiety medications and regained speech. This perhaps indicates that depression is also more common in this group and in fact the associated conditions reported as commonly occuring in those with the sensitive/avoidant personality traits include depression (whereas bipolar is more commonly associated with the artistic/cyclothymic personality which also has a solitary component to it).

According to some sites, selective mutism is also believed to run in families with a common incidence of another relative with the same condition. The incidence is cited as slightly higher in girls than boys but it may be that this is clouded by the greater likelihood that boys with the condition receive a diagnosis in the Autism spectrum instead, and that girls with an Autism spectrum condition are diagnosed instead with social phobia or selective mutism, on the basis that these conditions are expected more commonly in girls. Clearly, the field of selective mutism is still very much settling into its shoes. There are some websites which support the idea that the severe anxiety experienced by some people with selective mutism can in fact amount to a physical inability to speak caused by a primal fight-flight response. In an article titled *Mutism, Elective Mutism, Selective Mutism* authored by Svea Gold (2003), she looks at these conditions in terms of infantile reflexes. As we grow up, earlier reflexes are meant to become 'inhibited' to make way for progression to other reflexes which help us with later stages of development. Svea Gold found in working with selective mutism that a reflex – called the Moro reflex – involved in the 'freeze' reaction when faced with a threat, was still too present. She referred to it as a kind of 'fear paralysis'.

What is clear is that *many* Auties have severe motor-planning problems affecting the ability to articulate sounds to make up words or have receptive language processing problems. Any of these can mean a failure to develop language, but an emotionally hypersensitive child with a mistrust of a function that does not work easily, or is not like that of others, is more likely than others to develop an additional social-emotional inhibition in using it. In other words, certain personalities will cope better on a social-emotional level with overcoming language impairment than others.

A very large percentage of Auties also suffer from anxiety disorders, so it is not impossible that a child with Autism might progress in the capacity to acquire verbal language only to be then blocked by something like selective mutism. Certainly, selective mutism could easily be a feature of those with exposure anxiety or avoidant personality – conditions perhaps more common to those on the Autistic spectrum than the general population.

It is also the case that around one third of children with Autism do use verbal speech and the majority of Aspies have a relatively normal pattern of language development. Yet some verbal children do progressively become mute before being diagnosed as Autistic. In my consulting work in the last ten years I'd say this accounts for between half to one third of all the children with Autism I have seen. Most in this group were described as having a few words before losing speech, but some were described as being able to speak in whole clearly articulated sentences, using words as complex to pronounce as 'chocolate'. Most were described as losing speech around the age of two to three. I also met one child who became selectively mute around the age of three but lost speech entirely at the age of five after a family break-up and house move. I met another who began to become selectively mute at the age of five after starting in a playgroup, which extended to complete mutism at home with speech coming back intermittently after several weeks only to disappear again. I met one who had lost speech as late as seven years old after developing a stutter which progressively got worse. This person acquired typed communication at 17 (with much opposition from the special school) and communicated that it was the progressive grip of anxiety that made him mute. Today he is in a mainstream secondary college. All of these people were diagnosed with Autism.

Some people diagnosed Autistic who will only dare to whisper almost inaudibly with their reflection or under their breath to themselves, may in fact have selective mutism, not choosing to be socially mute, but unable to overcome severe anxiety and internal anti-motivations which counter the often extreme motivation to communicate interpersonally. And if we can accept this of those known to whisper or mutter to themselves, it is not a far leap to imagine there may be others for whom similar dynamics, though of a more severe degree, are at work who can not even dare to do that.

Contrary to the 'bull-at-a-gate' forced eye contact, overt pressure and expectation to speak currently used in most ABA (applied behaviour analysis) programmes with those with Autism, the recommendations in working with those with selective mutism involve employing an indirectly confrontational approach similar to that recommended by me in *Exposure Anxiety: The Invisible Cage* (Williams 2002) in working with those with exposure anxiety. Essentially this means being low key, playing hard-to-get, keeping things in small doses, leaving the person wanting, and being involved as though for our own rather than the child's benefit. Perhaps we would get so much further if we saw Autism as an umbrella term and began tackling the variety of elements that that umbrella is comprised of.

So where there is no obvious sign of degenerative disease in those with the demonstrated capacity to use verbal speech who progressively become mute, we might at least consider what the field of selective mutism has to offer us in terms of its own experience of what works and what doesn't, and use the memories of those adults who recovered from the condition. Why put all Auties into one basket when they may have extremely different speech therapy needs? Why re-invent the wheel when there are others outside of the Autism field who have been working on this issue since the 1930s? Who is to say they don't have much they might teach us?

If selective mutism is common in children with excessive shyness and fear of embarrassment, school phobias and depression, who may communicate only non-verbally or in a whisper, or only with one or two familiar people, and if a high percentage in this group also have developmental delays – how might this account for some people who were originally diagnosed with Autism as non-verbal infants but later re-diagnosed with Asperger's syndrome as adults? How many of these people had avoidant or schizoid personality and selective mutism? And if this really was the guts of their condition how much better could we have helped them had we known what was really going on under those labels?

Avoidant personality

Avoidant personality disorder is an extreme personality trait or type, and the jury is still out as to whether avoidant personality disorder and social phobia are the same thing or whether they simply often co-occur in the same people.

There may be some cases where avoidant personality disorder is at least partially underpinned by an untreated depressive state associated with low seratonin, and social phobia may sometimes be a product of an anxiety state (without mania) such as high adrenaline levels responsible for acute stress. Where high levels of noradrenaline are associated with mania and fight-flight states, and are likely at work in exposure anxiety, high levels of adrenaline are associated with acute stress but not mania.

Where someone has digestive, immune or metabolic disorders, imbalance in these important brain chemicals can occur in a range of combinations and there is no reason why some people can't have one or a combination of these imbalances or even fluctuations between them. Where these combine with dopamine irregularities, such a condition would be further compounded by impulse-control problems such as those seen in Tourette's and OCD. Enough of these straws on the camel's back in infancy may severely affect development on a range of levels to the degree that a child is labelled Autistic.

The possibilities of untreated depression aside, people with avoidant personality appear to be 'natural' introverts. As a consequence, they may find the world too socially invasive and emotionally demanding, and find it extremely challenging to understand why others may be so motivated to have them join them in their world. At first glance they may appear shy, withdrawn or passive, and they are often the target of bullies. Because of their aloof, withdrawn nature, some carers can be driven to over-protect such people, speaking on their behalf to the degree that the person is progressively released from the burden of having to communicate socially for themselves. (Perhaps such dynamics may account for why avoidant personality disorder and dependent personality often co-occur.) When expected to interact socially, they may take this as a totally unreasonable, even emotionally incomprehensible, expectation. Some may be so hypersensitive to unwanted social invasion that they may even find expectations that they learn to communicate and interact akin to being assaulted.

Avoidant personality is often found in people with depression, and when the depression is treated the person often begins to open up and find the social and communication intrusions and expectations of others more tolerable. In fact, if it weren't for the label 'Autistic', a therapist faced with someone with the chemistry of a person with clinical depression might half expect to find someone who was hard to motivate, rigid and resistant to accommodating new experiences, generally intolerant of attempts to engage socially or excite them, and generally rather uncommunicative or initiating, as having clinical depression.

Avoidant personality can involve dynamics of avoidance, diversion and retaliation responses, and many people with avoidant personality may respond well to the strategies used for exposure anxiety. Avoidant personality differs, however, from exposure anxiety in a number of ways.

My experience of what I call exposure anxiety is, I believe, associated with high levels of noradrenaline. High levels of noradrenaline are associated with manic, agitated, excitable, overstimulated, hyperactive states. Depression as the underlying feature in avoidant personality is associated with the opposite, low levels of noradrenaline; so perhaps this is why we might see a more sombre, passive, inactive state. At this point the picture may be more complicated as there may be no reason why one person might not fluctuate between these two extremely uncomfortable states. For example, in the case of rapid cycling childhood bipolar (manic depression) we see someone who sharply swings between both states anywhere between every few months and up to as frequently as every 45 minutes. So the two might occur separately, where one would treat either mania or depression as the underlying state, or in the same person where one would treat a general manic-depressive mood disorder, in that case with mood stabilisers. To give antidepressants or stimulants to the wrong person could do more harm than good, and the medication prescribed may depend on how the person presents during the appointment!

Avoidant personality also contrasts with exposure anxiety in the underlying causes of the avoidance, diversion and retaliation responses. In avoidant personality, these responses to the social initiations of others are more likely caused by the introverted and withdrawn state in which these are found as unwarranted social invasions and the acute fear that one will be expected to try something new in which one may fail, be imperfect or feel embarrassment.

In exposure anxiety, avoidance, diversion and retaliation responses are usually a natural response to protect oneself when already in a highly *overstimulated* state. In other words, the person may have already had so much more emotional and sensory stimulation than their body can withstand that these social initiations are seen as almost 'life-threatening'. Exposure anxiety is an animal instinct with a sticky switch and has nothing to do with fear of failure, fear of embarrassment or imperfection.

These two conditions differ in another way as well. The person in a manic state may well be overly empathic to the point where they pick up too extremely on the feelings of others and self-protect against them. A person with avoidant personality, who may suffer simultaneously from acute stress and anxiety, may also be so 'alerted' they may sense pattern acutely. If the same person also had high levels of dopamine, such as may happen in someone who also has Tourette's or OCD, they may also be extremely acute in picking up pattern. However, the person with avoidant personality who does not have high dopamine nor an acute anxiety state, yet has unipolar, may find it challenging to pick up on the feelings of others at all and may often be seen to be lacking 'naturally acquired' empathy (though can still learn it mentally and become good at behaving empathically). To further complicate the picture, someone with underlying childhood bipolar may fluctuate between an exposure anxiety state during manic phases and an avoidant personality state, with or without acute anxiety, during depressive phases. Where avoidant personality and exposure anxiety fluctuate in the same person, it may be a matter of stabilising the mood state (and there may be many dietary and nutritional avenues for doing this in addition to the option of minimal appropriate medication) as well as addressing any family and environmental social dynamics which compound this pattern of reactions. But first, in order to do any of this, we must recognise which states are at work at which times. If we are blinded by the idea that Autism is one distinct thing we may be very limited in doing this.

Separation anxiety disorder

Separation anxiety disorder is the fear of being separated from one's carers at an age when a child would normally have been expected to have outgrown this. There are certainly some cases of Autism where constant verbal or non-verbal questioning of where the parent is and when the parent will be back come to dominate a large chunk of behaviour management. I have visited some children in class where about 30–70 per cent of the child's speech or interactions throughout the school day, *every* day will be about seeking repeated constant reassurances relating to where the parent is and when the parent will be back. That's a big distraction from learning and focusing on other experiences, tasks and topics of communication and inter-action. My own view is that some Autistic children develop their primary trust and social connection with their reflection. Being removed from their reflec-tion and made to sit with others may be enough to inhibit them dramatically. Some, however, may begin to learn, relax and chatter when the mirror image is brought back into the social environment among others, allowing them to relax again, yet still remain in company with other people.

And this behaviour may not be merely about separation anxiety. It might equally be about distracting the teacher from taking them down any new path. It might also be about distress relating to home or the fear of being removed from the home (and a number of Auties must have had such fears prior to going into residential care or respite). In spite of significant informa-tion-processing challenges, and in spite of an inability to control their issues, some people may still be able to physically sense themselves to be a source of stress, a burden, the source of a parent's dissatisfaction and 'grief' that they are not 'normal'. This is very much the essence of the wonderful piece by Jim Sinclair (who is diagnosed with Autism) entitled 'Don't Mourn For Us' (Sinclair 1993).

There may be other cases where separation anxiety is not about fear of abandonment but about loss of power. If someone is accustomed to running the show at home and finds him or herself unable to have the same control and power at school, in a day programme or in residential care, then the person may be bound to fixate on getting back to the carer the person has control over.

There may be cases where someone has dependent personality and through playing on self-convinced 'incapability' manipulates the carer into taking full responsibility for him or her. It is imaginable that such a person might not only be distressed at being in an environment which does not allow them to 'get away with this' but also fear the loss of control over the carer during the time the carer is not directly being made to care for them. It may be possible, for example, that the carer will develop other interests, other contacts, even ones which compete for care or convince the carer to break with the current highly co-dependent pattern. The carer might have developed a relationship with a new partner, taken moves towards doing something purely for himself or herself, even been busy with arranging for someone else to take over the care for a while. For a person with separation anxiety disorder this fear could be compelling, even overwhelming.

Separation anxiety might arise as a result of real events involving previous separations and getting used to these is a normal part of becoming a healthy independent adult. Separations can be done in sudden and unpredictable ways which a person experiences as an extreme shock and threat of loss. Sometimes these things are inevitable. Sometimes separations can be done in a way that makes them an adventure with enough threads of familiarity to avoid panic. If an Autie has to stay away from home, keeping the same sheets, having the same clothes, using the same washing powder or smells, seeking to maintain other fragments of sensory or structural familiarity and, where possible, low-key pre-visits to become familiar in which user-friendly experiences help the person make good associations, may help make these experiences of separation less traumatic. But an Autie may also pick up on the anxiety and insecurity of the carer. If the carer is worried and beside themselves, an Autie may sense instability and a feeling of threat. So there is much that carers can do to get a grip on their own patterns as part of environmental medicine in helping those in their care.

Separation anxiety might also arise where someone has witnessed violence or abuse towards the main carer or where the main carer is overly emotionally or socially entangled with the person in their care. There are some carers who, understandably, have become overly entangled with the person in their care after escaping abusive relationships. There are also carers who, for other reasons, are very emotionally needy if not unstable, who have substance abuse issues, anxiety disorders, mood disorders, personality disorders or mental health issues and rely heavily on the person in their care needing them in order to have a reason to live or feel self-worth in society. Though someone may not intellectually and consciously be able to process or understand such things, we are all essentially animals and our bodies feel patterns of those close to us. Even those who are clearly incapable of helping may, at a gut level, feel extremely emotionally responsible for an unstable or disabled carer and feel a great anxiety when separated. Co-dependency in carers produces co-dependency in those they care for and this may well be taken as separation anxiety.

Obsessive thoughts can be a common part of both OCD and obsessive-compulsive personality. In OCD fears of the death or accident of someone close to you are one of the most common compulsive thoughts. It is theoretically possible that some people with separation anxiety disorder who also display traits of either of these other conditions may compulsively manifest the very thoughts that provoke anxiety underpinning separation anxiety.

Generalised anxiety disorder

People with generalised anxiety disorder remind me of the story of Chicken Little who was in a fluster because he thought the sky was falling. These people seem addicted to worry and will wind themselves up almost compulsively over one thing after another to the point that they may have very real physical signs of anxiety, including bowel problems, headaches, vomiting, dizziness and stomach pains.

Getting a grip on this disorder is like trying to tame a wild horse. If you are overwhelmed and just watch it do its thing, you are not going to be able to tame it. If you learn that it is your horse to take charge of, that nobody else but you actually can, then you have the foundations for practising self-calming strategies and 'reality testing' to help alleviate this terrible condition.

If you live in an environment where your carers are either constantly in the same kind of worried tizz or so constantly trying to calm you down that it actually makes you fixate even more on all the worries, then their getting a grip is likely to be essential for you to help yourself. The middle ground is that, instead of being either equally wound up or running to the rescue, they can behave in a low-key, almost blasé way, strong, steady, calm and self-owning, which can instil a feeling that these minor issues are basically not noticeable. This is akin to The Emperor's New Clothes where everyone acted as if the Emperor was wearing new clothes even though it was clear he was actually nude.

It may also be that some people feel understimulated, so are compelled to create a sense of chaos and melodrama where there was none, and that some people who are already highly overstimulated may be acutely sensitive to patterns which may lead to anxieties.

Whilst generalised anxiety disorder will certainly affect people who do not have personality disorders, it may be possible that those with certain personality disorders may be more prone to worry, over-concern or manifesting justifications to excuse them out of social inclusion or self-sufficiency, control others or make themselves the centre of attention. People with information-processing or sensory-perceptual problems, mood, compulsive or personality disorders are already more likely than others to feel destabilised by these things and perhaps more susceptible to these kinds of anxiety disorder.

Panic disorder

Panic disorder is a condition involving regular panic attacks. Panic attacks can involve sudden adrenaline rushes which hit for no obvious reason, but the result is that these give the person the feeling that something terrible is about to happen, they put the body into a fight-flight state. One of the problems with panic disorder is not the panic episodes themselves but the psychological, emotional and social impact these can have when one begins to fear being in any public space beyond one's control where these things might suddenly occur. So the panic disorder may begin to take over the person's life in the sense of it being 'a fear of fear itself'.

Imagine that you had experienced these overwhelming panic attacks in your own home and been unable in these blind panic states to think or communicate. Imagine how you might then feel standing on the platform of a train station about to enter a crowded carriage and suddenly gripped with dread that you might end up having one of these unexpected panic attacks whilst on the train. You perhaps imagine that others might seek to help you and that you might strike out at them, that you might even try to jump from the moving train without thinking just in order to escape whilst in the grip of a feeling that something terrible is about to happen. Just thinking about this possibility, your train might arrive but instead you might leave the station and simply go home. Imagine how you might feel about to embark on a new course that you'd looked forward to, but then you gradually start to fear that you might have such a panic attack during one of the classes and be completely out of control like a wild, frightened animal. You might think to yourself, 'I could never dare to go back, I'd be so worried, so ashamed, I wouldn't be able to explain.' Perhaps you'd simply back out of the course or fail to show up. Eventually, you may find that the only place you feel safe with the possibility of panic attacks is within your own home. You may feel nobody else would understand these and wish for everyone to leave you alone, for the only person you might trust in that state is yourself, if even that.

It is easy to see how panic disorder might underpin progressive agoraphobia for some people, and how socially limiting it might be.

Severe reactive hypoglycemia is a condition of sudden plummeting of blood sugar levels which can provoke sudden adrenaline rushes and bring on panic attacks. Some people may have these in response to food allergies within 20 minutes of having something they are allergic to. Some may have this as part of type 2 diabetes. Some will develop it as part of severe candida and leaky gut. The good news is that severe reactive hypoglycemia is relatively treatable and manageable in many cases. Supplements like glutamine and chromium are used in regulating blood sugar. There are diets which address allergies and food intolerances that reduce the incidence of hypoglycemic attacks, and diets which help maintain more stable long-lasting regular blood sugar balance.

Mania in bipolar is another condition which might suddenly provoke adrenaline highs and lead to states of panic. Omega 3 fish oils, low-salicylate diet and some types of mood-levelling medications are things which have been used by those with bipolar dynamics.

The Bach Flower Remedy combination called 'Rescue Remedy' is also used in acute panic attacks and has helped some people with panic disorder. Some people will try hypnotherapy or cognitive behavioural therapy, or try biofeedback and learn and practise self-calming techniques. Others may need a combination of approaches, sometimes including small doses of appropriate medication.

Post-traumatic stress disorder

When we think of post-traumatic stress disorder many people think of victims of war, hostage victims, victims of violent or hideous crimes, survivors of domestic violence or those who have suffered severe ongoing child abuse. We don't usually think of people with Autism, and if we do then we may fear this is harking back to the old 'refrigerator mother' theories. But we are all different, and what is a trauma to one person is not a trauma to others, and there can be some very good reasons why people with Autism may be far more likely to perceive some experiences as traumatic than someone without Autism.

A child with severe exposure anxiety might be tied to a chair in a closed room and not allowed to use the toilet or get a drink until he or she complies with forced eye contact, articulates a request or completes a seemingly useless test. If this happened once it's likely to be an unpleasant experience. But if this happened over a period of several months in the child's own home with the carers he or she had trusted as accomplices, this might be a very different, far more traumatising and confusing experience for the child.

That one was not safe in one's own home, perhaps even in one's own room and not even safe with one's own carers being home or present at the time may be an extremely traumatising experience from *the child's perspective*. From the child's perspective it may not be that he or she was being helped, but that the carers allowed 'strangers' to 'imprison', 'humiliate', 'deprive' and 'disempower' them in these seemingly 'futile' and 'self-serving' ways merely to force them to comply.

I met a child who had been through this, had been pinned down, tied to a chair and barricaded from exiting the room over a period of three months. At the end of the three months the child had become worse, not better and had developed a phobia of anything that resembled a 'teaching material'. The 'therapy' was stopped, but for a long time afterwards, the child would still go into a blind panic and attack simply on seeing such things brought into the same room. This led to the child now having an additional disability to what he had had before 'therapy'.

What this demonstrated for me was that there is no one-size-fits-all approach to Autism, that the idea therapists must 'rescue' the child from being a 'victim' of an 'epidemic' called Autism may instil a justification for a progressively 'no fail' militant approach that may sometimes be abusive and traumatising in some cases, that what is food to one child may be poison to another, and that a flexibility of approach may be essential. The child this family had after this 'therapy' was much more affected by his Autism than before they started. In this child's case, a different style of approach which involved no imprisonment and involved opportunities for discovery instead of highly directed forced compliance, involved play and recognition of the child's humanness instead of fixation on his pathological condition, involved co-opting the child's own interests instead of imposing the interests of others, may have produced very different results. Yet another child may have felt safe being externally controlled in a highly structured, highly directed, compliance-based programme.

I have seen similar issues where respite care transitions have been handled badly. Sometimes it's simply not possible for a child to have an opportunity to visit the place he or she will be staying prior to going there. Sometimes it's not possible to salvage a few familiar items to make the new room not so overwhelmingly foreign. Sometimes it's not possible for carers to explain to the child the necessity or circumstances to do with going into respite. And certainly, some people cope just fine going into care.

There are some non-verbal people to whom nobody explains things. They are assumed not to understand, or their aloof responses can make people feel they can't or don't want to understand. But there are ways of explaining upcoming scenarios in a concise, visual and experiential way to even the most aloof person with Autism. Communicating the upcoming change through playing this out with objects is one option, social stories are another, a story made up of photos showing all the steps as well as the resolution (i.e. that one will return home or that one will get used to the new place and feel safe and comfortable) can be so important.

Put yourself in the position of an Autie for a moment. You have been told you will be going into respite for a while. You hear this sentence as 'blah blah blah', the words are in a jumble, you have no picture or experience for the word 'respite' and nobody has told you the resolution or end of the story as in 'what this will mean for me'. You may either shrug this off as a bunch of words, understand fragments of it and walk around wondering what was so important, or worry about the fragments you have. You may have understood but have been given no opportunity, such as typed communication or paper and pen to draw with or objects to use, to play out what you've understood, to clarify anything or to express your concerns. You may be unable to ask for your things to come with you; or you might be scared that if they actually come with you, you won't be coming back. You might have no capacity to form a mental picture of where you are going to and may not even know the person who is taking you there. When you arrive, the people there may have no profile about you, and no idea whether you can or cannot cope with being called by name or being hugged, whether certain types of voices send you 'off', where your own room is in relation to the kitchen/lounge/front door/window and how disoriented you may feel adjusting to the difference. These people may have previously incorporated none of the smells, objects, foods, fabrics or your own sheets into this new environment. They may have no training in using the few available techniques for communicating with you.

For some Auties, going into respite becomes a routine. For others the original experience was so disorienting, disempowering and alienating if not associated with 'imprisonment', that they developed a post-traumatic stress response to the mere mention or possibility of going back into respite.

I have a saying that it is not always what's on the truck that counts, but often it is how it is delivered that matters, either just as much or even more. Whether it's about hospitalisation, getting blood tests, having your hair cut, meeting dogs, encounters with pigeons, being stuck with fans or fluorescent lights, having your fingernails cut, going into respite, restraint, experiencing therapy or any other potential source of 'trauma', it is not about your intentions as much as it is about the way your actions are *perceived*. Understanding the contents of the fruit salad involved in each person's Autism is essential to making plans for successful delivery of new experiences and change. If you know what the person's 'safe associations' are, utilise them. If you know someone tunes in or copes best when distracted, give them that distraction. If you know the person is traumatised by being disempowered, where possible (and however ludicrous you think it might be), give them a position of power over the situation, draw up the choices and the clear consequences, make things visual and concrete, give them a means of communication, even if it is a smile versus flatness in response to a statement (for questions require verbal answers but statements can trigger body responses).

With post-traumatic stress disorder the person will think of what has traumatised them over and over again, sometimes to the point that they will communicate or think about little else, and every new situation may threaten the same possible repeated experience. It may be they will even develop a post-traumatic stress response to things so broad as being kept inside, restrained, controlled by others or forced to comply.

It is possible to turn around a post-traumatic stress response, but usually it means dramatically changing the old tactics (which aren't working), sometimes in quite surreal ways, often using humour and silliness instead of run-to-the-rescue 'concern' (which can be perceived as 'control' and escalate a control/counter-control dynamic), and looking at the person with new eyes. It can mean taking the focus off the problem, acknowledging the fixation but co-opting the topic and re-routing it into something positive and enjoyable from the other person's perspective. If that's not part of the programme, sometimes it should be. There is little point creating a well-intentioned programme and then spending 90 per cent of that programme calming someone down who is gripped with anxiety from feeling 'robbed of control'.

Phobias

Phobias are defined as overwhelming unreasonable fears, and pretty much most people have had one. Some of us will be phobic of public speaking and exposure before others, of being in crowds, of the death of those close to us, of our own possibility of dying, of heights and flying, of closed-in spaces and being trapped, of suffocation and drowning, of being in the dark or storms, of getting needles or doctors or seeing blood, of dogs or being bitten or stung, or of being unable to get home. All of these are very common phobias.

As a consultant I have come across others, including strong aversions to certain letters and certain colours, which cannot easily be associated with sensory hypersensitivities. It is also possible that we can develop a psychological phobia of a sensory experience we remember we once didn't like, or associate with having imposed upon us by others against our will. This is not the same as a sensory hypersensitivity. We may be in danger of assuming that all sensory discomforts or phobic responses have a brain rather than sometimes purely psycho-emotional basis. To further complicate matters it may be that one person may have a combination of both so it would be important to consider which of that person's seemingly sensory challenges have a psycho-emotional basis and which do not.

People with Autism who have great difficulty gauging the degree of an emotional-psychological response to something may assume an extreme reaction or a non-reaction instead. This may not be about whether they can process the sensory experience properly, but whether they can gauge the emotional-psychological impact as well as other people.

There may also be certain undiagnosed personality disorders which might predispose people to having over-the-top reactions in order to justify avoidance, avoid self-sufficiency, control others or break a state of boredom. We need to keep an open mind in order to keep the options open on a broader range of treatments and more individually tailored approaches.

When we react to phobic responses to sensory experiences by running off to take out a house mortgage for sensory-integration programmes, or by assuming all sensory issues are about information overload, or pour ever-increasing truckloads of supplements down people's throats on the assumption that they *all* have severe gut/immune issues, we are forgetting these people as whole people and that one symptom does not amount to one cause in all cases. Sometimes the causes are different, sometimes there is more than one cause at work in producing any one symptom or set of symptoms. How the carers address their own issues, what they are modelling, their open-mindedness, level-headedness, good boundaries and ability always to be a person and always see the other person as just a person, are very much a part of the medicine too.

Secondary anxiety states

If you went to a psychologist specialising in anxiety disorders, you would probably be told that those with speech and language disorders or intellectual or learning disabilities were more likely than others to develop primary anxiety disorders. If you went to a specialist in mood or impulse-control disorders they would probably tell you that these problems commonly occur as co-morbid disorders, which is jargon for 'occurs together with other conditions' (and this includes Autism spectrum conditions). If you went to a specialist in personality disorders, they would maybe tell you that there is an extremely high overlap of some personality disorders with mood and anxiety disorders. But at present if you go to the psychologist specialising in the field of Autism, you may currently be told that the Autie's anxiety issues are caused directly by the Autism. In other words, you'll most likely be told the person does not have a primary anxiety disorder but a secondary one. The idea that someone could in fact have both may not be considered. If this happens, they are less likely to receive the individualised treatment needed.

Anxiety due to overload and sensory issues

There is no doubt that sensory-perceptual chaos, hypersensitivity, information overload and shutdowns can be a cause of acute or chronic anxiety. There is no doubt that many Auties become traumatised by having been held captive in environments they found disempowering, overwhelming, meaningless or sensorily confusing, and that these experiences can lead to phobic reactions to all kinds of things. There is no doubt that most Auties will experience more anxiety than others due to misunderstanding language, instructions or the actions of others. There is no doubt that many Auties will be educated in environments, and according to a social and learning style, that are dramatically out of sync with their needs. This aside, the environment can model a calm, relaxed attitude or it can equally run about projecting worry and anticipating misfortune. The environment can model self-calming strategies and provide the means and time and spaces for self-calming strategies to be employed. The environment can use techniques that augment receptive information processing and expressive communication and reduce sensory hypersensitivity in user-friendly ways, or it can choose not to. The environment can provide counselling, social stories, role plays, charts and visuals to facilitate people's ability to understand themselves, understand others, cope with change and make transitions, or it can choose not to. Many people feel that community education isn't their job, or is too hard or they're too busy. But in the absence of community education of any kind, bullying becomes a social option for ignorant and arrogant people to explore the nature of someone being 'different'. By speaking up and speaking out in the community about Autism we work to educate others so Auties might one day live in a more inclusive and understanding world in which ignorance and arrogance are seen as the real disabilities to be overcome. The environment can blindly assume that Autism is one thing and that the sources of acute or chronic anxiety are only about information-processing or sensory-perceptual issues, or where moves to address these things have not solved the person's anxiety, they can choose to be open-minded enough to look outside of the prescribed box at the wide range of other issues that may also be going on.

Anxiety due to impulse-control issues

If you have untreated rapid cycling childhood bipolar, OCD or Tourette's, impulse control is going to be a big problem. The problem is that if you are diagnosed with Autism and any of these conditions, it is fairly likely these other conditions will go untreated as your impulse-control problem will probably be assumed to be part of the Autism. This is equivalent to saying to someone with a severe impulse-control problem, 'You don't have bipolar/OCD/Tourette's, you simply have the consequences of a developmental breakdown we have called Autism, the underlying causes of which we are not clear on and which presently is believed to have no cure.' They may in fact have a severe information-processing problem too, and if the bipolar were treated they may well have less of a processing problem.

If you have a severe impulse-control problem caused by one of these other conditions (as well as being Autistic), you may be constantly reminded that you need to 'control yourself'. You may be more likely to be constantly punished and excluded for your impulsive behaviours, and others are fairly likely to treat your issues as though you are simply lacking in motivation or willpower and that you love being disruptive, annoying, a pain in the bum and disliked, even if, ironically, you may appear capable of incredible will, motivation, empathy and desire to 'fit in'!

It's very hard to sit still when your body feels electric or you feel you can't breathe unless you let your tic go or straighten the furniture or pick that sticker off the table so it's clean again. It's very hard to listen when your mind is racing so fast that your head feels like it's full of TV static or your mind or gut is gripped with a held-back compulsion to the point you can't think. It's very hard to control your body when it's in a state of intense heightened stimulation and reacting in impulsive fight-flight responses so that every intended 'no' is a 'yes' and vice versa, and you are compelled into extremes even if you are exhausted, let alone interested in remaining calm and level. And these can be exhausting battles in terms of suppressing the signs of tidal waves crashing and wild internal tugs of war. You may put all of your concentration into just remaining in your seat to the degree that you now have no ability to relax or concentrate on anything else, such as processing what you are seeing or hearing. So it's little surprise that people with severe untreated impulse-control disorders suffer acute if not chronic anxiety simply as a result of trying to hold themselves together without treatment which would stabilise their condition.

Anxiety due to untreated mood disorders

Rapid cycling childhood bipolar really qualifies as both an impulse-control disorder and a mood disorder. But there are other aspects to childhood bipolar than impulse control which might cause acute or chronic anxiety. The manic phase of rapid cycling bipolar can lead you to embarrass or endanger yourself or others without having any idea at the time of how irrational these things are. Once you are back in a stable part of the cycle, you can be gripped with shame, guilt, embarrassment, fear at what you have done.

In the depressive phase (which may be within the same hour, day or week) you may be gripped with acute phobic reactions and intense withdrawal, leaving you equally ashamed later when you realise how much you disrupted everyone or how silly the phobic response now looks in a stable phase.

People living on this rollercoaster can easily isolate themselves, preferring to experience the instability without having to face the sometimes very painful social-emotional consequences when they are back in a level state.

As if the condition itself isn't destabilising and alienating enough, how you may feel about yourself when in the level mood state may also be pretty bad. You may be given no counselling regarding your condition, sense of self or what others are doing to 'help' you. If you have 'dysfunctional speech', are aloof or have highly unpredictable behaviour, others may avoid providing any form of counselling, let alone alternative means of communicating (and some people who cannot speak in such states may still be able to type or point with support) on the assumption that you are not capable. So it is hardly surprising that people with these issues may suffer acute and chronic anxiety directly as a result of living with the consequences and social judgements that can result from living with this condition in an untreated form.

Untreated unipolar depression can also result directly in anxiety both through its impact on negativity, fear and lack of confidence as well as awareness that others will constantly expect, if not force, you to join in without you having any internal motivation or desire to do so. You may feel excruciatingly burdened by the feeling that everyone else's life is 'on hold' waiting for you, if not grieving on behalf of your 'losses' and their loss of a 'normal' child. You may feel unbearable responsibility for others, if not the constant promise of social invasion from others who are watching, waiting, wanting, even praying that you'd smile or find the desire to initiate. You may be provided no counselling (especially if you are avoidant, aloof or non-verbal) to help understand yourself, your situation and what others are doing to 'help'. You may be given no form of indirectly confrontational alternative non-verbal communication to respond to such counselling. These can be sources of acute and chronic anxiety directly associated with having a severe untreated mood disorder.

Anxiety to do with environmental issues

If anxiety is always put down to the Autism or to having a learning disability or having an information-processing problem, or assumed to be associated with gut problems or sensory-perceptual issues, then people will often overlook something very obvious. Sometimes we get anxious because something very obscure to someone else but precious to us has become misplaced, or because the TV show we considered 'our friend' has ended its season, or because someone moved the cooker so now we can't remember how to use the kettle, or because it was a day off and now we have lost all sense of where we are in the week. We might be wound up because an episode of our favourite programme on the TV raised something that disturbed us, or because someone shampooed the carpet and it doesn't smell like our carpet any more. We might be wound up because we outgrew those patent leather shoes we could see our reflection in so knew we were always in the company of someone 'like us' wherever we went. We might be wound up because we can feel in our carer's body that something has drastically shifted or is about to shift in their life and therefore affects our own stability. We might have 'woken up' and discovered that we were left behind as other children moved on, or that we couldn't 'scream' at will and were terrified of the idea of how we'd get help if we were in danger. We might feel the environment doesn't understand that our favourite object is 'our friend' we can connect with, with a feeling of 'depth' and 'withness' that our information-processing issues never allow us to have with people. We might feel the environment will never learn how to interact with us in a non-invasive way, or that it will never give us an alternative means of communicating when we cannot connect with speech. We might feel over-controlled, locked in, experimented on, pursued and watched. We might feel others can't see the person inside of us, or be afraid that they might. We might sense that our parent is more troubled than we are, and know that we will never be able to express this. We might have experienced the death or loss of someone who was a major part of our household, but because we have Autism nobody thought to help us with the grieving process we went through pre-consciously but showed no conscious indication of having. We may have changed our diet in a way that doesn't agree with out gut/immune function. It is always worth considering environmental issues that may underpin an increase in someone's level of distractibility, irritability or anxiety, without putting everything down to 'genetics', gut/immune or toxity issues as part of 'the Autism'.

Anxiety associated with other personality issues

Some personality disorders are underpinned by anxiety, such as avoidant, dependent, obsessive-compulsive or paranoid personality disorders. Some feature emotional extremes in which anxiety may be seized on as a justification such as in antisocial, borderline or narcissistic personality, or as a means of making oneself the centre of attention such as histrionic personality. Schizotypal personality might make someone more susceptible to anxiety if they are made to conform and stay in the reality of the 'external world'. Someone with schizoid personality might become highly anxious if he or she were followed around or constantly pressured to feel for others or share their own thoughts and feelings. Whilst many Auties do not have personality disorders as part of their 'fruit salad', some do.

In fact, in the 1960s and earlier, Autism was considered a psychosis and often referred to as a type of childhood schizophrenia. It's possible some of those children may have had schizotypal or schizoid personality disorder as part of their 'fruit salad' in the same way that today's Autistic children may have a higher proportion of people who would qualify as having avoidant or dependent personality disorder.

As a consultant, I have commonly met those with Autism who wouldn't be amiss in the schizoid, avoidant, dependent or obsessive-compulsive personality disorder groups, and it's important to ask oneself to what degree the information-processing issues and environmental responses to Autism pump up the volume on such personality traits. How many of these people are we labelling as having an anxiety disorder, or putting all their 'stuff' down to Autism, without focusing on the personality dynamics and how best to work with them environmentally to reduce their often debilitating impact?

I have more occasionally come across those who would fit the outline of schizotypal patterns, though without speech all one can rely on are behavioural patterns so it may be more hidden in non-verbal people than we know. Schizotypal personality disorder is not schizophrenia, nor do those with this necessarily go on to develop schizophrenia, though some do. Those with schizotypal personality are still capable of connecting to 'reality'. Schizotypal patterns might be more common in families with a parent with manic psychosis as part of bipolar or schizophrenia. Some people may easily confuse manic psychosis as part of the manic phase of bipolar with schizophrenia. According to the website for the National Autistic Society in the UK around one third of children diagnosed with Autism may have childhood bipolar. Not all people with bipolar will experience manic psychosis, and most will experience a lesser, non-psychotic, version – hypomania.

Similarly, the artistic personality trait is associated with fascination for objects and patterns with an interest in people being secondary. Those with this trait are discovery learners who learn through doing rather than passive cerebral learning and are said to be motivated to create and distressed when stuck in what they perceive as stagnation. In this context it is conceivable to imagine the anxiety of such a person when made to sit in a seat quietly, watch, listen and not fiddle. In the extreme, this artistic personality trait is called cyclothymic personality disorder, essentially akin to a low level bipolar state involving intense mood swings and bipolar disorder is more commonly found in those with this artistic-cyclothymic state than most others. It is not hard to imagine how an inherently artistic person with Autism might become highly distressed when put into a monotonous programme of repetitive passive learning and drills under a system of forced compliance in which any fascination with patterns and the sensory nature of objects over people would be actively discouraged as 'stimming' that was 'getting in the way of learning' rather than being the avenue towards it that it otherwise might have been.

Least commonly, I might come across someone who might fit the histrionic, paranoid, narcissistic and, perhaps, the more problematic antisocial and borderline personality disorders groups. Some of these have been people with Autism spectrum conditions who have been referred to me because the family is in great distress, because their child is at risk of having to go into a residential care placement or because the residential care placement itself is not coping with the person's Autism. I would say that in 10 years as a consultant in the field I could count on my fingers the number of people I've personally met who would fit these patterns. But for the sake of those desperately challenged families coping with these 'mysteries' labelled Autism, I take the time to acknowledge the diversity of all people, Autistic or otherwise, and their equal right to be understood.

Perhaps one of the greatest associations between personality disorders in those with Autism and anxiety is about what happens when we directly create social clashes which compound their multi-faceted disability. What happens, for example, when we have an extremely phobic, non-verbal, avoidant, dependent Autistic adult in a small special needs classroom with a booming, verbal, violent Autistic adult with all the features of undiagnosed antisocial personality disorder? What happens when we have a tiny special needs classroom of six Autistic students where most might fit the patterns of avoidant, dependent, obsessive-compulsive or schizoid personality, and there are three others with histrionic, narcissistic and borderline personality disorder respectively? What happens when we have Autistic people who would fit the avoidant, dependent, obsessive-compulsive mould and may thrive on structure and conformity and compliance, and two Autistic people who fit the idiosyncratic-schizotypal or artistic-cyclothymic traits who might react directly against this very structure but blossom in play therapy, drama therapy or discovery learning?

I think one of the consequences of lumping people together on the basis of Autism more than on the basis of learning style, motivation and personality disposition is anxiety and lost potential. Whilst we directly expose them to a diverse range of others we may be exposing them within a separatist ghetto of *extreme* others which may have little relationship to the usual social diversity of society. For some people this could increase their alienation and mistrust of 'difference' and increase their problems, not decrease them. It will also likely mean that only that group best suited to the current Autism approach of the day will prosper, and that those who don't fit this may be offered no fitting alternative. I believe the best way to create balance is not to lump a small group of imbalanced people together in a room with each other but to allow them to adapt to a more diverse range of modelling of less extreme personalities.

Whilst some mainstream teachers might feel challenged by this idea, I was heartened by a visit to an extremely challenged student with Autism. This student (who had had a range of interventions and environmental approaches already put in place) still had extremely disruptive behaviours, and the students in the class and the teacher were constantly distracted. I noticed, however, one very strange thing. No other children were disrupting the class and all were highly motivated to get their work done. I said to the teacher, 'How many students do you think would normally have been chatting amongst themselves, distracting each other, being reluctant to do their work in a classroom without this one person causing disruption?' Ironically, this one student had mobilised the entire classroom to want to learn and pay attention. My estimate is that her distraction, which amounted to the impact of maybe five others, meant that five others were instead motivated to learn and had no desire to add to the distraction in the class. In other words, the teacher, by having her there, broke even.

The nature of anxiety disorders

Are anxiety disorders voluntary or involuntary?

Unless you've ever had a chronic anxiety disorder it's impossible to imagine just how real these feel. They can be chronic or acute and I've experienced them in both phases.

In the acute phase you become gripped with a panic attack only when you are thinking about, approaching or engaged in an activity which triggers the anxiety. It may be something as simple as acknowledging you have a body and considering taking self-initiated action in dealing with its needs. It may be something as simple as awareness of the desire to speak, which risks the potential of connecting one's world to that of others. It may be something more specific, such as drinking tap water, holding a pen, being made to look at someone or say hello. It may be triggered by people speaking to you and the possibility they may emotionally affect you and rob you of the completeness of your own world. These acute attacks can be like feeling an impending earthquake coming, hearing a tidal wave about to come crashing down on you. They can be like a warning of a feeling of impending suffocation or drowning. They can be like a compelling physical warning you cannot avoid being alarmed by.

The chronic phase is an anxiety which no longer visits but seems to live permanently within your body. It is as if your body is no longer a comfortable place to live. It can make you feel imprisoned in a body you cannot use as yours. It can feel like an invisible armour of pins in which every move that defies your anxiety will stick you with pins so you progressively obey. Chronic anxiety can make you feel like you want to sleep all the time just to avoid the feeling. It can make you pace and flap and tense up and have tremors and jerks when you try to defy it in thought or action. Chronic anxiety can steal your connection with your body and voice, leaving you only that which doesn't threaten, perhaps humming, sometimes singing, the occasional pragmatic one-word command, the whispered speech often overlooked as 'muttering', the mouthing of dialogue at your mirror reflection. Chronic anxiety is an invisible cage, and the more others try to get in, the tighter the cage gets and the more you shrink within it. If I don't have much nice to say about chronic anxiety, it is because I lived with it for 38 years before I found treatment for my own case of it. Those on the Autistic spectrum who identify selfhood with their Autism and say they wish for no 'cure' are likely not living with a severe chronic anxiety disorder.

At its most severe, an anxiety disorder can be so compelling, so automatic, so overwhelming, it can be impossible to pull against it.

For some people, an untreated anxiety disorder may dominate their lives, affecting communication, interaction with other people, daring new activities and social involvements. Some will eventually learn to monitor their own anxiety levels and employ self-calming strategies and use typed communication to diffuse anxieties when connection with verbal communication is blocked or impossible. Some will learn strategies which involve putting on another character or voice in order to dare speaking. They may speak to their shoes or the wall where they cannot dare speak to a person. They may put on a characterisation of the family dog in order to dare to eat. They may pee in the backyard where they cannot dare use a shared toilet. Some will learn to assist others because it is too exposing of their own needs, wants and abilities to dare to do the same things for themselves. Some will attribute magical powers to the objects they carry as part of a self-calming regime in which they learn to 'dare' what the anxiety disorder would otherwise block them from doing. Some will make constant noises and movements in order to tune out self-consciousness or conscious awareness which might otherwise trigger acute anxiety and block their remaining abilities. Others will calm their anxiety through making noises and movements to reassure their anxiety that they are actively tuning others out.

Some will be helped through dietary interventions and nutritional supplements which address chemistry states underpinning anxiety disorders. Severe magnesium deficiency is one such issue, vitamin B deficiencies, hypoglycemic attacks and salicylate intolerance are among some of the others.

Some people will 'inherit' anxiety disorders which 'run in the family', such as social phobia, generalised anxiety disorder and agoraphobia, from what may be a combination of genetics, modelling and environment. Others will develop anxiety disorders partially in response to information-processing and sensory-perceptual issues and the developmental impact these things have, but those with mood disorders and those with certain types of personality disorders will be more affected than others simply because of the effect of 'too many straws on the camel's back'; too many stressors means something's got to give.

None of this is to say there are not some Auties who seem to be able to turn their anxiety on and off, and I cannot ignore those carers and teachers who have introduced me to these interesting, perhaps rarer, people. We need to keep in mind that new stereotypes in which we expect anxiety disorders and sensory hypersensitivities in those with Autism may mean that we sometimes give people permission to express distress whether or not they in fact have these issues. This may be even more important to consider where someone has patterns indicating a possible personality disorder which may lead to them using this display of distress to their social advantage but ultimately to the detriment of their own development or the respect, freedoms and rights of others.

So are anxiety states voluntary or involuntary? Sometimes one, often the other, perhaps even occasionally there are factors involved in which someone has bits of both.

Could a personality disorder pose as exposure anxiety?

There are people with schizoid personality disorder who are asocial and may be uninterested in forming social connections or even communicating with others, yet may experience great aloneness. This might be confused with having exposure anxiety, and such a person may well have both, but it is certainly possible to have avoidant, dependent, schizoid or schizotypal

personality disorder and not have exposure anxiety, even though the indirectly confrontational approach used for exposure anxiety may also be very
user-friendly to those in these groups. There may be those with histrionic or
borderline personality disorder who identify with a range of conditions they
may or may not have, and as exposure anxiety gets discussed it may be no
exception. Saying this, there is no reason someone with these personality
disorders would be immune from also having exposure anxiety. It is possible
that there might be a 'boy who cried wolf' scenario here where someone with
these personality disorders identifies a significant source of chronic stress in
themselves, but it is cast aside on the assumption that these people are more
likely than others to seize on conditions they in fact do not have.

Could a mood disorder be mistaken for an anxiety disorder?

Depression is often associated with fear, dread, phobia and negative thinking,
and it can be easy to confuse this with an anxiety disorder; but, equally,
anxiety disorders are more likely to occur in people with mood disorders.
Nevertheless, there are certainly those with depression who have no accompanying anxiety disorder and feel, instead, remarkably flat and difficult to
arouse. Saying this, there is a lesser-known personality disorder called depressive personality disorder, which is not depression, that is associated with persistent critical, negative and pessimistic thinking, where people avoid any
attempts to cheer them up or raise their hopes or expectations and feel far
more 'realistic' living in a mindstate of negativity they see as 'realism'.

Bipolar can involve crashing lows in which anxiety is common, as well as
agitated manic highs in which confusion and racing thoughts and feelings in
themselves can be so overwhelming and destabilising as to trigger acute
fight-flight states. This might be even more likely in those experiencing rapid
cycling childhood bipolar who have basically grown up with this intense
internal instability and extremity and have established little in the way of
stability to support them in the face of acute anxiety.

Effects of anxiety disorders
Anxiety disorders and health

Anxiety is closely associated with adrenaline, and the adrenal glands are an
essential part of the immune system. We need a reasonable level of adrenaline
to stay alert and responsive, but if we are constantly flooded with too much we

might equally spend all our time adapting by trying to calm ourselves and tune out regardless of the cost to development and communication.

Chronic high stress levels are associated with progressive recurrent and eventually chronic illnesses. High levels of emotionality have been linked with deficiency in secretory IgA necessary to fighting infections in the ears, nose, throat, lungs and gut, as well as being the messenger for signalling enzyme production necessary to digestion, essential in B12 metabolism, necessary for blood health, and implicated in the adequate production and balance of stomach acid for digestion and gut health. Chronic stress levels are implicated in leaky gut, in oxidative stress affecting the health of red blood cells and their ability to transport nutrients around the body and to the brain. Chronic stress levels are implicated in the cause and exacerbation of inflammatory states within the body. Exhausted adrenal glands are associated with chronic fatigue syndrome and accumulation of toxins as the immune system can no longer cope. Most importantly, anxiety disorders can severely affect functioning, family relationships, family structure and supports and be a major risk factor in depression, substance abuse and suicide.

Cognitive and behavioural implications of anxiety disorders

Anxiety disorders can be incredibly distracting. Imagine how hard it would be for you to keep up with a TV programme with someone doing something really worrying, even horrifying, in front of the TV. Not only would they be in your way, but their actions compel you to focus, instead, on them. Anxiety disorders are like having this stuff going on in your mind or emotions. Some people will play out mental scenarios, and those who 'think in pictures' may be compelled by their anxieties in a way comparable with daydreamers, being unable to stay tuned to the outside world because they 'drift off' into the internal one. It's pretty much just a different show that's going on inside. Some people with anxiety disorders will be unable to visualise mentally what is creating their anxiety. Both groups have advantages and disadvantages. One group may be unable to switch off the internal graphics. The other person may be unable to get a cohesive overview of their anxieties because they can't cognitively get a grip on them, either they are too fragmented, or they play out emotionally and physically rather than consciously and mentally. In either case, the impact on information processing in someone with mono-tracked processing in the first place may be enormous.

Exam nerves are a useful example of the effect on information processing as well as communication. When you 'freeze' you often can't think or express yourself.

Creating a calming atmosphere may help some of these people, and that may mean incorporating into the background, what is already user-friendly to them – music, smells, textures, patterns, lighting, placement of things within the room similar to what they are used to and feel comfortable or familiar with.

Whilst many will be easily over-stimulated there are some people who may actually involuntarily but instinctively manifest anxiety, provoking chaos in response to feeling too low, too flat or too bored. This could interfere with information processing and learning, and impact upon development and social inclusion. Producing an atmosphere more exciting, interesting and compelling than the anxiety-provoking one they would otherwise manifest may be more effective for some people than creating a calming atmosphere, but you may need to employ all of your surrealism, imagination, colour and dramatics in creating this.

We all learn differently. Some of us feel most 'present', most included, most receptive when we are 'peripheral' and 'fly on the wall'. I call this an 'indirectly confrontational' style of interacting and learning. Around a third of my lecture audiences will agree this is how they best function and there are entire occupations which rely primarily on this style as a 'skill'. Nevertheless, ironically, in society this style of being involved and learning is generally not accepted, especially by the two thirds who make and deliver education policies. Instead what is promoted is a directly confrontational style or watching directly, or interacting in a directly interpersonal manner. This might be compared with cats and dogs, with the cats behaving more like indirectly confrontational mini-islands and are essentially less socially invasive, pursuing or obviously demonstrative than the dogs. The dogs, by contrast behave in a generally openly, even blatantly directly confrontational manner in which direct competition, challenge, demonstrative expression and social pursuit is considered 'normal' and 'desirable'.

Essentially, however, around one third of my lecture audiences (many of whom are parents possibly somewhere on the spectrum) and many of those with Autism are not all like dogs. Some of us are far more like cats and find the dog's version of 'normality' alien, abnormal or at least not 'our natural system'. Whilst the 'dog-like' non-Autistic people are not forced to live according to the 'normality' of 'cat-like' Autistic minorities, the more 'cat-like' people often manifest anxiety in response to being made too consciously aware of what they are doing. Given something to fiddle with or focus on whilst tuning in peripherally works best for them. Yet this is the kind of strategy that would have 'dog-like' teachers assuming such a 'cat-like' person is, therefore, not paying attention! It's all about which glasses you are seeing the world through. Without these helpful if not essential (sometimes seemingly inappropriate) distractions 'cat-like' people may be less able to sit still, stay socially present and be open to incoming information, and in some cases it is only whilst distracted that they can speak directly from a pre-conscious state where doing so from a more conscious state is not accessible for them. Too often this may not be understood and the distractions may be removed on the assumption that the person can't concentrate or attend to a lesson or experience with these distractions present. The consequence, however, may be that the person then feels too overwhelmingly 'present', too joltingly conscious, and is almost triggered into fixating on a source of anxiety until it is exaggerated to a point of panic and finally used to justify escape and withdrawal. This is not to say this is true of all Auties or that stims do not sometimes get in the way of information processing, learning, communication and development or that they don't sometimes look weird but that for *some* people these things are *functional*, and we need to recognise when we are dealing with such a person and not sabotage their use of these 'artificial limbs' in some dogmatic, blind pursuit of a mythical 'normal' way of learning. People with abnormal brains do not have 'typical' ways of learning. We are big people. We really can face that.

Can people become addicted to their own chemistry?

People can become addicted to drugs. Drugs are chemicals that affect the body. We can also produce chemical states inside our own bodies, which maybe makes us capable of being equivalent to miniature, biological, low-level or high-level 'drug manufacturing plants'.

We produce our own chemistry states through how we react to stimuli in the environment. We can create patterns of reactions which progressively trigger high levels of particular chemistry states in the body. We can get so accustomed to these patterns of reactions and the chemical highs these produce that we can become addicted to them. Negativity is a particular chemical state. Mania is another. Anxiety is yet another. We can fixate on certain experiences, even seek to cause others to produce reactions in creating these experiences or perseverate on ideas or behaviours that produce these different states. Gut/immune dysfunction aside, we can raise or lower our adrenaline, our serotonin, our dopamine, all our major neurotransmitters, through the particular balance of foods we are drawn to, through particular sensory stimulations or through depriving ourselves of others which would balance them. Protein raises dopamine, carbohydrates raise seratonin, stimulants can raise adrenaline. Smelling foods can raise dopamine, withdrawing from sunlight can lower seratonin levels (as well as reduce immunity), watching violent computer games can make us immune to normal adrenaline levels and require higher and higher levels to get the same 'extreme', withdrawal into utter predictability can make us unfamiliar with and too sensitive to sudden adrenaline-producing experiences such as change.

Certain experiences will make addictions to our own chemical states more likely for some of us than others. If we experience our carers having similar patterns of avoidance or fixation, we can pick up these patterns as 'normal'. If we are born to a parent who has substance abuse problems, if not already with an 'addictive' nature, we might be primed with this physical response to experiences as 'normal'. If we are socially rewarded or protected in siding with our extreme repeated patterns of avoidance or fixation underpinning an imbalance of chemical states, then we are going to feel reinforced in continuing this way. Once we've known only the 'reality' of a chemically imbalanced state such as negativity, mania or anxiety from pre-infancy and long term, these patterns can become so integrated in our expectations of the social world, and 'reality' so integrated in our pre-conscious, if not conscious, sense of self and identity, it can be extremely difficult to adjust to anything different *even if* it is far more physically comfortable, safer, inclusive, etc. The saying 'better the devil you know' can certainly sometimes apply. Non-Autistic adults are no different. Most will remain stuck in patterns which limit their lives, depress them, make them uncomfortable or obnoxious to each other; but they will often find any excuse not to change, even though they may be unhappy with what they've got. Familiarity can be far more essential to us than all the positive things change has to offer us. Every motivation is blocked by an anti-motivation. Learning to counter the anti-motivations is the key to giving the power of change over to the hands of motivation. Sometimes we may appear to provide the old whilst peripherally delivering the new. Without realising, those who devalue the ability to take on new worlds may be praying to some god of compliance and losing sight of important issues such as identification, respect and humanity.

Anxiety disorders and IQ tests

Anything which can severely limit one's focus, attention, interaction, or communication, or drastically counter natural motivations is capable of messing with the impression of capability, which is what IQ scores are meant to be a measure of. It has certainly been my experience that people who have been helped to overcome or manage their anxiety disorders have then gone on to demonstrate intelligence, ability and potential that had previously not been seen in that person.

Treating anxiety disorders

Where to find help

Educational psychologists may specialise in Autism spectrum conditions, which may be shorthand for them understanding a fair bit about information-processing issues, perhaps these days even having some awareness of sensory issues and often having awareness of social-skills deficits and how to help these people practise and act as if they in fact have these skills. So these people can usually help people practise greetings, handshakes, eye contact, perhaps counsel them about handling their information-processing problems and how to choose opportunities they are more likely to succeed in on the basis of their type of information-processing and social-skills issues. These people may know about secondary anxiety issues caused by information-processing problems, but perhaps be a bit limited in clinical knowledge and practice when it comes to 'treating' or counselling people about primary anxiety disorders or secondary anxiety states relating to mood disorders, compulsive disorders, personality disorders or even environmental issues.

Clinical psychologists are more likely to understand about primary anxiety disorders, most will have a good awareness of family counselling and interrelationships between environmental issues and anxiety disorders, and some of them will also have some experience in the interrelationships between personality disorders and anxiety disorders, though most may be unwilling even to discuss the possibility of personality disorders in children. Many clinical psychologists, however, may have no experience with Auties and therefore not simultaneously understand the information-processing aspects as well as the anxiety issues, and might be limited in the ability to recognise which aspects of an anxiety disorder are related to the information-processing issues and which aspects are separate, even aggravating or causing the information-processing issues.

Cognitive behavioural psychologists are people who specialise in treating anxiety disorders and compulsive disorders, though they are not qualified to prescribe the medication which is often helpful to some of these people, and many cognitive behavioural psychologists will have no experience of working with Auties so struggle to work with the interrelationship or co-occurrence of anxiety or compulsive disorders in some people with Autism.

Psychiatrists have the capacity to prescribe medication but may be limited in their counselling experience, particularly with Auties. Naturopaths can recommend diets, supplements and even lifestyle changes that may help in working with anxiety, but some are more qualified than others, and natural medicine on its own may not be as effective as a combination of approaches or may not apply to the needs of particular people.

Play therapists, music, art and dance therapists, even hypnotherapists, may all play a part in helping specific people with anxiety disorders, sometimes in association with other professionals addressing other aspects of the problem.

What's needed is an independent assessment centre which can look beyond the label of Autism and fully assess the dynamics of various issues at work in an individual that are limiting or undermining their potential on a range of different levels. Such a centre should then make a full report indicating how these conclusions were reached, including recommendations of the types of approaches and therapies known to address these issues most successfully, including the many strategies and approaches the person or their carers can access and implement directly without cost.

Presently, such centres are only beginning to take shape, and often they are costly and therefore exclude a large section of society.

Can the environment be medicine?

More than any other medicine, I feel that people have the capacity to be medicine to each other, but you have to have the right prescription for the problem, and there is no one-size-fits-all prescription.

When we listen to music, it has the capacity to change how we feel in our body. Some music will get us revved up, some will calm us or level us out, some will transport us elsewhere or ground us here. People have minds and emotions, and when these play out day after day, place after place, they can create an overall 'feel' which I call 'the music of beingness'. Sometimes we will sit five minutes in the company of a stranger and something in us changes, though they have not said a word. Sometimes we will sit in the company of a carer who is playing a tune which doesn't fit with where we are or what we feel we need. We have the capacity to work on the music of our own beingness. How comfortable do we feel with ourselves? How inspired? How respectful? How empowered? How adventurous? How open? How self-protective? If the music of our own beingness doesn't sit well with ourselves when we are alone with nobody else's 'music' to tune into, then perhaps we have a bit of a journey to build the foundations of experience to rebalance ourselves so we can become that person, that medicine. Sometimes who we become is someone else's medicine, even if we've never met that person. It's OK to face up to it that someone else just might be the one with the keys in connecting with your own child. But that connection can be capable of restoring balance in imbalanced people, inspiring them to trust, to include, to adventure, to respect and to own themselves. This may be a community volunteer who has never met anyone with Autism. It may be someone who is also diagnosed on the Autistic spectrum, it may be an eccentric, an artist, a tradesperson, a great-aunt or the owner of the local supermarket. It may be a bag lady. Those who are looking for such medicine only in those with a professional title or university degree or in self-promoted 'gurus' are forgetting that education, professional experience and self-promotion may have little or no connection with the development of one's 'music of beingness' and the 'tune' their existence seems to 'play'. These people are often useful, and some are also 'magical' in the sense of also being great human beings, but they are not the only ones. I can name mine – one teacher in seven years of primary school, the non-English speaking owner of the Chinese café at the end of my street, a stranger at a bus stop who sketched trees, a stranger I picked from the phone book who spent a year teaching me to talk on a phone and who I never met, the tram drivers who let me ride the tram with no ability to speak to them or pay, my grandmother and anyone with the same feel as this self-owning person…my list goes on. Most would have no idea of the impact they had. All changed me dramatically over time for the better. How many of these contacts are most Auties excluded from meeting because of over-protection or lack of social inclusion?

Anxiety states and specific behavioural issues

Anxiety disorders might underpin specific behaviours/disorders relating to:

- communication
- being in one's own world

- eye contact
- learning and cognitive challenges
- toileting
- sleep problems
- stimming
- meltdowns
- self-protection responses
- challenging behaviours
- food behaviour problems.

Clearly, anxiety disorders such as selective mutism have a direct impact on *communication*, particularly loss of communication, and those with separation anxiety may be more likely to be inhibited in speaking to anyone outside of the main trusted carer. In the case of someone with Autism, separation anxiety may even occur when removed from the trusted company of their own mirror reflection. Sensitive-avoidant personality itself may make someone less likely to risk using language till a later age when far more certain of experiencing social success and acceptance in daring to try to communicate. The exposure anxiety felt by someone with a solitary-schizoid personality may give these people a stronger anti-motivation to developing and using social communication from a young age, as it would run the risk of inviting unwanted social entanglement and intimacy. As a result, such language might be more likely to be restricted to the 'purely necessary'. Generalised anxiety disorder may alter the nature of communication and interfere with retrieving or tracking what one has to say. Exposure anxiety might have a greater chance of shutting down receptive information processing than any other anxiety state.

Being in one's own world can mean many things, including the withdrawal caused by chronic or acute anxiety states. I believe this would be a heightened form of anxiety response in those who also had the types of personality traits which naturally found safety in withdrawal from intimacy, withdrawal from the social risk of rejection or failure, withdrawal from the threat of forced conformity or withdrawal into creativity.

Many personalities cope with anxiety by seeking *eye contact*. But those who associate making eye contact with inviting unwanted intimacy or inviting inclusion which could lead to social risk may be more likely than most to respond to heightened anxiety, not with seeking others through eye contact, but by ensuring security in closing others out by avoiding building those bridges through eye contact.

Where anxiety disorders go together with fragmented vision and impaired receptive information processing, these people would be less likely to seek such alienating and overloading experiences in times of heightened anxiety – experiences they'd perhaps risk getting through eye contact.

The ability to keep up with a simultaneous sense of self and other would diminish in a state of high anxiety so the alienation caused by eye contact would peak at these points. As a result this may be the very time these people are least likely to be comforted by eye contact, and rhythm and smell may be a far greater comfort.

Anxiety can result both from and in heightened adrenaline states. These cause sensory heightening and might result in the type of *diminished information processing* that results in sensory flooding where a huge wave of information is stored but not processed, resulting in chaotic sensory experiences. Quite simply, we learn best when we are most receptive and we are most receptive when we are relaxed. We process information best when we are relaxed. Some people are best relaxed when they are aware and keeping up. Some people are only relaxed when they are seemingly consciously unaware and preoccupied. Some people can learn and process information when in front of others. Others need solitude for that, or to be taught by the computer rather than through the social intimacy of involvement with another person.

Anxiety can give rise to various *toileting* problems. It can result in irritable bowel, which can mean fluctuating between diarrhoea and constipation, or simply diarrhoea. For some people, anxiety can cause an equally irritable bladder and frequent urination. For other people, anxiety can result in control behaviours such as holding on to the point that the bowel becomes too dry and stopped up. Some handle anxiety by being fixated on staying creative or by avoidance behaviours so delay going to the toilet. Others may hold on simply because access to the toilet would require asking or approaching others for permission, so it is far more comforting to go in one's pants than risk the anxiety state caused by pressure of social intimacy or being escorted or socially controlled. Some may be so anxious about what's unfamiliar they may hold on until they again get their own familiar toilet. Duplicate toilet seats, bathroom mats or other comparables may help. Others who feel comforted with their reflection may feel safer and more relaxed going to the toilet when in the company of their reflection on the back of the door.

Sleep is all about relaxation. Anxiety is one of the main things that can stop someone from sleeping. Understanding the basis of their anxieties is the key to a plan to counter these directly in the sleep environment and sleep routine.

Self-stimulatory behaviours can be important social blockers when people have been too invasive or directly confrontational to withstand. Just as we sometimes work through information overload when clicking a pen or fiddling with a ring, stimming can also be part of an 'information down-loading strategy' important to managing acute anxiety states. Stims can be self-hypnotic tools in returning one to a right-brain style of processing where things flow better and are more intuitive, albeit not based on conscious awareness or meaning. They can be wonderful rhythmic, repetitive self-calming tools in managing anxiety states. They may seem odd, and there are ways of channelling them into less noticeable, more low-key forms. But ultimately, they can be a resource, the removal and suppression of which may mean far bigger problems in anxiety management and alienation. However uncommon it may seem in mainstream society, stimming is a 'normal' behaviour within the 'normality' of that person, who is hopefully an accepted and equal part of a minority within society. But often stimming poses an anxiety challenge for many parents who see it as 'abnormal' and fear social judgement. Self-con-sciousness is 'in the eyes of the beholder' so to speak, and this is no justifiable basis for the alienating behaviour of fixating on 'normalising' someone with an eccentricity simply because of your own awkwardness or fear of so-called 'abnormality'. The narrow-minded of society have much to learn in overlook-ing, living alongside and seeing the person beyond the stim as a celebrated part of social diversity.

Anxiety is akin to panic, be that screaming, crying or simply a blank expression and 'blown fuses'. Managing *meltdowns* is often synonymous with managing anxiety, and babying people won't do that. Monitoring and bio-feedback techniques, modelling anxiety self-management and calming tech-niques, time-out cards, self-explanation cards, adjusting environments to best fit the person's strengths and interests, social stories, in some cases reverse psy-chology and in others 'reality testing' and the 'tough love' approach are all tools that may be employed with different people at different times to manage the anxiety associated with meltdowns.

Self-protection responses are frequent with anxiety, and people so often run to the rescue, throwing fuel on the fire. Many people merely need a safe space, a guarantee of reasonable periods of social non-invasion from others, a guarantee of limited short tolerable periods of social contact and information-processing demands, the right to the time and space to find the desire to chase something all within a safe, adaptable, respectful and accepting environment. Managing self-protection responses means acknowledging how carers may be unintentionally provoking these. The solution may be an indirectly confrontational approach, which entails the non-Autistic people in the environment learning how to use a system of 'simply being' that is socially non-invasive, self-owning and essentially foreign to them. Such is their own 'disability'.

When we are acutely anxious we are often in a panic state and feel trapped, overwhelmed, confused and disempowered. It is natural to feel fight-flight states, which may drive you either to implode and shut down, or explode and attack either self, others or property. Whether you engage in such *challenging and self-injurous behaviours* will depend on:

- your natural personality traits
- modelling in your environment (including that on TV and in computer games)
- (to a far lesser degree) general sanctions and consequences.

The effectiveness of sanctions and consequences often relies on:

- multi-track processing
- conscious ability to understand these things with meaning and make inferences before the event
- a mood state in which there is more than apathy but also in which there is enough consistency and cohesion to retain and recall sanctions and consequences in future situations
- those sanctions and consequences actually fitting into the natural framework of motivations and distresses specific to the collectives of personality traits of each individual.

If someone has mono-tracked processing, relies on right-brain pre-conscious processing rather than conscious awareness and meaning, has a mood disorder and has personality traits in which the usual sanctions and consequences end up acting as either irrelevant or as 'rewards' then the anxiety response and its impact on self-injurious and challenging behaviours is going to prevail.

In my view, one-size-fits-all approaches like ABA currently still seem to be based on the vision that there is one 'normality' (the non-Autistic one). In this way it may not yet have the philosophical base to envision Autism spectrum conditions as part of a wider range of 'normality'. That may, in time, change. Till then, there is a pragmatic, holistic and anthropological (stand-in-their-shoes) approach to work out the best cohesive programme to tackle these issues for any one individual.

Anxiety disorders generally result in the person feeling utterly robbed of control, disempowered. Because of this it is a common, natural, generally unconscious and generally involuntary self-protection response for people to seize control over the few things they can control. This often means bodily functions, including breathing, eating, drinking, sleeping and excretion.

Anxiety disorders can mean not only greater insistence on sameness affecting *food and eating behaviours*, self-restriction or binge diets or binge eating, but also inability to eat when being observed, to eat among others or to conform in eating what others would prefer them to eat. Anxiety disorders can also lead to diminished gut/immune function, which means food allergies, food intolerances, immune deficiancies and nutrient deficiencies may be more common, all affecting eating patterns and eating behaviours. Zinc deficiency, in particular, can underpin pica, the eating of non-food objects, though someone with right-brain dominance who lived by pattern, theme and feel without much conscious interpretation may also eat non-food objects because of similar feel or association with things they like and would like to make part of self, things which resemble food experiences.

CHAPTER 8

Being Joined at the Hip

Dependency Issues

Max struggled with a bear. Mary struggled with Max who was struggling with the bear. Max was now torn between handing the responsibility for the struggle over to Mary, who was clearly 'trying to help', or simply thumping Mary so as to better get on with the focus and struggle of fighting off the bear in the first place!

Mary was exhausted when Max disappeared leaving her to struggle directly with the bear. Max of course was dismayed for surely she had set herself up as the capable one? Mary re-engaged Max with the bear but stood watching, waiting, at the ready to 'help'. Finally she jumped in again, but because it was Max's bear she was impotent to help so she simply got in the way. Max thumped her. Mary was confused. After all, she was trying to help. Finally, Mary walked off and confronted her own bears along the way. Max considered, surely she would not have left me with this bear of mine had I not been at least a bit capable to deal with it. Then, observing Mary's skill in handling her own bears, and with the freedom to focus on his own issues, he used some of Mary's own patterns. Soon, the bear, rather bored and not getting his usual 'fix' of excitement from the struggle, moved on.

Learned dependency and co-dependency

Most families are OK about discussing their child's dependency. What they are often not OK about is discussing the ways in which a disabled child, like any other emotional living thing, can come to pull emotional strings on the carer. Where a carer and a person affected by Autism get into this entanglement, it can reach a point that the person is affected by 'learned dependency' and the carer equally affected by 'co-dependency'. In terms of potential and reaching independence, these are not good things.

There's an assumption that people only ever pull strings consciously and with great multi-tracking and conscious awareness, so one must be 'manipulative', even calculating, to do such things. We can, however, react unconsciously to all kinds of patterns, and very young babies as well as animals do just this, yet we would not see them as being consciously manipulative.

To say people with disabilities are somehow immune, or should be immune, from even considering this issue, is to deny that the child is still an emotional being with a capacity to feel pattern. This doesn't make the disability an acquired one, though there are many studies full of examples where learned dependency and co-dependency have made an existing and very real disability worse. Carers need to cast aside self-defensiveness and ask themselves honestly whether they are using 'love' and 'help' in a way that contributes to the self-image of the person with disabilities as dependent, incapable and helpless, or whether this love and help really empowers them to explore through trial and error and self-initiated discovery their own independence, capability and self-sufficiency. Most of us learn self-initiation because we need to. We learn that we need to because we are left wanting. We learn that we need to because our carer is not always more capable than we are. How many Auties get these opportunities?

There is a saying 'Do as I do, not as I say,' and sometimes we may verbally encourage someone to believe in their capability, yet our eagerness to take over and invite dependency, or our quickness to correct/fix/help, is a louder message which says 'You wouldn't be able to do this without me,' 'You always get this wrong.' It doesn't matter if they have learning difficulties or are clumsy or have acute anxiety or, or, or. There are some extremely disabled people who are unable to process even half of what they have learned to do, and those who continue to wear their clothes back-to-front or inside-out but who can, nevertheless, dress themselves. There are those who cannot hold cutlery but can feed themselves quite adequately by hand. There are those who have never spoken who have come to type-speak. Some people won't be affected by subtle patterns constantly suggestive and reinforcing of their own incapability. But some who are emotionally hypersensitive, even if it is merely hypersensitive to the non-verbal patterns of others or how they react in their bodies, may well overreact in a way that contributes to their disability.

I have met severely disabled people who cannot pull down their own pants, wipe themselves or hold a spoon, but who can switch on a DVD player, disassemble a light switch, open a bottle of Coke, snatch food, swipe objects off a table top and pile furniture up to reach cheese in the highest cupboard. I have met mute people who hum all day or mutter at their reflection, but cannot 'speak'. I have met others who progressively stopped using speech as their parent or sibling eagerly guessed and verbalised their needs for them. Some of these people certainly would have had significant impulse-control problems making volitional or controlled actions difficult but not utterly impossible. I am not doubting the level of their disability for a moment. Some would certainly have had compounding mood, anxiety and information-processing issues that would have made it harder for them to develop self-help skills or communication. But it is at least conceivable that some, though certainly not all, of these people, just may have become a fraction more 'disabled' than they otherwise might have been, because they have never been left to handle the consequences of their own incapacity before they quickly, compassionately, received 'help' and 'rescuing'.

At this point it is understandable that any reader would say, what do you, someone so undeniably 'high-functioning', know about being disabled? What do you know about being helpless, terrified, unable to communicate, to organise yourself, to co-ordinate your actions, to understand instructions or language, unable even to recognise what you see or to control an acute anxiety state or extreme shift in sensory experiences?

I have had extreme emotional fits since infancy, manic oblivion, crashing despair, overwhelming phobia, acute rage, and I've had them in school and as an adult. I've had severe sensory-perceptual fluctuations, the equivalent of what someone might experience on LSD, with all the associated phobia and fascination. I've been meaning-deaf till late childhood to the degree that I functioned much of the time like a deaf child, guessing meaning. I have had the visual equivalent to the degree that I have not understood that that moving thing is a car, and such a state of all-self/no-other and vice versa to the degree that I had no idea that a car would hit me if I walked in front of it. I have had such extreme fight-flight states and disorganisation that for about 20 years I would step into a boiling bath (not having regulated or checked the water) and then freeze unable to step out. I have burned toast, locked myself out, flooded baths and got my clothes in the wrong order (if not back-to-front or inside-out) more times than anyone I have ever known who has lived independently. I have washed myself and lost track that my other arm exists to wash the rest of me. I have had involuntary compulsive behaviours and vocalisations which have drawn fear, surprise, annoyance and external attempts to control me that have made my challenges worse. I have been utterly terrified of daring to show others what I thought, liked or felt, feeling this threat like the threat of impending death, which often meant extreme helplessness, frustration, isolation and missing out. I have been frustrated, sad and angry at things being more difficult for me than other people, and been angry at a world of opportunities full of technology and instruction manuals and verbal explanations I can make little use of without lots of direct patterning, and then lose the ability with each change of context. Nevertheless, I grew up in an environment where my own carers had sometimes related (and some unrelated) challenges to the degree that they were not capable of 'taking care' of me, or 'helping' me (in fact my mother greatly opposed anyone 'helping' me, for which I am actually very understanding and grateful).

Life was not easy for someone with my challenges and there are certainly those with bigger challenges than mine. But it is the fact that it has not been easy that has had me dedicate much of my life to pursuing the treatments to finally significantly minimise these different challenges. I am, nevertheless, a person who is certain I am capable no matter what disabilities make things harder for me, and it is that attitude, that absolute assumption that I am responsible for how I help myself or how I seek help, that has been an invaluable asset in my life, that makes me aware that even a small dose of sink or swim can help some people with related challenges.

There is a saying which goes 'If you say so, then so it will be,' meaning if we say 'I can't' then this will remain our reality. Real growth takes calm, steady determination and self-belief; one step at a time climbs the mountain. Stroke victims and those who have suffered illness and injury later in life have often had a similar journey in gaining what ground they can. Those who've had a condition or range of compounding conditions since infancy have a harder struggle because they have no memory of who they might otherwise have been, and struggling against the confines of their condition may feel like struggling against 'self'. As adults, this is a personal choice. With children, carers are left to make that choice on their behalf. I believe we can give different gifts; 'dependency' and 'empowerment' are two of them, and the choice is ours as to what we define as the most loving thing to give.

Some people develop additional 'disabilities' involving obsession or fixation on a pathologically possessive relationship with a co-dependent carer. Others may withdraw further into themselves because of the social invasion of a carer desperately watching, waiting, wishing, wanting, and ever overly eager to jump to the rescue.

I remember working with one fantastic and wonderful older boy with marked immune and gut problems, some movement and co-ordination problems, significant information-processing and communication challenges and acute anxiety. As he was now in late childhood, his parent was worried that he'd never have independence. We did what we could first to improve his information-processing and anxiety issues, then we focused on the rest. He was 'unable' to open doors, climb steps, walk along a street without assistance, take action to solve dilemmas, and so on, and was considered quite significantly disabled.

His mother, who I greatly admire, loved her child deeply, but equally associated 'love' completely with her role as his helper and rescuer. Furthermore, she was utterly convinced of his inabilities and his need to rely on her at all times, and at the same time was perplexed as to why he appeared to have no desire or motivation to help himself. Added to this was a great awareness of social judgement, of wanting to be seen to be a 'good' mother who never left her child to struggle, to feel helpless. This also meant she had never left him to find his own self-motivation to help himself.

It was clear her boy was extremely dependent on her, even possessive and controlling, if not fixated on his greatest 'support'. I accepted that his challenges were very real but could see that, in spite of his challenges, he had potential he was simply not using. My work with her was painful to us both. I instructed shop assistants to address him directly (I had previously met and discussed his needs with them privately before we did this) and we walked away leaving him behind (as already organised with the shop assistants), compelling him eventually to help himself and follow, even necessitating his having to open doors for himself (with the expected great displays of incapacity and distress). We walked ahead of him up the street and in spite of his mother's utter belief (and near phobia) he would not know how to or be able to follow, I told her that if he felt the slightest chance she would come and rescue him, he would not follow, and I insisted she did not look back or stop. She had a great fear he would simply wander onto the road, but I assured her he would more likely do this if she showed signs that to do so would have her run to save him from such chaos. She trusted me, and we behaved as though we were busy and assumed his capability. We entered my office, closing the door behind us and leaving him in the street a few doors away. With us out of sight he ambled his way to the office and hovered 'helplessly' outside of the door before finally tapping. I answered, greeted him, then came back in the office leaving him standing at the door, behaving as though it was entirely his responsibility to enter or stay there, not mine. I instructed his mother to take her gaze off him, and he eventually tapped again; at every point she felt certain of impending doom. This time, fed up with waiting for us, he opened the door and let himself into the office, and we warmly included him as we would have any child his age. With great determination she courageously continued this 'tough love' back home, often needing a lot of help to sustain her strength to do so. In spite of his resistance (including self-injurious behaviours he directed at her in anger at being left to care for himself) he progressively showed many abilities he had never had, and they developed a very different relationship and one in which 'love' was redefined as something mutually enjoyable and empowering. He is now a teenager, living away from home and attending boarding school. He remains a child with marked disabilities, but a more independent one. They both equally still struggle with co-dependency and learned dependency issues but they have the road map to what a loving and caring relationship can be without these things.

Dependency issues don't affect all Auties, but I have seen them affect enough of this group for this problem to be worth a mention. With help in supporting the carer over feelings of guilt, fear, social stigma, social isolation, poor self-esteem or even extreme emotionality and desperate need to feel loved and loveable, the potentially compounding and disabling problem of co-dependency is so avoidable. What's more, carers locked into the addictive pattern of co-dependency in which their entire self-image and self-esteem are tightly bound up with their ability to 'save', 'rescue' or be always ready to spring into action to 'help' their child are more at risk of social isolation, poor self-esteem, lack of personal identity outside of being 'the carer', exhaustion, depression and suicidal feelings. They may experience acute guilt and shame at even the possibility of owning up to not being able to cope or at daring to leave their child to struggle and discover his or her capacity in any way. Co-dependency is, however, a relatively treatable addictive social pattern of responses which can be helped through a combination of approaches, including good respite services, counselling, hypnotherapy where counselling cannot help and, for some carers, nutritional or medical intervention to manage anxiety states and depression.

Certainly, there are some Auties who because of acute anxiety become frozen and truly unable to function, and there are environmental strategies to minimise anxiety, and medication and dietary interventions which can address some of the underlying causes. There are those with extreme impulse-control problems who cannot use volition even when they are compelled all over the place; again environmental strategies, medication and dietary interventions have been found to help some of these people. There are those with severe nutrient issues affecting brain function, sensory integration and perception, for whom treatments in the gut/immune field have been able to improve functioning. And there are those with very real physical disabilities and actual brain damage and toxicity issues who truly must depend on others to some degree for some functions. But very few people have to depend on others completely at all possible times for all possible things, and many people with all kinds of disabilities, even sometimes quite severe disabilities, learn to compensate if given the opportunity to do so – some speaking via everything from voice communicators to head pointers and facilitated (assisted) typed communication, some needing to eat with their hands where they cannot co-ordinate utensils, some needing shoes and clothes they can slip into and out of without reliance on assistance, but many still needing some empowering help to wash, groom themselves, fully dress or even hold their body upright.

Some families respond to the first appearance of their child's developmental problems by ignoring the problems, hoping they'll 'get over it' or feeling 'I don't have time for this rubbish'. They may as well be saying to the child 'I can't hear you.' Some people will respond by turning up the volume of their helplessness to the degree that the parent is forced into taking over the hard work for them. Once the child is rewarded in this way for avoiding having to struggle with and challenge his or her own disability, this can easily be the start of a pattern of dependency on the part of the child, and progressive co-dependency on the part of the carer. Other carers have learned to associate 'need' with 'I am loved,' 'I am loveable' and jump too eagerly at the chance to rescue, completely unintentionally reinforcing the child's self-image as 'helpless', 'incapable' or 'stupid'. When the carer tries to break out of this pattern, the child has sometimes already learned that if he or she becomes even more incapable, throws fiercer tantrums, gets more self-injurious, begins to refuse food, and so on, the carer will eventually 'behave themselves' and play by 'the rules'.

Now at this point, some carers might be feeling, 'Woah, that's real taboo, you can't say that. My child is not manipulative, my child is severely disabled. My child is not intelligent enough to work that out.' One's own children are almost always angels, and those with Autism are generally seen as being without 'guile' or 'intent'. The myth that guile is necessary to being survivalist or manipulative compounds this view that people with Autism couldn't possibly manipulate anyone. Anyone who's had a cat or dog with toileting, eating or going-outside dramas will know that dogs, and especially cats, develop power dynamics with their carers all the time. And they are non-verbal, have no formal education and don't have fluent receptive language skills. What they map is patterns of action = response. They feel it in their bodies and their behaviours become entrenched as a result.

Many who work as carers with some of the very elderly in nursing homes have faced similar challenges where some who are still relatively capable, though things are surely a struggle to them, will, when a carer can do it instead, find themselves at that moment most utterly 'unable' to do something. It's nothing to do with intelligence or deliberate spiteful emotional manipulation. It's about sensing and patterns, and sometimes it's about confusing 'controlling others' with 'being loved' and 'feeling secure that one will not be left alone', confusing 'making someone feel needed' with 'showing someone they matter'. And it is not just the 'client' who can confuse these things till the confusion is an assumed 'reality', it is often also the carers who have been brought up to believe they are only truly nice, worthy or loveable people if they are helping, saving, rescuing, giving. In the meantime, the carer may even resent their progressive imprisonment into, and social isolation in, the carer role but feel too guilty or ashamed to admit they have a life too and a right to be loved, not for what they can do, but simply for being 'just a person'.

This pattern is reinforced by the cruelty of society judging those carers who dare to leave their child to struggle with a button, dare to leave their child scream in the supermarket without buying him or her one more chocolate bar or leaving in shame. This pattern is reinforced by other carers who hide that they are not coping, certain they will be judged as social failures when they are in fact having very normal reactions to carrying a heavy load, a load so much heavier when they no longer give anything to themselves, no friends, no chat on the phone, no right to ten minutes of laziness. And once their child has learned to take the carer's freedom and self-love as a threat of 'abandonment' or withdrawal of 'love' (i.e. loss of control over them), these can be the very moments when the child employs his or her greatest demonstrations of need, pain, helplessness, frustration, boredom or despair. The child does this not because he or she is heartless or resentful, but because when we have a disability it is so much easier to delegate the hard work to someone else.

The carers of a child with a developmental disability can be warm, playful, silly and love their child as a person, but for a disabled person to seize the hard work, for their own sake, the parent needs to leave them to find a reason to do so. One of those reasons is 'because I had to'. This is 'tough love' and tough love is not violence, it is not demoralising forced compliance, it is not being cold and uncaring. Tough love is about walking away sometimes, about not jumping in, about getting on with your own thing, about doing half the job rather than the whole job for someone. Tough love is about not hovering over their shoulder. It's about acting like you are too tired, too busy, too distracted to help sometimes. Sometimes, tough love is the most empowering thing you can give someone faced with a struggle, and it can even lead some people to surprise themselves with what they can do when it's 'survival'. They may kick and scream all the way, especially if you are watching from across the room, biting your lip and wringing your hands (very bad modelling). But you as the carer will still know that in choosing to turn away from co-dependency, choosing to use tough love, you did what you did out of love. In my own (biased) personal view, 'love' is 'to empower' people.

Recognising someone with learned dependency

Information on learned dependency is currently very limited. It is something spoken about by teachers, but it is still quite taboo socially because the carers who unwittingly 'train' their children to be dependent do so mostly unconsciously, mostly with no idea this is harmful to their child, and they do so often out of a great desire to help, care and love. To describe what learned dependency is and what it looks we have to look at the lives of those most likely to develop learned dependency.

Learned dependency is a tool used by religious cults in getting their members to let go of their own independent thought and lose confidence in their own ability to make decisions and take actions independent of the cult. Learned dependency is also a subject which comes up in the field of substance abuse, where an addict may have come to believe they are not responsible for their own actions and decisions in coping with their addictions, and instead blames the co-dependent carer who is so constantly seeking to 'help' them. Learned dependency is also a common topic in the field of mental health where a patient may have become overly dependent on a therapist or care staff in institutional settings.

Learned dependency is raised in the field of brain injury where a patient who is physically capable of improvement fails to believe in their own potential and take action to better achieve it. Unlike those with Autism who may have been affected since birth or had regression into Autism in infancy, those with brain injury have often had a previous level of ability prior to their brain injury. This does not mean that those with Autism are not sometimes equally capable of reaching a higher level of ability than the disability of learned dependency might allow them.

Whilst some Auties certainly struggle to manage and overcome their challenges wherever possible, it has been my experience as a consultant to be told again and again that I am different to the children of the families I am seeing because, they tell me, 'my child isn't motivated' to help himself or herself, to speak, to learn new things. What child is when the job is a hard one and the anti-motivations are higher than the motivations? But this is all the more reason why those with such challenges need not be burdened with one more such as learned dependency.

Could an Autie be capable of malingering?

Malingering is feigning or exaggerating physical or psychological incapacity for personal benefit. To answer whether Auties are capable of malingering, we need to ask whether non-Autistic people are capable of malingering and whether carers have ever modelled such behaviours or created the circumstances where malingering was seen as 'natural', 'normal', a way of getting advantages or simply a matter of survival.

How many non-Autistic people have feigned or exaggerated the degree of a headache to get out of something, feigned or exaggerated a back ache to get someone to do the heavy work, feigned or exaggerated an anxiety or discomfort or state of their car or finances or the cleanliness of their house to get out of going somewhere or seeing certain people? How many non-Autistic people have feigned or exaggerated an illness or responsibility in order to get a day off work, or as children did so to get a day off school or even had their carers do this on their behalf? How many non-Autistic people have stayed up late knowing they are making a cold worse or will be too tired to work the next day, but then failed to later mention how they contributed to their own state? I think it's pretty likely that many non-Autistic people do these things at least some time in their lives, and some are much better at getting away with these things than others. It's also true that malingering is believed to be a feature of certain types of personality disorders, and it is possible that Auties are no more immune from the possibility of also having personality disorders (as part of their Autism package) than any other human being.

Whilst feigning something is certainly the same as lying, is it still lying to exaggerate, if not falsely gauge, the level of one's challenges? And what if such an exaggeration was instinctual and not conscious? Can we view it as having the same malevolence, selfishness and intent as when a non-Autistic person exaggerates an issue for the purpose of avoidance or perceived benefit?

The question then is, if they have a level of information-processing, sensory or anxiety problems, is it possible that some Auties might be motivated to avoid facing their challenges if they learn they can gain control over the environment by playing on the sympathies of their carers?

Some Auties actively struggle against overwhelming odds under their own steam. Some struggle in certain circumstances but are much better at coping in other circumstances. Some Auties will be seen to struggle extremely until they get the exclusion or inclusion or reward they want, and then the problem seems to have taken care of itself. I don't think we can make assumptions as to whether Auties are capable of malingering, and we should certainly never psychologically and emotionally abuse people in assuming that they are. But we can say that it does not take conscious awareness or extremely high IQ to malinger, and dogs and cats can pick up these patterns, and Auties are as human and instinctual as anyone. I don't think any of us would call our dog or cat a liar. I think we need to keep an open mind that with giving understanding and sympathy to Auties for the very real challenges they truly do struggle with, we don't inadvertently disempower them in excusing them out of challenging themselves in the name of being 'sympathetic', 'understanding' and 'caring'.

Recognising someone with co-dependency

If we are to guard against promoting learned dependency or even malingering, we need to look at one of the most common environmental causes involved in promoting these patterns in others – co-dependency.

Co-dependency is a social pattern which is considered a form of mental health problem. Those living with alcoholics, drug addicts, people with mental illness, emotional problems, personality disorders or disabilities are far more likely to develop a co-dependent relationship with those in their care than most people would. This does not mean such co-dependency is good for the recipient, nor does it make the carer a saint or an angel: it progressively imprisons them and robs them of their own identity and social supports and ultimately is as unhealthy for the carer as the recipient. Co-dependency is by nature to be 'emotionally incestuous', to have boundary problems, to be over-involved. To the recipient, this can feel overwhelmingly invasive, it can extinguish connections with wider 'others', it can be confusing to the point where one cannot develop an independent selfhood or feel responsible for one's own abilities or expression, it can even become an unquestionable habit outside of which one finds any other kind of relationship 'foreign'. Those in care need to be people in their own right, to have their own identity and be in the company of someone who also models these things in their own life.

It is absolutely certain that almost all non-Autistic people have developed some degree of co-dependency. It is also true that many people in society will negatively judge those who do *not* behave co-dependently in relating to a loved one with challenges. It is also true that some cultures promote co-dependency as a 'norm' more than others. Finally, it is true that there is a distinction between 'caring' and co-dependency. Caring can be empowering to the person in one's care. Co-dependency, however, is never empowering. When we become co-dependent with the other person, we invade their boundaries, we become controlling and disempowering, and we create an obstacle to them reaching out to take control over their own lives.

In a way, co-dependency is a great example of a strength that has been so overdeveloped it becomes a pathology. We could say euphoria is a great feeling, but acute mania becomes a functioning problem to the person with mania and usually to those around them. We could say that an obsessive nature is part of being a good observer just like a compulsive nature can make you a great 'doer'. But to excess, the same things can mean being a workaholic, a compulsive gambler or an alcoholic. Co-dependency is about being so over-whelmingly great at worrying, caring, helping, fixing, saving the other person that you outshine them and diminish the chances of them daring to compete with your proven capability – and in the process, you build your addiction to taking responsibility for other people's opportunities to make mistakes and to eventually diminish their search for any reason to want to save themselves. In this sense, you increase their reliance on you instead of on themselves, and with this, anxiety about losing you increases, to the point where some people will make themselves less capable just to ensure you'll stay, and others will compulsively run from your perceived 'interference'. Only wanting to be needed and helpful, in the end you may have built up such a pedestal upon which you place your own sainthood that you may feel guilty and selfish at then naturally wanting a life of your own, only responsible for yourself, and you become exhausted.

The other person may be in a terrible 'catch 22' as well. If they follow your lead, you may pride yourself on having helped them achieve to the degree that it may feel to them like it's your achievement more than theirs. Solitary people who fear intimacy and entanglement may be truly stuck and traumatised by this 'choice' to rely on you or to run and remain incapable. At least they can't flag your achievements as due to their 'caring' or take on your helpful instruction as theirs, at the cost of feeling invaded and reduced to being 'one of their achievements'.

On the TV we have so many sit-coms and soaps promoting 'loving' relationships where Dad or Mum is so close to the son or daughter they share the same tastes, confide like best friends, their social world revolves completely around their child, they feel they know exactly what their child thinks or should think or feel, and the children strive to make Mum or Dad proud because they have always been there for them. In real life there are those parents who are so entangled and co-dependent with their children that they lose the strong boundaries needed to guide their child. They are so concerned with being liked or needed that they fail to take risks in leaving their child wanting long enough for the child to struggle to find their own capability, and if the child seeks to make life hell for the parent instead of using or developing his or her own abilities, the co-dependent parent will too easily cave in for fear of being seen as uncaring or risking the child's approval or 'peace'. The fact is that development is about conflict and struggle, and to teach any child it is all about 'peace' means someone's going to get the easy way – and it's generally going to be the child who has learned to play on the co-dependency of the parent. However much sit-coms and soaps have become the new psychologist promoting co-dependency and teaching us this is an ideal relationship between two people, the reality is that whilst some would dream of this as ideal there is equally a fair percentage children who would withdraw, get on a self-assertive (if not self-destructive) bender or need a shrink if they felt this over-important or entangled with their parents.

Could learned dependency really hurt anyone?

For many carers, their child's Autism began around the same time as they started worrying something was 'wrong'. This is not to say that such worrying progressively caused the development of learned dependency, or that it promoted the child's development of dependent personality disorder, or that it increased a sense of social invasion or audience to the degree that it led to a sensitive child developing avoidant personality disorder or exacerbated exposure anxiety, because it is certainly true there are many people with an Autism spectrum condition who have none of these issues. But it is also true there will be some who do.

The effects of learned dependency on health are usually those of the carer's progressive stress levels and social isolation, if not psychological, emotional and, ultimately, physical health. Those with learned dependency may go without rather than help themselves, to a more extreme degree than most people, even where they might actually be capable. In this sense they may choose to go cold rather than challenge the assumption they couldn't get themselves a coat. They might choose to go hungry rather than challenge the assumption they can't feed themselves. They might choose to stay up rather than challenge the assumption they can't put themselves to bed when they are tired. They might choose to be bored rather than challenge the assumption they can't openly take action to occupy their time. In this sense learned dependency might have an impact on psychological, emotional and physical wellbeing.

Effects of learned dependency and co-dependency

Learned dependency and information processing

Those with information-processing or sensory-perceptual problems are more likely than other people to develop learned dependency, simply because life is more challenging for them, so leaning on someone else, copping out, giving the responsibility to someone else more 'intact' can seem so natural a thing to do, if not seemingly 'expected' or invited by others. Learned dependency itself can mean someone is more limited in opening themselves up to opportunities for learning and development, and this might mean they will have fewer foundations to keep up with information processing. Otherwise, learned dependency should not directly affect someone's ability to process incoming information even though it could severely restrict them in acting upon this information. In this sense, learned dependency could have the same degree of impact upon ability as anxiety disorders, and in both cases information processing may be far more intact than outward ability may give away.

Cognitive and behavioural implications of learned dependency

Learned dependency is going to restrict the way someone will take on learning. Someone with learned dependency is more likely to become prompt-dependent and be unable or unwilling to independently demonstrate what they appear to have learned.

Learned dependency is also likely to limit the people someone will work with. Where a carer has set up a situation of learned dependency, those at the school who do not 'follow suit' are going to appear 'unreasonable' by comparison and meet a lot of resistance, and those who do always 'help' will be much more accepted. So it's important that in breaking down learned dependency an approach is adopted which is followed through in a variety of settings.

If someone has a committed view of themselves as incapable except when their helper is present, then this is going to have a big effect on where, when, with whom and how they can communicate and interact. This is not to say they don't have other very significant challenges along with learned dependency, but just because they have those other challenges doesn't mean learned dependency isn't in there as one of the big contributors to limitations.

Some people will become extremely anxious, if not utterly phobic, if abandoned by their helpers to the point where they have to save themselves and prove their capability. I have put people through this, and when they do manage to climb those stairs, open that door, get themselves out of that swing seat or whatever ability they had for years behaved as if they didn't have, I can assure you these people are not happy about their achievements. Knowing this is the deal, I have never overtly watched, never addressed them directly afterwards about their achievement, never allowed myself to be seen 'waiting' or 'present'. In response to their achievements, I have behaved as though the achievement didn't exist. I have had them cry and attack over such 'defeat' and humiliation of being left to save themselves and prove their own capability. I have had them almost immediately 'pay back' the person who put them in this position through self-injurious behaviours.

Learned dependency has different faces depending on how others pander to it or not. Some people flippantly say 'anything for an easy life', and this may well be where some cases of learned dependency begin.

Learned dependency in its most extreme may have a placid face and be about passivity, as long as someone else is responsible. It may be about being controlling when the carer is busy, or has their own priorities or tries to budge them out of learned dependency. It may be about tantrums if the rules are changed. Learned dependency may mean subtle emotional manipulation in which someone who cannot show the capability of asking may use noises, self-endangerment or other provocations to bring the carer running. Learned dependency at its worst may mean passive-aggressive behaviours. If a child engages in these behavioural patterns consistently, then this runs the risk of becoming integral to that child's identity and part of their 'personality'. Passive-aggressive reactions are those of the emotional blackmailer, the drama queen whose head falls off over the slightest thing. One moment they may be distraught, the next moment spiteful, one moment eager and enthusiastic, the next intolerant, critical and fussy.

Effects of learned dependency on carers and the family

All kudos, admiration, sainthoods and martyrdom aside, learned dependency burns carers out. It may also entangle the Autie recipient of this caring in a series of catch-22s. The Autie may explore capability and lose face and face shame and guilt over having let someone else carry them for so long, or they can continue to feel frustrated, even imprisoned in their own pattern. They may break away from their own assumed incapacity, but face the uncertainty of not knowing who they are, being utterly without structure except that they must learn to construct and provide for themselves and have no idea whether they are still 'loveable' this way (for many will wrongly assume that to be carried means one is 'loved' or 'loveable'). They may improve, but if their carer believes they had this ability all along will he or she be angry, rejecting, even abandon them? Then there is the choice to continue in the learned dependency role but run the risk of the carer experiencing burn-out, with all this means, for hearing a carer cry, scream, hate their own life or sometimes even regret your own or their responsibility for it.

Recently, particularly in the English-speaking world, there has been a spate of tragic killings of children with Autism by a burnt-out parent (see www.geocities.com/growingjoel/murder.html). The stories, again and again, are not of incapable people but of a parent who had previously been so 'capable', felt so depended upon, so certain their child could not possibly survive without them. When these people have, themselves, lost all love of life, they have taken their child with them, if not just killed the child, because they could see no other way forward. For no other reason than taking such burn-out seriously, we need to look not only at what it means to help these children out of extreme dependency but also at what it means to help their carers face letting go.

A lot of relationships cope fine with having one person, even several people, in the family with Autism spectrum conditions. Where a child is severely affected by information-processing problems, health issues, anxiety disorders, mood disorders or compulsive disorders, families often come to understand these things and manage to cope, not only addressing the issues, but remembering to be people in their own right, and to see the child as a person too. There are certainly some personality disorders which are not easy for any family to live with. Antisocial personality disorder, for example, is usually not easy for any family to cope with, particularly where this affects someone who also has an information-processing problem. But perhaps the biggest impact on the family is that of dependent personality disorder or learned dependency. Here, more than most other things which might form part of someone's Autism picture, a couple can feel that the child with Autism has 'come between them'. One parent may feel the other doesn't understand how much care and attention this child needs. The other parent may feel there is no space left in their partner's life for caring about, listening to, or being there for anyone else, including them. The co-dependent parent may drift away from their own identity and personhood to the degree that their partner can't find anyone in there any more except the carer of the child with Autism. The co-dependent parent may feel their partner is unsupportive, uncaring, selfish. The partner may feel the co-dependent carer is not allowing the child space to learn for himself or herself, or over-worries and over-protects to the child's own detriment and the detriment of the relationship and the sense of family as a whole. One partner may progressively see a condition where he or she once saw a child, see only a carer where he or she once saw a spouse.

In a healthy family – in which one is always a person, not just a condition, in which there is security and opportunities for survival and discovery, experiences as well as boundaries, humour as well as sense – inclusion and opportunity to be in one's own space is important to all family members. This can be a family with two carers, a family with one parent, a family with many children or only one. But a family in which one is too important, in which life is always serious, in which inclusion is claustrophobic and without boundaries, is not a healthy space for anyone's development. If you change the undercurrent, so you change the tide and vice versa. Families experiencing difficulties with these balances need help in addressing the imbalances, and that doesn't merely mean 'services for Autism', it means services for families. It doesn't merely mean seeing a child with Autism as a strain upon, or a wedge between, carers but helping the carers themselves to address their own mindsets, get flexible, explore new patterns; and sometimes their child's Autism may change a little as they change too. The Autism will, at some level, remain, but a child with Autism can be more or less well adjusted. Healthy plants grow in healthy gardens.

Effects of the carer's co-dependency on health
We cannot give and give and give without something in our soul crying, screaming, if not fracturing somewhere in there. Some of us learn to give com-

pulsively, and we are told we are so wonderful, so caring, so loving, so thoughtful. Illness is merely imbalance. Even being too giving can make us ill and cause illness in others. We are often so fixated on those who take, seeing them as selfish. We openly accept that those who cannot help their disability are free to take and are not selfish to do so but needy. If someone had learned dependency, they would run a great risk of moving from angel to demon if they were to face up to the possibility that they are not as incapable as they are allowing themselves to be.

Denial is a form of stress. If we hold something down, even acknowledgment, it takes energy. I met the carers of a girl unable to do anything at all for herself. Yet she had great fine motor control and could pinch herself wonderfully in provoking others to rescue her from her own self-injury. She had even disassembled light switches and she could hum. Yet she had no self-help skills, no communication, no apparent ability to learn. She was just one of so many enigmas: people with gross motor and fine motor skills when involved in their own fixations, entertainments and distractions, who nevertheless appeared unable to do anything towards their own communication and independence; people who could hum and whisper and sing and take other people's hands to do the things they 'couldn't' do for themselves. The word 'Autistic' has become a word that somehow explains all these enigmas, and yet these carers may still be left with a nagging sense that their child may actually be more capable than he or she can show, or they may suppress that because they have this word 'Autism' which now explains it, only it doesn't.

Co-dependency is like a drug for those addicted to this pattern of 'caring', 'helping', 'rescuing' – and getting them to face up to the fact that one may empower someone more greatly by stopping carrying them, covering for them, saving them so quickly, can be like putting an addict through withdrawal. Yet their worry can be equally exhausting, and the two feed each other. The co-dependency feeds the worry, and the worry justifies the co-dependency which then feeds the worry, and around and around it goes. Yet nobody offers help to the parent of an Autie who is on this roundabout, for it is almost always assumed that the Autism has necessitated the co-dependency, rarely that the co-dependency has intensified aspects of learned helplessness, if not avoidance, which are considered part of the Autism. The tide and the undercurrent affect each other.

Can people become addicted to their own dependency or co-dependency?

Being carried is surely addictive for those who have never known any different. Others will not allow anyone to assist or take responsibility for them and would rather their head were to fall off first. Yet both types of people exist within that word 'Autistic'. I think that patterns which have become integral to our sense of self and our sense of the world become something we live and breathe and part of our patterns, and our patterns are about emotional chemistry. An addiction is about feeling distress, discomfort, even pain, when a pattern we are deeply used to is altered or removed. In this sense, we can experience the loss of a deep love like a withdrawal from an addiction.

Dependency issues and IQ tests

There are people who score below their actual potential all the time for all kinds of reasons. One of those will be where a person fears proving their own capabilities before others and one of those reasons may be that of learned dependency.

I remember a man with Autism who had been being taught the ABC for 14 years in a special school before he finally told them, through typed communication, that he wanted to learn about art history and physics. When asked why he had continued for so long to give them the impression he had severe learning difficulties, this man explained that as they'd assumed him incapable he had given them exactly what they had expected. Asked about whether this wasn't incredibly frustrating to him he explained that he'd found it amusing to 'play this game' with them and was watching their gullibility and stupidity. This same man had self-directed, often non-functional speech, and when I asked him why he didn't try to control and use his speech for communication rather than typing he expressed through typing that one of the reasons he was afraid to speak like this was that after so many years of being 'non-verbal' (he always referred to himself as 'non-verbal') it would shock his carers too much.

Helping those with learned dependency and co-dependency issues

As the focus is on the disability rather than on learned dependency as one basis for the severity of severely impaired level of functioning, most available therapies do not address this issue at present. In fact schools are divided, with some seeking to empower their students rather than promote learned dependency, others actively accepting, if not inadvertently encouraging, learned dependency and prompt-reliance, and others which have no policy of helping the carers as part of helping the child break away from such patterns.

Some have gone the other way and removed typed communication on the basis that it promotes a child's belief that he or she cannot speak or can only speak with the physical assistance of a facilitator supporting, guiding and sometimes prompting the typing (strange logic that any school should feel it can treat a severe communication disorder by removing a communication technique). My view is that where a person has severe motor-planning, infor-mation-processing, anxiety, impulse-control or compulsion issues affecting their communication, such support may be essential if there is to be any com-munication at all. Certainly, there will be those who appear to have any of these issues but for whom a learned dependency issue is the far greater aspect of the disability. But removing typed communication may not mean the person will revert to speaking verbally, and many would instead return to screaming, pulling or challenging behaviours. Typed communication, like any tool, can be a bridge to progressive independence as much as it can be a chain that ensures dependency. Sometimes it's not about the package, it's about how it's delivered and what you do with it.

It has been my experience that there is currently nothing specific in the Autism field to help families address their own co-dependency, only offers to help support families to maintain their co-dependency. Most current Autism programmes involve carers, teachers or therapists 'saving', 'rescuing', 'prompt-ing', 'controlling', 'mirroring', 'merging with' and 'fixing' the Autistic person. To my knowledge, there are currently no programmes which work on helping co-dependent carers learn to play, be silly, get into their own space, stop jumping to the rescue, stop taking the bait of emotional blackmail sometimes involved in challenging behaviours, stop projecting worry, or to learn to delegate responsibility to others not to do the same, but to spend time being people with a person who happens to have Autism. There are, however, a number of clinical psychologists and hypnotherapists who are aware of learned dependency and co-dependency issues who are trained to help carers change the way they view their lives, themselves and the people in their care in order to set them free, whilst empowering those in their care to build an independent identity and to grow.

Dependency and specific behavioural issues

Dependency issues might underpin specific behaviours/issues relating to:

- communication
- being in one's own world
- eye contact
- learning and cognitive challenges
- toileting
- sleep problems
- stimming
- meltdowns
- self-protection responses
- challenging behaviours
- food behaviour problems.

In my view, someone with any one of the following conditions would have *communication* challenges:

- oral dyspraxia
- selective mutism
- right-brain processing without left–right integration
- (in social communication) left-brain processing without left–right integration
- gut/immune/toxicity or other health issues impairing information processing.

And there are those with certain personality traits who would be predisposed to have greater social-emotional or anxiety challenges tackling their communication disorder than others would. Add to this recipe co-morbid mood or compulsive disorders and you increase the challenge. Give these people the soft option of learned dependency within a close relationship to a carer or series of carers who worked in a co-dependent manner, and you would multiply the chances that that communication disorder would be greater and harder for that person to overcome with any degree of independence.

There are two forms of '*being in one's own world*'. One is to be disconnected from others. The other is to attempt to merge with and lose oneself in others to the degree that there is essentially no interaction between self and other because self has become a mere extension of other, an appendage. Being in the world means having a distinct self with a separate will and expression and an identity separable from one's carer. Being dependent on someone doesn't mean one necessarily has no independent sense of self, but where there is learned dependency and a co-dependent carer it may become harder to develop or ever dare assert that separate sense of self. For those with the devoted-dependent personality with a natural fear of acting independently and a desire to be looked after at all times, this would likely be harder than most in any case, but it is these people more than any who need their carers not to feed into their challenges, but to provide enough semblance of incapability and unavailability in themselves to provoke a progressive safe acceptance of their own capacity for independent action.

Anyone with learned dependency may have learned or come to map and feel which triggers most encourage a co-dependent carer to take over. Some may learn that *eye contact* brings this. It is possible that others may learn that shutting down or indulging in the behaviours associated with shutting down will bring these people running to take over. Part of this, for some people, may be actually failing to use eye contact. This is not to say these people are manipulative or conniving, merely that they have found what brings them the quickest comfort. Animals learn this naturally on an instinctual level by mapping pattern. They do not sit down and strategically plan it out. It just evolves that way.

There are personalities in which it is unnatural to learn to depend on others. There are other personalities where dependency on others is their most natural and highly developed response. Someone with the latter type of personality quickly learns, for example, that the expression of sensory hypersensitivities provokes their greatest sense of comfort in being 'taken care of' and being excused from involvements and activities which would progressively lead to or require their greatest weakness: that of acting independently. This is not to say that people don't also have very real sensory challenges or sensory heightening, but that there are some personalities which would be predisposed to hiding these things from others to avoid interference or help and who would therefore naturally challenge themselves to continue in spite of confusions and discomfort, and that other personalities would be the opposite, particularly if a co-dependent carer unintentionally promoted learned dependency.

We could take one imaginary person with one of the four more 'Autistic' personality types – the solitary, the idiosyncratic, the artistic and the sensitive – and give them the same actual degree of *cognitive 'impairments'*, and I'd expect their adaptations in terms of *learning* would each be quite different. The solitary personality would possibly keep their cognitive impairments under wraps, to themselves, and seek learning through predominantly solitary activities. The idiosyncratic personality would possibly deflect from any conscious acknowledgement of their cognitive impairments and swing against external attempts to help which had any hint of expectation to conform. The artistic personality would possibly ignore the cognitive impairments and find whatever patterns were available for aesthetic pleasure and creativity and would not tolerate well the stagnation, passivity and lack of creativity involved in the offer of dependency. The sensitive personality would be perhaps the most likely to fear failure so much, rely so strongly on assured acceptance, be so unsettled by breaks with routine and so reassured by being told exactly what to do and how to do it and, especially if they also have the devoted-dependent personality trait, be more likely than the others to fall comfortably and without struggle into the learned dependency trap within a co-dependent relationship with a carer and do little from their own side to break from this. In terms of learning, these people may be the ones who seem most compliant, but in terms of independence, so central to learning as 'self', these people may be the most challenged.

Those with the devoted personality may rely more strongly than most on being told what to do and when to do it. Under the weight of additional burdens, such as information-processing challenges, I believe that natural personality traits 'blow out' so that they move towards the exaggerated disorder forms of the same traits. The disorder form of the devoted personality is that of dependent personality disorder, in which there is an exaggerated fear of abandonment and assumption of helplessness.

There are probably no skill deficits that tie up a carer as much as an apparent *inability to feed oneself or use the toilet independently*. Theoretically, if someone had a combination of the sensitive-avoidant personality, which struggles with change, loves routine and struggles to take risks, and the devoted-dependent personality, in which there is a sense of emotional comfort in being taken care of and a release from exaggerated fears of having to act independently, then in a co-dependent environment which unintentionally promoted learned dependency I believe that long-term toileting problems might well be one of the most common results and yet be no real true reflection of that person's actual intelligence or cognitive ability. The catch-22 is that once someone with Autism is seemingly unable to feed or toilet themselves, the assumption that they must therefore be severely mentally retarded then gets them off the hook from any other assumed capabilities. In fact, I have met a small handful of Autistic adults around the world in this same group who have been, nevertheless, able to walk, use fine and gross motor skills, type, and use a computer, and some who have even achieved university degrees, while remaining essentially non-verbal and not yet independently using the toilet. We really must ask ourselves whether we are ready to consider the interrelationship between emotion, personality, motivation, daring and capability in looking at our own responses in bringing up Auties with these types of challenges. If we continually sweep these people aside as mentally retarded or learning disabled we may never move forward from the comfort zone of the 'cared-for dependant' and the 'self-sacrificing helper'.

If someone with dependent personality is irrationally and phobically fixated on fear of abandonment, then taking themselves to bed, putting themselves to *sleep* and sleeping alone may be quite an emotional challenge for them, with the comfort of joining in their carer's bed as the promise of a reward if they appear incapable enough in doing so. To someone with an irrational fear of abandonment may come an additional comfort in doing this if they are also far more dependent on or possessive of one of their carers than they are of the other. Insisting on their inability to sleep alone, and invading the relationship their carer may have with an adult partner, directly ensures they have not been 'excluded' or 'closed out' by the intimate relationship their carer has with the partner. Sadly, this short-term fix of an irrational fear may actually lead to the carer's own adult relationship breaking down and the less co-dependent partner leaving. This could mean the dependent person now achieves total control over their carer who is now less socially supported and more isolated, and more desperate than ever for their child to 'get better' that their now unchecked co-dependent behaviour actually increases. At the same time, any heightened resentment or feeling of being overly burdened by their child's dependency may reinforce their child's sense that 'if I became independent my carer would leave me'. If you don't like the game or its outcome, the lesson is that as soon as you recognise this is the game, don't play it.

If someone with dependent personality being cared for in a co-dependent way realises that *stimming* excuses them out of assumed capability and leads to the carer leaving his or her own activities and needs to attend to theirs, then this could conceivably naturally reinforce the positive associations stimming has for that person and make them less likely to limit or suppress their stimming in favour of seeking out independent activity. Taking their greatest fears as those of abandonment and having to act independently, it might be that ignoring and moving away from their indulgence in stimming could help trigger them to stop and pursue you if only to find another, more constructive way to make you 'take over'. But it is essential to be aware that this would probably not be so for the solitary personality, who would find your absence and their solitude a reward, and your involvement and intimacy and intrusion may well drive some to stim to close you out. So, these are not one-size-fits-all strategies for Autism, but far more individualised applications for specific people who also happen to have Autism.

Tantrums are a normal part of development in two- and three-year-olds who are making the transition from the dependency of babyhood to the independence of toddler and childhood. There are some people whose personalities are naturally far more 'self-owning', independent, autonomous, nonconformist, adventurous or confident, who may be less likely to throw tantrums in order to reinforce their dependency and their carer's co-dependency. Personalities such as the sensitive-avoidant or devoted-dependent may struggle more than most to make that transition without finding it terribly difficult, and those with additional information-processing or other challenges will find this even more so. The deciding factor for whether they get past this stage or not may well rest on the degree of respectful and empowering 'tough love' and the lack of co-dependency in the carers they grow up with.

As those with Autism become older children and teenagers, these tantrums may well be called meltdowns, when there may be very good emotional-personality reasons to keep an open mind that some of them are in fact 'regressions' and 'tantrums' in simply finding it too emotionally challenging to dare, to take risks or to act independently.

In terms of *self-protection responses*, the learned appearance of helplessness (or the lack of spontaneous emotional motivation to defy this impression) is a type of self-protection response for some people. A self-protection response in someone with a solitary or vigilant personality may revolve around fear of social invasion or subordination. For someone with the idiosyncratic or leisurely personality, it may revolve around fear of forced conformity or compulsory activity. For someone with the artistic personality it may revolve around fear of being blocked from one's own expression of creativity. For the

avoidant personality self-protection, by contrast, may revolve around minimising the expectations of others that you might take risks, function outside
of routine or work with strangers. For the dependent personality, self-protection may mean minimising risk of imagined abandonment and fear of independent action by maximising those behaviours which reinforce dependency
and promote the co-dependency of one's carers.

Challenging and self-injurious behaviours can occur for a whole variety of
reasons. One of those reasons may be the natural but perhaps irrational
distress of those with dependent personality who may engage in the types of
behaviours which may provoke guilt and responsibility in a carer and bring
them 'running back to the rescue'. In this way they get a 'fix' in terms of the
comfort of 'being taken care of' as much as from the reassurance that they
have power over the carer's ability to leave them, including leaving them to
have to act independently. I have personally worked with some people with
Autism who have blatantly used self-injurious behaviours to provoke a carer to
take over, to punish the carer for having left them to do something for themselves (even when they achieved it), to create a wedge between their carer and
others in the home, or friends and strangers visiting the house and sharing the
attention of the main carer. This is absolutely not to say that self-injurious or
challenging behaviours function this way for all people with Autism, just that
I have seen this in this subgroup and honestly have to acknowledge what I
encountered. In each case, the response of the carer was to run to the rescue
compulsively and instantly, which they'd been doing for years.

Those with learned dependency involved with co-dependent carers may
be more likely than other people with Autism to appear *unable to feed themselves*,
in spite of having good dexterity and fine motor skills in their own obsessive
interests or stims.

CHAPTER 9

Bad Parenting or Bad Match?

Boundary Issues

Two neighbours from hell, Fred and Joe, live next door to each other. Each thinks it is he who is 'normal'. Fred wants some roses so goes and picks Joe's roses. 'There is no reason to ask,' he thinks, 'I don't mind after all if he comes and picks mine.' Fred sees Joe in the front room of his own house, eating his breakfast in his pyjamas, and waves hello from Joe's own front yard on which he is standing. Joe looks quickly away and draws the curtains, sneaks out the back of his house grumbling to himself and tends to his 'neighbours begone' 60-foot conifers that border the two houses. Fred goes back home feeling sorry for Joe that he's so uptight and self-protective.

What are boundary issues?

Most non-Autistic adults have a sense of 'boundaries'. Boundaries are like a kind of circle we might draw around ourselves, a little way outside of our body.

A boundary is like a safe space we exist within. A boundary is like a safe place for our soul to feel free to express itself through the body, within the realm of the external world. When we feel something is invading our boundary uninvited, we might run away to protect the integrity of our boundary. We might reject or retaliate against the sensed invasion. If we feel powerless against it or feel the invader is oblivious, dogmatic, relentless, fixated, on a mission or deeply invested in an imagined right to invade our boundary physically, mentally, emotionally, socially, morally, we may simply withdraw back into our body, back further to where we cannot even connect to our body. We can 'pull up the drawbridge'. Those who invade our boundary may continue to do so, but they can have a shell, a body we have abandoned, a compliant reflection of themselves given back purely to the prompt.

Some people have no boundaries, they don't care about 'invasion', are open to it, even welcome it, seek it, thrive because of it. Dogs are often far better at being like this than cats or horses.

Some people have no respect for the boundaries of others, and again, think about dogs. Some people have no respect for the boundaries of others but they have a strong need for a wide boundary around themselves. I've met some ginger tom cats who qualify for this one. Some people have a great need for a strong sense of boundaries dividing themselves from others, sometimes physically, sometimes psychologically, sometimes emotionally, sometimes socially, sometimes morally.

A partner can choose or find themselves with someone with similar boundaries to their own, or with someone with a dramatically different sense of boundaries. These differences can bring out change in each of them, or they can clash in ways that inhibit their growth, not enhance it. We can also listen to each other and adapt and adjust in ways that help the garden of our family be a healthy space. People can have children with very different boundaries to their own, and the carers may have a shared assumption that the child's sense of his or her own boundaries is 'abnormal', or one parent may have this feeling but the other may find no problem at all with the child's reactions in protecting his or her own boundaries or having virtually none.

Again these differences can make everyone adapt and adjust and grow, or they can clash, lead to dynamics involving invasion and control, and lead to self-protectiveness and withdrawal. Auties are not immune from being part of this very natural human process. In fact, if anything, they may be far more sensitive to feeling these clashes than many.

We can react to the environment by progressively expanding that sense of boundary outside of ourselves so that our sense of 'invasion' is easily triggered. We can react to the environment by progressively decreasing that sense of boundary outside of ourselves so we become progressively more tolerant of small, fairly non-invasive forms of social contact.

Having an information-processing, sensory-perceptual, mood or compulsive disorder will certainly affect how we feel about those boundaries. Anxiety disorders can be provoked by the ways others impinge upon our sense of our own boundary and can be progressively reduced where we give consistent clear signs that the nature of our interaction, communication and involvement is self-owning (we are just being present within our own space) and 'non-invasive'. Some personality traits, and their exaggerated 'disorder' forms, involve an extreme need for strong boundaries, others involve having very poor boundaries to our sense of self, and yet others involve invading the boundaries of others.

We can learn from the environment that invasiveness is taken as a normal thing. We can learn from our environment that self-protection seems justified. Non-Autistic people may differ from Auties in how they invade or self-protect, but essentially invasion and self-protection are the same things no matter how we dress them.

Some degree of correction or annoyance is healthy and normal. An excess degree, however, may be like a tidal wave which sweeps straight over whatever's in its path. The tiny blossoming flower will be crushed by the tidal wave and stand no chance. Perhaps only the cement and steel pillar will have a chance. Having poor boundaries can be about being too quick to correct, or too stressed at, the mess or noise or explorations of others to the point where we seek to overly suppress or control them.

Being helped has a healthy place, after one has had the opportunity and time and unobserved space in which to explore and try and fail and try again in discovering one's own potential for oneself. Being helped too eagerly, watched too intensely, carrying the emotional investments of others too heavily, may be a robbery, an invasive sense of audience, an invisible tightening fence and a burden, if not an indulgence, one cannot dare to sell out to.

Having people be proud of you can be a healthy thing for most people at some level. Some need this overtly, others self-sabotage if the limelight is too harsh, too weighty or socially invasive.

Having others be too proud of you may also be a burden involving an unsustainable self-expectation you may fear you could never live up to. Some would rather give up before trying. Being advertised for the benefit of someone else's sense of achievement may make you an object more than a person, and it doesn't matter whether what is being flag-waved is the burden of your disability on the shoulders of the martyrs or saints that carry you or whether it is someone's focus on something you had half a chance of feeling pride in for yourself. If you sense someone else steals your achievements for their own social pride, you may feel invisible and your life may not feel like your own. Even those achievements which once felt like yours, may now be little more than someone else's medals of service pinned, claustrophobically, on your chest.

Having people love you blindly might be ok if you also know how to love others more than use them, if you have learned through your own efforts how to equally love yourself, and if you are equipped with reason and motivation to challenge and set boundaries for yourself. But being loved so blindly that nobody dares set boundaries or perimeters for your behaviour may mean you have nothing to kick against in finding out who you are. There are people loved so unconditionally that they feel the need to create a provocation worthy of an imposition of boundaries, and there are those loved so uncondi-tionally by people they themselves have not yet wrestled with enough to respect and love back that the love may seem like a force-fed handout they have not earned and may neither devour nor stomach. Unwanted love given too freely can sometimes be a bitter fruit.

Having enough food, water, light, air, shelter and clothing are essential to all of us at some time. But it is the absence of entertainment which drives us to seek it, the absence of toys which drives us to create them out of sticks and sand and saucepan lids. Being showered with material 'love' of the TV, computer games, DVDs or videos as babysitter can be an addiction but also a robbery of the motivating force of boredom and loneliness. The simplest of things shine by contrast – this shower of material 'love' appears empty by contrast with, for example, the piece of string one discovered for oneself in its infinite patterns and the sense it is so 'mine'.

Being exposed to language can be an important foundation to developing communication. But being chased with torrents of language, feeling watched and waited for like a rabbit which may move only to be pounced on by the expectant and hopeful fox, may paint language not as an invitation but as a social invasion to protect oneself against. In an urban society in which televi-sion and radio fill every once empty piece of solitude, there is now often little space left to discover the stillness of silence.

Having perimeters to grow into can be a solid structure in which we can find 'ourselves' within a mass of exploration and interaction. But if, too early, those perimeters are too narrow, if we are judged too 'abnormal', too 'quirky', too 'weird', too 'aloof', too 'slow', too 'late', then we may be boxed before we even have a chance to self-discover, to know or own who we are. Why should we bother? The journey is over before it has even begun.

Boundaries are not just about adults. Teenagers have them. Children have them. Infants have them. And babies have them.

Boundaries are not just about conscious awareness. Boundaries are something our bodies feel, our psychology adjusts to, our emotions react to. Boundaries are something animals experience. Even worms and plants will react to a breach of their sense of boundaries. You don't need a high IQ in order to sense. In fact, there may be a case for being more highly sensing if your intellectual abilities are actually lower and less reliable than your pre-conscious state.

Having bad boundaries is not just about the common definition of 'child abuse' in its various forms, it is broader and often subtler than that. We all experience boundary issues where these often don't formally qualify as abuse. Boundaries and how we respect or disrespect them, how they clash with someone else's or how we adjust where we can to help everyone grow, are an invisible world which we all have, whether we are conscious of it or not. Understanding how to work with boundaries is a large and overlooked part of environmental medicine.

Effects on boundary issues
Boundary issues and health
In having poor boundaries, we may become overly sensitive to the push and pull of others.

In having overly strong boundaries, we may self-protectively extinguish the ebb and flow of our connection with the external world, which is to close ourselves off from our own 'life force' (growth, expansion, interaction) and embrace the stagnation of our 'death force' (that which denies flow, is about contracting and restricting contact and interaction).

In spending our time reacting to our own hypersensitivity or mourning our own entrapment we may be expending energy, feeling despair or anxiety, destabilising our own environmental supports. Where carers are trapped with their own neediness, a desire to give which will not be let in, a need for pride which others will not fulfil, a desire for order which will not be tolerated, a desire for flexibility which will be met with resistance, a desire to know and connect which will not be trusted, a need to be valued which will not be recognised, here carers expend energy in frustration, suppression, isolation and mourning.

When we exhaust our energy again and again and again, we can re-examine our mindsets or find other ways to fulfil the same needs. If we choose not to take that path we choose to lose hope, to resign ourselves, to grab what straws we can rather than find the haystack. The tide and the under-current affect each other, and change in one causes change in the other. Ulti-mately, one road will lead to health and free others to change too. The other road will lead eventually to ill health, socially, emotionally, psychologically or physically. And it may be about making choices, even hard choices.

Cognitive behavioural implications

Having an extreme lack of boundaries, having withdrawn deeply within yourself, or being hyper-vigilant and self-protective about your boundaries are all issues which have the capacity to distract from the experiences you are in and divert energy away from information processing you don't deem imme-diately relevant to your situation. Having boundary problems can mean that you either never shut up, and have difficulty controlling or channelling your speech to meet your needs, or that you can't connect with your body easily in speaking up, speaking out and connecting with others. And there will be people who swing between one state and the other either because of an infor-mation processing challenge in tracking a simultaneous sense of self and other, because of mood or anxiety issues or because different environmental dynamics are triggering different feelings about their own boundaries.

To make matters even more confusing, an environment can have two or more major carers over a short period of time in which different carers trigger dramatically different boundary relationships in the child. One carer may cause an extreme self-protectiveness of one's own boundaries and a with-drawal from expression through the body. Another may be completely without boundaries themselves and yet so non-invasive that one finds oneself opening up without limits. Another carer may be highly aloof but extremely structured such as in the old institutionalised residential settings or in some hospital wards. The end result may be a shifting or sharply fluctuating boundary state which lacks enough continuity to become integrated into any one sense of personality. Theoretically, there is no reason why someone in this kind of situation may not eventually develop collections of distinct personality traits, which may take many years to integrate because each is such an extreme and so distinct from the others.

Addressing boundary issues
Helping those with boundary issues

Our relationship to our own boundaries is ingrained, unconscious and automatic. We can change our psychology and, often, our gut instincts will still not listen. Hypnotherapists specialise in changing patterns that our conscious mind cannot change for us. There are even some who work with children and work with emotional and body reactions through taking children on adventures through storytelling and myths that progressively build different patterns of reactions. Some professionals may be able to adapt these techniques for children with receptive-language and information-processing challenges. This is not to say these approaches are for everyone, or that boundary issues affect all Auties.

Some people will explore boundary issues through dance, art or music therapy. Some will work on boundary issues through massage or reflexology, or through using Bach Flower Remedies or Bush Flower Essences to alter family dynamics. Some family therapists and clinical psychologists will have experience in counselling and educating people about boundary issues. Some cognitive behavioural psychologists may be able to prescribe exercises that help people change their current boundary relationships or help them to make outlines and plans about what's not working and how they might go about constructively changing those things.

The conformist and the rebel

There are many things which make us what and who we are. Sometimes social judgements drive some of us to part with ways we would otherwise find 'natural'. Sometimes social judgements drive us to do the opposite – swing against them, become more rigid in our defiance.

This pattern is true of any people facing social pressures. Some bend and conform, others rebel. Auties are no less human. Some bend and conform, others rebel. The achievement of making someone bend and conform may not be all it is made out to be, and many who do so do so at the expense of finding their own selfhood, the driving force in independently finding one's place in the world. Rebelling can mean one cuts off one's nose to spite one's face, or it can be part of developing a strong sense of self, even the platform from which we come down in discovering humility and respect for those we once were so busy pulling against. Sometimes we learn a lot from having a war, including how to let go, to change sides, to reconcile, to negotiate, to be the diplomat even within our internal world. Whether we conform or rebel and whether we do so to our benefit or detriment depends on the sensitivity of the environment in the part it plays in this dance of the soul. We are never alone in our conformity or rebellion. We are siding with (or selling out to) something. We are pulling against something we perceive to be opposing us.

I have seen amazing things done with reverse psychology and the 'good cop/bad cop' scenario. If we are busy telling a rebel what they must do, perhaps we will get much further in agreeing with them that they must not. Perhaps if we present a rebel with two choices, one slightly worse than the other, he or she is led to choosing the better of two evils rather than simply rejecting outright our offer of 'reward' too quickly renamed as their perceived 'defeat'.

Boundary issues and specific behavioural issues
Boundary issues might underpin specific behaviours/issues relating to:

- communication
- being in one's own world
- eye contact
- learning and cognitive challenges
- toileting
- sleep problems
- stimming
- meltdowns
- self-protection responses
- challenging behaviours
- food behaviour problems.

Communication has many different uses. These include:

- self-entertainment
- practical uses
- social interaction
- emotional self-expression
- social control (for both communication and its absence).

Where boundary issues occur within an environment, the social-interaction and emotional self-expression uses for communication may be the most likely to be affected, and the social-control uses for both communication and its absence may become far more relevant.

Nothing may compel someone quicker into *their own world* than the boundaries issues of those in the 'external world' of 'other'. This may be a much bigger issue for certain personality types such as the solitary, the idio-syncratic, the vigilant, the artistic and the sensitive personality types. Equally, in reverse, nothing may so relax and disinhibit these same personalities as when those in their environments get back into their own space, stop being so intense, so overly enthusiastic, so invasive and controlling. We are all moved differently by music, and one of the most therapeutic forms of 'music' in my view is the 'music of beingness' unique to each human being. When we bring the music of our own beingness back into harmony with the perhaps different 'tune' of someone else, this is one of the greatest forms of environmental medicine – and it changes both people.

Eye contact can be a way of making people back off and a way of inviting them in. Some people will stare someone down to gain space and take back empowerment when they are feeling disempowered. Other people will empower themselves through avoiding the eye contact that would normally invite social inclusion of others. If you already feel others have 'over-included' themselves, avoiding eye contact with them may be a very natural way of saying 'too much', 'stop force feeding me'. Interestingly, where this is occurring, advice to carers to get back into their own space, get some self-ownership about their own identity, needs and interests, play hard to get, leave the other person wanting long enough for them to find the motivation to chase them, has sometimes been reported as the strongest 'medicine' they've found in getting their Autie to seek eye contact, relax and sometimes even socially pursue them for a change.

Giving people the indication 'you are causing me discomfort' can also function as an indirectly confrontational self-directed expression to others of 'get away from me', 'no I don't want to come in there with you', and the more it's used in front of others in the general public the more powerful it often is in inhibiting others from being as socially invasive or controlling as they might otherwise be. This is not to say this is consciously manipulative. It may be as simple as having learned 'this seems to help'.

There are those who *learn* through assistance and instruction and those who are non-verbal learners who learn through discovery when unobserved, uncontrolled and unguided by others. If you take those in the second group, and watch, control and constrict access to doing things 'their own way', you may well find you have drawn on their greatest weaknesses and they now appear far more muddled, overloaded, cognitively challenged and with learning difficulties. In fact it may equally be due to the incompatibility of your own approach with their preferred learning style and personality traits.

Many of us might drive but completely forget how to drive when a criticism-on-legs backseat driver does their big-time 'nag thing'. Then they say, 'See, you needed my help, if it wasn't for me watching out then you would have…' But chances are that if they didn't increase stress, self-consciousness and disempowerment, and decrease your ability to tune into your own instinct or learning, you wouldn't have messed up at all. I remember being on trains and knowing my stop perfectly well based on the visual patterns outside but having no idea of the name of my station, and being asked how many stops it is and what the name of the station was that I needed. In the end I couldn't find my own system at all. In similar situations, I ended up giving over all control to the other person and looking like a complete idiot when my own (admittedly less conventional) system actually was working fine without their interference. I remember many times being grabbed from crossing a road only to cause me instinctively to jump away from them and in front of an oncoming car; and people who would seek to get me to watch, look left and right and cross when there were no cars only to find that with delayed processing nothing registered with meaning or significance this way so I ended up walking in front of the moving object I hadn't processed was a car. I learned instead to break away from these seemingly 'mad' people so I could feel the rhythm of the moving objects, cross calmly into the spaces, avoiding the rushing movements, and progressively cross the road whether it was a two-lane road or a four-lane motorway, much to their absolute horror. But without the ability to process in the active moment the meaning of the whizzing objects, I could still know not to walk in front of them and I had the absence of the kind of fear and threat of panic that would have come from a crystal-clear idea of what these were or their significance (as would normally be so with non-Autistic people).

If one cannot emotionally endure asking for help or permission, receiving assistance, fuss, being in the limelight or on the receiving end of overt praise, then avoiding *using the toilet* or even demonstrating a need for it can also function as a form of social control in temporarily avoiding or reinforcing the over-involvement of others. Other personalities who thrive on routine, familiarity and dependency may become so accustomed to others taking over the responsibility of toileting on their behalf they may not find the personal drive or daring to take over.

Those who cannot cope with forced conformity (the idiosyncratic personality), compulsory activity (the leisurely personality), stagnation (the artistic personality), being subordinated (the vigilant personality) or handling social-emotional intimacy they have not overtly sought (the solitary personality) may all struggle more than most with being made to go to bed and go to *sleep* when this is handled in the conventional way. In the first case (idiosyncratic) you would use reverse psychology, in the second (leisurely) you would give a semblance of freedom of choice by presenting the good cop/bad cop style of options, in the third (artistic) you would let the creative pursuit go to bed too, in the fourth (vigilant) you would give the person responsibility for putting something else to bed, and in the fifth (solitary) you would remove social fuss and involvement from the bedtime ritual and increase social involvement if they stayed up. In other words, how we use our own boundaries can be used strategically to helpfully affect the way others respond with their own.

Stimming may be accentuated by the need to reinforce one's own boundaries, and often when others become less socially invasive, less controlling, less fixated on the person with Autism this additional driving force of stimming decreases.

We all have our privacy needs, our personal space; Auties are no exception. The problem is that when a parent is overly conscientious, even obsessive-compulsive in their fixation on their child's 'special needs' or extremely self-sacrificing and co-dependent, it is part of society's present values to sympathise with this, encouraging the parent to continue this way, even if such an approach is as dysfunctional as the phobic or dependent responses the Autie may give to it.

Pursuing, disempowering, fixating upon someone with an Autism spectrum condition, constantly filming them, overtly observing them, seeing them as a project, controlling and forcing conformity on them at every turn is pathological and in such a context *meltdowns* by any name are a natural, even healthy, response to an extremely unhealthy situation. I'd like to say this type of thing is uncommon in the families of those with children on the Autistic spectrum and in residential care homes and ABA programmes. I'd like to, but as yet, it is still too common, way too common, and often the main focus of attention in the treatment of Autism.

Self-protection responses can be a normal part of responding to boundaries issues. It is sometimes more the case that the boundaries issues need to be sorted so the self-protection responses no longer require attention or intervention.

Despairing, disempowered, alienated, frustrated people are more likely to engage in *challenging and self-injurious behaviours* whether they have information-processing and other issues or not. One of the sources of that despair, disempowerment, alienation and frustration is unaddressed boundary issues in the environment. Zoo animals in similar distress also respond with challenging, even self-injurious behaviours until the environment is changed.

People who are coping with boundaries issues can respond with controlling the only things they can. For some people this will be self-comforting behaviours in relation to *food and eating*, for others it may be about refusing to 'share' in the same food as others or insisting on eating only that which others don't want you to have or wish you'd 'get over'.

CHAPTER 10

A Matter of Perspective

Trauma, Neglect, Abuse and Grief

Sure the cat died, but that was cats for you. They don't live long.

Max had lived for the cat. It was the only non-verbal self-owning person in the household. Max and the cat had an understanding. Neither chased the other. They'd just quietly 'be' in each other's presence. Nobody thought of that as a relationship. When the cat died it was put in the rubbish bin and taken away. Then they got themselves a dog. They'd always wanted a dog.

Most adults have experienced an episode of trauma, neglect, abuse or grief at some time in their life. Age is no guarantee against such things and no degree of 'protection' can completely shelter a person from glimpses of these experiences on our televisions, in our newspapers, played out in our video games, our DVDs and on the internet – they are part of what happens in the world.

Some people have experienced these things in other times of their life, such as in their teens, childhood, even infancy. Some people have experienced these things in a small dose, but that small dose created one rather large thorn in their side. Some exceptionally hypersensitive personalities may only have experienced these things in subtle ways, and it is by virtue of their hypersensitivity that these things would have had such an impact.

Some people have experienced these things covertly before things were swept under the rug. Some have experienced these things openly in a place where the common values were to ignore such things or assume them as 'normal'. Some people have had denial poured on top of tragedy. Some people have been encouraged to wear their victimhood like a badge like an old general (sometimes to their own psychological, emotional or social detriment).

There is no one form or degree of trauma, neglect, abuse or grief and no one way of responding to it. What is certain is that it is such things that can break us, and sometimes, equally, we become something different, even sometimes something more, because of these things; and those on the Autistic spectrum are not immune.

Defining the issues

What defines trauma?

According to Merriam-Webster's Online Dictionary (2005b), trauma is 'a disordered psychic or behavioral state resulting from mental or emotional stress…'.

The traumas of my own childhood were numerous, but many of them are events nobody would even have thought mattered much. For example, leaving the welfare daycare centre, its familiar room of rows of cots, its grass, its wire and frosted window, the Sister who was familiar to me, this daytime world I'd known from six months to two and a half, and losing it all suddenly in one day was a trauma nobody noticed or knew of. Somewhere I promised myself that as all things could end so abruptly, nothing I could not control could be allowed to become too familiar, too important.

When I let my mother's bird escape from the aviary out into the blue sky and it left our lives never to come back, followed by the cat running away, were traumas to me, for there were parts of our home which could leave and never come back, parts more socially friendly to me than most humans. I so desperately wanted to be an animal, not a human, to fly and leave the confines of a world I didn't belong in, and not to be left behind.

When the green plastic ball I had carried with me for three years 'disappeared', I was traumatised, as if a part of me or a great friend had gone. I became determined that all attachments to objects would be secret and private, and where possible with things which could never disappear, like air particles and running in circles with sticks which could be found anywhere and were always replaceable.

Being taken back to the park by a child who had found me, taken me home and made me part of her house, had stuck with me as a trauma for years in which I was deeply struck by my inability to communicate, to build or hold a relationship with this person or ever find her or be found by her again. I became determined that nobody could ever discard me because I would connect with them all within the internal world, not the external world, but when I recreated this feeling of friendship with my mirror reflection I still spent 20 years crying to my reflection because this 'other girl' in there would not 'let me in'.

I was traumatised by my own emotional fits, in which I attacked myself and had no idea who, what or where I was. I was traumatised by being trapped in a room I was not allowed to leave without asking, when I was unable to ask. I was traumatised by being watched and spoken to directly when all familiarity and security was based on having a clear separation between my world and the external world. I was traumatised by the realisation I was alienated from others, and sensing I was also alien to them.

I was traumatised in realising that meaning existed, and I was nine years old and a world away and didn't feel I stood a chance in hell of being in 'their world'.

I was traumatised by awareness that people put on façades and would be convinced these were real, and could even be repulsed by me or attack me if I saw that they were not.

I was traumatised by the idea that others would deny me the equality and freedom of other children if I was not seen to be 'normal'.

I was traumatised by the fact that in society, I was treated as stupid, powerless and disposable yet felt myself equal in worth to any other human being.

I was traumatised by society's emphasis on social dialogue as a sign of intelligence, when mine could badly let me down in spite of my being as worthy of respect, inclusion and opportunity as anyone else.

I was traumatised by the fact that I had, wherever possible, to hide disability rather than ask for help if I was to have the status of a person and not a child or a pet.

I was traumatised by being capable of deeply loving yet unable to tolerate touch, express love or openly accept its expression towards, or connection with, me.

None of these things would have been remembered by others as traumas. And strangely, it is these simple things which stand out among some of the biggest impacts on my sense of myself and of the world. These became the basis of my greatest fears, the escape or conquering of which became the sources of my greatest securities. What this says to me is that trauma can happen where we cannot predict it or head it off, for to do so would extinguish life and cripple a child far worse than traumatic experiences themselves. We are broken as well as shaped by traumas.

There are children who were traumatised by their first social experiences with other children, and children who were traumatised by having scratchy clothing imposed upon them for the sake of 'looking nice'.

There are children who were traumatised by losing a toy down the toilet and then fearing they themselves may disappear down there.

There are children who were traumatised by an overreaction to them making a mess, making too much noise, touching dirty substances, or simply by suddenly finding themselves being laughed at or suffocatingly fussed over by a crowd of towering yet adoring adults.

There are those who have been traumatised by violence, shouting or slamming of doors, and those who have been the object of their carers' disputes who fear being torn away from one parent and abandoned by the other.

There are those with early experiences of hospitalisation they assumed to be abandonment and a sudden loss of all things familiar with no ability to ask or understand they would again go home.

There are those traumatised by their own lack of communication or social phobia in a society where this can cost them inclusion, equality and opportunity. And there are those traumatised by being by nature asocial, asexual, detached and even harmlessly devoid of empathy for others foreign to themselves in a society which teaches them this is 'abnormal' and they must learn to act otherwise.

There are those who are traumatised by being acutely sensing in a world which relies on interpretive thinking, having largely lost its ability to sense and most of its respect and use for this function.

There are those who are traumatised by being people with fragmented vision in a world which insists on fluorescent lighting that makes their fragmentation worse. There are those with sensory hypersensitivities who are traumatised by being made to sit in a room with noisy fans, and those with severe receptive language problems who have been traumatised by spending years in a world which assumes them stupid yet provides no gestural signing or visual cues for them to process incoming language.

There are those traumatised by being alienated by both having an Autism spectrum condition and being homosexual, bisexual or transgender without realising these 'differences' are naturally more common among those on the Autistic spectrum than in the general population.

Trauma is not a word made up by Auties, but having Autism can make you a lot more susceptible to the impact of everyday trauma invisible to most non-Autistic people. At the same time, in my experience, there is currently virtually no focus on trauma counselling, advocacy for those who cannot communicate their needs, or skills training for Auties specifically aimed at explaining their needs to others.

What defines neglect?

Dictionary definitions of neglect include entries such as 'a deliberate lack of care and attention' or 'disregarding responsibilities and lacking concern'. It can also be defined as 'to give little attention or respect to', 'to leave undone or unattended to especially through carelessness'. (Merriam-Webster, Incorporated 2005b)

Usually when we think of the term 'neglect' we think of depriving someone of something. We are all pretty clear that children have basic needs which must be met for physical survival. We are all pretty clear that children have psychological and emotional needs for some degree of stimulation, involvement and experiences. But what we often completely fail to realise is that it is possible to neglect a child's need for solitude, trial-and-error learning, self-discovery and, most of all, for motivation. If our jug is too full we do not want it to be filled up further.

We usually think of neglect as something someone has done deliberately out of their own selfishness. Accusations of neglect can be a big, nasty old bashing stick used by people against each other, and the phantom of these accusations can haunt carers and be imagined, if not actually seen, in the glares and huffing and eye-rolling responses of strangers in supermarkets and on the street, of the extended family at the family get-together.

But we all neglect, all of us do it. We neglect ourselves and our own needs to the degree that we may lose sight of who we are, and with that our love of life, our physical, emotional, psychological, social or moral health. We may neglect ourselves by over-focusing on something or someone else to the degree that we are then so empty we are actually not there to be a healthy role model anyway. We may neglect ourselves to the degree that we lose the sharing of that self with a partner and so progressively lose the health of that garden called the family in which children are meant to grow up. We may neglect our relationship to the community, to nature, to ongoing life experiences to the point where we are isolated and vulnerable and far more likely to fixate on our ever more minute point of focus, which is usually not healthy for anyone. We may neglect *balance*, and when we neglect balance, we can't clearly see our own lives or the lives and diversity and equality of those around us.

Neglect can happen when we are not aware of the nature of someone's needs. This can happen when their needs are dramatically different from or foreign to our own. It may happen if carers are told, or assume, that the needs of their Autistic child are a sign of their 'abnormality' and that their own are 'normal', and that they therefore have a right, if not obligation, to ignore the child's needs in asserting their own version of 'normality', failing to realise that the child's reality is also 'normal' to them. A century ago, deaf people were denied access to sign language on the basis that they needed merely to fit themselves into the 'normality' of a hearing world. Today, to deny a deaf child access to learning or experiencing signing would be considered a form of neglect. Still, there are Auties with severe central auditory processing disorders, which amounts to the same thing as meaning-deafness, many of whom are often still denied access to signing or fluent visual cues in assisting them to understand what is otherwise little more than 'blah blah'. These are not the only needs not being met.

All people are different. Their information-processing capacities are different and some will overload more quickly than others. If we overstimulate such people, force-feed them with information beyond their capacity to process it, we may deprive them of the opportunity to experience information processing as something user-friendly, something they find a rewarding experience, such that they can remain motivated to chase another small dose of it at a later stage.

If a child has sensory hypersensitivities or exposure anxiety and we insist on being in that child's face, watching, waiting, wanting and ever ready to pounce, or fail to ensure a sensory environment the child can find sensorily tolerable, then we may neglect that child's emotional needs and set the child up for potential trauma about social encounters and environments the child cannot control.

If a child has a personality disorder which leaves them unable to withstand large amounts of social contact or unable to empathise with others who are not like themselves, it might be neglect to deny such a person a reasonable degree of solitude and opportunities for solitary self-directed learning and exploration. It might be equally neglectful if, in helping them with with social skills and employment opportunities, we did not provide them opportunities in which they could be useful rather than social. It might be neglectful if we provided them with no opportunities to relate via something else, such as the computer or being part of a walking group or chess club in which the focus was on the activity, not on the person. If we provided them with activities and opportunities involving only face-to-face, directly confrontational interpersonal interactions in which they were expected to empathise, we might be neglecting their social needs by offering them only that which they find inaccessible and a source of constant social failure. If we were to provide stairs for someone in a wheelchair and call that the provision of an opportunity for access, we would be equally neglectful in facing up to and working with their needs. We would be imposing some assumption of our own version of normality in a way that completely disregards, demeans, devalues, if not segregates and limits, them.

If we were to fail to provide strong boundaries, privacy and a reasonable level of personal detachment for someone with dependent personality, so that they might never be forced to explore their own potential, then this might be a form of neglect for we fail to meet their needs in reaching their potential necessary to independent survival. If we constantly prompt to the degree that a child is never left with the consequences of his or her own apathy or learned helplessness, and is deprived of the opportunities to discover his or her own, perhaps delayed, thought processes or emotional responses, then this may be neglect.

Looking at the child with avoidant personality who is so hypersensitive to awareness of his or her own imperfection, so anxious of embarrassment, so nervous of trying anything he or she might not be brilliant at, perhaps we can look at a carer's own excellence. It is often inspiring to model excellence, but to others it can be both inspiring and overwhelmingly intimidating. If we so excel and outshine a reticent child in our own abilities, to the point where we succeed in impressing them but they will now never dare to compete or try for themselves, perhaps, no matter what we *tell* them, we may be inadvertently showing them that they could never be so good. In this we may deprive them of the opportunity to believe they too could excel or be as impressive, and so we neglect their need. Then the carer will always be made to speak, or draw, or read out loud on behalf of the child who has become certain he or she could never be that good and is unmotivated accordingly.

If we over-protect a child to the degree that he or she is deprived of social opportunities, involvement in the community, trial-and-error learning, or of being left wanting long enough to begin to explore, then this may be neglect. If a child then develops social phobia or generalised anxiety disorder and becomes progressively more socially limited and has a reduced capacity to function, then we may have neglected that child's needs for self-initiated exploration and opportunities to develop self-confidence, and deprived them of any other social role model which could help instil a sense of the world as a place they can trust, explore and know they, like any of us, can deal with.

If we fail to allow a child (with respect and moderation) directly to experience the consequences of his or her actions, where this is safely possible, and to make these links overt in a way the child can keep track of and base future choices upon, then we may be depriving that child of the capacity to make these links, learn from them and modify their own behaviour, which is essential for family stability, for their own stability and for future social inclusion and opportunities.

If in early infancy, we fail to limit the flood of passive experiences (e.g. via electronic media) and simultaneously provide children with few opportunities sensorily and physically to explore the world interactively, this introduction to 'normality' may so much flood their senses with endless passive experiences that they have now got no life experience to slot those experiences into, and their sense of the world is now an internal, theoretical sense of the world: the world in one's head, not something our body or gut may be yet able to relate to. In this we may be depriving that child not only of opportunities for wider physical development and sensory integration necessary to brain integration and gut/immune health, which is such a large part of being active and interactive, but also of the opportunity to realise that sensory and physical interactive experiences in the external world provide a basis for comprehending and relating to passive experiences within one's internal world. If this leads to a progressive unfamiliarity with physical and sensory interactive exploration in the external world and a limited capacity simultaneously to process a sense of self and other, the internal and external realities, then we may be limiting their future development, and in doing so we have neglected their needs.

What defines abuse?

Definitions of abuse include 'to put to a wrong or improper use' (Merriam-Webster's Online Dictionary 2005b). When we think of abuse we usually think of bruises, swearing, degradation or sexual abuse. This is the narrow definition.

In the broader definition, smoking, excessive dieting, even some types of body piercing or fashions that involve wearing clothes that are uncomfortably tight, or exposing one's body in the middle of winter to the point one gets sick might even be seen as a form of self-abuse.

Passive smoking is seen as a form of abuse of the rights of others to health and a healthy social environment.

Even constant correction could qualify as improper or excessive use of one's authority and power over someone else, and most of us have been driven to distraction, if not despair or rage, in the company of a compulsive nag or worrier.

Homosexuals, psychologically manipulated, emotionally blackmailed, if not threatened into living a heterosexual lifestyle, might well feel they've been abused. People with severe cerebral palsy who have faced imposed social segregation, negative assumptions about their intelligence or denied access to an alternative means of communication might well feel they've been abused.

Women pressured into having or keeping children they didn't want or couldn't cope with may feel they've been abused.

People who have been given work obligations beyond what they can possibly meet, or who go unpaid for someone else's weak boundaries of 'working hours', may feel they've been abused.

Abuse is in the eye of the beholder. If we feel we have been treated in a way which is cruel or inhumane, involves improper or excessive use of ourselves, involves unreasonable confinement, intimidation or punishment which we see as having caused us pain or mental anguish, then we may feel abused.

There are Auties who have had collectives of strangers move into their own private bedroom, where these strangers have then established a routine of barricading them within this once trusted room, sometimes even pinning them down physically to a chair, until compliance has been forced out of them. Some of these people have been kept involved in an activity considerably longer than they have the capacity to keep up with in terms of information processing, where others have used their power to hold them there against their will. They may feel inflicted upon by activities with no perceived purpose or interest and be forced to complete these activities before they can exit even for the toilet or a drink. Whilst a significant number of children with Autism in such behaviour modification programmes are said to improve, it is possible that some of the equally significant number who fail to improve may perceive these programmes as 'abusive', and that the 'success' figures do not show how many later go through 'regressions' in late childhood, teens or early adulthood because the changes were never part of their own real identity, motivation or choice.

There are people who are unable to tolerate eye contact or physical holding who, instead of the other person avoiding their eye contact and all physical contact in order to provoke an exploration of these perceived 'taboos', have been subject to forced holding and forced eye contact in which their own will, motivation and choice is irrelevant and from which they have been released only after they comply. Often once they comply, perhaps quite confusingly, they are given chocolate or other 'rewards'. Some of these people may perceive such programmes as abusive. To then receive a reward for tolerating perceived abuse is perhaps very morally questionable. There are abusers who have abused developmentally typical children who have done similar, implicating the child in his or her own abuse, and this second aspect of the abuse has been equally damaging to those children. Therapy often has to counter the damage not only of the initial abuse but also of the child's self-blame and guilt in accepting the reward for his or her compliance with the abuse.

There are kind people with no cruel intent who, through no fault of their own, have a personality disorder which makes them unable to empathise with others. They may be very openly and personally put down again and again and again to the point that they are clear they are a very bad person, having been given no strategies for dealing with society's inability to understand or cope with someone without a natural capacity for empathy and no counselling in helping them feel like an equal and valuable member of the community. Some of these people may feel they have been abused.

There are people with undiagnosed and untreated mood disorders who have been constantly told to 'snap out of it' or 'control yourself' to a degree that they have developed social phobias and anxiety disorders and blame themselves for the product of an untreated chemical imbalance that is not addressable through mind over matter. Some of these people may feel they have been abused.

There are people with information-processing styles in which they can only really tune in when they have a distraction going on in order to partially tune out. There are also those with such severe exposure anxiety who when made to notice they have noticed are instinctually compelled into avoidance, diversion and retaliation responses. And there are those with scotopic sensitivity syndrome and other visual-perceptual problems who are often able visually to perceive a scene as a whole only when using vision peripherally, whose vision fragments when they look directly at something. There are those unable to see as a whole under fluorescent lights or comprehend speech when a fan is going. There are those who can correct an error, tick a box on a multiple-choice questionnaire or respond in a triggered way to statements, but are unable to respond or access language in response to an open-ended question. Any of these people may be persistently forced by others against their will, for no other reason than the other person's assumption of what is 'normal', to use their senses, information-processing, retrieval and consciousness mechanisms in ways that actually limit or shut down their ability to function. Any of these people may develop phobias and anxieties they would otherwise not have, and may perceive arrogant and ignorant impositions of someone else's version of normality to be a form of abuse.

There are those with restless leg syndrome or food allergies underpinning hyperactivity, in whom suppression merely makes their mind race and triggers impulse-control problems. These people may instinctually know that if they have the opportunity to run off this chaotic energy they would be again able to manage their behaviour. Yet they may be deprived access to intervals in which they can employ this self-management strategy, only to be nagged, chastised or deprived of expected 'rewards' because they were 'unable to control themselves'. Some of these people may perceive this as abuse.

There are intelligent but trapped people who are treated as though they are mentally retarded, and there are those who are emotionally and socially, if not communicatively, retarded who are denied the right to play according to their actual social-emotional age on the basis that they are considered 'too intelligent' for that. Both groups may well perceive themselves to be abused.

There are those segregated from others on the basis of their label, and there are those who in spite of their label face insistence they accept a form of inclusion they are unable fully to process or tolerate. Some of these people may see these things as abuse.

There are those who have found communication through typing who have then had their access to typing denied, and so have been effectively silenced. Surely some of these people might well see this as abuse.

There are those with gut/immune disorders who lose their ability to manage their behaviour, emotional states or information processing when they are given food or chemical substances their bodies can't cope with. There are also those with neurotransmitter imbalances who have severe mood, anxiety or compulsive disorders who may experience extreme and unnecessary distress and impairment when they are denied access to appropriate medication to reduce the severity of these conditions. There are also those who are given even life-threatening and disabling excessive, irresponsible doses of inappropriate medications with insufficient supervision. Any of these situations could be seen as forms of abuse.

What defines grief?

A dictionary definition of grief is 'a deep and poignant distress caused by or as if by bereavement' (Merriam-Webster, Incorporated 2005b). The developmentally typical adult's view of what might provoke grief may be very different to that of an Autistic child. Auties may be more deeply and socially attached to their own reflection, or favourite TV character, or favourite climbing tree, or shoe or cat, bedroom or backyard than they may be to a human being.

The loss of a valued object to a social, communicative, emotionally stable and non-anxious developmentally typical child may be a very different thing to the same loss experienced by someone who is socially and communicatively isolated, emotionally unstable and chronically anxious. For one person this is the loss of an object in a world of human connections. For the other this may be more like the loss of a trusted friend.

Where such deep relationships are made and lost, some people learn to adapt to loss, others learn instead not to form attachments. The environment can recognise those needs and bridge the gaps created by those losses.

The environment might progressively use someone's 'object friends' as a bridge to a non-invasive, self-owning, 'Autie-friendly' social and interactive world of people. If the delivery of such a strategy was Autie-friendly enough, some people might accept this. If, however, the environment invasively seizes uninvited control and ownership over someone else's 'object friends', it may be experienced as if anyone's friend were co-opted by an 'outsider' in order to blackmail or secure interaction beyond the child's free will. These 'object friends' may then be seen as taken prisoner, but to save them would mean approaching the prison guard or showing them what matters to you. Perhaps better to cut one's *losses*. If one's 'object friend' is used by an 'outsider' in a way that portrays the 'object friend' as now being on the side of the 'outsider', it may be reasonable that the 'object friend' is now in the role of 'traitor'. What does one do with 'traitors'? One cuts them off, rejects them, discards them, behaves as if they never existed or never had importance. And yet, any of us who has had a friend and been 'betrayed' and had to 'cut them off' or 'let them go' knows that this is not so easy. We may be threatened or bitter or resentful, but still there is *loss*. And loss means grief, and grief shapes our future approaches to attachments, be these objects, places or people.

Just as a shy and socially reluctant child may require a social support or friend present when adapting to more challenging, daunting or new social contacts, some Auties will use the presence of an object as a means of being able to stand being in a room with others. If something works for you, you stick to it.

My ever-consistent, completely unfailing social support was a green plastic ball, and there are photos of me with that ball from two and a half years of age to the age of five. Even when it was taken out of my hand, one photo shows my hand remaining cupped as if it is still there.

Two and a half years is a long time in the life of a child who has only been on the earth for five years. It is half a lifetime. Two and a half years is even longer to have a consistent 'social' and 'supportive' presence when one's life is full of the instability of a mood, anxiety, compulsive or information-processing disorder or chronic ill health. It may be even longer in the life of a child who has lived in the care of several different environments, experienced several house moves, experienced several different carers or has lived through upheaval in the relationship between its carers, loss of a carer or a sibling or even the family dog.

To the developmentally typical adult, removing a plastic ball when a child is about to start school may seem sensible. To the Autie, losing the only reliable consistent sense of 'supportive other' when expected to embark on a major course of change and new experiences may be the straw that breaks the camel's back. To the carer it is only a ball, and what is important is the people world. But if a mood disorder or information-processing disorder means the people world often makes no consistent sense or is so overstimulating that it causes a fit, if the people world is unable to save you in the midst of a shutdown or acute episodes of mania or depression, if nothing it does makes sense at those times, and if your body perhaps is ill all the time from the stress and exhaustion and nobody can fix that either, then that ball looks like one very important concept and it offers far more than people ever could. That ball may be the symbol that no matter how meaningless it gets in a shutdown, no matter how lost one gets in the extremes of a mood disorder, no matter how sick the body gets and how painful or frightening that may be, the ball will complicate nothing, exacerbate nothing and never disappear from your capacity to sense its presence, no matter how much your information processing shuts down. To take that away is to say, 'Now you are utterly alone with all of that and condemned to a purely human world incapable of supplying that same perceived "understanding".' That is loss and it is also loss of empower-ment.

Loss can be experienced when moving house. When a developmentally typical person moves house, he or she may be able to ask for and understand an explanation, to seek comfort or process that comforting. The Autie may have no such luxuries. When a developmentally typical person moves house he or she has usually processed this not just through their body but more so conceptually in their mind. Hence the house move becomes a concept they can manipulate and resolve. When an Autie moves house, he or she may know their world almost exclusively through their body. When they move to the new house the rooms are in all the 'wrong' places, the furniture and windows and doors are not where they should be. Just as one's body clock can be sent out of kilter in moving to a new country, some people have a kind of 'body map' of familiar spaces. This body map may be their version of the concept of their home. Where a mind can quickly adapt, someone who has no mental concept of having 'moved house' may have no ability to adapt and alter their 'body map', and they may continue even for years to wait for the old house to 'come back' and continue to impose the old 'body mapping' on a building which it does not fit. When one's perceptions don't 'work right' it is normal to mistrust, to freeze, to become afraid to explore. Loss of familiarity, especially the familiarity of one's 'body mapped' personal and exploration spaces, may be a destabilising loss to some people, which, together with other forms of upheaval and change, may build to a level of trauma and accompanying anxiety responses. Developmentally typical people, unfamiliar with 'body mapping' and what moving house may feel like to someone who relies on this (just as a blind person feels space with their hands, the kinesthetic person 'body maps' with their senses), may feel there is no big deal with moving house. But for some kinesthetic Auties this, like any other loss, may lead to a feeling of helplessness, and of futility in again building up a sensed familiarity when clearly it can be swept away utterly beyond their control, overnight, with no going back. Carers can bridge these losses in considering the new layout and how they might best match it, in bringing along or adding familiar features, smells, textures, surfaces, patterns, sounds or acoustics, and continu-ing old routines for a while until the remaining unfamiliarity has been adapted to and 'mapped'. Those with a split between intellect and sensing or who rely only on sensing may be unable to be comforted through verbal or even visual explanations, but creating an external physical small-scale model of the previous home and the new one may help some people adapt.

When adults lose a partner, child or even a family pet, they may assume this has little effect on their Autie child. Dogs are seen to mourn the loss of their owners because they are directly confrontational, highly sociable and openly interactive animals. Cats, on the other hand, are more aloof in their attachments. Where dogs will initiate physical contact, cats often will merely come and 'be present' in one's company. Cats also experience loss. They just experience it differently.

Some Auties form deep attachments to others, though they do so in a virtually unobservable way within their own internal world. When someone we love dies, we also are with them in the nostalgia of our own internal world. But others generally can't see this attachment, so they often assume it's not there.

I loved my cat and would stare through it, breathing as it breathed, merging with its beingness. Yet I didn't pat it, and around others wouldn't even look at it. I formed my attachments in an indirectly confrontational way. But I experienced loss as deeply as, perhaps even more deeply than, those who did not sense people so strongly or have such a depth of relationship with them in their own internal world, as opposed to merely an interaction with them in the external world. There are, of course, others also labelled Autistic who do not form attachments in their own world or externally, but this does not mean all Auties are the same.

To an Autie, a parent, a sibling or the family dog may be equally sensed as 'people' and members of the family. The Autie may never pat the dog or chase it any more than they may pat or chase their sibling or parent. But the loss of any of the important characters in their life can be a loss as great as for any person, even though it may take longer to register because this character may linger longer in that person's internal world than it might with developmentally typical people, and the Autie may for some time continue as if the character were still around, with a progressive, intangible 'missing' feeling creeping into their life like an ivy ultimately breaches stone walls.

Developmentally typical people use care services like they use any service. For them it is a service, not an alternative 'home'. The Autie will settle and relax into a daily care facility and firmly adapt to the environment or particular carers. When the service is no longer used by the parent, the Autie may simply be removed with no thought that he or she may have formed deep, non-verbal attachments, if only within the confines of their unobservable internal world. An aloof, indirectly confrontational, functionally non-verbal person with no alternative means of communication may be unable to express that they have felt the equivalent of losing an adoptive daytime parent or alternative 'home'. Some more sensitive people who form deep internal attachments, however little they may externally show of these (and some men are good examples of this), may move on to new social experiences with the old haunting reminder of loss in the background. Instead of embracing new connections, new opportunities for closeness, they may even more strongly protect themselves against becoming familiar, relaxed and close, and thereby protect against the potential of future loss and grief.

Many more couples experience family break-up today than 30 years ago. Often the children remain with the mother, sometimes with the father, sometimes moved on to grandparents, aunts or uncles, or even into fostercare or adoption. When one parent has left an abusive relationship and taken the child with them, this is generally ultimately a necessary, brave and healthy decision. But the escaping parent may assume the child was as glad to leave as they were, and the child's reality may be overlooked, perhaps understandably by necessity.

A child may be traumatised by experiencing carers involved in domestic violence, abuse or the consequences this has for the adult victim. But the same child may still have a very separate relationship with the abusing adult. The abusing adult may have been the only person in the home who gave the child the solitude he or she felt relaxed in. The abusing adult may have been a source of humour, distraction or 'rough and tumble' play which helped the child cope with or escape for a moment from his or her own challenges. The abusing parent may have been someone who could be present but non-invasive or was associated with a welcomed lack of information overload or verbal overstimulation. The abusing parent may have been the more socially confident parent and the source of the child's inclusion or excursions into the community. The abusing parent may have had a workplace the child felt safe and at home in, felt able to explore, or even found a social role within. The abusing parent may have had extended family or friends or a family pet the child had formed a special bond with and is now cut off from. The abusive parent may have had a communicative style the child felt confident and relaxed with, however badly he or she treated their partner. The abusive parent may merely have been a source of material rewards, sensory fascina-tions, or simply sensory or activity patterns which were part of the structure of the child's life. None of this is to say these things can't be replaced and bridges built, but sometimes the trauma of the escaping parent blocks them from wanting to bring back any reminder of the old life, positive aspects of which are important to the child. Like any form of loss and grief, with sensitivity, we can be helped through it and build bridges to new realities. But if our loss and grief is unseen, overlooked or ignored, then we equally can go on to invest much more of our cognition, emotion, physical, social and communication responses in protecting ourselves from attachment, familiarity, relaxation and the impact of loss and grief we may have come to associate with that.

Effects of trauma, neglect, abuse and grief issues
Effect on health
When we experience trauma, neglect, abuse or grief then we might experience helplessness, devaluation, depression, fear, distraction, withdrawal, agitation, exhaustion, or a combination of any of these things. High levels of stress, depression or exhaustion may progressively reduce our health, most particularly the health of our gut, where most stress is first felt, the health of our blood, which is directly affected by gut function and the impact of oxidative stress, and the health of our immune system, any and all of which may ultimately impact on our information processing, inhibit the development of brain organisation and disturb neurotransmitter balance necessary to mood and impulse control.

The secondary effect of this may be that once a child's development is severely impacted upon by these things, then this affects the lives of other members of the family, and family stress may be increased as a result of these challenges, which then, of course, might further impact upon the child, perhaps especially so with particularly sensitive and highly sensing children.

This is not to say this pattern fits all Auties, and some may be far from highly sensitive or highly sensing, but others may have progressively made themselves that way because it seems to 'work' in limiting the impact of perceived trauma, neglect, abuse and grief. And of course there may be others for whom the impact of trauma, neglect, abuse and grief has played no part in the severity of their Autism.

Cognitive and behavioural implications
Baggage, and how we carry it, suppress it or run from it, can be one of the major sources of influence in our lives. Our baggage and our relationship to it may affect how we consider, approach or tolerate new experiences with people, places, animals, objects, events and activities. It may affect how we make ourselves vulnerable in future, how we will avoid doing so and how we

will fill up the voids left by these compensations. It may affect how we monopolise and ensure the securities we have left or how we choose never to invest again. It may affect how distracted we are with these 'fleas', how tightly we control our lives or our impact on others. Conversely, it may affect how we refuse to care for ourselves, our future or our impact upon others. Baggage may affect how much we invite, how much we take, or how much we give and what motivates us. Auties are as human as anyone.

How baggage affects people got thrown out with the bogey man of the 'refrigerator mother' theory. However narrow or inappropriate the resurrection of that bogey man may be, ignoring the fact that Auties accumulate baggage, if only for some at a gut and body level, is to dehumanise them and reduce them purely to medical models.

I believe that Autism is like a fruit salad and the numbers of types of fruit, the ripeness and size of each piece of fruit, how long each has been left in the fruit salad and the way the environment has adapted to the presence of those fruits all determine the severity of a person's Autism. I believe those with 'grapes' representing issues such as felt or perceived trauma, neglect, abuse and grief as part of this fruit salad, deserve to be heard, understood, empowered and helped with respect, equality and the empathy developmentally typical people so pride themselves on having.

Effect on carers and the family
When someone reacts to perceived or felt trauma, neglect, abuse or grief, it affects the whole family.

Most carers love their children, Autistic or otherwise. Many siblings care about, if not love, their brothers and sisters, Autistic or otherwise. Some do not but even in families which do, trauma, neglect, abuse or grief may be utterly unseen, if not utterly unavoidable.

When a family member cannot see or understand a source of perceived trauma, neglect, abuse or grief, they feel helpless. Often their desire to help, to save, to rescue, to protect only increases the pressure and makes the problem of a child's self-protection, resignation, withdrawal or distraction worse.

Perhaps all we can hope for is that this topic will stimulate discussion on the sources of these unseen issues and how these can affect Auties, what things to look out for and how to pick up the pieces, fill the gaps and build the bridges in respectful and Autie-friendly ways. What is essential is to move on from the idea that the severity of someone's Autism always begins with health issues, or that educational or communication deficits should always be the central focus of services, or that teaching social skills can merely be superimposed on deeply entrenched self-protection mechanisms sometimes blocking the experiences which would lead to developing these skills, or that compliance matters more than motivation. Perhaps we need to wonder for a moment whether play, music, dance or art therapies might not be of equal importance in building those bridges, filling those gaps, salvaging that respect, recognising that humanity and igniting a love of life, spirit of adventure, and tapping into natural motivations.

Can some people become too 'invested' in their trauma, neglect, abuse and grief issues?

Before I encourage people to be too understanding, it's important to remember there are some personality disorders in which it is natural to cling on to perceived past trauma, neglect, abuse and grief and as Auties are as human as anyone, some of them will have these types of personality traits.

Depressive personality disorder is not depression but a chronically depressive and pessimistic outlook in which it is natural and normal to view new experiences critically and with cynicism and negativity. People with this disorder may be deeply annoyed at attempts by others to cheer them up or make them look on the positive side – they feel more stable predicting the worst.

Paranoid personality disorder may involve seeing the potential for being victim to trauma, neglect, abuse and grief at the hands of others in situations where these do not objectively exist.

Histrionic personality disorder is associated with dramatics and melodrama. People with this condition may be not more 'sensitive' than others but more likely to fabricate or exaggerate the impact of minor experiences of perceived trauma, neglect, abuse and grief in order to monopolise on sympathy and attention. As with 'the boy who cried wolf', this is not to say that someone with such a disorder may not sometimes actually experience severe trauma, neglect, abuse and grief; it might be equally important not flippantly to disregard someone's accounts simply because they have this kind of personality disorder.

Narcissistic personality disorder is associated with a need to feel special and privileged. People with this disorder are predisposed to take extreme offence at being treated as less than they assume their worth. Allowing such people to deal directly with the consequences of their own actions might well be taken as an extreme insult to their specialness and sense of privilege. So, perceived trauma, neglect, abuse and grief issues might produce more extreme responses than the events themselves usually warrant.

Antisocial personality and borderline personality disorder can both be emotionally explosive, and the responses of those with these conditions to perceived trauma, neglect, abuse and grief issues might be expected to be easily overblown with violent or self-injurious responses, more so than might occur in other personalities. This is not to say these people have a monopoly on violence or self-injury, which can be part of someone's Autism for a whole variety of other reasons unrelated to these personality disorders.

Personality disorders aside, there are opportunities for social acceptance and inclusion which revolve around being in therapy for issues like trauma, neglect, abuse and grief. Whilst these are supportive to many people who have been through such things on all kinds of levels, there are also those who have earned special privileges on the basis of being a 'survivor', which may make them less able or likely to then move on. Whilst therapy may be essential for many people, I have had some clients on the Autistic spectrum who have been encouraged by a series of therapists to indulge in the replaying of their experiences to the degree that they have come to use these experiences to shock, distance, test, impress or earn the respect of others. Rather than helping, this seemed to hinder them from moving forward with any new social identity. Therapists working with people on the Autistic spectrum might need to remember that these people may quickly fall into structures and patterns in ways a developmentally typical client may not, and that where a developmentally typical person may let go of a pattern when it has worn out its usefulness to them, some people on the Autistic spectrum may wait for permission to move on to a new pattern.

Helping those with trauma, neglect, abuse and grief issues

Currently, there is an emphasis on education, communication and gut/immune issues as the keys to reducing the severity of someone's Autism. It's equally possible that some people's education, communication and gut/immune issues are underpinned by unresolved and compounding social, emotional, psychological and communication responses to perceived or felt trauma, neglect, abuse and grief. It is time the field recognised that none of us copes when our load of baggage has become too great and that Auties accumulate experiences too, even if some remain unable to deal with these impacts consciously or even block conscious recognition or awareness of these things.

None of this is to say that educational psychologists, speech therapists, naturopaths or teachers are not of value and important in sorting out and working through the challenges of what's in the fruit salad, but hypnotherapists, play therapists, music therapists, dance therapists, art therapists, if not respite care, should be considered as being of equal therapeutic value where these people are the best people for the job in addressing trauma, neglect, abuse and grief issues. And counsellors, friends and even the community have roles to play too in helping carers to create and maintain open, natural, fun, healthy and relaxed environments as part of helping them to deal with these issues.

How might social patterns help?

There is a time and way to work through trauma, neglect, abuse and grief issues and there is a time to play and just be.

Sometimes, a new routine, good boundaries, self-owning people, silliness and surrealism are a big part of environmental medicine in filling those gaps and building those bridges. Sometimes, this happens because we don't focus on the issues rather than because we do. Sometimes, we keep the issues in the back of our mind, not the front of our minds and we simply get on with making a healthy, balanced, natural, relaxed environment and let past experiences progressively unravel. Sometimes, the answer is a combination of both.

Modelling a healthy, balanced, relaxed, natural, fun and open response to life can't be underestimated as one of the most healing things in that garden called 'home' or 'family'. Some people will trust their reflection, nature or animals before they will again trust people, and staying in your own space in gentle respect is certainly a great social statement to someone going through their own healing at their own pace which is all any of us can do.

Trauma, neglect, abuse and grief and specific behavioural issues

Trauma, neglect, abuse and grief issues might underpin specific behaviours/issues relating to:

- communication
- being in one's own world
- eye contact
- learning and cognitive challenges

- toileting
- sleep problems
- stimming
- meltdowns
- self-protection responses
- challenging behaviours
- food behaviour problems.

Some personalities may respond to trauma, neglect, abuse and grief by being utterly crippled by it, and any existing *communication* problems may become worse. Other personalities may become far more private, detached, mistrustful and self-sufficient because of it, and again this might have a big effect on the development of communication and social communication. Others may overcompensate through complete denial of these issues and seek to 'blend in'. This second strategy could lead to a lot of stored language which is not necessarily connected to what the person really thinks or feels. Others may become overly passive, eager to please and utterly conforming, which may lead to difficulties with speaking up, speaking out or asserting individuality or independence through communication.

Trauma, neglect, abuse and grief may compound the necessity and comfort of *one's own world* but equally can become a driving force for moving on from these dark, difficult and helpless spaces into being progressively more a part of the external world. Some personalities are more likely to react in the first way, others in the second way, and we all have combinations of those. Some may have combinations of traits that, in the face of challenges, push them strongly into their own world. Others may have combinations that do the opposite. And others may have traits which drive them in both directions with equal force. Under the burden of perceived trauma, neglect, abuse and grief issues, it is my opinion that those in this last group may face a fiercely fluctuating split within this basic relationship to life and struggle to go forward as a 'whole person'. Add to this the information-processing challenges of an Autism spectrum condition and you have someone who may struggle more than most to resolve these things without the types of therapy that work on a less conscious level, such as music, art, or movement/dance therapy or hypnotherapy.

The emotional and psychological challenges of perceived trauma, neglect, abuse and grief commonly cause *eye-contact* problems in developmentally typical people, so it stands to reason that Auties who already have these problems may be increasingly challenged by the additional burden of trauma, neglect, abuse or grief.

Severe trauma, neglect, abuse or loss in early infancy have been found to have the capacity to interfere with neurological development, including left–right hemisphere integration. In this sense, there may be very real physical reasons why those who have had these experiences may develop the sensory problems common in Autism spectrum conditions. It is equally possible that those with Autism spectrum conditions who also happen to grow up experiencing perceived trauma, neglect, abuse or loss in early infancy may be more affected in their sensory-perceptual areas than otherwise. As mood also strongly affects sensory responses, the psychological-emotional impact of perceived trauma, neglect, abuse or grief issues might conceivably increase the impact of mood on these people's sensory responses.

So much of *learning* is about motivation, self-love and social safety. Without a strong love of life, interest in life and a feeling of social safety, learning can be severely affected for non-Autistic people too. Add to this the fact that early severe trauma, neglect, abuse or grief may impact on health and the development of brain organisation, including left–right hemisphere integration, and there are some fairly concrete reasons why these things might also result in increased cognitive challenges for those people, particularly if they already had an Autism spectrum condition and were therefore doubly burdened.

When people are distressed because of perceived trauma, neglect, abuse, grief, there is usually an effect on *toileting, sleeping and food-related behaviours*. When people with Autism feel safer, are happier in themselves, less alienated from their environment and feel understood and respected in their own right as equals among others, they, like any human being, will have fewer toileting, sleeping and food-related behaviour problems than someone who hasn't got these very simple things.

Stimming can be about many things including being a source of self-comforting, of maintaining familiarity or of controlling the environment from 'getting in'. These three needs may be more likely to increase when someone with an Autism spectrum condition has also experienced what they perceive as trauma, neglect, abuse or grief.

Meltdowns are not just about the demands of the moment or the day or the week. We all have a certain threshold above which we can't withstand any more, and often what burdens us is cumulative. This may sometimes be outside of conscious awareness, though still tying up our processing resources, if only in our use of those resources to keep those discomforts at bay by putting them 'on hold'. Perceived trauma, neglect, abuse or grief can all decrease that threshold of tolerance for people with Autism spectrum conditions, who would otherwise cope better under a diminished burden. Many people in this situation struggle with the cognitive or communication resources to resolve or heal from these issues, so this process is delayed; and just because something is out of conscious awareness doesn't mean it doesn't affect that person.

It is natural to develop *self-protection responses* to avoid further suffering, and whether we do this consciously or unconsciously makes no difference to whether our development can become more limited because of this. It stands to reason that someone with an Autism spectrum condition who is already struggling with self-protection challenges due to information overload, sensory chaos, mood, compulsive or personality-related issues is at greater risk of these becoming more intense, more compounded and ingrained if they perceive themselves to have also suffered from trauma, neglect, abuse or grief.

Challenging and self-injurious behaviours are very common parts of expressing extreme stress and distress. Whilst information-processing problems, anxiety, mood and compulsive challenges and personality issues can all result in these things, so too can trauma, neglect, abuse and loss. Very often it is assumed that if someone has a label of an Autism spectrum condition then their challenging or self-injurious behaviours are due to the Autism alone; this is to dehumanise these people. People with Autism who are already self-injurious or challenging are more likely to be more so when additionally struggling with perceived trauma, neglect, abuse or loss, particularly if it is in some unseen or unrecognised form and they do not have the cognitive or communication resources to resolve these things themselves or assist others in doing so.

CHAPTER 11

Who Am I
and Which Side Am I On?

Identity Issues

Mary's bag was full, very full, as she lumbered up the street with it. In it was Mary the 'case' and Mary 'in her own world', Mary the 'broken goods' and Mary who was a 'laugh', Mary the 'label' and Mary 'the person', Mary the 'problem' and Mary the 'project', Mary 'the little girl' and Mary 'the sexual being'. As she stopped by a shop window, she couldn't recognise herself.

What is identity?

The difference between the child who develops severe information-processing, mood, anxiety, compulsive, personality or environmental challenges before the age of three and the child who develops these after the age of three is that the child who is unaffected until after three years old will have some level of more usual brain organisation and an intact sense of identity as a social, emotional, communicative success. Once identity is intact, many children will struggle against their challenges just to maintain what they know of their own 'usual' state. The same may not be true of those who have been severely affected before establishing any cohesive sense of identity within themselves or in relation to others.

Dictionary definitions of identity include 'who a person is, or the qualities of a person which makes them different from others' (Cambridge Dictionaries

Online 2005), 'the distinguishing character or personality of an individual; individuality' (Longman 1984).

These little clips give us important windows into what identity is. Perhaps even remembering how we all have separate email identities can be a wonderful way to think of the links between identity and privacy. Email aside, it is true that when we develop distinct identities within a household it is our ability to separate one identity from another that allows each to experience our own autonomy and degree of privacy within a shared household. Sometimes carers can be so eager for sharing, inclusion and being needed, they forget this unseen world of identity.

The me and the not-me

'Ego-*syn*tonic' is a term which means something feels like it is part of the self and integral to who someone is. 'Ego-*dys*tonic' is a term which means something feels like it's foreign to one's sense of self, it feels alien, invasive and often disables the expression of the self. Among the 'fruits' which can make up someone's 'fruit salad' labelled an Autism spectrum condition, there can be conditions which are ego-syntonic and those which are ego-dystonic.

Obsessive-compulsive disorder can involve compulsions and obsessive thoughts that are annoying and distressing, and that can feel imprisoning to the self within. Tourette's can involve motor, vocal and breathing tics, which are also involuntary and can feel alien and invasive, contorting and control-ling who someone appears to be. Both of these things are often experienced as ego-dystonic, which means they are experienced as alien, invasive, involun-tary and external to the self within. Some people ignore their compulsions and tics and some people are so dominated by them that they are extremely distressed by their imposition on their expression of selfhood.

Obsessive-compulsive personality disorder, in fact all personality dis-orders, are described as being ego-syntonic, which means the person is very unlikely to struggle against these states because they see them as being part of their selfhood. So someone with dependent personality, avoidant personality, schizoid, schizotypal, paranoid, depressive, antisocial or any other of the per-sonality disorders will be very poorly motivated to change, may try for a while perhaps compliantly to act like they have changed, but basically slip back into the old patterns because they feel alien when that they are out of these patterns.

Anxiety and mood disorders can be ego-dystonic or ego-syntonic, which means a person can identify with their anxiety or mood disorder or recognise that these things are not 'who they are' even if they cannot be rid of them. Some people may blame the environment and side with their own anxiety or mood disorder. Others will see the anxiety or mood disorder as the destabilising 'enemy' and seek to control, manage, counter, work with or address these issues and see these problems as something travelling along with them but not part of their sense of self. Whether a person experiences their anxiety or mood-disorder issues as part of them or alien to them will often be affected by how chronic the issues are, as well as the modelling of the environment and how the environment responds to these issues.

Information-processing problems can be ego-dystonic or ego-syntonic depending on how fluctuating these are. If the problems markedly peak and trough depending on environmental overload, the impact of anxiety or mood disorders, intermittent epilepsy episodes or intermittent gut/immune issues, people with these information-processing problems may see overload, shutdowns and 'meltdowns' not as part of who they are but as temporary, invasive losses of connection with their whole, integrated or more connected sense of selfhood. They may become angry with the overload and shutdowns themselves rather than the environment, with resulting despair or even self-injurious behaviours.

The motor-planning and brain organisation issues of dyspraxia, dyslexia, chronic severe information-processing issues underpinned by gut/immune issues, or even the left–right integration issues which can underpin the dominance of interpretive versus sensing-based styles of information processing, can all be ego-syntonic, meaning they are usually taken as being part of one's selfhood. When you attempt to impose a new way of processing or responding to information on a system which doesn't fit, people with these issues may feel you cannot accept them or they are not acceptable for what they are, which in their world is the same as 'who they are'; and far from embracing this 'help' they may resent it, retaliate against it, withdraw, self-protect or even retaliate against the environment.

The lack of understanding or counselling about the interrelationship between these ego-syntonic information-processing experiences and identity can be a major source of alienation and despair for these people, and that needs to be understood by developmentally typical people. Yet it is true that many people can progressively adapt better, even sometimes overcome their dyspraxia, dyslexia or left–right integration issues, or even move from sensing to developing interpretive information processing, but how these people adapt emotionally and psychologically to these shifts in selfhood is rarely considered. These people are often left feeling separated from their previous self and somehow uprooted, even experiencing alienation from their sense of selfhood and not yet settled into any new one. They may feel in limbo, similar to the adjustment a person deaf or blind from childhood may feel when hearing or sight is restored as an adult. For some, in spite of advancement, it may be easier to revert to a lifestyle in tune with the old patterns they had moved on from. There is currently little research into the links between identity and resistance to embracing improvements brought about through interventions in these groups.

Attachment

One of the ways we build identity is through having enough stability that we get some consistent flowing sense of self, as well as enough diversity to make that sense of self broad enough to handle some flexibility in the experiences we relate to or allow to affect us. But attachment is another very strong aspect of identity.

Without attachment, we are alone. Alone we cannot reflect on the difference between ourselves and anyone or anything else. There is no boundary, no sense of entity to stop us from simply merging with new experiences, becoming one with objects or the feel of a place, with nature or merging into the feel of another person. It is when we form an attachment that we learn to discriminate and it is when we learn to discriminate we learn what we are not.

Gut/immune, information-processing, sensory, anxiety, mood, personality or even environmental issues can interfere with development to the degree that attachment becomes limited, contorted or delayed. But few Auties develop no attachments at all. Most Auties at the very least become attached to certain types of foods or packaging, certain behavioural patterns, certain sensory experiences, certain daily structures, certain places, certain objects or videos or games or TV programmes, certain shoes or cups or pieces of clothing, certain music or colours or sounds, their own echo, shadow or reflection, and often even certain people. Because the attachments of most Auties are different to those of non-Autistic people, non-Autistic people often overlook that they have any attachments at all. If the dog could tell us it might say the same of the cat, but to the cat, the dog sees only its own reality. It is blinded by assumptions of its own reality as the only 'normality'.

Many Auties will be delayed in the process of forming attachments to people, however aloof or unusual those attachments might ultimately be. For some children this may not begin until toddlerhood or mid-childhood. For others it may not begin until late childhood, their teens or even adulthood. There is an assumption that in taking away an attachment to objects or one's reflection that Auties will then move on to people, but some simply decide that loss is too great and cannot risk something even less certain, such as attachment to people. Some developmentally typical people decide to try to 'invade' via what the person with Autism is attached to only to have this bridge burned. Building bridges is not about invasion. It is about respecting people's own pace, their time and space and inspiring and enticing rather than forcing or blackmailing people. Sometimes playing hard to get and leaving people wanting more achieves far more.

Attachment to sensory experiences is a foundation to attachment to objects. Attachment to objects means one is learning where one's own body begins and ends and how to interact physically and sensorily with the external world. It is the foundation of a sense of self and other which is the basis of a later simultaneous yet separated sense of self and other necessary to a sense of 'company' and the experiential concepts of 'social' and 'us' and 'with'. Attachment to one's reflection is an extension of attachment to objects and is a big part of getting used to human company in a very safe way for the reflection can never chase you, touch you or bombard you with anything unfamiliar you have not already had some experience of processing. Attachment to one's reflection is a foundation of becoming aware of what is same and what is different. The limitations of the reflection's ability to expand one's own world, and the eventual inability to join the reflection within the same world, can be the motivation to explore the potential of real humans, if only within controllable and restricted boundaries, before one can accept them being too distinctly different from oneself.

Attachment to the objects of others and to places can be part of knowing people by proxy, as a cat new to your house might. When we feel safe and uninvaded in getting used to the company and interaction with someone's belongings, home and space, it is just an extension of that bridge to explore being in the company of the people themselves, however indirect, aloof or hit-and-run these first steps may be.

Attachments to people may first be on a sensory level or as collections of information before we are ready to form attachments with them on the basis of their differences to us. Accepting what is foreign to us, that with which we do not resonate, may be much harder than forming attachments to that which is neutral or 'like us'. If you want to be in the company of a cat you may need to learn to speak the subtle behavioural language of cat before you progressively relax and fall back into being the dog you really are.

Through attachments we work out what we are and what we are not, we work out what we like and what we are uncomfortable with, we work out where self ends and other begins and eventually some of us may even find that both can continue to coexist without the processing of one or the other 'disappearing' (I got this at age 30 so it can take a long time and it still comes and goes). We have only two choices in helping Auties to make these natural developmental progressions. We can respond in ways which help in this process (which may even mean backing off, giving space and not 'helping') or we can, however unintentionally, hinder or sabotage this process.

Problems of self and other

A simultaneous sense of self and other is an important part of having a comparison through which we know what self is and what it is not, where self begins and other ends and vice versa. These are important foundations of a sense of identity.

One of the implications of information-processing problems, mood or anxiety disorders and some personality disorders is that one may swing from a state of all-self/no-other to a state of all-other/no-self, and rarely if ever get to hold onto the processing and awareness of a simultaneous sense of self and other. This means that in a state of all-self/no-other, one may be oblivious to one's impact on the other person or even of the other person's existence. In a state of all-other/no-self, one may be acutely aware of a sense of the other person but utterly unable at the time to connect to one's own thoughts and feelings, as if one is watching a movie, become akin to a computer simply accumulating information, or feel as if one has 'disappeared'. The end result from the developmentally typical person's perspective may be that 'something is missing'.

There are several ways an Autie with these issues might artificially compensate for a lack of simultaneous sense of self and other. One is in merging with 'other'. When one 'merges' there may be no sense of self, no sense of other and no simultaneous yet separate sense of self and other. When one merges with 'other' one may feel not 'with' but 'as' 'other'. For many Auties this may be a salvation from loneliness and aloneness and the closest translation they know. It may also be a cultural phenomenon as much as an information-processing one; and perhaps deserves a degree of respect, for respect breeds respect and that is what building bridges between different cultures is all about.

Another artificial way an Autie may compensate for a lack of simultaneous sense of self and other is through TV shows, videos, computer games, typing or email. When one is able to merge with characters one is watching passively, the interaction is an internal thing and this requires less information-processing ability than interacting with a living real person.

Interacting with one's reflection may be another way an Autie may compensate for a lack of simultaneous sense of self and other as what is coming back from the reflection has already been processed by the person expressing themselves so it may be the only cohesive experience of interaction that person is capable of keeping up with.

Playing out interactions through drawings, photographs or representational objects may allow some Auties to keep up with these scenarios in a similar way to watching and replaying the events in videos or TV shows. Playing out interactions through drawings, photos or representational objects, however, may allow people to put themselves into these scenarios in a way that isn't possible with TV shows. Because the person can visualise the entire interaction externally, including themselves, there may be no switch between all-self/no-other and all-other/no-self. The focus becomes on the topic, the objects, the issue; and this becomes one piece of information. When interaction is interpersonal between two living people, it involves keeping up with not one but three different realms of information: self, other *and* the topic. When someone is mono-tracked or limited in their ability to keep up with incoming information, often sense of self, sense of other or keeping track of the topic itself becomes lost.

Unfortunately, most developmentally typical people are unaware of the value of compensations or the possibility of expanding people's social world through these potential 'bridges'. Instead, these 'bridges' are often cast aside as 'abnormal', 'inappropriate', 'too eccentric' or 'too Autistic'. Often, Auties are instead merely taught to act out social skills they may be unable to relate to, actually experience internally, or keep up with with any internal cohesion. This is very similar to a century ago when signing was considered too 'abnormal' to be encouraged and deaf people were expected merely to learn more 'normal' patterns of interaction and communication, whether they could keep up with them or not, such as only lip reading and speaking with voices they themselves could often not hear. Today we apologise for such arrogance and ignorance of the past. Yet the parallels exist for many Auties.

The danger of too much familiarity

People with dependent personality or borderline personality may be very vulnerable to making themselves over-involved with others to the point that separation becomes a threat that dominates their ability to manage their own behaviour. But just because something is a drug doesn't make it healthy to keep feeding that drug habit, and an addiction is not a choice.

We often think that attachment is love, but love does not shrivel or stagnate our lives, it empowers and inspires us. Addictive attachments *can* shrivel and stagnate the lives of those caught up in them. Yet if we are from a background where this is our only model of 'love' then we may ignore any healthier options in favour of chasing what is unhealthy but familiar.

The danger of over-involvement is huge for the identity of children with special needs. Without knowing ourselves as distinct from our carers we become extensions of them, appendages, and the idea of helping, stretching or saving ourselves is irrelevant to a life where no separate selfhood exists, and the taste of it by comparison with merging into someone else seems like the bitter threat of abandonment and exclusion, not an offer to be loved in our own right and on the path to feeling our own achievements and feeling our own way to freedom.

Looking at this from the other side, the website www.geocities.com/growingjoel/murder.html lists cases of murder and manslaughter of Autistic children, and some Autistic adults, since 1997 in modern countries with existing welfare services. Currently there are over 20 cases listed there, from stabbings to drowning, to suffocation, shooting and strangulation, mostly committed by burnt-out parents and carers unable to cope. Most of these parents and carers cared deeply for their Autistic children, yet overvaluing their version of love so extremely they remained without enough love to save their children by giving them up to the care of authorities. Unlike in killings of so-called 'normal' children, virtually none of these cases resulted in prison sentences. One actually resulted in the parent responsible being then given a job in an Autism society. Clearly being over-involved can be dangerous on so many levels, and parents may need help not only in coping with extremely dependent or challenging children but in better managing and turning around their own co-dependency issues.

Sensing and merging

Some Auties have such severe receptive-processing issues that they can struggle in developing 'interpretive' information processing. In other words, they may struggle to use their mind to grasp concepts or make sense of things. Instead, they may rely on their senses and on kinesthetic processing and the pattern, theme and feel their body 'maps'. This is what I call 'sensing'.

Many people confuse 'sensing' with being 'psychic', as if highly sensing people can 'read minds'. I see sensing not as an ability to read minds but as an acute ability to feel pattern and theme and feel through one's body. It is an unconscious, instinctual process, but some people can be so highly developed in this ability that they need only the first few bars of the song, so to speak, and they have a feel for how the tune will play out. Sensing people may sense from a few fragments of pattern felt in their body what the next expected run of patterns is likely to be. So they may appear 'psychic', as much as the family dog might.

The thing about sensing is that if you are remarkably good at it and remarkably bad at keeping up with interpretive processing, you are going to struggle with holding concepts in your head in a conscious way because you are far more oriented to holding 'mapped' patterns in your body in a pre-conscious way. If you don't hold concepts in your head, including those about yourself or others, let alone concepts about yourself in relation to others, then it can be extremely difficult ever to achieve a conscious, mental impression of self-awareness necessary to identity. But identity is not just about a conscious mental impression. We can have a pre-conscious *feel* of our own identity, even a 'body mapped' sense of someone else's 'entity' or 'beingness', in the same way that the dog has a feel of its own beingness and a feel for yours. It is not the same as a developmentally typical conscious mental awareness of identity and probably a lot less rigid and fixed (because most interpretive people get stuck on ideas), but it is a sense of identity nevertheless.

One of the functions of interpretive information is that of 'getting to know'. When someone relies on interpretive information processing they have to try to get information out of you in order to build up a mental concept, idea or intellectual body of knowledge about you, or themselves for that matter. But with sensing, you don't have to do this. In fact, when people try to give your 'mind' information, it can be a distraction from the process of sensing, for sensing is most acute when intellect is not switched on. With sensing, you don't seek information, you absorb it, you pick it up, and you do this not by experiencing it externally, but by merging with the source of the experience as though you become one with it; you may get acquainted more than you get to 'know'. So not only may someone who relies on sensing have acquired a good 'feel' of your pattern, theme and the feel to you, your 'music of beingness', but they may still strongly lack a comparison of themselves with you as they know you through merging with you, and in merging there is no separation between self and other in this simultaneous sense of self and other.

For developmentally typical people, a simultaneous sense of self and other may be present most of the time, and a normal part of having multi-track interpretive information processing. So the highly sensing Autie may swing between deeply having a feel of their own identity and deeply having a feel of your 'entity', but with little comparison between the two necessary for developing a mental concept of their own separate identity. In fact, the concept of comparison may not exist unless such an Autie is involved in watching themselves and the other person played out through representational objects in caricature, where they might view this as a whole single external and interactive 'movie'.

Loneliness, isolation and merging

An Autie can excel in the system of sensing not only because interpretive information processing (mind and intellect) is so slow, delayed in its processing, quick to overload and shut down or scrambled in its wiring, but also because the development of proficiency and depth in the capacity to use sensing can be driven by loneliness and isolation. Either deaf, blind or deaf/blind children often behave 'autistically' until they are helped to link to the world in ways which can reach them on an interpretive level. But there are Auties who are so consistently meaning-deaf and meaning-blind in spite of adequate sight and hearing that these challenges amount to the same degree of 'deprivation', isolation and loneliness. For these people, merging may be their salvation and a means of adventuring through the window created by mapping the pattern, theme and feel of others.

It is a life really 'by proxy', but with my first nine years spent largely in that system of sensing, I feel it was a place of richness and connection, although those connections were of an Autistic style. It is possible to compensate for meaning-deafness and meaning-blindness among other sensory-perceptual challenges and confusions, and certainly if the environment does so in an Autie-friendly way the person is more likely to make bridges to the world of developmentally typical people.

There are some eccentric developmentally typical people who rely largely on sensing rather than interpretation, and many Auties can navigate most things through sensing if they are not convinced by people that, in the absence of interpretive information processing, they are utterly incapable and should instead rely on people with 'minds'. And the way a highly sensing Autie comes to think of their own capability and self-reliance or assume themselves incapable and dependent is certainly a matter of identity which the environmental approach plays a big role in deciding.

Mind and identity

Ask people who they are and they will often describe how they 'think'. For them, they are their minds, their thoughts, their conceptual frameworks. For most developmentally typical people, mind can have much to do with identity and they cannot imagine identity without it.

But there are many Auties who far from thinking in pictures or experiencing mind, feel the world rather than conceive of it. The world for them may be a place they sense and they may grasp concepts only through direct sensory experience of them at the time.

Most babies are so busy being they are likely not so much consciously aware of thoughts as gripped by feelings which drive wants. But by toddlerhood, most small children experience conscious thought and wonder and imagine and think and make things up. Most Aspies develop conscious thought fairly early on, but many Auties may not and they may appear to be 'somewhere else', 'not home'. They may experience thought, but it may be pre-conscious, fragmented, ungraspable, tumbling or what I call 'confetti thoughts drifting'. They may be what I call 'sleepwalker/sleeptalkers'. Their mind isn't quite aware, 'online' or able to stay that way yet. For them, the only consistent thing may be the more pre-conscious world of 'sensing' in which sensory experiences, pattern, theme and feel dominate.

Most children have begun to establish some sense of coherent, fluent, conscious thought by the time they are about three years old, and so their language shows this and their identity begins to form. Some Auties do not develop a conscious grip on fluent, cohesive interpretive thought processes until they are about five and then begin to explore the use of interpretive speech. Some do not develop these mental processes until they are in late childhood, and there are some who start using interpretive language around 8 to 12 years of age, and of course others who this eludes right into adulthood. I have even known two adults in their thirties who 'woke up' and began using interpretive speech. Of course, other adults who can't organise this verbally are able to do so through the much simpler motor-planning task of typing. What these people often share in common is the feeling that stepping into 'having a mind' is like becoming a new person.

It can be an extreme jolt to identity. Some people are happier about losing their 'old world' than others. Personally, I made this jump when I was nine and became consciously aware that fluent meaning existed in language and reading. At first, this was exciting and I was eager to grasp this new system, but progressively a dread about being so far behind other children began to set in, as if there were little point trying to get good at something I'd never be as good as others at. I also had panic attacks about a fear this would mean I would lose my 'old world' and my own 'language', as by then I spoke almost fluently in songs, jingles, advertisements, made-up words, movements and sounds which stood for experiences. The fact that others didn't share this language didn't make it any the less 'mine', and there was a lot of alienation, resentment and sudden frightening realisation I was 'different'. Even though I'd receptively grasped that 'their language' had fluent meaning, this didn't mean I could yet use it, and it took another two years before I could use it in speaking to my shoes (for daring to speak to people was largely impossible, and even 'yes' and 'no' were hard), and it took another two years before fluent 'litanies' emerged (and some of you who've lived with such two-hour litanies will know that the welcome relief of hearing fluent language soon wears off).

In any case, acquiring receptive interpretive language can completely alter identity and in my case I felt I'd gone from being an animal to also being a mind, a person. The fact this ability would shut down after five or ten minutes until I was about 20 made it the dangling of a carrot I could reach but not keep.

I went from about 10 per cent receptive language at the age of nine to 50 per cent at 20 and 50 to 70 per cent by 30, and each time it altered my identity and it altered my feeling of my place in the world, my sameness, my differentness, and it altered my feelings about others, who and what they were and my empathy towards them or lack of it. Receptively I went through the following sharp shifts of identity, from identifying myself as:

1. a deaf child who could hear, to

2. a meaning-deaf child who was building bridges to the world of those who could hear fluently with meaning, then to

3. a person bluffing and pretending I didn't have receptive processing problems, then to

4. a person who had very low expectations of her social worth because she was still largely meaning-deaf and therefore more stupid and worth less than others, then to

5. a person who believed that with determination I could learn and deserved the same opportunities and worth and equality as others, then to

6. a person who felt sad that I now liked and cared about and enjoyed the company of the aliens around me and whose conversation and reading I would never find easy or very enjoyable, to

7. a person accepted as an equal by my friends and peers in spite of my challenges, who uses what strategies I have to keep up, has great confidence I can function well on familiar topics, knows I am free to reject anyone who negatively or patronisingly judges my worth or intelligence by my challenges, and who is self-confident and self-accepting enough to feel loveable and included by my partner in spite of ongoing receptive language processing problems.

Expressively, I went through almost as many major identity shifts, moving from being:

1. someone who could only communicate in my own language, to

2. someone who could use 'theirs' but in an extremely painstaking 'walking through mud' type strained attempt, which also changed my identity.

Here, I had to choose between the identity of being 'the person in my own world who could always survive as an animal' to 'the crazy girl who could speak fluently but not be understood' to the 'probable moron who struggled to get out three sentences in two minutes and had to cut down significantly on what she had to say because of the incredible effort and strain involved in the task'. From here I went to:

3. the person giving up in arrogant scorn at those who were different and striving for pride as an alien who would never succeed as one of 'them', to

4. acting like the problem didn't exist, putting on characterisations in order to speak 'as them' and being a person who was committed to not worrying or caring about the problem as long as I 'passed', to

5. an exile from her own land who had taken on someone else's system and culture and had to stay there in order to survive in the world, to

6. someone who is now safe and free to speak her old language at home and communicates fluently in 'their' language when typing or 'at work' as a consultant.

These are only my journeys with identity affected by my own communication challenges, and all of these shifts in identity altered the presentation of my apparent Autism.

There are those with articulation or anxiety problems who have never spoken but are as whole and intelligent as any person, whose identity will be shaped by this and whose identity issues may severely distress that person and compound their apparent Autism.

There are those who have come to prove they can speak through typing and, nevertheless, had their communication disbelieved or taken away. Such things will affect their identity and show in despair, resentment or distraction, and will compound their apparent Autism.

There will be those who know they make sense inside but what comes out is jumbled or incomprehensible, and whether or not they develop, or are provided with, strategies to manage their communication will equally affect their identity and affect the impression of their Autism.

It is not uncommon that someone might protect and preserve their old sense of self by rejecting or regressing from a new system they have acquired. Sometimes it may be the very enthusiasm or forced compliance of others that makes them overly aware they have shifted from the old self to this new self. Helping people make such transitions in identity involves recognising this struggle may exist for them no matter how excited or happy you may be about their change. Helping people make these transitions may mean helping to distract them from awareness of their achievements, rather than making them too overtly aware, and giving them time and space to get used to these 'new shoes' before discarding them as not feeling 'like theirs'. There is currently a complete lack of professional awareness and services in this area of training and support.

Body and identity

Ask some developmentally typical people who they are and some will describe themselves as 'still young', 'middle-aged', 'elderly', 'a big person', 'petite', 'in good health', 'frail', 'athletic', 'overweight'.

Some Auties won't have any problem with body-connectedness at all and will have cohesive visual perception with which to see themselves, good receptive processing in getting feedback about touch and where their body begins and ends, and no problem gauging sensation. Others may be extremely confused about these things because of problems with brain organisation, neurochemistry imbalances, toxicity issues or gut/immune disorders affecting feedback.

Some who have experienced severe ongoing ill health, persistent and repeated experiences of epilepsy cutting them off from awareness of control over their body, severe ultra-rapid cycling bipolar making it excruciating at times to experience emotions through having a body, extreme depression limiting motivation to explore or use the body, extreme neglect or ongoing physical abuse throughout early infancy, may have developed a heightened capacity to detach themselves from all awareness of their body and its needs or a failure to re-attach themselves. By the age of three some people in this situation may have developed an identity which is devoid of any identification with having a body. External attempts to change that may be experienced not as help but as infliction, invasion, intrusion and alienation.

Who are you when you perceive yourself as having no 'body'? Who are you when you perceive your own body as something foreign, alien, stuck on, even imprisoning the self rather than being the means of expressing it? How does one build relationships with others when one perceives one's selfhood as having no relationship at all to them having a body, or one fails even to perceive that the body can be used in building communication or relationships with others? Who am 'I' when, in spite of the presence of a body, the sense of 'I' has no physical existence? And what does this identity issue have to do with the particular presentation of someone's Autism?

Alienation is an important issue. If we as Auties feel alienated from the world of others, we will not relax with them, respect them, open up to them, explore their world. If we perceive ourselves as having no body or being uncomfortable with having a body, then we are more likely to be alienated by those people, environments and in those activities which most want, need, require us to have one. This is of course a catch-22. It is as essential to help someone to build identification with their body, come to be friends with it and actively use it as it is to reduce the possibility that he or she will feel alienated in that process.

If Auties feel alienated from others, they may comply simply because others have the position of power in their lives. Auties may, however, then set up an even stronger opposition against identifying with and using their body. After all, if their use of their body is so obviously not about their own will but about how others have imposed their wishes on them, then it is almost natural for them to begin to distinguish what is 'self' from what is 'not self'. They will not think of their body as really theirs, or part of their 'self', because it is not their own will which is driving the compliance to use it but the will of others. So the million-dollar question is how do we inspire someone in this situation to discover the desire to use their own body?

To start with, we should address who it would please for them to do so. For only if it is clear to *them* that it would bring them pleasure for them to use their own body would they begin to process the feedback from their body as associated with their own will, desire and enjoyment.

The key to finding what will motivate someone is to have a sense not of what you want or enjoy but what they enjoy. Some children love coloured lights, others love certain types of sounds or echo-acoustics, some love certain textures, some love certain smells or tastes, some love watching patterns and lines and symmetry, some love watching movement, vibration or being swung or bounced or tickled. If you think of these things as the delivery van, you can bring in all kinds of goods through the use of an acceptable form of delivery.

There are coloured lights and music machines which will react to movement such that in using one's body one can make a light show happen. With technology, pictures, letters, sounds or words can be set to appear when linked to the triggering of a coloured light or sound.

There are vibrating cushions and bootees which massage feet, and massage pads and massage chairs for massaging the entire body without any of the emotional confusion of including other human beings as one gets to know and befriend one's own body.

There is the possibility of creating perfect and harmonious patterns and order, then setting one piece annoyingly out of place to the degree that it triggers at least the desire to correct this disharmony. Parts of a harmonious collection can be left, trail-style, throughout a passageway with each on a picture or word which is then passively taken in as the desired objects are gathered back into the collection. The same can be done with Thomas the Tank Engine 'tracks' with 'station stops' which each deliver a new experience, or with food trails where each tiny morsel along the track is sitting on a new object, picture, number, letter or word.

There are hammocks above which pictures and words can be projected on the ceiling for passive learning. There are bouncers and trampolines which can be linked up to sound triggers, so through bouncing and jumping one triggers a range of recorded sounds, even words.

There are essential oils which can deliver differing smell sensations to different objects, a series of pictures, a collection of letters or numbers or words. There are feathers and brushes one may be stroked or tickled with where these experiences can be linked with the projection of colours, sounds, pictures, words, numbers that they can take in passively.

Without identification with one's own body, one may struggle to find the motivation or familiarity to use speech or develop self-help skills. Even in the absence of identification with one's own body, some people may still be able to connect to speech or self-help skills whilst tuning out awareness of what they are doing. They may do this through what might be globally labeled as 'self stimulatory behaviours'. The problem here is in telling which people use these 'stims' to enable communication and self-help skills to break through and which people are so compelled toward stimming they are unable to focus on or connect to communication or self-help skills. If we assume that what we call 'stimming' never has a use in facilitating the release of useful skills then we may disadvantage that section of the Autistic community for whom it does. Any technique that seeks to reduce self-consciousness or self-awareness in order to counter 'blocking' and facilitate a flow of action is, unfortunately, still often seen as looking 'too Autistic'. So, ironically, what may work may not be used.

Some will not only struggle to identify with having a body but also a mind or even emotions. Some will only have the problem in identifying with their body. Their identification with their mind may be quite intact, though they may be unable to express such awareness physically. Some will learn to type with physical facilitation, and some of these people may progress to typing their communication with varying degrees of independence. Mostly, however, people with struggles in connecting with their body, or identifying their body as theirs, will be made consciously to tune in, made overtly aware of what attempts they do make and be overtly 'rewarded' for any demonstrations that they are exploring identification with their body. This is almost a form of 'cultural ignorance' because it assumes that the non-Autistic form of using consciousness, identity and cognition relating to functioning ability is the best possible system to facilitate potential in all people on the Autistic spectrum for whom consciousness, identity and cognition may be very differently structured and very different processes. Such ignorance may be extremely unfortunate for those people for whom this may burn their only bridge to capability.

Communication and identity

Who are we if we cannot speak? Do others still imagine that we have thoughts and feelings? Do they believe that if we had thoughts then surely we would be driven to speak them? Do they imagine we are selfish, uninterested? Do they feel we are damaged, broken, somehow less of a bargain than a speaking child? Are we seen as someone less in the world if we do not speak, assumed to be so much more in our own worlds instead? Do those who do speak drudge about in grief and despair worrying themselves to distraction about our inability to communicate and burden us with such fears about ourselves, feelings of being this weight upon others? Are all who can't speak essentially made up of similar ingredients to each other in the same way that verbal people are assumed to be somehow a group with some kind of shared reality? And what do those who cannot speak think of the world of those who can, and of the world of words and its grand importance 'out there'?

Whilst Aspies generally do speak, a significant proportion of people diagnosed with Autism do not, though around one third generally have echolalia – speech which is an immediate or delayed repetition of things said by others – and other so-called 'dysfunctional language'.

I was in this second group. I developed so-called 'dysfunctional language', meaning that it was very difficult for others to understand me. Eventually, I made a leap to so-called 'functional language', meaning basically that now I could make myself understood by developmentally typical people. But during my own language journey, according to my father, I had days, weeks and even months at a time when I stopped speaking. A visitor to the house who had met me around 200 times had never heard me speak, though I felt I chattered to myself all the time. She did recall me muttering but said nobody could tell what I was saying. So the world of people who do not speak and the world of those who do has a space in the middle where people like me would have been found.

To talk about the world of non-verbal people, we should ideally hear it from them. Many are able to tell us through typed communication, though their communications are certainly often drowned out by most verbal people on the Autie spectrum. Non-verbal communicators sometimes present at lectures through typed communication, but mostly they are represented by those who speak verbally. To make matters worse, whilst many verbal Auties and Aspies accept non-verbal people as their equals, it is far rarer that non-verbal people occur in the social circles of verbal Auties and Aspies, and it is becoming more common that non-verbal Auties will now type-speak with other non-verbal Autie spectrum peers, especially via computers. But what of those non-verbal Auties who do not type even though they have been provided the opportunity to develop typed communication – do they think the same as non-verbal Auties who do type?

To answer the question of whether the internal worlds of non-verbal people are comparable, you need to look at all the issues that can make someone non-verbal. Some people may be non-verbal because of brain organisation issues so they can't put the ideas together or retrieve the connection to their body at the same time as their thoughts and feelings.

Some may have had functional agnosia or visual fragmentation so severe they may have been unable to form the links between images and words to acquire much functional speech beyond things they can experience in other ways.

Some may be so meaning-deaf to their own speech, or process it in a way that makes it sound jumbled, distorted, distracting or fragmented to a degree that sticking with speech becomes more trouble or more disturbing than the effort is worth.

Some may be non-verbal because of oral dyspraxia, reducing their ability to articulate.

Some may be non-verbal because of gut/immune issues or toxicity issues severely affecting their ability to process, order, retrieve or monitor their own communication.

Some may be non-verbal because of imbalanced brain chemistry leading to severe impulse-control, mood, anxiety or compulsive disorders, and interfering with the motivation or control of functional speech.

Some might be phobic, detached or unable to identify with their mind, emotions or body to the degree that they are functionally non-verbal.

Some might have developed selective mutism as part of a progressively severe personality disorder inhibiting them from the ability to use speech interpersonally or personally.

Some may have been so consistently meaning-deaf to incoming language as well as visual meaning that they live in a world of sensing in which interpretive language is something that may as well be of another world.

Do all of these people experience their lack of speech or dysfunctional language the same way? I doubt it. Do all of them experience thought in the same way? I doubt that too. Do they all think in pictures? I'm sure many do, but certainly some do not. And the way one experiences oneself as a communicator will affect not only how others understand, misunderstand or project realities onto you, but also how you feel about those misunderstandings, projections and the difference between yourself and others, if in fact you are equipped to hold those two concepts simultaneously and consciously. And, to make this even more confusing, there are those who can do so but not consciously, who may display amazing insight when in a pre-conscious state and struggle extremely when consciously aware.

Finding a shared reality with people who lack functional language may mean learning what this means for the person in this situation regardless of any label they may share with others whose seemingly similar communication challenges may actually be dramatically different.

The words 'I' and 'you'

There are people who will struggle with the relativity of who is 'I' and who is 'You', but there are others who, because of issues like exposure anxiety, may simply be utterly allergic to conscious awareness of their own existence. For some of these people, the ability to refer to themselves in the second person form 'You' or third person form 'He' or 'She', or formally by name or impersonally and detached using 'a person' or 'one', allows them to communicate. Take this away by overtly forcing them to acknowledge and 'properly' use 'I' and 'You' and you may find it costs them a lot of their social-emotional daring of communication. If non-Autistic people can learn to translate foreign languages then they can learn to translate for the small language nuances associated with markedly different social-emotional realities.

Dependency and identity

Co-dependency

Co-dependency can subtly imprison the identity of the dependent person. One stops being a person and begins being a burden, a cross to bear, a victim to be helped, saved or assisted, something broken which cannot believe in its own potential capacity for self-initiated improvement, a tool more than a person. Breaking away from a co-dependent carer means disloyalty and fear of abandonment.

I remember a man who used typed communication at a very high level and had some 'dysfunctional' speech but claimed he couldn't speak. Finally, he acknowledged he had been whispering to himself and knew he could speak, but he couldn't possibly dare to do so in front of his mother because she'd 'die of shock'. How many capable carers set up impossible situations like this where a precedent has been set for years in which they feel useful and helpful and get social praise for their martyrdom and sacrifice as they explain that their child is 'non-verbal' or 'severely low-functioning'? Then the child is unable to defy loyalty to such an assumption, to shock the parent, dramatically alter the parent's identity, shatter the parent's public persona, rob the parent of their perceived source of self-esteem and purpose, and possibly run the risk of abandonment or of annoyance as to why they didn't show these abilities sooner!

Learned dependency

How many of us can realise our abilities when we are hooked into a pattern of being perpetually helped, sometimes before we've even experienced any discomfort or annoyance? And what if we screamed? What if we became annoyed? What if we experienced discomfort? Well aren't these things part of life? Isn't expressing these things loudly part of learning to express oneself, that to do so is safe, and that through doing so we can eventually learn to gauge a level of justifiable reaction and modulate the extremity of our reactions? But if we are taught right from the start that all discomfort, annoyance or screaming is bad, or if we are slow to develop and we are waking up to this important developmental phase at the age of three or five or seven instead of between one and two, should we then be robbed of going through it and coming out the other end merely because our carer is socially embarrassed or worried about social exclusion or disapproval? And where is this going in society with an ever tighter definition of 'normal', where the diversity of yesterday becomes the labels of today?

In a state of learned dependency, we are given the identity of perpetual follower, never leader or equal. In a state of learned dependency we are given the identity of being a receiver, never a giver; of being a learner, never a teacher; of being capable not of discovery, only of compliance. Some personalities will be eager to please or live up to these very low expectations and here we must ask who it is who has the disability – the 'client', the 'carer', the 'professional', even 'society'.

Discovery learning and identity

There are always the goods and the form of delivery, what's on the truck and how we drive the truck to its destination. Learning and development is the same. There is the learning experience and how we deliver it.

If we had a TV with only three stations and all of those stations had similar shows and those shows all had the same type of format of delivering that information, then it's the same as saying we have three trucks, all with very similar goods and all being driven and delivered in a very similar way. Even if we agree that the goods are valuable and useful, we could almost be convinced that this had to be the best way to deliver them, the 'normal' way, even the 'only' way because we've been shown nothing else. Now education is like this too. We are told about the skills of reading, writing, maths, science, art, music, dance, technology, sport, languages, etc. (and these days a lot of schools have dropped art, music, dance, technology, sport, languages), and we generally agree these are valuable things to learn. But when we get the goods, we also get their delivery, and we don't even notice or question whether there are other, perhaps even better ways of delivering these goods.

Take a hamburger, for example. We buy the hamburger and we barely notice what it's wrapped in. It might be in a cardboard package, it might be wrapped in paper. It might be that some of us would be more likely to eat it if it was served to us on a paper plate, or a china plate. Someone else might be unable to eat it till later and be more likely to eat it served cooked but cold and wrapped in cling film. You see my point?

Anyway, we get delivered education in a cost-effective way that allows governments to pay teachers less money to teach more students in one classroom. Even private schools are businesses that set out to give a reasonable delivery for a reasonable price, and that means how to deliver what they can to a large group of students all in one go. Because of this they follow a particular method of delivery. You've mostly all seen it, it used to be called 'chalk and talk' back when blackboards were still used. But it hasn't changed much. It still involves 'excessive instruction', 'following orders', 'copying the teacher's example', 'coming up with answers the teacher has already taught you to give', 'complying', 'proving you have memorised what you've been primed with' and basically very little discovery, no real 'Eureka', just plenty of 'good boy'.

This type of instruction isn't just done by teachers, it's done by carers who grew up learning that this is how you 'help' or 'show' or 'teach' someone. So when a child is not compliant, not a follower, not good with receptive intake of excessive instruction, not good at waiting for the conclusion, but is excited about exploring the experiences and finding their own conclusion, the child is seen as 'a poor learner', 'not ready for mainstream schooling', etc. In fact, I've found that some Auties, when relaxed and not compelled into self-protection mechanisms, compulsions or information overload, are the most experimental and inventive children I've met. They are more likely to explore angles, lines, patterns and new sensory experiences and materials in innovative ways you'd not normally find in non-Autistic children.

Control these children and you often bring out the worst in counter-control or anxiety responses, but provide them with a socially non-invasive space with self-initiated access to sensory experiences along the lines of their own fascinations and you can often be surprised. Invade, and this group generally respond badly, but will be involved for your own benefit, seemingly to their exclusion, though many will continue to explore, even cashing in within their own controlled space on some of the new patterns you've 'discovered'.

This is 'discovery learning'; and we don't learn about it because it is manoeuvred and facilitated, but not controlled, by adults in charge, and not able to be easily wrapped in an economical package like the excessively instructional approach involved in most teaching. I have created discovery learning programmes for people with Autism and I'd have no problem with recommending the incorporation of a chunky piece of elastic around the participants' waists to allow a carer safely to remain relatively attached to the person doing the exploring and discovering found in open spaces of parks, gardens, art centres, factories, markets, quarries, warehouses, escalators, elevators, apartment buildings, cemeteries, malls, hotels, car parks, car washes, laundrettes, post offices, train stations, public transport, rubbish dumps, etc., etc. Being unable to interpret written and spoken words, I ran out of classes to create this for myself and visited all of these things. Even without functional language, these experiences created frameworks, systems, perspectives, assurances, feelings and unspoken questions, and what was so essential was that these were my choices, my learning, my pace, my mind and feelings and body. These things are the foundation of a strong sense of identity, and most people with Autism will be controlled out of such opportunities by virtue of their label, by virtue of 'services', by virtue of fear of social judgement in a society with public liability dramas hanging over everything in which progressively narrower definitions of 'normal' are growing like an ideological takeover.

I felt plenty of 'ah' and 'aha' from discovery learning, something I never got from excessively instructional education in any form within the schools I was meant to learn in. Each new self-directed discovery learning experience had a framework to slot into which I could never have achieved sitting in a classroom being reminded daily of my inabilities and the comparative power of others, and I was not subject to the constant overt (and abnormal) control of others over me, the constant feeling of being watched, of expectation and being measured against myself or others. I wandered through such places and by the time people had noticed a child wandering about I was gone and off on the next adventure. But similar visits can today be diplomatically arranged with those who believe in social diversity and equal access to learning opportunities, and who understand the safety measures in place. Facilitators will get plenty of 'no' but it's the 'yeses' that count.

Diversity and identity

Some of us are flexible, can cope with inconsistency and are happy to be dominated and cope with many bosses. Many of us require structure and knowing where we stand and getting only one non-conflicting set of rules to follow, and are happy to submit to the control of someone else so we only cope with having one boss. Some of us cannot receptively keep up with or relate to the foreign (often verbal) structures of others and by contrast work well when we have created a structure for ourselves. Some of us are inventive, exploratory, entrepreneurial and eccentric by nature, unable to grasp or sustain hierarchy, and we cope with no bosses over us, merely alongside us in a world in which our right to be our own boss is also respected. In other words, we are not all one flavour; some of us are strawberry, some chocolate, some hazelnut...

For any Autie or Aspie it is probably a good thing if the environment has a cohesive approach which fits with that person's frameworks and challenges, regardless of what's 'mainstream' out there. This means that a developmentally typical parent or partner might need to do a bit of attitude shifting. It means recognising that projecting a foreign reality onto someone may not be the best way for them happily to come to the party of their own accord, but we may be able to change the way we deliver some of these foreign options. In terms of education and services and employment we need to recognise that what's on offer may not always be the best fit. There may be a neighbour who has a more constructive and positive relationship with the person with Autism than the school psychologist. There may be new friends the family hasn't yet met who are more accepting of diversity than the circle the family currently surrounds itself with. There may be social involvements which don't rest on a person's weaknesses but on their shared active interests that revolve around 'doing'. There may be entrepreneurial opportunities nobody has ever modelled because they were all too busy slotting into the 'mainstream'. If a miniature community doesn't yet exist in which there is a cohesive and accepting atmosphere, then nobody is going to create it if you don't make a start yourself, however tiny those first little steps may be.

Just because an increasingly multinational, 'big business', 'big brother' society is progressively erasing our vision of future opportunities for those who fail to grasp hierarchy, 'kiss arse' or 'follow the leader' doesn't mean these people are necessarily broken or of less worth. The problem is this is often the very message they are being given about themselves, and this is a social crime against diversity to which most of society is an all-too-willing accomplice. There are opportunities for these people but they may be on the peripheries of society and those peripheries are nevertheless a very real, essential, colourful, valuable part of society.

The person versus the condition

Many 'high-functioning' people with Autism or Asperger syndrome say they 'are' their Autism or Asperger's, that the two are inseparable and that to take away their Autism or Asperger's would be to take away their selfhood.

It may be that the decision as to whether one is one's Autism or Asperger's comes down to whether what underpins those conditions is 'ego-syntonic' (experienced as part of one's selfhood) or 'ego-dystonic' (experienced as something external to one's selfhood). Personality disorders, brain organisation and style of information processing are all things we can experience as part of our own selfhood. Anxiety disorders, tic and compulsive disorders, mood disorders and fluctuating gut/immune dysfunction which can create information-processing and sensory-perceptual fluctuations might all be more likely to be experienced as external to one's selfhood unless the environment continually identifies these things as 'us'. If we are constantly defined by conditions we have, but feel imprisoned by them, then we may struggle to know where the 'us' really is. Furthermore, if the environment's approach actually exacerbates our condition, it is easier to identify with the condition as part of our selfhood and the environment as being 'the problem'.

Information-processing differences, mood, anxiety, compulsive or personality disorders or environmental issues can shape our interests and shape what we will avoid becoming our interests.

Information-processing differences can shape the formation and expression of personality. So can mood, anxiety or compulsive disorders or environmental issues. Personality traits, including extreme forms such as personality disorders, will largely shape the way we respond to opportunities and experiences – communication, interaction, our relationship to thought, feelings and body, our sense of self and of society and our responses to the environment, our take on what motivation is all about and what our anti-motivations will be. Knowing the difference between what is our condition and what is just part of being ourselves can be important in finding shared ground with others, in deciding what to defend and identify with and what just to leave to take care of itself as we seek instead to focus more on our personhood than on our condition. If the environment sees our condition first and personhood second, this is usually how we will see ourselves. There's a fine line between explaining someone's special needs and setting them apart or segregating them. It's also important that the person with Autism can be realistic about opportunities which might best fit their collection of challenges, without being condemned to this realism.

If we set up a person to identify their selfhood only by their condition, then it is their condition they will defend if the external world seeks to change what they see as their selfhood. If we bring someone up to focus on their personhood first, as if the condition is merely the details, such a person will be more likely to focus on life and less likely to fixate first on their condition. When a parent is co-dependently fixated on, perhaps even forced to exaggerate, the severity of their child's condition for the purpose of securing maximum funding, there are still people in there. The parent is more than merely a burdened, self-sacrificing carer. The child is more than just a bundle of Autism.

There is an assumption that if a child is severely affected by a developmental condition, we can't see what they like, want, are interested in; but I don't believe this is true. Even the most severely affected people with Autism will have at least subtle physical body, sound or movement responses to different types of sensory experiences and patterns, and from this we may know what kind of music, sounds, smells, textures, colour, patterns, lights, tastes, movements, themes, places, people or voices they like. Furthermore, many who are severely affected in so many ways may still be capable of communication through assisted typing such as facilitated communication. Communicating, even through typing, may be someone's first opportunity to manifest their existence of mind or feelings out into the external world, and that may be a big part of knowing themselves, feeling themselves to be an individual and more than just a condition. Without that, many will not know on whose behalf they are trying for.

Segregated environments

So having rattled the cages of 'mainstream' society, let's take a look at the challenges of segregated environments and what these mean to identity.

One of the issues with segregated environments is that these are places where a small section of the community has been gathered together on the basis of being 'different' in some extreme way and removed from direct involvement with those who are 'usual', 'common' or, dare we say it, perceived as 'normal'. This means some very important things.

One is that the people being segregated from 'the mainstream' are given examples of their own stuff as 'normal', but the problem with this is that we don't have segregated shops, footpaths, parks, etc., so these people's 'normality' can get some pretty brutal responses.

Sure we want society to stop defining 'normality' in ever more impossible tiny boxes and to respect, even celebrate, diversity, but how can people learn to do or value that when those who are 'different' are kept conveniently away from them until adulthood?

Why should developmentally typical people respect what they've had no personal experience of or involvement with? Sure, you can moralise at them, shame them, nag them that they should, but unless they have formed connections and shared environments with people very different to themselves, why should they rock their grand pedestal of assumed 'normality'? Why should they share their resources with those they assume are damaged, broken or inferior because if they weren't they'd have gone to the same schools, playgrounds, shops, etc. as anyone else?

So integration isn't just about the now, it's about laying social foundations for a hopefully more tolerant world.

I remember meeting up with a friend who had known me when I was nine. She was laughing about how I used to run at the furniture, bash myself in the head and scare everyone with my behaviour. She was imitating how when I had tried to speak with meaning it was like someone verbally constipated who was trying to access and get out words in a strained and excruciating slow pace, which she described as 'like watching paint dry'; she remarked how, by contrast, when talking to myself I could talk fine. Then she said, 'But I never thought there was anything *wrong* with you, you were different but to me you were, you know, just Donna.' What's more those who had encountered my stuff, my ways, then recognised similar stuff in others when they met them. My needs aside, had I not been in mainstream environments, these people would have been more socially limited, and guess who I grow up to have to encounter in the street, down the shops, etc…yes, these other people. I'd like to encounter those who have had experiences in which they saw the person beyond the condition.

When we socially segregate Auties, we lump them in with others who may share a label but are not necessarily 'the same'. If we have one child whose mood, anxiety, compulsive or information-processing issues have upped the tempo on personality states to the degree that he or she has dependent personality disorder, we may have them in the same cosy and intimate sparsely populated room with someone who's personality state has equally become exaggerated but within a framework of antisocial personality disorder. Whilst we all have different personalities, I believe that clashing mixtures of extreme personality and emotional states may sometimes be more likely in small populations of severely developmentally challenged kids than in the general social mix of a mainstream environment.

This is not to say that bigotry, prejudice, fashion and plain old 'shared realities' won't cause segregation within mainstream environments too, but at least one is being prepared for dealing with a world of developmentally typicals as an adult. For the truth is, we don't grow up to move out to islands inhabited only by those like ourselves, except perhaps some specialised residential care units. Even then what do we do? Be afraid to leave the unit in case we encounter the foreignness of developmentally typicals unaccustomed to us?

I recently visited a specialist centre working with Auties where they had a wire fence. On the other side of the fence a skateboard park had been built and the Auties could clearly see and hear the skaters. The parents had asked for a wall to be built to protect the Auties from the noise of the skaters and the traffic. I was asked my opinion. I said to provide a box of headphones, and if the noise was that big a problem then the Auties could choose to do something about it. I was asked, what about the wall? I said, if you build a wall now, you will take away this window on wonder, this vision on sport and skateboarding some of these children might otherwise one day have aspired to. You would build a wall and then expect them to cross a road, go to a shop, walk through a crowd, where you will not be able to build a wall. Yet if they learn they have a choice of utilising headphones, they can go anywhere. Most of the walls we build, however, are social prisons and they may be built as much by those with misplaced and excessive 'care' as those who don't care at all.

Giving Autistic people developmentally typical identities

Some developmentally typical people can suffer badly from having bodies, faces and clothes which don't measure up to what they see and hear over and over and over in magazines, TV, pop videos and in shop windows; and therapists, psychiatrists and cosmetic surgeons are out there earning a living from such insecurities and anxieties as you read this. Some may resent having anything but blond hair or having to wear glasses or not being part of the 'in-crowd' or not owning whatever piece of technology or skateboard or, or, or... With little credible counter-culture, for some people this barrage of social imagery and how they don't 'measure up' to it can lead to low self-esteem and, in some cases, affect their confidence later in life.

On top of this, Auties also have a culture waved in their face which they usually have even less chance of measuring up to – non-Autistic styles of processing information, non-Autistic means of coping with sensory environments, developmentally typical styles of coping with social-emotional experience, developmentally typical styles of communication, sharing developmentally typical interests and abilities, even developmentally typical expectations and aspirations and developmentally typical patterns of identifying with developmentally typical heros. In other words, Auties can be expected, subtly and overtly, to develop developmentally typical identities – a developmentally typical sense of self.

We would never expect a wheelchair user to identify with being someone who didn't use one. We would never expect a blind person to go around acting as if they had sight. We would not expect someone with a hearing impairment to follow a conversation as if they could hear fine. We wouldn't expect someone with cerebral palsy to act as if they had complete control over their body. But we often expect an Autie to behave as though a multi-track world is ideal, enjoyable, appreciated and desired. We often expect an Autie to behave as though they have the same intellectual or interpretive interests as anyone else, even if they struggle extremely with receptive information processing and live in a world of pattern, theme and feel in which information is processed well after the event, often pre-consciously. We often expect an Autie who has no simultaneous sense of self and other to pretend or behave not only as if they do have such a sense, but also to initiate activities they may then be unable to keep up with socially and act like this process is great.

They may be expected to comment on or be attracted to bodies they can't even actually see as a whole, and to play along about being interested in being physically, socially or even communicatively involved in a way, at a level and for a length of time they may be unable actually to stand or process.

We may expect an Autie to want to eat with others where the Autie may be better able to eat without anxiety and have a hope of experiencing the eating much better when eating in isolation.

We may expect those frozen in self-protective states to speak up verbally, and deny them the ability to use typed communication instead on the basis that when they were relaxed we heard them say 'orange juice'.

We may expect that an Autie who can get an academic qualification can multi-track in the social-communicative world of employment in an ongoing way when they simply can't.

There are people who lose cohesive visual perception under fluorescent lights, lose track of their body when sitting still, or lose the ability to understand language when fans are going. Yet these people are often expected to behave as though these issues simply don't exist. Now, tell me, how many developmentally typical people do you know who would cope with that level of alienation from their own reality and still respect and open up to those making these assumptions?

We all have a right to be who we are and what we are, including a right to be a person in transition with a right to grow and challenge our own limitations and to change. We all have a right to use what tools work for us and to seek tools where we have none. We all have a right to say, this doesn't fit and can we adjust this. We are all of equal worth in our differentness; and this is not the world of the majority, this is everyone's world. If I'm an apple, I don't want to spend years in therapy trying to fix myself up from being what I assume is a failure as an orange. I don't want to hate myself, be angry at myself or hate others or be angry at others or at life itself for my being taught, pressured or encouraged to aim not to be my best at who and what I am but to be my best version of someone else's utterly foreign system and reality. If I am to be taught what is useful, it would begin with being taught to accept and love myself, to understand respectfully and with equal worth the difference between my own system and that of others, and to be included in ideas and plans of how different worlds can meet and how my own abilities can find a place of appreciated expression within a diverse world.

When others impose an identity upon me of a system that is utterly foreign to me I feel I am invisible, invalid and unworthy as what and who I really am. This is no way to build bridges between two worlds. If Autism is a condition of too many straws on a camel's back, the camel certainly doesn't need the added straw of alienation.

Maximising potential

It's a great thing to encourage people to reach for the stars, whether they are aspiring to non-Autistic models of achievement or those of any human being. It can certainly be a bad thing to underestimate someone's potential, and some of the most severely affected people with Autism have achieved some amazing things, some small, some large. Some have typed poetry, prose and books, some have produced moving and compelling artworks, some have produced amazing music, some have astounded people with their collections or moved people with their capacity to sense. Some have been masters and wonderful examples of Simply Being. But it can be equally damaging not always to remind people that whatever they will achieve, they will do so in their own way and that it's OK to adapt a goal or plan along the way. It's OK to remind people that sometimes in aiming for a goal, we find out more of who we are and how we work, and sometimes that leads us onto a different track where we better realise our own potential. There are blind people who have flown planes, deaf musicians, and paraplegics who have climbed mountains; but there are also people who have achieved things which were so much more easily achievable. I would love to have been a singer; but I spent 38 years with exposure anxiety, so I became a recording artist who sang only in a studio with no direct audience. Sometimes there are ways of shaping our goals to see our dreams more than our limitations.

Personality disorders and identity
Schizotypal personality disorder and being 'too fluid' about identity
When we talk about the relevance of identity to functioning, there are those who have a very fluid experience of mind and identity. One example may be that of idiosyncratic-schizotypal personality.

How can we help someone have a sense of self when they are oriented and motivated to disappear back into their own world off onto a series of fluid tangents, almost as though they desire no fixed identity? Can they still learn to function without a conscious sense of self? What about communication? How can someone with extremely fluid thought and little conscious sense of self tell you about their thoughts and views? Is it possible that an extremely fluid sense of self is nevertheless one form of a sense of self? Are we able to accept this if we are strongly expecting or wanting something else, particularly if we are limited in our vision of how such a person may ever 'achieve' anything or be 'successful'?

Yet fortune tellers, psychics, palm readers, poets, songwriters, children's performers, drama therapists, music therapists, artists and art therapists, buskers, comedians, mime artists and impressionists would all need a high degree of this 'fluid' nature; yet I wouldn't be one to say they have never achieved anything. And for that matter, what kind of minds wrote the strange poetic teasings of the Zen koans if not some very fluid thinkers? Yet what if such a person is born into a family which cannot relate or model or even imagine these things? It's an interesting question. In any case, perhaps it is not a strong conscious sense of identity which we need and that having one stands in the way of us so easily using the skills we have. It may be that for those who have never developed any one strong conscious sense of identity, as long as this trait is channelled in a direction which the person themselves feels 'at home' with, then it doesn't matter. I once wrote 'I am always myself, in the becoming of it' and there are certainly those who might be more limited in having an overly rigid defensiveness about sticking to one narrow experience of identity.

Obsessive-compulsive personality disorder and being 'too rigid' about identity

The opposite to the very fluid sense of self with idiosyncratic-schizotypal personality might be the rigidity of conscientious obsessive-compulsive personality. What if we develop an awareness we like Thomas the Tank Engine and this is like a major interest and an equally major full stop? We might want every aspect of our life to be channelled through Thomas the Tank Engine, like siphoning a lake through a straw. It's doable, and I remember sitting in the car with one such absolute obsessive with whom I channelled all other kinds of topics through the use of the additions Thomas, Gordon, Percy and the words train, station and tracks. It's amazing that you can refer to stopping at the supermarket station and buying some Percy brand breakfast cereal before getting back onto your tracks to head back to the home station where you will have to cook up some dinner fuel for Thomas Senior and Thomas Junior and little Gordana before all the carriages go to sleep for the night. Perhaps rigidity seems so rigid to equally rigid minds. Perhaps rigidity is not such an obstacle when manoeuvred by a fluid mind.

Borderline personality disorder and identity problems

The mercurial personality is one of several personality traits that occur in the general diversity of society. When someone has this trait in the extreme it becomes dysfunctional in some way and, therefore, is called a 'personality disorder'. The extreme of the mercurial personality trait is called borderline personality disorder.

Far from having little or no emphasis on identity and far from having a very narrow and rigid sense of identity, those with the mercurial-borderline personality can have a strong need for identity but build this around idealised others without having a strong identity of their own. This might lead people with the mercurial-borderline personality to over-invest in those they idealise at the expense of developing a sense of self, but there are certainly constructive occupational outlets in which this would be a talent more than a disability. Method actors such as Dustin Hoffman specialise in empathising with and 'becoming' the character they are seeking to play, and there are some people who are capable within certain roles specifically because they have taken these on as a 'role' or character. So an unstable sense of identity may become a greater disability when someone with this is channelled in a direction where it is important that they have one relatively stable sense of self. Channelled into a direction where their disability becomes an ability, this would be less of a problem.

Dual personality and bipolar

The artistic-cyclothymic personality as well as a rapid cycling bipolar state itself might leave a person feeling very confused about who they are. Are they Jekyll or Hyde? Are they the excitable, agitated, perhaps even bombastic, manic, obnoxious, euphoric extrovert, or are they the phobic, fussy, obsessive, worrying, rigid, depressive and shut down introvert? The shades in between may, by contrast, be so subtle or undemanding they are barely noticed. In terms of identity, who is the self one decides to share with others? And if they so like or care about one side of the self, will they equally like or care about the other? How does one trust the social world when one is mostly at least two, if not three people (including the stable self in the middle of fluctuation between the two poles)?

One of the most wonderful things ever said to me (before I was on medication that addressed the bipolar dynamic) was when my husband Chris said he loved me and I asked 'Which me?, Which part?', and he said, all of them, equally. I asked him how he could love someone who was never one person. He said nobody is totally one person, just that my extremes were more extreme and that he loved the many Donnas as different shades of one Donna.

We need to be aware of what we are expecting of people with bipolar or the artistic-cyclothymic personality. These people may never be able to guarantee consistent dependability in one relatively stable emotional state. Yet in any part of their state they may be passionate, creative, expressive people, and there are opportunities which do not always require dependable commitment. Instead of setting people up for opportunities they may be unable to sustain, it may be best for them to aim to excel in opportunities that can accommodate the fluctuations they may be unable to manage fully. Without such a vision or plan, what place in the world do you imagine they should be hoping for? One they could actually feel whole and accepted in and a position in life they are consistently able to live up to without fearing constant embarrassment, failure and rejection when others find they cannot always function merely as 'one person'?

Multiple personality disorder (MPD) and dissociative identity disorder (DID)
One can live in one's head, even create or discover or divert into characters in order to survive, communicate or live with an anxiety disorder and yet not have multiple personalities. One can have split brain or 'mono' information processing and constantly lose track of what one has said or done, of having crossed a room or of what one's body was doing, without this meaning one has multiple personalities at work. One can survive extreme childhood trauma, abuse and loss, and live with post-traumatic stress responses that include diverting into characterisations, and not have multiple personalities. One can live comfortably with the fluid and flexible nature of having several different identities without this being an illness or a case of multiple personalities.

There is a controversy as to whether multiple personality actually exists as a condition and today it has been replaced by the term dissociative identity disorder (DID). Is it possible there may be some cases where someone with dependent personality may have formed a deep personal attachment with a therapist and felt compelled to discover new personalities to justify staying in therapy and avoiding fear of loss or perceived 'abandonment'? Is it possible that some cases involve idiosyncratic-schizotypal personality in which flight into one's own world and characterisations may be a central feature? Is it possible that some people seen as having dissociative identity disorder are experiencing uncommon but 'normal' split brain phenomena, but who, in a world of people with common brain integration, struggle to slot easily into the same opportunities or social-communication realities consistently so seek to solve this through therapy?

In any case, there are patchwork people who are accommodated within society and others who are badly matched with their environment, occupation, or self-expectations, and who will feel they are 'failing', 'broken', needing 'help'. Is it OK to be one identity one day and another the next? If you have built a life that has diverse opportunities and social acceptance to sustain this reality, then yes, it is OK. A patchwork quilt is still one quilt.

Sexuality and identity

There are some males on the Autistic spectrum who identify strongly with women and are estranged from their male bodies and the gender-related expectations these bodies stand for. There are certainly females on the Autistic spectrum who are confused about their gender or sexuality when expected to identify with feeling female or with heterosexual friendship and relationship styles that don't fit them. In fact, one of the world's current leading experts in the field of Asperger's syndrome, Tony Attwood, found that bisexuality, homosexuality and transgender issues were higher in people on the Autistic spectrum than they were in the non-Autistic population (Hénault 2006). I have met a number of openly gay and bisexual adults on the Autistic spectrum, as well as those who would fit the transgender category. I have written about gender and orientation issues in my own life in my fourth autobiographical instalment *Everyday Heaven* (Williams 2004).

I was once asked whether I felt that being homosexual or having gender identity issues could underpin someone's Autism. I did feel that any experience which dramatically alienated a child from their natural sense of self, or of their natural experience of or expression through their body, would only add to anxiety or depression issues which could theoretically affect everything from eye contact to interaction and communication. Take for example a very gentle, dainty, effeminate male toddler born into a family with brothers and a father who present the opposite and perhaps even feel a little alienated from such an effeminate boy, wondering, 'OK, so how do we include this kid?' Take the opposite example of a tough, adventurous, very physical, science-minded female toddler with no interest in her looks, clothes or usual 'girl toys' who is born to parents just waiting for a sweet, dear little feminine girl to take care of and spoil and show off. Add to that perhaps a brother who is openly encouraged (unconsciously and otherwise) in all the areas she is not. That could become one rather confused and alienated little person. If such a child already had other issues, this wouldn't take the burden off.

And what if you were female but identified strongly as 'male' and were being dressed all the time in girls' clothes and were expected to stay clean and look good? Or vice versa where you were male but identified emotionally as 'female', yet were banned from dressing up in 'nice things' and seeking attention, and were expected, instead, to go play rough and tumble? Wouldn't this be a bit confusing? And how confident would such a child be when introduced to the playgroup or primary school where he or she couldn't find a single other soul 'like themselves'? Enough yet to cause social phobia or selective mutism in an already sensitive personality? I'd keep an open mind.

What is more certain is square pegs in round holes may not round off, they may just feel out of place, uncomfortable, not accepted for what they are. Accepting one's own orientation means having a right to change if that comes naturally to you to do so, or not. Accepting diversity doesn't mean actively pushing people in a direction you feel they should be heading. It does, however, mean accepting they could best be whatever it is most natural for them to be and facilitating them in reaching their full potential on terms that make sense according to their own system. Helping people function as best as they can means helping them feel they are not alien, that they are understood and that there is a place for all of us in this world. There are many wonderful and successful bisexual, homosexual and transgender people in the world, and there is no reason why some of those can't also be people somewhere on the Autistic spectrum.

Social politics of disability and identity

There are various angles to the links between the social politics of disability and identity.

From the Aspie point of view, a current social politic involves proudly identifying selfhood with the condition. I can understand where selfhood and the condition are inseparable, but also the places where serious disabling and troubling co-morbid conditions are treatable and, therefore, in a sense, relatively separable over time from one's selfhood, and often healthily so. I agree that the information-processing style of Aspies and Auties should be respected, appreciated and perhaps sometimes improved to its greatest potential, but not pushed aside or merely overlayed with a style that doesn't connect. At the same time, co-occurring conditions such as gut/immune dysfunction, OCD, Tourette's, bipolar, depression, anxiety disorders, scotopic sensitivity or central auditory processing disorder, selective mutism or even schizophrenia for that matter, should be treated if people are severely disabled, distressed, dangerous to themselves or others or uncomfortable with these things, and severely challenging personality disorders should be respectfully managed and channelled into constructive directions for the benefit of the individual, the family and the community.

From the developmentally typical person's point of view, there is often a call for cure which needs to be tempered with 'cured of what?' If they are seeking to treat co-occurring conditions, such as gut/immune dysfunction etc., in people on the Autistic spectrum (and thereby dramatically reduce much of the severity of someone's Autism in many such cases), then I think many folks with these issues might ultimately be grateful for the equilibrium, reduction in chaos, increase in stability and improvement in functioning. But if they are merely lamenting a label, a package, or dreaming not of a much less burdened Autie but of a developmentally typical person they wish to emerge, this is alienating and emotionally damaging to the person with Autism. They won't become a developmentally typical person even with all the help they can get. They'll just be an Autie with a greater chance of reaching what potential they have. So realistic, grounded, informed plans of assistance aren't insulting or hurtful, but romantic. A bleeding heart, blind pursuit wrapped up in an overt display of family grieving over Autism as a tragedy may not be very good for the identity of any person on whose behalf these displays are so 'lovingly' indulged. So with all due respect to my non-autistic readers, have your grief in your own space and time, express yourself, and get any potentially harmfully unrealistic dreams and desperate prayers out of your system as you must. Then take off any martyr's badge you find you've been wearing and lower your flag, and then constructively deal with what actually is in front of you with all the objectivity, humanity, respect, empathy, understanding and pragmatism you can find in gently and peacefully finding answers whilst, most importantly, getting on with playing, being and living life with who you actually have there. Because, if you ask yourself what you'd have wanted had you been the individual human soul in their place, that is maybe what you'd have asked for.

Zen and identity

Zen is a form of Buddhism in which it is realised that attachments are futile because all we become attached to is impermanent. The goal of Zen, as I understand it, is to let go all attachments, to body, to mind, to emotions, to belongings and materialism, to our place within hierarchy, to others. Those who do not follow Zen Buddhism may find this bizarre, pointless, a 'giving up of life', but to the 'Buddha' who achieves this state it is not the experience of giving up life but of being born to a true experience of life without the illusions of attachment. I raise this because I have heard from many people over the years who have been fascinated by the way some 'severely affected' Auties appear to have achieved this state.

Far from being seen as a defeat or a loss, their achievement of such a Zen state of non-attachment is seen as a place of stillness, peace and clarity. I'm not sure I'd say I've seen many Auties in such a state, but the Zen Buddhist perspective would be that those for whom such a Zen state comes so naturally would be distressed and confused by a society which seeks to have them embrace a very non-Zen reality. This non-Zen reality would be one in which they fully develop the intense and obvious attachments so desired by eager parents and professionals seeking to demonstrate their child's advancement toward a state of 'higher functioning'. Regardless of your own religious orientations, it's worth considering this very different perspective simply on a philosophical level.

If it is true that some Auties would feel at peace living wildly, naturally, with only the most basic of needs, finding entertainments in the simplest of transient experiences and discarding them in the next instant with the impermanence they really have, then have we any facility for such people truly to experience this peace? In western society, if not worldwide, have we not erased all possibility of such a haven for these people?

And what if the point of life for a natural Zen Buddhist is to let go all paths to identity? At our most basic, pure reality as humans, can we not function peacefully as the human animal we truly are without the confusion and commitment, if not weight, of identity?

Personally, identity is a very transient thing to me. I have a vague feel of it, I know how my personality manifests itself, I have an idea which mechanisms within my chemistry, frameworks, experiences drive those manifestations of my personality, and I have a vague, floating sense of identity which I am not particularly attached to and am happy to lose most of the time. It is this that allows me to be the natural systematician, 'empath' and anthropologist (studier of other cultures) that I am. I do not feel lost without fixed identity. I am not threatened by merging with others, because I walk through them and come back to 'me' rather than stay 'as them'. Many who meet me open up in ways they often would not except in the company of an animal, and I feel this is because there is something about my relationship to identity which makes me more like an animal. I'm comfortable with that, very comfortable. Equally, given a Zen haven in which I could 'play' and 'be' in the fluid and mindless way that is so natural to me (when not writing, for writing is always of mind, however clever the pre-conscious ranting of it may be), then, yes, of course I'd be in heaven on earth, and there'd be plenty who wouldn't mind that either. Would I equally handle having to gather or hunt my food, make my own clothes, build my own shelter and fire for warmth, given that if I had this haven why should anyone else carry me in such luxury? Well, possibly, yes, because I certainly have a very feral streak (not to be confused there with Meryl Streep, which merely sounds similar to a right-brain person ever alert on the basis of pattern, theme and feel). Having been forced into independence from a very young age because of harsh circumstances, I'm actually happy to try my best to work and pay for heating and clothes and food and shelter like most people, however much I need to adapt my employment to fit with the various Autie challenges and natural Autie structures I actually live with. And I can always steal Zen moments in between doing my best to carry myself as best I can in this complex, often urban, mass-production, shop-bought, corporate, multinational, social reality we call 'being in the world' (gulp).

Parents have a choice which reality they want to help their Autie children towards. But the fact is that in most modern societies, cave-man reality isn't an option. Many Auties wouldn't be prepared to survive on those terms, and creating a Zen Buddhist style retreat for natural 'Buddhas' within our common urban jungles is generally out of the financial reach of most families and unlikely to be considered for government funding.

Effects of identity issues

Cognitive and behavioural implications of identity issues

Identity issues can cause a degree of alienation, isolation, depersonalisation and nervousness as to interfere with the ability to tune in to and communicate with the world around you, and that will have an impact on social-emotional and communication development. Identity issues can cause depression, they can underpin the development of anxiety disorders, they can exacerbate the stress effect upon compulsive disorders and can accentuate personality disorders. Anything that severely increases chronic stress levels will not be good for gut/immune function and that's not good news in the information-processing department. Severe identity issues may also impact upon exploration, social involvement or interest in physical/sensory exploration to the degree that developmental opportunities might be lost. If this happens before the age of three, brain organisation might be less developed than it otherwise might have been.

Effects of social patterns on identity issues

Social patterns can reinforce or turn around how people develop identity issues or defensively self-protect because of identity issues. If someone blames themselves for their condition they are more likely to struggle to overcome its challenges or supress any signs of it. Those with special needs who have grown up in mainstream schools have been subject to the 'sink or swim' effect of social patterns on identity and the issue of self versus condition where they have struggled to suppress or minimise appearance of the condition to be seen instead as a self. Others, however, have been seriously damaged by it. Equally, empathically identifying someone in terms of their condition may do little to help them seek a strong selfhood beyond the expectations others have of their condition. Yet there is a middle ground where one's condition is accepted as being no reflection one way or the other on their selfhood or worth but those in the environment make an active attempt to look for the personhood of each individual, regardless of any condition they have. A change in environmental attitude, dynamics or approach changes how people identify in relation to their condition and this will become part of their social-emotional development. The people in our lives can be medicine or poison, and what is medicine to one person at one time may be poison to another and vice versa.

Identity issues and testing

If we identify ourselves as being without mind, we will fail to be interested in developing that mind. If we identify ourselves as having no body, we will be uninterested in, even oppositional to, using our body in any exercise to prove our capability or potential. If we identify ourselves as in a totally different reality to others, we may not comply with their structures, their rules, their tests. If we identify with dependency, we will avoid efforts to have us prove our abilities. If we identify ourselves as being constantly invaded, we will not welcome the invasive efforts of any tester who openly observes us or puts us under a spotlight. If we identify ourselves as non-conformist, we will respond to conventions and protocol with surrealism and creativity not 'appropriate' or 'required' in the task. If our audience alienates us, we will be less likely to co-operate, which will be taken as a reflection on our ability.

Helping those with identity issues

Clinical psychologists and counsellors work with non-Autistic people with identity issues but may be limited in understanding these issues in people with Autism spectrum conditions. Because they, themselves, come from a non-Autistic reality and framework, they may be at risk of unwittingly projecting these onto people they generally don't fit. Psychologists and counsellors experienced in working with people on the Autistic spectrum might have the other type of problem in that their vision of the condition might restrict them from thinking broadly outside of the stereotypes, particularly as currently these people are more aware of information-processing issues than they are of the entire fruit basket which may be at work in any one Autie or Aspie impacting upon identity, including environmental clashes of a nature which wouldn't normally be such an issue with developmentally typical people with identity problems.

Family therapists look at the entire family rather than just the individual, which may be more helpful, but again there is that balance of finding someone with experience with people on the Autistic spectrum but who is equally not rigidly tied into seeing their clients through a stereotype. Personally, I feel social psychologists might be more aware of identity issues than some other types of psychologists, and might better understand the culture of the person they are seeking to understand. It is perhaps someone with these kinds of skills who might work well in this area. Cognitive behavioural psychologists are good at helping to discern and define a person's experienced 'reality' and then weed through this, testing this reality along the way.

In working with identity I will use Bach Flower Remedies, but I'll also identify who someone really is, who they are expected, or pressure themselves, to be, to what degree their life makes them feel good about themselves and promotes their potential in sync with who they are, and to what extent their life is creating unreasonable and unsustainable anxieties, pressures, demands or self-expectations which are resulting in any kind of breakdown or ill health. Then I will look at who they are trying to please and aspire to being, and I will bring in a fair dose of reality about that vision.

At the same time I will work with them to see what is there to celebrate about who and what they really are and what existing or theoretical friendships, opportunities, activities or occupations might best fit with that. Then I would work with them to get agreement to commit to trialling a change of direction and work on a step-by-step plan of exercises that would gradually get them to a more fitting place.

Most essentially, I would make it very clear that nobody can change anyone else and that the desire to change can only come from the person themselves. I have worked with environments to create circumstances in which that desire for change will emerge naturally. Of course, that's an ethical issue. In terms of ethics, I do this if the person themselves was in danger, ill, distressed or dramatically at risk of lost potential and facing a bleaker future being 'where they were'.

I completely acknowledge the right to choices in our own lives, but I believe in informed choice, without assuming that all reactions express choices. If a self-defeating pattern is all we know, we may not have enough experience upon which to make a truly informed choice until our experiences have broadened. In the case of minors, for example, they are not always deemed to have freedom of choice if their range of life experience and development has been too limited for them to be truly capable of informed choice. Similarly, how much choice does the addict know? If we are addicted to a particular pattern then the first question is: Does this pattern assist this person or is it truly self-defeating? Different people will answer this in different ways. But an addiction is a compulsion. And a compulsion has none of the freedom integral to choosing to side against it. Therefore, where there is no freedom, there is also no choice.

Identity challenges and specific behavioural issues

Identity issues might underpin specific behaviours/issues relating to:

- being in one's own world
- eye contact
- learning and cognitive challenges
- toileting
- sleep problems
- stimming
- challenging behaviours
- food behaviour problems.

Alienation is one of the driving forces which compel any of us to find solace in being *in our own world* when we feel unsafe, unaccepted or unacceptable as ourselves within the external world. Identity challenges have everything to do with alienation. It stands to reason then that someone with information-processing and other challenges who also lives with these identity and alienation issues is going to have less confidence and natural drive to move beyond being in their own world than those without these additional challenges.

Eye contact is often all about connecting and inviting others in. If you feel the social world or the external world can't connect with you for who you are and how you naturally function, then it's harder to reach out to what is foreign and views you as foreign, or to people you sense would only ever accept you on their terms, presenting in their own image.

If you are enthusiastic and socially comfortable somewhere, you are more likely to challenge the restrictions of your own sensory problems than if you already feel alienated and socially uncomfortable. If you identify someone as 'the person with the sensory problems' then you have to take account of how this would affect different personalities. One person may 'live up to their reputation' and feel unable to show when they are not so overloaded or challenged. Another person may swing against your expectation and progressively work to relax and function better in spite of continued sensory issues. Another person may simply feel better understood and see this as a safety net so that if things were bad you'd understand and if they weren't so bad on the day that would be OK too. Someone else may enjoy the attention and power over the environment and exaggerate their sensory issues. So how others identify us affects how we come to identify ourselves or swing against that as the case may be. Identity challenges can, in this sense, be a big part of out-weighing some of the burden of sensory issues.

People *learn* best and process best when they are physically, sensorily, emotionally, psychologically and socially comfortable. If you feel you cannot be yourself, would not be accepted or acceptable as yourself or feel under direct or indirect emotional or social pressure to be what is so counter to your true nature and selfhood, then it is not going to be so easy to pay attention, embrace learning or try to the best of your ability. People with Autism may appear unable to process such social awarenesses directly, but we don't just process these things intellectually, we also sense them, we feel them as patterns through our body. We don't have to be conscious of them or cognitively understand them to experience and respond to these challenges.

If you feel you don't belong and that the external world does not accept you as yourself, it becomes harder to respect their needs for you to conform. Respect breeds respect. If it is easier to go to the toilet in your pants or in your own sacred spaces, why should you conform to the needs of someone you feel would love you so much more if you were not 'like you'? If it is easier to eat what you'd normally fancy or in your own time and spaces, then why should you conform to the desires of those who on so many other levels you sense want you to be someone else? Sometimes, the pressures to be something or someone you are not is like zipping a big person into tiny clothes. Eventually, you pop out at the seams. *Toileting, sleeping and eating* are the stress points that work this way. If an animal is distressed this is where it will show. Humans are animals too. When a person with Autism is hemmed in during their general daily activities in ways that seem 'non-self', then the need to compensate with 'me-ness' is more likely to pop out at the seams in toileting, sleeping and food-related behaviours. Often when you change the social, educational or communication environment, improvements start to show in the seemingly unrelated areas of toileting, sleeping and eating.

Self-stimulatory behaviours can have many different functions, from self-calming to helping download when in a state of overload, from sensory fascinations to mistaken Tourette's tics and OCD compulsions, and simple misunderstood natural expressions of interest and emotional connection. But stims, like any part of self-expression, can also be part of someone's identity, what they feel makes them 'them'. When we feel we are not understood, accepted or acceptable for who and what we are, some of us will seek to be like others at any cost; and that cost is sometimes depression and alienation from self. Other personalities will swing the other way and indulge all the more in those things which set us apart from others, secure in our own cohesive sense of identity. Stims can be part of this and there are certainly those who have become more militant, proud and indulgent in their stims as an assertion of their identity when their 'Autistic identity' is under pressure or threat. When these same people feel socially comfortable and accepted for who and what they are, the stims may simply be not so necessary as a form of comfort.

If we run the risk of being alienated, we put more effort into self-management in the face of overload. If we already feel alienated, we have nothing to lose. There is far less natural motivation to 'hold it together', 'calm oneself down', 'seek help'.

There is no-one more self-protective than the person who feels alienated from others and the world. Undoing the basis of that alienation means not only helping Auties to understand the reality of developmentally typical people, but also building bridges from the other side in which developmentally typical people demonstrate a heartfelt appreciation, understanding and respect for the information-processing and personality differences that may be a large part of someone's Autism. When they do come to this sort of understanding, it's amazing how speaking the same language can lower the walls.

Feeling trapped, alone, alien and unlikeable, unacceptable, and unwanted for what and who one is, is one of the greatest sources of disempowerment, frustration and despair. These feelings have to go somewhere. If they don't sink into the mire of depression, they may fuel *challenging and self-injurious behaviours* or up the tempo on those already fuelled by the forces of other burdens.

PART 3

The Fallout

CHAPTER 12

The Fallout

In the face of the 'fruit salad' model, what do we do with the Autism versus Asperger's debate?

Let's take six people and call them A, B, C, D, E and F, who we know are somewhere on the Autistic spectrum and let's consider how we are going to know which of them fall into the Aspie group and which fall into the Autie group. Now, what we need is a checklist of how to tell the difference.

So, we decide our main difference is 'level of ability' and we define 'ability' as 'having a normal IQ', 'being able to communicate socially', 'having provable literacy and numeracy skills', 'being relatively able to control their behaviour'.

Now we find that A, E and F are 'high-functioning' in this way so we label those three as being Aspie.

But, hang on a minute. B has amazing balance and an acute sense of perfection and can rollerskate amazingly. C is astoundingly intuitive and highly sensing and can hum reams of classical pieces off by heart. D can say the alphabet backwards, has a huge repertoire of advertisements he can reel off and knows the word for pizza in 17 languages. Do these not qualify as high levels of functioning?

So maybe if we take verbal ability as the defining feature. Then we might find that A actually only communicates about football cards and stickers. E can do all the rote learned social patter he has learned at the social skills group but can't tell you how his day was. F can talk but can't simultaneously process any responses the other person makes at the time, or can listen and understand but can't simultaneously process any personal thoughts or feelings.

On the other hand, B has a great old time non-verbally when interacting with people through physical play. C has a wonderful interactive dialogue with people through music therapy and improvisation. D is extremely interested in languages.

Maybe we could take personality or mood as defining the difference, with those who are depressed with tendencies toward schizoid, avoidant or obsessive-compuslive personality over to the Aspie side and those with bipolar or dependent, schizotypal, passive-aggressive, masochistic personality traits over to the Autie side. Here we'd find another combination again.

Maybe we should take interpretive thinking as the defining feature of Aspies. In this case we might find that D, who we thought of as Autie, was actually incredibly Aspie, and although E can put on the appearance of an interpretive thinker he is actually much much better when encouraged simply to map pattern and work by pattern, theme and feel in navigating the world via sensing.

So these are all theoretical divisions, but it is enough to make the point that the division between Auties and Aspies is not as clear cut as it has been made out to be. There are those who fit aspects of both, sometimes at the same time, who may swing between a distinctly Aspie and then a distinctly Autie presentation at other times. There are non-verbal and late-speaking people who fit Aspie presentations, and there are verbal people who clearly fit the presentation we associate with Auties.

This is not to say that those with extremely ripe fruit in their fruit salad, overflowing in its diversity, should be represented by those whose fruit salad is quite different, nor that there should be assumptions that those with an overflowing fruit bowl can't one day progressively have that collection well managed.

The slippery nature of fruit salad
The dynamic and fluctuating nature of Autism-related challenges

A mood disorder may come and go, or be permanent but treatable and treated. An anxiety disorder may be more provoked in certain environments and happenings than in others. Pathological personality disorders may be reduced through adapting environmental management in a way which leads to belonging, acceptance, inclusion and the channelling of natural traits in constructive, even productive and respectful ways. Environments may be able to learn to make the world more sensorily user-friendly and more interpretively accessible to people with information-processing and sensory-perceptual challenges. Alienated families may one day be given real, informed, holistic instruction and support to adapt in ways which are healthy and productive to all involved. Those with left–right integration issues may sometimes adapt constructively to these processing differences, to shifts between two very different processing styles, and through patterning programmes, biochemistry and gut/immune programmes greatly improve processing. Those without communication may be trained in alternative communication forms which allow them to express as much or as little as they wish or can cope with. Those tortured with severe compulsive disorders may sometimes get real, humane and respectful treatment. Sick children may sometimes get help for the health issues that they have and those who do not have gut/immune disorders may not, through ignorance, be forced to consume buckets of nutritional supplements which do not actually apply to their particular physical constitution.

In this sense, the degree of challenges underpinning someone's disability may possibly be altered, but clearly this will not happen for the majority of people through any one-size-fits-all approach.

Labelling mixed fruit: What happens when conditions interact and compound?

The *first step* is recognise that conditions such as Autism, Asperger's, PDD, PDDNOS, ADD, ADHD are not single conditions. They are a compound of co-occuring conditions. These labels are merely responses to different collections of fruit salads. We might as well say, 'the functionally non-verbal and dysfunctional fruit salad', the 'intelligent, logical, literal, awkward, clumsy, intellectual, formal fruit salad', the 'distracted, dreamy, inattentive fruit salad', 'the volatile, active, manic, inattentive, distracted fruit salad', etc.

The *second step* is to recognise that the fruits in the various fruit salads are relatively identifiable and that there are ways of responding to these which will make the developmental impact of each either better or worse.

The *third step* is to recognise that the environment is an active part of achieving re-balance, and that this doesn't always mean controlling the person with the condition but often means the environment has to alter its own style, values, strategies. This means addressing concepts of what 'help', 'love', 'caring' most constructively can mean in the context of each case. Sometimes it means dramatically altering present rigid definitions of what is considered 'normal'.

The *fourth step* is to recognise that there are relationships between the different pieces of fruit that make it more difficult to differentiate the pieces of fruit. For example, if someone has OCD together with avoidant personality they may struggle to dare new things but have no apparent struggle at all when it comes to compulsions.

If someone has schizoid personality making them an intensely private, distant and solitary person, but also has bipolar resulting in constant hypomanic and manic episodes, they may be both distant and solitary yet impulsively driven to episodes of extreme extroversion in which they accidentally draw high levels of attention to themselves in spite of detesting attention!

If someone has extreme exposure anxiety yet is plagued with Tourette's tics, they may feel crippled by the spotlight of attention while their tics constantly draw attention. If someone has central auditory processing disorder (CAPD), so that they are effectively meaning-deaf much of the time, but also has mania, they may chatter all day in spite of being unable to understand what is said to them.

If someone has CAPD, schizoid and schizotypal personality they may be both solitary and highly idiosyncratic, they may make up their own language within their own space but be unable to learn yours or even find any natural motivation to use their own made-up language interpersonally.

If someone has sensory-perceptual, information-processing issues or works purely by sensing rather than interpretation yet has avoidant, schizoid, masochistic or dependent personality, exposure anxiety or severe depression, they are not going to be naturally inclined to help you to understand their needs.

If someone has OCD, Tourette's or an anxiety disorder combined with schizoid personality or avoidant personality together with social phobia and selective mutism, they are not going to be naturally motivated to explore or discuss their condition so that you can actually help them, especially if you don't provide them with a non-verbal, indirectly confrontational means of communication via which to begin to do so, and a user-friendly social delivery that respects their natural personality frameworks.

The *fifth step* is finding 'systematicians': those who can naturally map out the systems behind a given issue. These would be people who can think more holistically about how each piece of an Autism 'fruit salad' is interconnected with the rest. It would be people who can navigate patterns and provide a programme outline, instruction, training and support to those involved with someone with an Autism spectrum condition.

Are there any basic cluster types?

In my experience as a consultant I'd say I have noticed patterns emerging. I'd say that most of my clients over the years perhaps fall into three broadly identifiable clusters with a range of variants on each cluster. We might think of them as three kinds of fruit salads:

- the 'this is me' fruit salad
- the 'highly irritant' fruit salad
- the 'no frills' fruit salad.

Cluster 1: 'this is me' fruit salad – Avoidant/schizoid groups

There are a handful of personality types that when under additional chronic stresses since infancy might become so extreme that, together with the impact of the particular associated disorders related to each, may make someone appear more 'Autie'. These might, for example, include the idiosyncratic-schizotypal, the vigilant-paranoid and the artistic-cyclothymic, all of which are said to have a solitary component to them. But the only two personality disorders currently considered Autism spectrum conditions are those of avoidant and schizoid personality disorders, so it is these I'll look at here.

CLUSTER 1A: AVOIDANT PERSONALITY TYPE OF ASD

This group might include those who started out as sensitive children who developed the more full-blown traits akin to avoidant personality. Together with a tendency toward depression, social phobia and a sliding scale of selective mutism, those in this group may present a very real physical inablility to speak caused by a combination of a depressive state and an excessive fight-flight response. As with any depressed population, those in this group may be more likely than others to be rigid, withdrawn and have more limited activity and a tendency to be emotionally over-sensitive to sensory experiences. The expected depressive and phobic state might easily limit the exploration of social skills, communication or being actively involved in their own learning, and if this began in early infancy this may be enough both to have a functional developmental delay and to diminish brain integration, the development of which relies on such explorations. Once brain integration has been disrupted, problems of information overload, shutdowns in processing associated with that overload, secondary anxiety reactions and sensory hypersensitivities relating to this could conceivably snowball.

There is a common relationship between depression and OCD and generalised anxiety disorder, and because of this it may be that around one third of
those fitting Cluster 1a would also have additional co-morbid conditions like
OCD or generalised anxiety disorder. As these are generally believed to be at
least partly inherited conditions, perhaps around half of these would have a
parent who recognised the outline of these conditions in him or herself.
Because of the nature of extreme sensitivity if not mutism in those with traits
fitting avoidant personality, high to extreme levels of co-dependency are
more likely to develop in the parents of these children. Avoidant personality is
considered an ego-syntonic condition (one which the person identifies as part
of the self), and so those in this group may be less naturally motivated to help
themselves. Because of this, environmental approaches might need to cash in
on the dynamics of the personality state to counter this through tapping into
the person's own motivations and anti-motivations, such as the need for
acceptance, approval and routine.

Co-dependency, when occurring in only one parent, and perhaps especially where the other parent responds in a way which is excessively passive,
solitary or authoritarian, may also put such families at greater risk of family
breakdown. I believe that extreme co-dependency of a parent also unwittingly runs the risk of promoting and reinforcing learned dependency, anxiety
disorders and poor identity development in people in this group. The
resulting fallout of such a snowballing situation runs the risk of increasing a
parent's chances of progressive social isolation, eventual emotional exhaustion or even breakdown.

Because of the anxiety and depression levels in this group, there may be
signs of mild gut/immune problems, associated with low mood or chronic
anxiety, and poor appetite, associated with low zinc and candida issues found
in lowered gut/immune function.

If non-verbal, this group may have had speech but lost it between two and
three years when social and communication expectations increased and worry
about them compounded the situation. This cluster can occur in children with
patterns associated with either right-brain dominant (reliant on pre-conscious
information processing based on sensing pattern, theme, feel) or left-brain
dominant processing styles (reliant on conscious information processing
based on interpretive thinking), presenting a more Autistic or more Asperger's
pattern.

This cluster might be altered with the addition of any one or more
extreme personality traits akin to the frameworks of personality disorders,

most commonly: obsessive-compulsive, schizoid, passive-aggressive, depressive, dependent, paranoid. These would add the features of the additional personality disorders to the basic original cluster.

Common diagnoses of those in Cluster 1a might include Kanner's Autism, Asperger's syndrome or PDD.

CLUSTER 1B: SCHIZOID PERSONALITY TYPE OF ASD

Slightly different to those with avoidant personality, those with schizoid personality may have started out as solitary, private, serious children with limited emotional expression. Like those with avoidant personality, those with schizoid personality may also have developed conditions associated with schizoid personality such as depression, social phobia and selective mutism, which may all be associated with a strong anti-motivation pulling against moves to initiate social contact and involvement necessary to the development of communication and interaction.

Being towards the depressive end in terms of mood, those in this group may be more rigid, self-excluding, and have limited social activity and social communication, and a tendency to be emotionally over-sensitive to sensory experiences as the chronic 'invasions of others and their world'. Those with schizoid personality and its associated conditions might limit their open or overt exploration of social skills, communication or (where the only learning offered is in a social context) active involvement in learning. This may be enough both to have a functional developmental delay and to diminish brain integration, the development of which relies on such explorations. Once brain integration has been disrupted, problems of information overload, shutdowns in processing associated with that overload, secondary anxiety reactions and sensory hypersensitivities relating to this could conceivably snowball.

As with Cluster 1a, those fitting Cluster 1b are more likely to have associated anxiety disorders or OCD. Because of the extreme solitary, private, even seemingly rejecting nature of those in this group, some parents may fail to bond with such children and find their nature 'disturbing' and 'alien'. This may lead to overcompensation by parents who may go out of their way to 'help' such people, potentially leading to a cycle of self-protection on one side and guilt on the other.

Because schizoid personality is also an ego-syntonic condition (one which the person identifies as part of the self) those in this group may also be less naturally motivated to help themselves. So, as with Cluster 1a, environmental approaches would need to cash in on the dynamics of the personality state to counter this through tapping into the person's own motivations and anti-motivations, such as the desire for solitude and the discomfort with intimacy and entanglement.

Here too there may be signs of mild gut/immune problems, possibly associated with low mood or chronic anxiety in feeling socially 'invaded', and poor appetite associated with anxiety over eating with others or accepting their food.

This group would be the most likely to speak late, if at all, and some may have lost speech at between two and three years of age when social and communication expectations increased and worry about them compounded the situation.

Those in this group may be right-brain or left-brain dominant and appear more Autistic or more like someone with Asperger's, depending on which is their dominant function.

This cluster might be altered with the addition of any one or more extreme personality traits akin to the frameworks of personality disorders, most commonly: obsessive-compulsive, avoidant, passive-aggressive, depressive, dependent, paranoid. These would add the features of the additional personality disorders to the basic original cluster.

Common diagnoses of those in Cluster 1b might include Kanner's Autism or Asperger's syndrome.

Cluster 2: 'highly irritant' fruit salad – Irritated brains and disturbed brain chemistry

This cluster primarily contains a combination of conditions generally associated with far more disturbed brain chemistry and toxicity issues. The co-morbid conditions of those in this group could include features of epilepsy, rapid cycling childhood bipolar, Tourette's tics, OCD and an acute fight-flight state not associated with lack of confidence or fear of failure (as seen in avoidant personality). I call this anxiety state exposure anxiety and associate it with involuntary avoidance, diversion and retaliation responses.

Exposure anxiety can easily be confused with avoidant personality and vice versa and the two can co-occur. A key difference is that those with avoidant personality may be dependent on encouragement and low-key praise, but the abilities and self-control of those with exposure anxiety may actively deteriorate when praise or attention is shown to what they have been able to achieve. Exposure anxiety should also not be confused with dependent personality, though, again, the two may co-occur. One of the key differences is that when left entirely alone and seemingly unobserved, people with exposure anxiety are sometimes capable of things they would never normally be seen to do when observed or when feeling they risk being observed, whereas those with dependent personality in the same situation may be so convinced of their own incapability this will not happen.

Bipolar, Tourette's and OCD are all considered ego-dystonic conditions (running counter to the sense of self). This means many people feel trapped inside of these conditions. I believe this is also true of exposure anxiety, which I refer to as 'the invisible cage' (this is quite different to avoidant personality where the person sees this personality state as 'part of themselves'). Nevertheless, the younger the onset of these states the greater the likelihood that these issues may contribute to identity confusion or become bound up in identity. Unlike personality disorders, however, those with these issues may be more likely to be motivated to challenge their own condition. However, I believe that the nature of the conditions themselves may often make this difficult, if not impossible, regardless of intact motivation. I believe this might be comparable to how people struggle with cerebal palsy. Degree of motivation may be intact but will often not be enough to conquer the challenges significantly. Working directly to reduce any sabotaging conditions may be the most likely successful route to freeing up the natural motivations of people in this cluster.

In my experience there is a higher rate of chronic infections and more severe bowel problems in this group indicating more physiological issues at work.

Those in this group tend toward a bipolar dynamic in terms of mood, with associated high impulsivity, hyperactivity, attention problems, behaviour-management problems, difficulty modulating emotional responses and erratic and fluctuating communication.

Associated with Tourette's tendencies, this group tends to have a higher incidence of echolalia, sometimes echopraxia (involuntary mirroring of actions), involuntary movements/sounds/facial and body contortions and distressing involuntary breathing-related compulsions.

Associated with exposure anxiety, when in a high-mood phase, those in this group often squeal and are highly excitable, and they often come and join social company but end up sabotaging themselves through involuntary avoidance, diversion and retaliation responses. As a result, those in this group are socially more likely to be seen as highly unpredictable, nonsensical or frightening, and therefore more likely to be overly controlled by others, which seems to exacerbate their exposure anxiety.

The OCD in those in this group is quite unlike obsessive-compulsive personality and is often quite distressing and overwhelming to the child. Temple Grandin is a well known public speaker and author now re-diagnosed with Asperger's who is certainly a very conscientious personality with obsessive interests who strongly promotes the expansion of obsessive interests. Whilst I agree with her, I have to point out that Temple has never written about suffering from OCD, which puts her in a difficult position in telling OCD from the obsessive interests of someone with OCPD. Those carers working with people with OCD as part of their autism could, after hearing Temple, mistake OCD compulsions as voluntary interests in need of expansion. Where OCD-related compulsions are mistaken for the obsessional interests of OCPD, there is the danger that people have been advised to try to extend manifestations of the OCD which would only confuse and further entrap a person with this sort of compulsive disorder.

Unlike those in Cluster 1, those in Cluster 2 seem to either fail to acquire speech at all or develop idiosyncratic or 'dysfunctional speech'. Quite differently to those in Cluster 1, where those in Cluster 2 fail to acquire speech there seems to be an associated severe receptive language problem in which grasping meaning at the time when people are speaking is so limited that it amounts to being deprived of meaningful input from which to build language. Nevertheless, many of these people show signs they have understood things, though generally after the event has passed. Those in this group seem more reliant on pattern, theme and feel, so a capacity for 'sensing' may be not only acutely developed, but so overdeveloped that it becomes a problem. Imagine that you had such a fierce intellect that you constantly craved information to the point where you had a head full of constant thoughts and drove everyone nuts. Then imagine the opposite where you sense the slightest shifts in the patterns around you and you are one step ahead of what anyone else has yet realised consciously or through direct experiences. You may feel compelled to attack a stranger who has not yet had the chance to demonstrate whether they will or will not ever act on what you've sensed about them. You may sense the friendship breaking before there are any surface signs to the degree that you almost bring on the break-up by reacting as if the seemingly inevitable has already manifested. If you love someone in an integral way for who they are and they only deeply love you on a surface level, it is a terrible thing to have an exceptional capacity to sense.

This cluster can occur in children with patterns associated with either right-brain dominant (reliant on pre-conscious information processing based on sensing pattern, theme, feel) or left-brain dominant processing styles (reliant on conscious information processing based on interpretive thinking), though the chaos, disruption and extreme adrenaline state of those in this cluster may predispose them toward more right-brain styles as a kind of 'bottom line' which remains more consistent for them. Language acquisition for these people might be very 'foreign' and if it occurs may, therefore, go along the less usual path. After the age of three, this processing style may become part of an integrated sense of identity affecting motivation to use the more interpretive left-brain processing style generally expected if not required in most conventional education programmes. Because of the constant disruption and chaos, those in this cluster may run a greater risk of disrupted feedback, which may limit brain integration. So problems of left-right integration and dyspraxia (including oral dyspraxia which can contribute to being non-verbal) may be quite common in this group.

Sensory distortions, sensory crossover (synaesthesia), sensory-perceptual problems, problems processing information cohesively, difficulty consciously retaining or accessing information may all be quite common in this group because of their quite unusual neurological organisation.

Because of the common destabilising dominance of rapid cycling childhood bipolar those with the artistic personality trait already more susceptible to the extreme mood fluctuations of cyclothymic personality disorder may be even further destabilised by the addition of a bipolar disorder. Because of the impact on such a variety of overwhelming distortions and disruptions to the processing of incoming information those idiosyncratic personalities more susceptible to schizotypal personality disorder may appear even more effected by these issues than those in Cluster 1.

In addition, because of the severe impact on the family that such a fluctuating and unpredictable child can have, families may have the kind of reactions you might expect from people under circumstances of severe chronic stress. This can mean higher likelihood of family breakdown, resorting to authoritarian or heavy-handed approaches, exhaustion and emotional challenges from the impact on social life, the impact of the child's behaviours in public and the impact such challenging behaviours have on other children in the home. Because of this, the families of children in this group may be more likely to become alienated from such a challenging child. This then comes with its own psychological and emotional effects of progressive social limitations on the child.

The entrapment involved with having a range of involuntary conditions one may not identify with, together with the confusion of erratic chaos and emotional extremes caused by the conditions, and the greater likelihood of inability of the environment to see the person rather than the condition, may more commonly lead to additional emotional disturbance, identity, or psychiatric issues, perhaps including secondary personality disorders where existing personality traits become exacerbated under extreme circumstances. Some of those perhaps to watch out for might include masochistic, antisocial or borderline personality disorder.

Common diagnoses of those in Cluster 2 might include Autism with ADHD, atypical Autism, PDDNOS.

Cluster 3: 'no-frills' fruit salad – Information-processing issues only

I see those in Cluster 3 as having a kind of 'no-frills Autism'.

Essentially I see those in this group as having information-processing challenges as their primary condition, with resulting secondary learning challenges, sensory hypersensitivity, rigidity associated with information-processing challenges and anxiety responses associated with shutdowns when overloaded.

I believe that those in this group may fall into one of three subcategories: those with left–right hemisphere integration issues, those with dyspraxia (which may include oral dyspraxia) and those with health issues affecting the consistent and sufficient supply of nutrients to the brain necessary for ongoing comprehensive information processing and retrieval. So we could call these Cluster 3a, 3b and 3c.

CLUSTER 3A: LEFT–RIGHT HEMISPHERE INTEGRATION ISSUES

Left–right hemisphere integration problems can occur for a whole variety of reasons, including abnormalities in the parts of the brain stem which relay messages between the left and right hemispheres. These abnormalities may be associated with growth in that area, or with damage from infection, toxicity (including pre-natal substance abuse but also certain metabolic, immune-system or digestive abnormalities leading to toxicity) or head injury.

Where there is limited or severely delayed left–right integration in someone with right-brain dominance there may theoretically be a significant impact on language processing and conscious interpretive thinking central to 'functional' verbal social communication. There may also be struggles to succeed in conventional education programmes, where teachers expect reliance on conscious accessing in retrieving information and those with right-brain dominance may work much better with triggering techniques such as discovery learning and statements and actions to provoke sensory and emotional responses, rather than questions which address 'mind' and 'intellect'. It may be that, personality issues and exposure anxiety aside, inter-personally those who are right-brain dominant may best keep up in a rela-tively indirectly confrontational world, and tend to be oriented toward sensory experiences. Without integrated left-brain processing to assist them, there may be a struggle to conceptualise consciously about the other person necessary, for example, to altering one's behaviour out of consideration for the other person's feelings. The experience of being social may work best when the other person is not tiringly attempting to constantly jolt conscious awareness or interpretive processing.

Enjoyable social experiences may be reliant on interacting thorough doing and intermittently merging with the feel of the other person's patterns: in effect, to experience them *as* them. These people may be highly developed in intuition, even appear acutely sensing, sometimes incredibly aware of pattern and systems though the relationship of these to interpretive meaning may be lost at the time. Those who have a lack of integration but switch between left- and right-hemisphere processing may later be able to co-opt such mindless accumulation of 'pattern'. Without left–right integration to assist them, processing may be more likely to be partial, to backlog under pro-gressive processing delay and to result in shutdowns in various other process-ing areas. What is experienced may be more mono-tracked than multi-tracked including challenges in keeping up with a simultaneous sense of self and other, necessary for good social communication skills or even for a good grasp of why people interact or what the feeling of being 'with' really is.

Where there is limited or severely delayed left–right integration in someone with left-brain dominance there may theoretically be a significant impact on awareness of emotion or ability to interpret or discuss feelings. There might also be an inability to rely on intuitive ways of picking up patterns, theme and feel, which are useful, but not utterly essential, in acquiring many subtle social skills and life skills.

There may be those who will switch between one style of processing and the other with the benefits and disadvantages of each of these limited unintegrated information-processing styles. One of the problems for such people is they can't do this at will, and very subtle experiences can suddenly shift the style of processing, leaving the person disoriented, and sometimes even traumatised, by these constant shifts. To imagine this, think about losing 'mind' every now and then regularly throughout an hour, day, week, always for varying lengths of time. Or imagine one moment being in a culture and language you understood, then in a blink and with no volition of your own and no expectation of the change, thrown out of there and finding yourself in one in which meaning does not exist for you. Add to this that everyone else around you may be acting as if nothing has changed, even expecting you to continue functioning in a way you cannot. Imagine also what it is to be in one culture, surrounded by one language, and to feel there is a missing dimension there but be unable to find it except for a kind of intangible aura of the other. How certain would you be of 'reality'? Those who are very lucky will learn to adapt their lives to accommodate this as safely and constructively as possible.

In either mode, the associated processing style and social, communication and learning styles will still not be those of the majority of non-Autistic individuals. Many parents would see that as a tragedy. Others would go so far as to say that the 'normality' common to non-Autistic people with integrated left–right brain processing isn't always to their own advantage or that of society either and many of the ills humans have done to each other would have been less likely had they not had such efficient processing. In this context, working with what amounts to half a brain may have its advantages too and there are many accepted social means non-Autistic people seek to quieten the awareness and busyness of their own brains.

Patterning exercises such as Brain Gym are the most commonly used current approaches in addressing left–right integration issues, and there are specific programmes to address these. Nevertheless, some people benefit more than others through such programs, particularly those who begin before the age of ten.

CLUSTER 3B: DYSPRAXIA

Dyspraxia is comparable to a department store in which the various departments have few internal phone lines to let each other know what is happening. One of those phone lines is about muscle feedback, and there is usually clumsy movement and very poor handwriting.

Oral dyspraxia occurs in some people with dyspraxia and can occur in different degrees, so one child may merely have slurred speech, another may have a number of sounds he or she can't make and another may be unable to form enough letter sounds to form words. People with oral dyspraxia usually have a normal level of motivation to communicate. If, however, they have a sensitive personality they may be overly sensitive to feelings of failure or incompetence, heightened by the usually well-intentioned help of others. This could expand into avoidant personality with associated selective mutism on top of the oral dyspraxia problem. In effect, you'd then have a motor-planning issue and a motivation issue at work underpinning lack of verbal skills.

Similarly, if someone with oral dyspraxia had a solitary personality in the first place and found themselves pursued and flooded with the attention of others by virtue of having a language problem, this might, theoretically, exacerbate these personality traits to a point that the person is progressively closer to schizoid personality. In such a state there might be, in addition to the motor-planning problem, an extremely highly developed anti-motivation regarding any attempts to initiate, practise or tolerate the social communication involved in improving the oral dyspraxia. Again, the result could conceivably be mutism.

People with dyspraxia have considerable organisational, sensory-perceptual and learning challenges, clumsiness and general motor-planning problems that could conceivably undermine confidence and flexibility. This might be heightened in those with sensitive, solitary or conscientious personality traits who under extreme challenges might lean towards avoidant, schizoid or obsessive-compulsive personality.

Patterning exercises such as Brain Gym are the most commonly used current approaches in addressing dyspraxia. But once again, some people benefit more than others through such programmes, particularly those who begin before the age of 10.

CLUSTER 3C: HEALTH ISSUES AFFECTING SUPPLY OF BRAIN NUTRIENTS

Some of the health issues that might contribute to serious information-processing impairments were mentioned back in the Cluster 2 section. It would suffice to say that in general these health issues might result in similar problems to those in Clusters 3a and 3b, except that treatment relating to Cluster 3c might involve addressing gut/immune, toxicity or metabolic issues where possible on top of patterning programmes. Some cases will be more improvable than others.

Common diagnoses of those in Cluster 3 might more commonly include PDD, dyspraxia or learning disabilities.

How the professionals might one day meet the needs of those within these different clusters

The challenge is that those in Cluster 1 have different and often incompatible needs from those in Cluster 2 and different needs again from those in Cluster 3.

Cluster 1: 'this is me' fruit salad – Avoidant/schizoid groups

Those in Cluster 1 may need an emphasis on a compatible environmental approach and a sensory environment with an emphasis on a relatively low-key and indirectly confrontational style. This can include low-key delivery of rewards, encouragement and praise and provision and training relating to voice communicators where they are also mute. These people may need family counselling and support in avoiding excessive co-dependency and a programme designed to address the signs of developing any co-morbid personality disorders which will compound or complicate their situation.

Cluster 2: 'highly irritant' fruit salad – Irritated brains and disturbed brain chemistry

Those in Cluster 2 may need assistance in managing brain chemistry on a variety of levels. This may mean examining everything which impacts on the balance of neurotransmitters – from diet and nutrition, to sleep and light and addictive patterns – and working carefully to avoid developing or snowballing control–countercontrol dynamics so common to this group. It may involve adapting the environmental approach to work best to respectfully and non-invasively model strategies through which people can progressively manage their own arousal and anxiety levels. It may involve addressing overload factors in the sensory environment and adapting the social delivery of interaction for those with overarousal and acute self-protection responses. It may involve communication techniques which augment and retain meaning inherent in language, not merely through reliance on static pictures but in drawing out experiences through gestural signing and communication via objects. It may involve an educational approach that respectfully acknowledges how to use triggering, rather than relying on an expectation that others will consciously access information, and that permits a means of typed communication, which for some people may be the only way to get around involuntary self-sabotage of their own attempts to communicate verbally. Those in this group may require indirectly confrontational counselling about their own condition through facilitated or typed communication or play therapy. Their families, too, may need counselling and emotional support, if not also respite care to help them have time for other children and to stay together. Most importantly meeting the needs of those in this cluster may involve the presence of others with the kind of orientation and attitude that involves seeing the person beyond the surface presentation while respectfully not shoving this awareness in the other person's face.

Cluster 3: 'no-frills' fruit salad – Information-processing issues only

Those in Cluster 3 may at least require assessments from occupational therapists, physiotherapists and, if necessary, speech therapists trained in working with dyspraxia, if not several years of therapy from these professionals. They may also need a respectful and modern approach involving the humane and prompt provision and training in transportable hand-held equipment for typed communication where oral dyspraxia or dysgraphia will otherwise severely limit the person's development, life chances and social inclusion or lead to personality complications compounding mutism. These people may need the provision of a sensory environment that minimises their processing issues, and the use of language around them in which visual and/or gestural cues are given at all times to help them keep up. Those with these challenges may benefit from adapted counselling about their own challenges, as might the families of those supporting these people.

Shaking up the system – And some reasons why there would be strong resistance to doing so

Most professionals are progressive, many parents are open-minded and only care whether something 'works'. Other professionals have built their high-paid careers and services upon a thesis that Autism is all about x or y or z and, like politicians caught with their pants down, they will defend their outdated stance regardless.

Many of the one-size-fits-all Autism approaches today are based on the big money-spinning businesses which have sprung from someone's 'miracle story' or the dusty thesis of one university professor who has been applauded by his close circle of colleagues even when many of those on the Autistic spectrum themselves have found such assumptions narrow, biased, ignorant and downright incorrect. There remains a belief that if something has sold well, or has been rubber-stamped by virtue of someone's professordom, then surely it holds water just like is promised. But I've seen so many people for whom the promise ended up being empty, who nevertheless keep pouring in the money to *their* programme, keep endorsing it. I've met people who have taken two mortgages for this stuff, committed themselves to 10 years with one programme and felt too guilty to dump it regardless of it failing them and their child. What madness is this? It's the promise of an easy solution where someone else will take care of it. It's also about status and power and big business delivered with sweet-talking public relations. And it's about time we used our own brains. Don't read the company's own self-endorsements, go to a series of chat rooms and ask out in the general public about their own independent experiences.

If the product we are offered shows us no sign of starting to deliver results in a year, take no emotional blackmail, owe no excuses to marketeers and sales people, just move to something else. If something is going to work, then, if you've got the tools appropriate to the particular job and followed the instructions, I'd expect to see changes begin in 30 days, improvement by 90 days, adaptation to a new direction beginning by six months, and being settled into and identified with that new direction by two years.

Some of the most successful interventions have been quirky individualised programmes arrived at through a combination of intuition, adaptation and open-mindedness. Some of the most challenging cases have been those let down by fervent and dogmatic adherence to one-size-fits-all approaches that clearly had failed particular individuals. These people almost always improved, sometimes dramatically, when an individualised programme was brought in.

The Autism 'supermarket' – What might a multidimensional approach look like?

Over the last year I have been working as a consultant to educators in schools and those in social services who specialise in intervention services. My reports detail my analysis of individual cases and provide a working model for these people to learn from in building up more refined pictures of the challenges and strengths of the people they work with. This book will, I hope, go a long way to providing open-minded practitioners in fields like social services, education and health a framework to begin to identify their clients' needs more specifically than an umbrella term of Autism, Asperger's, PDD, ADD, ADHD, etc. They should be able to fill out a profile identifying challenges and styles in:

- information processing
- health issues
- sensory perception
- anxiety
- mood
- compulsive states
- personality
- identity
- alienation issues
- environmental dynamics issues
- other environmental issues.

On the basis of this profile they should be able to design:

- a developmental programme to minimise all currently recognised blocks to development on all levels
- an outline of preferred learning style
- an outline of most beneficial social delivery and communication styles
- an outline of overriding dominant motivation/anti-motivation profiles
- an outline of recommended environmental changes and adaptations
- a full outline of all recommended or required support services specific to the various levels of the complete profile including befriending, broader family support services and counselling, if needed.

What kind of designers and co-ordinators might be able to create programmes and services?

Ultimately, are we looking for a new type of practitioner? After all, if we needed someone to do these profiles with the possibility that this will mean referring people on to a range of conventional and alternative services, or even families designing their own programmes, could we really give this job to a

GP, a teacher, a psychiatrist, a naturopath, or any one of the people who might be involved in the programme itself? Some of these people might not easily, open-mindedly, and without bias, recommend services and programmes their own profession didn't fully go along with or would not financially benefit from. So are we looking at a new kind of family services professional? And if so, what would be the qualifications? How would such a professional know what he or she was viewing and be able to tell one component from another? Is this a profession or is this a trait?

Are we talking about someone with the objectivity of the solitary personality, the heart of the self-sacrificing personality, the capacity to map patterns of the artistic personality, the attentiveness and multi-layered perspective of the vigilant personality and the surrealism and open-mindedness of the idiosyncratic personality? Could people with different collections of natural traits do the same job?

Would we need perhaps an anthropologist trained in objectivity and the ability to slip into foreign cultures and understand them as best as possible on their own terms? Would we need perhaps someone with an encyclopaedic knowledge of a vast diversity of structures and professions, and contemporary knowledge over a wide range of fields, highly skilled in fossicking through vast amounts of internet searches for the more credible and reliable information to fill the gaps they couldn't for themselves? Would we need someone highly sensing enough and devoid enough of mind to 'feel' their way through mapping these systems and intuiting these profiles from often functionally non-verbal people who have confused observers for half a century? Would they need to know what it is to have experienced so many of the states of their clients, or would it be enough to learn of these things and their signs. And yet even if we found such a person, we would need them to be verbal enough to communicate back in language used by the rest of the world, even write reports. Are we looking for a cross between Tarzan and Sherlock Holmes? I'm sure they're out there somewhere in a range of forms.

Could we derive reliable in-depth profiles from anyone who was designed by nature to see only what they wanted or expected, or were trained to see, who was more fixated on their own entertainment or self-image, or who was perhaps less vigilant or too directly confrontational, too desiring of social and personal connection, or simply limited to imagining their own style of processing and experiencing? We may need to think beyond mere university qualifications.

Why naming the fruits in an Autism spectrum 'fruit salad' may be important to funding

What if we are currently putting all available funding into directions which address the symptoms but in many cases fail to address, or even aggravate, the mechanisms which generate some of those symptoms?

We talk about people with Autism requiring lifelong support, but what if the support which sustains Auties, in spite of unaddressed mechanisms, became support involving addressing those mechanisms directly in an ongoing way? Wouldn't we then maximise the real potential of people with Autism beyond their mere dependence upon non-Autistic people?

What if the largely non-existent but desperately needed respite care was not so urgently needed, if generally treatable conditions such as rapid cycling bipolar, depression, Tourette's, OCD and anxiety disorders were recognised and addressed in these people? How much less funding would be required to pay for expensive, imported behaviour management programmes? How much less funding would be required for behaviour management if those non-verbal people who were found able to use electronic communication aids were given them, with assistance as required; and how much less inappropriate medicating if these people could explain their experiences and feelings for themselves? How much less funding would be required in special education if the educators, carers and families of every person with severe central auditory processing disorder were taught to use fluent gestural signing and communication via representational objects? How much less funding of supported workers would be required to help people access facilities if the sensory, social and communication environments were made compatible with the sensory-perceptual needs, personality and anxiety states and processing styles of those who used the facilities? How much less funding would be required if the vast diversity of personality traits in people with Autism spectrum conditions was understood, accepted as equal and constructively channelled towards their strengths instead of their weaknesses, and towards their motivations instead of spending so much energy countering their natural anti-motivations?

With all the funding saved, there would surely be some money available to train people to unravel and map the profiles essential to meeting these people's needs so much more finely, humanely, respectfully and constructively. With all the funding saved there could be a reallocation of funds for families who today cannot afford special diets, nutritional supplements or professional counselling for their own adjustment issues. There could be a reallocation of funds toward research into areas affecting those with Autism spectrum conditions, about which very little is currently known, into dyspraxia and its treatment, into how people can compensate when they grow up without interpretive processing, into the relationship between motivation, personality and disability, into the dynamics which exacerbate natural person-ality traits to become personality disorders in developmentally disabled children, and into the ability of families to treat their children through altering environmental dynamics and approaches.

There is so much we don't know, but with much available funding going into treating symptoms and not causes, into sustaining environmental approaches and dynamics which sometimes exacerbate underlying condi-tions, into crediting only paid professionals at the expense of overlooking the role of the community and the family and the individual themselves, we may not be working as effectively as we could be. This can all be improved.

Early intervention may end up with a different definition. Integration aids would have to address more finely with whom they are required and in what capacities. Special schools may be left progressively with fewer children if more end up being better able to be mainstreamed. Mainstream schools might develop a new protocol in accepting people with 'cluster conditions'. Work training schemes could be more finely aware of working with the strands in a 'cluster condition'. Day centres, respite and residential services could be much better informed in adapting to individuals. There would be broad social opportunities for educating the community.

The politics of 'treatment' and 'cure' – The 'normality' argument

When it comes to the politics of 'treatment' and 'cure' everyone has their own take.

Those who see Autism as a culture may resist having their selfhood analysed as much as their condition. Some conservatives may feel challenged in being expected to be open-minded to any new structure of understanding things which hasn't been rubber-stamped by the most renowned and rubber-stamped dinosaur in this very fast-moving field. Some pragmatists may find the task a logistical challenge but see the practical applications. Some professionals may feel nervous that they are merely part of a much wider multidisciplinary team which includes parents and people on the spectrum themselves. The moneyspinners may well lament, for it could be the end of a golden era of believing in one-size-fits-all, magic bullets and magic wands.

The individual stands to be seen as all they see as self, all that shapes that self and all the mechanisms at work which challenge or contort that sense of self, and has only empowerment, respect, inclusion and equality to gain. 'Normality' would become irrelevant as an ideal or a goal when the focus is instead on promoting dignity, potential, diversity and a healthy definition of what it really means to be loved and to love.

Conclusion

What makes someone non-Autistic is not simply the feature of being 'neurotypical'. Many non-Autistic people have significant information-processing differences through substance abuse, brain injury, immune system collapse, toxicity issues, dementia, Alzheimer's, or simply having been born with brain 'abnormalities' causing them to be outside of the neurotypical, and yet they are not on the Autistic spectrum.

Many non-Autistic people have significant gut/immune problems that have originated in infancy and yet they have not developed Autism spectrum conditions.

Many non-Autistic people develop acute anxiety disorders, even in early childhood, and do not become Autistic.

Many non-Autistic people develop various types of bipolar or depression or compulsive disorders, even in early childhood, and do not become Autistic.

Many non-Autistic people are recognised as having personality disorders in adulthood that are traceable back to early childhood, and will also not be considered Autistic.

Many non-Autistic people have experienced or perceived significant abuse, trauma, neglect, grief, alienation and identity issues going right back to early infancy and have not developed Autism.

The answer as to what causes Autism spectrum conditions will certainly involve age of onset, because part of an Autism spectrum condition is being significantly affected in early childhood development. Another part will certainly be the establishment of a particular information-processing and learning style, and a pattern of social-emotional responses and communication differences, which will be bound up with identity formed in the first three to five years of a child's life. But I don't think this is enough to explain the onset of Autism.

Five boxers in a boxing ring will all require a different number and type of knocks before they start to stumble, fall or be knocked out. I think Autism is similar. What it takes to alter development dramatically in one person may be a lot more than is required to alter it in another person. Some personalities will be more vulnerable than others to the impact of information-processing, gut/immune, communication, sensory-perceptual, anxiety, mood, compulsive or environmental challenges.

In the face of these same challenges, some environments will bolster certain personalities and completely fail others, who may ultimately be diagnosed with Autism. Some personalities will be diagnosed with an Autism spectrum condition where their main challenge is that of information-processing issues, others where the main challenge is a combination of other things which have a secondary effect on information-processing issues and development.

Some people will have only an orange, an apple and a pear in their fruit salad: personality, environment and information-processing challenges. Others will have to have many more pieces of fruit in their fruit salad to result in the developmental impact called Autism. This book has been an attempt to demystify the diversity of presentations that get called Autism spectrum conditions. It is my hope that we one day see these as Autism spectrum cluster conditions and are able to identify the pieces of this Jumbled Jigsaw. We can do this in freeing potential as much as we do so in celebrating the beautiful behavioural mutations which are the fabric of social diversity. If we do, then we will have given much not just to those on the Autistic spectrum, but also to a world so much poorer without their inclusion.

Sources of Help:
Professionals, Places and Services

Acupressure therapists
Alternative practitioners specialising in a non-invasive health treatment through using pressure points based on Eastern medicine.

Audiologists
Conventional mainstream specialists in hearing problems.

Auditory training consultants
Alternative practitioners specialising in retraining how the brain perceives sound.

Behavioural therapists
Conventional and alternative therapists specialising in programmes to train people out of undesirable or 'dysfunctional' behaviours and train them in desirable and 'functional' ones.

Brain Gym practitioners
Conventional and alternative therapists specialising in patterning exercises to assist in neurological integration issues underpinning learning problems and developmental difficulties.

Care assistants
Voluntary or paid community workers working either within a centre or as visitors to those in their own homes.

Chiropractors
Alternative practitioners specialising in spinal alignment.

Counsellors
Often alternative practitioners offering therapy through discussion, ideas and sometimes practising techniques.

Cranio-sacral therapists
Offering an alternative chiropractic/osteopathy-based technique to free up and balance the flow of cerebral spinal fluid to the brain, important in information processing and health.

Dieticians

Professional advisors on healthy diet and dietary interventions some of whom are more open to test-diets, holistic, natural and alternative medicine than others.

Endocrinologists

Conventional mainstream doctors specialising in the function of glands which make hormones.

Gastroenterologists

Conventional mainstream doctors specialising in gut function.

GPs (General practitioners)

Your local doctor who has an overview of general medicine without usually having a speciality in any one branch of medicine or social group. The GP is a source of referral to other medical specialists but may be more or less informed or open to telling you about holistic, natural or alternative medicine approaches or environmental strategies.

Herbalists

Alternative practitioners specialising in natural medicine using natural herbal treatments.

Homeopaths

Alternative practitioners specialising in natural medicine using small amounts of therapeutic substances to trigger physical and emotional changes in the body.

Hypnotherapists

Conventional and alternative therapists specialising in getting around mental blocks, addictions, motivational and attitude problems by addressing these on a pre-conscious level.

Immunologists

Conventional mainstream doctors specialising in the immune system and allergies.

Irlen consultants

Alternative practitioners specialising in visual-perception problems.

Libraries, book stores, the internet

Public community learning resource for those who learn through reading in less directly confrontational atmospheres.

Masseurs

Alternative practioners specialising in stress management and detoxification through massage.

Naturopaths
Alternative practitioners specialising in natural medicine including dietary interventions.

Occupational therapists
Conventional mainstream therapists specialising in helping people to use what skills they do have to develop leisure activities, occupations and self-help skills.

Opthalmologists
Conventional mainstream specialists in visual perception.

Optometrists
Conventional mainstream specialists in sight problems.

Osteopaths
Practitioners specialising in treating detoxification processes through manipulation of the soft tissue and lymph system of the body.

Paediatricians
Conventional mainstream doctors specialising in children's general health.

Parks, public gardens, laundrettes, airports, train stations...
Public community learning and inclusion resources for those who learn through direct experiences, need direct interaction with places, spaces or objects rather than people and conversation – great social support resources for those who cannot easily cope with direct contact with people and live with loneliness, alienation or depression.

Personal trainers
Alternative therapists specialising in a variety of exercise programmes suitable to help optimise peak fitness, stress management or sports vocation.

Physiotherapists
Conventional mainstream therapists specialising in helping people to develop physical and co-ordination skills to develop leisure activities, occupations and self-help skills.

Play/music/art/movement/dance therapists
Alternative therapists specialising in non-verbal therapies to build social interaction, communication, conflict resolution and stress reduction/management.

Psychologists
A variety of conventional mainstream specialists in disturbances in thinking, learning and information processing.

Publishers, galleries and cafes
Outlets for direct expression within the community through writing, art, music.

Reflexologists

Alternative practitioners specialising in non-invasive acupressure treatments and massage focused on pressure points on the feet to treat health conditions and for relaxation and stress management.

Reiki therapists

Alternative practioners specialising in stress management through 'spiritual healing'.

Respite carers

Voluntary or paid workers giving families respite through holiday, day care or residential services.

Sensory integration specialists

Conventional and alternative specialists in sensory integration.

Social workers

Conventional mainstream specialists in helping people with practical matters affecting care, respite, health benefits, pensions, financial management, equal rights and access to information, counselling, management, services, education and employment.

Speech therapists

Dedicated specialists in speech development, some of whom will work more narrowly or broadly than others. Some will open-mindedly support facilitated, augmented and typed communication, others will not.

Support groups, friendship circles and community houses

Public community learning and inclusion resource for those who learn through direct hands-on or discovery learning methods – the greatest social support network and resource for those with developmental disabilities who may be limited to their local community, and for those living with chronic loneliness, alienation or depression.

Teachers

Formally qualified or otherwise experienced knowledgeable and hopefully wise professionals able to supply approaches and structures within which people are enabled to learn. Nevertheless, teachers will have more or less awareness or openness to alternative teaching and learning styles or structures.

Teaching assistants

Experienced or voluntary workers present to assist the teacher in providing assistance to students preferably without being co-dependent or promoting learned dependency.

Workers and workplaces

Public community learning resource for those who learn through direct hands-on or discovery learning methods.

Autism Spectrum Cluster Checklist

After reading chapters 1–11, you can use this checklist to rate which types of conditions are most likely to be present

Rate each feature on a scale of 0–3 as follows:

0 – doesn't apply	2 – moderate/sometimes
1 – mild/occasionally	3 – severe/usually

Information processing

Indications of information-processing issues (indications of mono-tracked, delayed, fragmented, partial or tumbled processing)

0 1 2 3
☐ ☐ ☐ ☐

Differentiate from: gut/immune/toxicity issues, sensory-perceptual disorders, communication disorder, motor-planning disorders, anxiety disorders, depression, compulsive disorders, avoidant/schizoid/dependent personality, unaddressed experienced or perceived trauma/ grief/neglect/abuse.

Indications of motor-planning issues (movement co-ordination)

0 1 2 3
☐ ☐ ☐ ☐

Differentiate from: sensory-perceptual disorders, gut/immune/toxicity issues.

Indications of left–right integration issues

0 1 2 3
☐ ☐ ☐ ☐

Differentiate from: gut/immune/toxicity issues, sensory-perceptual disorders, motor-planning disorders, unaddressed trauma/grief/neglect/abuse.

Indications of visual-perceptual issues (meaning-blindness, word-blindness, print misperceptions, page distortions, difficulty seeing or processing the face/body/objects/places as a whole, loss of processing of visual context, lack of ability to see in one straight line, inability to consistently use two eyes together or one eye appearing not to 'register' incoming information)

0	1	2	3
☐	☐	☐	☐

Differentiate from: gut/immune/toxicity issues, motor-planning disorders, anxiety disorders, compulsive disorders, avoidant/schizoid/schizotypal personality, unaddressed experienced or perceived trauma/grief/neglect/abuse.

Indications of a central auditory processing disorder (meaning-deafness, constant mishearing, extreme challenges in tuning out irrelevant sounds)

0	1	2	3
☐	☐	☐	☐

Differentiate from: effects of hearing loss/uneven hearing, communication disorder, gut/immune/toxicity issues, visual-perceptual disorders, motor- planning disorders, anxiety disorders, depression, compulsive disorders, avoidant/schizoid/ schizotypal/ dependent personality, unaddressed experienced or perceived trauma/grief/neglect/ abuse.

Indications of gut/immune/toxicity/nutritional issues

0	1	2	3
☐	☐	☐	☐

Differentiate from: effects of drug medications, anxiety disorders, mood disorders, compulsive disorders, environmental issues or long-term health impact of chronic emotional extremes affecting those with a range of personality disorders, unaddressed experienced or perceived trauma/grief/neglect/abuse.

Anxiety, mood and compulsive issues

Indications of anxiety disorders (not directly associated only with sensory or information-processing issues)

0	1	2	3
☐	☐	☐	☐

Differentiate from: effects of information-processing/motor-planning/left–right integration/sensory-perceptual issues, gut/immune/toxicity issues, communication disorders, mood disorders, compulsive disorders, long-term impact of chronic emotional extremes or environmental clashes affecting those with a range of personality disorders, experienced or perceived trauma/grief/neglect/abuse.

Indications of obsessive-compulsive disorder

0   1   2   3
☐   ☐   ☐   ☐

Differentiate from: effects of information-processing/motor-planning/left–right integration/sensory-perceptual issues, gut/immune/toxicity issues, communication disorders, mood disorders, long-term impact of chronic emotional extremes or environmental clashes affecting those with a range of personality disorders, unaddressed experienced or perceived trauma/grief/neglect/abuse.

Indications of Tourette's

0   1   2   3
☐   ☐   ☐   ☐

Differentiate from: effects of information-processing/motor-planning/left–right integration/sensory-perceptual issues, gut/immune/toxicity issues, communication disorders, mood disorders, long-term impact of chronic emotional extremes or environmental clashes affecting those with a range of personality disorders, unaddressed experienced or perceived trauma/grief/neglect/abuse.

Indications of rapid cycling bipolar

0   1   2   3
☐   ☐   ☐   ☐

Differentiate from: effects of information-processing/motor-planning/left–right integration/sensory-perceptual issues, gut/immune/toxicity issues, depression, communication disorders, anxiety disorders, long-term impact of chronic emotional extremes or environmental clashes affecting those with a range of personality disorders, cyclothymic personality disorder, unaddressed experienced or perceived trauma/grief/neglect/ abuse.

Indications of depression

0   1   2   3
☐   ☐   ☐   ☐

Differentiate from: effects of information-processing/motor-planning/left–right integration/sensory-perceptual issues, gut/immune/toxicity issues, bipolar, communication disorders, anxiety disorders, long-term impact of chronic emotional extremes or environmental clashes affecting those with a range of personality disorders, serious/depressive personality disorder, unaddressed experienced or perceived trauma/grief/ neglect/abuse.

Environmental issues

Indications of experienced or perceived injury, trauma,
abuse, neglect, grief

0	1	2	3
☐	☐	☐	☐

Differentiate from: effects of information-processing/left–right integration/
sensory-perceptual issues, gut/immune/toxicity issues, destabilising/traumatising
effect of rapid cycling bipolar/compulsive disorders/communication disorders,
depression, anxiety disorders, environmental clashes associated with personality
traits/disorders.

Indications of chronic alienation issues (associated
with environmental dynamics being out of sync with
the person's own dynamics)

0	1	2	3
☐	☐	☐	☐

Differentiate from: direct effects of information-processing/left–right integra-
tion/sensory-perceptual issues, gut/immune/toxicity issues, destabilising/
traumatising effect of rapid cycling bipolar/compulsive disorders/communication
disorders, depression, anxiety disorders, environmental responses to personality
disorders, unaddressed experienced or perceived trauma/grief/neglect/abuse.

Indications of frustration in communication (directly
associated with no access to a means of understood
expressive communication)

0	1	2	3
☐	☐	☐	☐

Differentiate from: effects of information-processing/left–right integration/
sensory-perceptual issues, gut/immune/toxicity issues, destabilising/traumatising
effect of rapid cycling bipolar/compulsive disorders, depression, anxiety disorders,
personality disorders, unaddressed experienced or perceived trauma/grief/
neglect/abuse.

Indications of chronic worsening under particular
environmental conditions

0	1	2	3
☐	☐	☐	☐

Differentiate from: effects of information-processing/left–right integration/
sensory-perceptual issues, gut/immune/toxicity issues, destabilising/traumatising
effect of rapid cycling bipolar/compulsive disorders/communication disorders,
depression, anxiety disorders, personality disorders, unaddressed experienced or
perceived trauma/grief/neglect/abuse.

Identity issues

Indications of identity and alienation issues (associated
with severe disruption/disturbance/distortion to sense
of identity, extreme alienation from self or hatred of own
conditions, extreme and problematic identification with
own conditions, extreme environmental/emotional/
psychological pressure to be something/someone one is not)

0 1 2 3
☐ ☐ ☐ ☐

Differentiate from: effects of information-processing/left–right integration/
sensory-perceptual issues, gut/immune/toxicity issues, destabilising/traumatising
effect of rapid cycling bipolar/compulsive disorders/communication disorders,
depression, anxiety disorders, personality disorders, unaddressed experienced or
perceived trauma/ grief/neglect/abuse.

Referral List Based on Checklist

Obviously, where your score in the Autism spectrum cluster checklist was 0 for any item you would not need to follow up on those things. Those whose score was 2–3 on any item would need some help rebalancing, or most comfortably and constructively living with any of those items. Those whose score was only 1 on any of those items might need no help in living with these things, as most people will experience some of these issues some of the time and this is just part of being a complex, responsive, sometimes overloaded or stressed human being. Those who have known what it is to be a 1 on some of the Autism spectrum cluster checklist items may be able to draw on these experiences as a small window into what these things might be like in greater extremity for others, especially when a vast number of such challenges and extremities come together in the one person, starting in infancy generally before conscious awareness and reasoning. What's important in responding to Autism spectrum challenges is not to get overly concerned that people who have a 1 in some areas are necessarily going to develop into having a 3 in those areas or that those who are at 3 can't sometimes be brought back around 2, or sometimes even 1. But let's also realise that these issues interact, and motivations are a huge part of someone helping themselves; if these are not tapped into, you can try all you like to help a 3 to become a 2 or a 1 but they will fight you to remain responding as a 3. On the other hand, if they want to go from 3 to 1, and if the help necessary to their issues is available, there is nothing that will stop them.

Information processing
Indications of information-processing issues
Referrals could include those for a chiropractic assessment, cranio-sacral therapy, a neuropsychologist, a gut/immune specialist in holistic medicine, a Brain Gym therapist, a specialist in infantile reflexes and patterning, a sensory integration specialist, a naturopath, an open-minded, enlightened and supportive dietician, or paediatrician or GP to monitor dietary changes or supplement regimes, an educational psychologist, a specialist in assisted-communication techniques, a supplier of communication devices and toys/entertainments used in building motor-planning/sensory integration and sensory exploration.

Home programmes could include adequate exposure to sunlight, an exercise programme, a homemade obstacle course for patterning, homemade items for sensory exploration, relatively safe materials left for discovery and trial-and-error learning, a range of gym equipment, electronic equipment for interactive learning and communication, a homemade sensory sensitisation and desensitisation programme.

Indications of motor-planning issues

Referrals could include those for a chiropractic assessment, cranio-sacral therapy, a neuropsychologist, a gut/immune specialist in holistic medicine, a physiotherapist, an occupational therapist, a Brain Gym therapist, a specialist in infantile reflexes and patterning, a sensory integration specialist, a naturopath, an open-minded, enlightened and supportive dietician, or paediatrician or GP, to monitor dietary changes or supplement regimes, a specialist in assisted-communication techniques, a supplier of communication devices and toys/entertainments used in building motor-planning/ sensory integration and sensory exploration.

Home programmes could include an exercise programme, a homemade obstacle course for patterning, homemade items for sensory exploration, relatively safe materials left for discovery and trial-and-error learning, a range of gym equipment, electronic equipment for interactive learning and communication (including typing where dysgraphia severely affects handwriting), a homemade sensory sensitisation and desensitisation programme.

Indications of left–right integration issues

Referals could include those for a chiropractic assessment, cranio-sacral therapy, a neurologist, a gut/immune specialist in holistic medicine, a physiotherapist, an occupational therapist, a Brain Gym therapist, a specialist in infantile reflexes and patterning, a sensory integration specialist, a naturopath, an open-minded, enlightened and supportive dietician, or paediatrician or GP, to monitor dietary changes or supplement regimes, a specialist in assisted-communication techniques, a supplier of communication devices and toys/entertainments used in building motor-planning/ sensory integration and sensory exploration.

Home programmes could include an exercise programme, a homemade obstacle course for patterning, homemade items for sensory exploration, relatively safe materials left for discovery and trial-and-error learning, a range of gym equipment, electronic equipment for interactive learning and communication (including typing where dysgraphia severely affects handwriting), a homemade sensory sensitisation and desensitisation programme.

Indications of visual-perceptual issues

Referals could include those to a behavioural opthalmologist, an Irlen specialist (or, in the UK and USA, obtain a small collection of more affordable sample lenses from Brain Power International to test at home in one's own time), to a chiropractor for a chiropractic assessment, a neuropsychologist, a gut/immune specialist in holistic medicine, a Brain Gym therapist, a specialist in infantile reflexes and patterning, a sensory integration specialist, a naturopath, an open-minded, enlightened and supportive dietician, or paediatrician or GP, to monitor dietary changes or supplement regimes, an educational psychologist, a specialist in reading recovery, a supplier of toys/entertainments used in building sensory-perceptual skills.

Home programmes could include homemade items for sensory exploration and alternative forms of object/facial recognition, relatively safe materials left for discovery and trial-and-error learning, picture-based electronic equipment for interactive learning and communication, lighting changes to the home and other environments, sunglasses to explore, visors for use under fluorescent lighting, coloured plastic overlays for computer screens, coloured paper for printing and writing on, the brightness and colour control altered on the TV, tolerance of unfamiliar explorations of depth/distance/form, ability to explain to the public and relax about alternative uses of senses and vision to compensate for perceptual challenges, a humane understanding of the effect visual-perceptual problems can have on looking at faces and therefore on eye-contact behaviours, gestural signing and communication via objects where visual processing of static pictures is limited and, finally, an attitude that accepts that those with severe visual-perceptual challenges who use their senses differently may be different but are equal to anyone else.

Indications of a central auditory processing disorder
Referals could include those to a sign language course, training in gestural signing and using representational objects in augmenting receptive language processing and communication, a music therapist, an audiologist, a behavioural opthalmologist (sorting visual-perception issues can reduce auditory-processing burden), an Irlen specialist (or, in the UK and USA, obtain a small collection of more affordable sample lenses from Brain Power International to test at home in one's own time), a neuropsychologist, an educational psychologist, a gut/immune specialist in holistic medicine, a Brain Gym therapist, a specialist in infantile reflexes and patterning, a sensory integration specialist, a naturopath, an open-minded, enlightened and supportive dietician, or paediatrician or GP, to monitor dietary changes or supplement regimes, an educational psychologist, a specialist in reading recovery, a supplier of toys/entertainments used in building sensory-perceptual skills.

Home programmes could include adapting the environment and communication styles to maximise receptive language processing, homemade items for sensory exploration in learning to differentiate different layers of noise, homemade tapes/games exploring recognition of alternations in voice tone, opportunities for less verbally based discovery and trial-and-error learning, picture- and possibly print-based electronic equipment for interactive learning and communication, headphones to explore in controlling environmental sound.

Indications of gut / immune / toxicity / nutritional issues

Referrals could include those to a specialist in holistic natural medicine, an allergy specialist, an immunologist, a gastroenterologist, an endocrinologist, a naturopath, an open-minded, enlightened and supportive dietician, or paediatrician or GP, to monitor dietary changes or supplement regimes, a hypnotherapist, a chiropractor, a cranio-sacral therapist.

Home-based programmes could include a basic gut-support supplement programme, a basic immune-boosting supplement programme, a low-allergenic/low-toxic diet, a rotation diet, a 30-day (preferably supervised) low-salicylate/casein-free/gluten-free/sugar-free diet supported with supplements where necessary, homemade social stories/visual charts/contractual agreements in coming to terms with health/dietary issues, removal of suspect products from the family home, lists/written instructions to relatives/school regarding health/dietary issues, modelling a positive and easygoing attitude.

Anxiety, mood and compulsive issues

Indications of anxiety disorders

Referrals could include those to a cognitive psychologist, a neuropsychologist, a psychiatrist, a hypnotherapist, a Bach Flower therapist, a naturopath, an open-minded, enlightened and supportive dietician, a music/movement/art/drama therapist, a cranio-sacral therapist, a chiropractor, a specialist in infantile reflexes, a support group, suitable activity programmes, a specialist in alternative communication techniques and devices.

Home-based programs could include a structured daily diet and exercise regime aimed at lowering chronic anxiety states, modelling of self-calming strategies, removal of any models which reinforce fixating on or siding with anxiety disorders, a home-designed small-steps 'reality testing' contract in challenging psychological/emotional effects of anxiety disorders, homemade social stories/visual charts/contractual agreements in coming to terms with anxiety issues without controlling the lives of others, lists/written instructions to relatives/school regarding anxiety issues and the approach used at home, the use of an indirectly confrontational approach, modelling a calm, stable, positive, easygoing and non-co-dependent attitude.

Indications of obsessive-compulsive disorder

Referrals could include those to a cognitive psychologist, a neuropsychologist, a psychiatrist, a hypnotherapist, a Bach Flower therapist, a naturopath, an open-minded, enlightened and supportive dietician, a music/movement/art/drama therapist, a cranio-sacral therapist, a chiropractor, a support group, suitable activity programmes, a specialist in alternative communication techniques and devices.

Home-based programmes could include a structured daily diet and exercise regime aimed at lowering chronic anxiety/overarousal states, modelling of self-calming strategies, removal of any models which reinforce fixating on or siding with anxiety or compulsive disorders, a home-designed small-steps 'reality testing' contract in challenging psychological/emotional effects of anxiety or compulsive disorders, homemade social stories/visual charts/contractual agreements in coming to terms with anxiety and compulsive issues without controlling the lives of others, lists/written instructions to relatives/school regarding anxiety and compulsive issues and the approach used at home, the use of an indirectly confrontational approach, modelling a calm, stable, positive, easygoing and non-co-dependent attitude.

Indications of Tourette's
Referrals could include those to a psychiatrist, a cognitive psychologist, a neuro-psychologist, a Bach Flower therapist, a naturopath, an open-minded, enlightened and supportive dietician, a music/movement/art/drama therapist, a cranio-sacral therapist, a chiropractor, a support group, a specialist in alternative communication techniques and devices.

Home-based programmes could include a structured daily diet and exercise regime aimed at lowering chronic anxiety/overarousal states, modelling of self-calming strategies, removal of any models which reinforce fixating on or identifying selfhood with anxiety or compulsive disorders, a home-designed contract in socially managing challenging effects of compulsive disorders, homemade social stories/visual charts/contractual agreements in coming to terms with issues relating to compulsive disorders without controlling the lives of others, lists/written instructions to relatives/school regarding compulsive issues and the approach used at home, the use of an indirectly confrontational approach, modelling a calm, stable, positive, easy-going and non-co-dependent attitude.

Indications of rapid cycling bipolar
Referrals could include those to a psychiatrist (with knowledge and experience of all forms of bipolar as well as awareness of cyclothymic personality), a cognitive psy-chologist (experienced in working with those with rapid cycling bipolar to behaviourally self-manage their states), a neuropsychologist (who can test for related biochemistry/epilepsy issues, if not also provide biofeedback techniques), a Bach Flower therapist, a naturopath (open to working in close liason with a GP or treating psychiatrist), an open-minded, enlightened and supportive dietician, a music/movement/art/drama therapist, a cranio-sacral therapist, a chiropractor, a support group, a specialist in alternative communication techniques and devices.

Home-based programmes could include a structured daily diet and exercise regime aimed at lowering chronic anxiety/overarousal states, modelling of self-calming strategies, removal of any models which reinforce fixating on or siding with anxiety or compulsive disorders, a home-designed contract in socially managing challenging effects of bipolar disorder, homemade social stories/visual charts/contractual agreements in coming to terms with issues relating to bipolar disorder without controlling the lives of others, lists/written instructions to relatives/school regarding bipolar issues and the approach used at home, the use of an indirectly confrontational approach, modelling a calm, stable, positive, easy-going and non-co-dependent attitude.

Indications of depression

Referrals could include those to a psychiatrist (able to distinguish depression from all forms of bipolar), a clinical psychologist (experienced in working with those with depression to behaviourally self-manage their states, a neuropsychologist (who can test for related biochemistry/epilepsy issues, if not also provide biofeedback techniques), a Bach Flower therapist, a naturopath, an open-minded, enlightened and supportive dietician, a music/movement/art/drama therapist, a cranio-sacral therapist, a chiropractor, a support group, a specialist in alternative communication techniques and devices.

Home-based programmes could include a structured daily diet and exercise regime aimed at lowering chronic anxiety/overarousal states, modelling of self-calming strategies, removal of any models which reinforce fixating on or siding with anxiety or compulsive disorders, a home-designed contract in socially managing challenging effects of depression, homemade social stories/visual charts/contractual agreements in coming to terms with issues relating to depression without controlling the lives of others, lists/written instructions to relatives/school regarding depression issues and the approach used at home, the use of an indirectly confrontational approach, modelling a calm, stable, positive, easygoing and non-co-dependent attitude.

Environmental issues

Indications of experienced or perceived injury, trauma, abuse, neglect, grief

Referrals could include those to a social worker experienced in working with these issues, a psychologist/psychiatrist (with experience in working with these issues and open to them affecting children with multiple challenges), a clinical psychologist (experienced in working with those affected by these issues to come to terms with them, resolve them and behaviourally self-manage their effects, as well as in stress management), a specialist in alternative communication techniques and devices, an art/music/play therapist, a Bach Flower therapist, a support group, a counsellor/hypnotherapist able to help such a person cope but also to help their family or partner come to terms with facing up to these issues and to the impact of these issues on the person they care about.

Indications of chronic alienation issues

Referrals could include those to a social worker, psychologist or psychiatrist (with experience in working with these issues and open to them affecting children with multiple challenges). Such a professional should be experienced in helping clients and their families/partners to come to terms with these things, resolve them and behaviourally self-manage their effects, as well as in stress management. This could mean addressing these chronic alienation issues on all levels within a cluster condition including the environment's inability to understand, respect, come to terms with or work constructively with information-processing, sensory-perceptual, communication, anxiety, mood, compulsive and personality issues, as well as being open to working positively with any additional experienced or perceived abuse/trauma/ neglect/grief issues. A referral to a specialist in alternative communication techniques and devices, an art/music/drama/play therapist, a Bach Flower therapist, a support group, a counsellor/hypnotherapist able to help such a person cope, but also able to help the family or partner come to terms with facing up to these issues and their impact on the person they care about, might also be relevant.

Home-based programmes might include: exploring alternative communication techniques (including facilitated and typed communication, art and the kind of communication via representational objects as used in play therapy), the use of music to help people come to terms with emotion, release emotion or find emotional peace in coming to terms with such experiences, social stories, exploring relationships to nature, the sensory world and the world of animals, providing a user-friendly creative outlet for emotional expression/resolution, and providing a new healthy environment in which one can begin to grow safely, feeling safe, respected, understood, equal and accepted.

Indications of frustration in communication

Naturally, the most important referral would be that to a specialist in the very vast range of alternative communication techniques and devices. Other referrals could include those to an advocate in equal rights for those with disabilities, and to a social worker with experience in working with these issues and open to these affecting children with multiple challenges, including having the label 'Autism' or 'severe learning disabilities' (or equivalent). Such a professional should be experienced in helping clients and their families or partners to come to terms with these things, in practically resolving these issues and in helping people to deal with the immense trauma and perceived abuse that can sometimes be part of finally being given a non-verbal means of fluent communication. Addressing this issue could mean addressing chronic alienation issues, including the environment's inability to understand, respect, or work constructively with information-processing, sensory-perceptual, communication, anxiety, mood, compulsive and personality issues, as well as being open to working positively with any additional perceived abuse, trauma, neglect or grief issues that come up through establishing non-verbal means of communication.

Other referrals might include those to an art/music/drama/play therapist, a Bach Flower therapist, a support group, a counsellor/hypnotherapist able to help such a person cope and to help their family or partner come to terms with facing up to these issues and to the impact of these issues on the person they care about.

Home-based programmes might include: open-mindedly exploring alternative communication techniques (including typed communication, art and the kind of communication via representational objects as used in play therapy), the use of music and other forms of non-verbal communication to help people come to terms with emotion, release emotion or find emotional peace in coming to terms with such experiences, social stories (if necessary adapted for those with significant receptive auditory processing issues), exploring relationships to nature, the sensory world and the world of animals and a full programme of respectful and user-friendly non-verbal activities/involvements to fill the social/emotional gaps where verbal communication is not accessible, providing a user-friendly creative outlet for non-verbal emotional expression/resolution, and providing a new communication environment in which one can begin to grow feeling respected, understood, equal, accepted and with a feeling of hope for belonging as a person with something to 'say'.

Indications of chronic worsening under particular environmental conditions
Referrals could include those to a social worker, psychologist or psychiatrist (with experience in working with these issues and open to them affecting children with multiple challenges). Such a professional should be experienced in helping clients and their families/partners recognise patterns of chronic worsening under particular environmental conditions and be able to isolate when worsening effects derive from specific challenges. They would have to be able to differentiate between worsening effects derived from challenges due to information-processing, sensory-perception issues, communication limitations, anxiety/mood, compulsive/personality disorders or other personal challenges, including experienced or perceived abuse/trauma/neglect/grief issues or alienation issues associated with the environment not understanding or respecting these things. They would also need to be equipped to offer suggestions for how to change the environment or its approaches to remedy these worsening effects.

A referral to a specialist in alternative communication techniques and devices might also be an essential part of this. Other referrals could include an art/music/drama/play therapist, a Bach Flower therapist, a support group, a counsellor/hypnotherapist able to help such a person cope and to help their family or partner come to terms with facing up to these issues and to the impact of these issues on the person they care about.

Home-based programmes might include exploring alternative communication techniques (including facilitated and typed communication, art and the kind of communication via representational objects as used in play therapy) in fathoming environmental issues at work in worsening someone's ability to function or cope, the use of music to help people come to terms with emotion, release emotion or find emotional peace in coming to terms with such experiences, social stories, exploring relationships to nature, the sensory world and the world of animals in environments not associated with the previous worsening effects, providing a user-friendly creative outlet for emotional expression/resolution outside of the usual environments approach, providing a new healthy environment in which one can begin to grow feeling respected, understood, equal and accepted, and with a feeling of hope for belonging.

Identity issues

Referrals could include those to a social psychologist, developmental psychologist or clinical psychologist with experience in working with identity issues and open to them affecting children with multiple challenges. Such a professional should be both experienced in working with the person affected by these identity issues and able, if ethical and requested to do so, to work directly with families/partners to change their own approaches so that these identity issues can be resolved. A referral to a specialist in alternative communication techniques and devices might also be an essential part of this. Other referrals could include an art/music/drama/play therapist, a Bach Flower therapist, a support group, a counsellor/hypnotherapist able to help such a person cope and to help their family or partner come to terms with facing up to these issues and to the impact of these issues on the person they care about.

Home-based programmes might include exploring alternative communication techniques (including facilitated and typed communication, art and the kind of communication via representational objects as used in play therapy) in fathoming environmental issues at work in worsening someone's ability to function or cope, social stories, exploring relationships to nature, the sensory world and the world of animals in environments not associated with the previous worsening effects, providing a user-friendly creative outlet for emotional expression/resolution outside of the usual environments approach, providing a new healthy environment in which one can begin to grow feeling respected, understood, equal and accepted, and with a feeling of hope for belonging.

References

Cambridge Dictionaries Online (2005) *Cambridge Advanced Learner's Dictionary.* Cambridge: Cambridge University Press. www.dictionary.cambridge.org

Crook, W.G. (1986) *The Yeast Connection: A Medical Breakthrough.* Vintage Books.

Dyspraxia Foundation (n.d.) 'Dyspraxia explained: An overview.' Available at www.dyspraxiafoundation.org.uk/an_overview.htm

Gedye, A. (1991) 'Tourette's Syndrome attributed to frontal lobe dysfunction: Numerous etiologies involved.' *Journal of Clinical Psychology 47,* 223–252.

Gold, S. (2003) *Mutism, Elective Mutism, Selective Mutism.* Eugene, OR: Fern Ridge Press. Available at www.fernridgepress.com/mutism.1.htm

Gray, C. and White, A. (2002) *My Social Stories Book.* London: Jessica Kingsley Publishers.

Hénault, I. (2006) *Asperger's Syndrome and Sexuality: From Adolescence through Adulthood.* London: Jessica Kingsley Publishers.

Leicestershire County Council Specialist Teaching Service (2003) 'What is autism?' Available at www.leics.gov.uk/what_is_autism_handout

Longman (1984) *Longman Dictionary of the English Language.* Essex: Merriam-Webster.

Merriam-Webster, Incorporated (2002) *Merriam-Webster's Medical Desk Dictionary.* Springfield, MA: Merriam-Webster Incoporated.

Merriam-Webster, Incorporated (2005a) *Merriam-Webster's Medical Dictionary.* Springfield, MA: Merriam-Webster Incorporated.

Merriam-Webster, Incorporated (2005b) *Merriam-Webster's Online Dictionary.* Merriam-Webster Incorporated. www.merriam-webster.com

Miranda, R. (2004) 'Anxiety Attacks in Social Anxiety Disorder – Incidence, Onset, History, Evolution.' *Social Anxiety Shyness Info.* www.social-anxiety-shyness-info.com/art/sad/social-anxiety-attacks.htm

McWilliams, M. (2005) 'Famous Bipolars'. www.maramcwilliams.com/resources/famous.htm

NeuroPsychiatry Reviews (2000) 'Childhood-onset bipolar disorder: The danger of misdiagnosis.' Interview with Demitri Papolos. *NeuroPsychiatry Review 1,* 3. Available at www.neuropsychiatryreviews.com/jun00/npr_jun00_bipolar.html

Sinclair, J. (1993) 'Don't Mourn for Us.' Available at http://ani.autistics.org/dont_mourn.html

Williams, D. (1996) *Autism: An Inside-Out Approach.* London: Jessica Kingsley Publishers.

Williams, D. (2002) *Exposure Anxiety: The Invisible Cage.* London: Jessica Kingsley Publishers.

Williams, D. (2004) *Everyday Heaven: Journeys Beyond the Stereotypes of Autism.* London: Jessica Kingsley Publishers.

Wrongdiagnosis (2003) 'Statistics by country for social phobia'. Adiware Pty Ltd. www.wrongdiagnosis.com/s/social_phobia/stats-country.htm

Index